ATHENIAN MYTHS AND FESTIVALS

Athenian Myths and Festivals

Aglauros, Erechtheus, Plynteria,
Panathenaia, Dionysia

CHRISTIANE SOURVINOU-INWOOD
Edited by
ROBERT PARKER

OXFORD
UNIVERSITY PRESS

*This book has been printed digitally and produced in a standard specification
in order to ensure its continuing availability*

OXFORD

UNIVERSITY PRESS

Great Clarendon Street, Oxford OX2 6DP
United Kingdom

Oxford University Press is a department of the University of Oxford.
It furthers the University's objective of excellence in research, scholarship,
and education by publishing worldwide. Oxford is a registered trade mark of
Oxford University Press in the UK and in certain other countries

First published in 2011
Reprinted 2012

British Library Cataloguing in Publication Data
Data available

Library of Congress Cataloging in Publication Data
Library of Congress Control Number: 2010935054

ISBN 978-0-19-959207-4

Author's Preface

I am very grateful to Professor Robert Parker for discussing many of the issues involved in this book and especially for kindly reading, and commenting on, a draft of most chapters. I am also grateful to him for lending me his copy of Mansfield's unpublished dissertation. More generally, I am extremely grateful for his insightful and learned input and warm encouragement. I would also like to thank Professor Chris Pelling for encouraging me to produce this book.

Editor's Preface

For several years before her sudden death aged 62, from an undiagnosed cancer, on 19 May 2007, Christiane Sourvinou-Inwood had been working on two books. One, provisionally entitled 'Reading in Close Focus: "Wild" Girls and Animals', was a study of the relation between girls and animals in Greek language and cult. It was a continuation of one of her earliest and most abiding academic interests, the attempt to understand the cult at Brauron where Artemis was served by young girls known as 'bears'. The other, the present book, had a later and, in some ways, contingent origin. In writing her *Tragedy and Athenian Religion* (2003) she was much preoccupied with the City Dionysia; so too in her posthumously published detective novel, *Murder at the City Dionysia* (Vanguard, 2008). A short article published in 1998, but coming to her attention only rather later (Lambert 1998), argued, contrary to the general assumption hitherto, that members of one of the restricted religious societies known as *genē* had an important role at that festival. The book started as an evaluation and rejection of that claim. From her negative conclusion about the role of a *genos* at the Dionysia, she moved to a broader consideration of the differential involvement of *genē* in different festivals; in attempting to explain that phenomenon she was led in turn to consider in detail the activities at certain festivals; from the festivals she was drawn back to the web of mythology underlying them. This movement is very characteristic of Sourvinou-Inwood's work. We think of her, rightly, as a scholar capable of powerful abstract thought (and abstract expression!); but she almost always moved out from, and back to, very specific problems.

Of the two projects, the one begun later overtook the first. 'Reading in Close Focus' never came near completion, though I hope that publication in some form will be possible. The present book, after many expansions and reshapings, had reached something close to a final form: the disks entrusted to me by her husband Michael Inwood contained an all but continuous text which faded away only at the very end, and footnotes that were about 95 per cent complete.

I offered to edit the work for publication, and my proposal was accepted by the Oxford University Press subject to the proviso that the typescript should be compressed by about a sixth. Some of the editorial changes I have made in consequence (far too numerous to list or indicate except in rare cases) would doubtless have been made by Sourvinou-Inwood herself had she lived to revise her text. I have abbreviated wherever I felt able to do so without cutting the sinews of the argument, excised subsidiary considerations that the author herself admitted provided only weak support for a major thesis, eliminated answers to anticipated objections, omitted some polemic, consigned detail in abbreviated form to footnotes. I have also engaged in some light stylistic retouching, tried to clarify some passages of detailed textual argument by quoting and translating the relevant Greek texts in full, and occasionally reorganized sections. The typescript contained abundant references to works published up to but not after 2005. I have not attempted a systematic updating, but have added in square brackets a few references to works known to me of central relevance to the argument. For advice and encouragement, I am most grateful to Emily Kearns.

The author's working title for the book was *Festivals, Myths, and Genē: Plynteria, Kallynteria, Panathenaia, Dionysia*. I have ventured to change the title to that which the book now bears, partly from a fear that the unfamiliar term *Genē* in the title might act as a deterrent, but also from a feeling that, though the book started from the *genē*, it moved beyond them as it grew in the way described above.

The editorial interventions that I have listed mean that, at a local level, there is an element of hybridity about the work; there exists a weak possibility that a given phrase or formulation is mine, not Sourvinou-Inwood's. But I have striven conscientiously not to alter or abbreviate the essentials of her argument; and I do not doubt that those familiar with her previous work will hear her unmistakable voice on every page.

R.P.

Contents

List of Illustrations

Abbreviations

Abbreviations of periodicals and works of reference aspire to be those recommended for use in the *American Journal of Archaeology* at http://www.ajaonline.org., with a few supplements listed below. For ancient authors, standard source collections, and works of reference not listed by *American Journal of Archaeology* the abbreviations in *OCD*³ (see below), supplemented by those in Liddell, Scott, and Jones, *A Greek English Lexicon with a Revised supplement* (Oxford 1996), have been followed, with a few trivial divergences. Comic fragments are cited from R. Kassel and C. Austin, *Poetae Comici Graeci* (Berlin 1983–), tragic fragments from *TrGF* (see below).

EGF	M. Davies (ed.), *Epicorum Graecorum Fragmenta* (Göttingen, 1988)
Inscr. Dél.	P. Roussel and M. Launey, *Inscriptions de Délos*, vol. v.2 (Paris, 1937)
LSCG	F. Sokolowski, *Lois sacrées des cités grecques* (Paris, 1969)
LSS	F. Sokolowski, *Lois sacrées des cités grecques: Supplément* (Paris, 1962)
Neue Pauly	Hubert Cancik and Helmuth Schneider (eds.), *Der Neue Pauly: Enzyklopädie der Antike* (Stuttgart, 1996–2002); English edn. as *Brill's New Pauly* (Leiden, 2002–)
*OCD*³	S. Hornblower and A. Spawforth (eds.), *The Oxford Classical Dictionary*, 3rd edn. (1996)
RO	P. J. Rhodes and R. Osbrone, *Greek Historical Inscriptions, 403–323* (Oxford, 2003). Reference is to inscription number, not page
TrGF	B. Snell, S. Radt, and R. Kannicht, *Tragicorum Graecorum Fragmenta* (Göttingen, 1981–2004)

1

Festivals and *Genē*

Reconstructions, Problematik, Methodologies

This book investigates in detail aspects of a few Athenian festivals and cults and their associated myths, the exploration of which also involves the wider mythology of early Athens.[1] It offers two major (and, in different ways, sustained) ritual reconstructions and also a set of associated explorations. One of these explorations pertains to the Panathenaia, especially, but not only, the *peplos* offering; it includes an attempt to read the *peplos* scene on the Parthenon in the context of the frieze as a whole, and, above all, in the context of the religious system of fifth-century Athens. Another exploration involves the investigation of an aspect of the City Dionysia, and of the cult of Dionysos Eleuthereus in general, that I had not discussed in my extended investigation of this festival and cult in *Tragedy and Athenian Religion*, the gentilicial involvement, if any, in this cult and festival.[2] Finally, a third exploration investigates the myths associated with the cult of Athena at the Palladion. The first of the two major reconstructions I set out is a reconstruction of a festival nexus that consisted of two associated festivals, the Plynteria and the Kallynteria; the second is a reconstruction of some general trends that, I will

[1] See the discussion of Athenian festivals, including the nature of our access, the ways in which modern studies have structured that evidence, and the important questions concerning these festivals (such as definitions, changes, celebrants) in Parker 2005a: 155–73.
[2] Sourvinou-Inwood 2003a. On the City Dionysia, see now also Parker 2005a: 316–18.

try to show, governed the association between polis festivals[3] and
the hereditary religious societies known as *genē*, a reconstruction
of some of the parameters that helped determine the extent and
nature of gentilicial participation in the different Athenian festivals,
parameters that may be conducive to a greater or lesser gentilicial
participation.

After the discussion by Parker there is little more to be said
about the nature of the Athenian *genē* and their origin.[4] But given
my subject, and since the issue has been raised again recently,[5]
I should perhaps nevertheless say something about my own perception of their nature and set out some of the parameters within which
I believe the Athenian *genē* are to be perceptually located.

On my understanding, whether or not the *genē* were the structure
through which, during the emergence and crystallization of the polis,
a Eupatrid aristocracy was defined[6] from out of the leading families
of (at least some of) the communities that went into the making of
Athens, as I believe they were, there can be no doubt that, as Parker
put it,[7] the system of *genē* was the structure through which the

---

[3] Specifically whole polis festivals, as opposed to festivals celebrated by polis
subdivisions such as demes; on cults and festivals of the polis subdivisions, see
Sourvinou-Inwood 1990a: 310–12 = 2000: 27–9. On whole/central polis festivals,
see Sourvinou-Inwood 1990a: 310 = 2000: 27. In these places I used the term central,
but 'whole polis' carries less baggage and may be less misleading.

[4] Parker 1996: 56–66. For earlier discussions, see Roussel 1976: pt. 1, esp. 65–78;
Bourriot 1976 passim; Humphreys 1983: 35–44. [In very brief summary, the *genē*
were, in the classical period, 'hereditary groups based on descent in the male line, all
legitimate children (or perhaps all sons) of a father who belonged to a *genos* being in
principle admitted shortly after birth' (Parker 1996: 560). (But Blok and Lambert
2009 argue strongly that a priesthood could pass in the female line where the male
line failed to provide a candidate.) Only a minority of Athenians were *gennetai*,
members of a *genos*. Though one meaning of *genos* is family, clan, most *gennetai* will
not have been able to trace kinship ties with one another, because the supposed point
of contact lay in the very distant past (for the connection between *genos* membership
and 'straight descent' from way back, and so with autochthony, see Blok 2009a and
2009b). In the classical period *genē* are defined, above all, by religious functions, their
association with a particular polis cult or cults. R.P.]

[5] Lambert 1999a: 484–9. [On the uneven prestige of different *genē* and *gennetai* see
Lambert forthcoming c.]

[6] See esp. Humphreys 1983: 42; Parker 1996: 63–5.

[7] Parker 1996: 65.

allocation of priesthoods and responsibilities for the organization and conduct of public festivals were organized in archaic Attica.

Polis religion was created as the religion of the Athenian polis, when that polis emerged and crystallized, out of the religious systems of the local communities which had undoubtedly interacted with each other in varying degrees depending on proximity, the prestige of each cult, and probably also other factors; these religious systems had themselves developed as a result of the (to a greater or lesser extent) disintegration of the religious system of the Mycenaean kingdom of Athens, above all the collapse of the framework for administering cult controlled by the palace. These local communities, especially the more substantial ones, had more than one cult, but clearly only some of those local communities' cults became whole polis cults of the Athenian polis, while others remained local community (eventually deme) polis cults. This process of the creation of the religion of the Athenian polis also encompassed the creation of the *genē* since, obviously, whatever they may have been before, it was their becoming part of the polis that transformed them into (the earliest forms of) *genē*; no institution can remain 'the same' when it becomes part of a different system—let alone a radically different one, as in this case.

I believe that the hypothesis that best fits the data known to us concerning the Athenian *genē* is that when polis religion was created, responsibility for the different cults (and the privilege of holding their priesthoods) was shared between the leading families of (at least some of) the different local communities that crystallized into Athens and defined themselves as the *genē* that constituted the Eupatrids. The allocation of the different cults to the different *genē* was presumably based mostly, but not necessarily exclusively, on a pre-existing association.

But this suggestion of a pre-existing association must not be confused with the notion that the cults had 'belonged' to those leading families, that they had been their private family cults. There is no shred of evidence to support the theory that the families which (on this reading) developed into *genē* had ever owned the cults with which they were involved in the historical period; on the contrary, what evidence there is suggests that they had been the cults of the whole community, in which those leading families may have had a de facto leading role, and with which they may or may not have constructed a mythological connection before the emergence of the polis.

The absurdity of imagining that the cult of Athena Polias had ever been the private cult of a family group has been pointed out by Parker.[8] Then, as I hope to have shown elsewhere, the notion that in the 'Dark Ages' communal cult was not practised in separate ritual spaces, that it was domestic and associated with the chieftains' houses, is mistaken; public cult was indeed practised in set aside spaces before the eighth century.[9] In addition, it is clear that the fact that more than one *genos* is involved in some very important cults, such as the poliadic cult of Athena Polias and the Eleusinian cult of Demeter and Kore, is not consistent with the notion that cults had previously been owned by a family, but is consistent with the reconstruction involving allocation; that is, that during the process through which the polis emerged, responsibilities for, together with the priesthoods of, particular cults were shared among different *genē*.

To put it crudely, using a metaphor derived from modern cultural assumptions: on my reading, the organization of the newly crystallized polis religion and the allocation of particular cults to particular *genē* was 'centrally' planned and decided, in the sense that the decisions would have been taken by whatever body was acting as a 'central' (in the sense of whole polis) authority while the polis was being created—for example, a council which, like a modern Parliament, reflected local units, such as one consisting of the leaders of each local leading family that was to become one of the *genē* that made up the Eupatrids; but those decisions about such organization largely, albeit not wholly, refracted, or at least took account of, earlier local circumstances.

Before the emergence of the polis different local cults are likely to have had different visibilities and prestige, reflecting, among other things, mythological associations. Whether or not this was the case, some of the local communities' cults became whole polis cults, while others remained local community, eventually deme, polis cults. On my understanding, it was the priesthoods of whole polis cults that were assigned to *genē* along with the associated responsibilities. The

---

[8] Parker 1996: 24, 61.
[9] Sourvinou-Inwood 1993.

cults that remained local community polis cults would have been managed at the local level—which, at that time at least, would have entailed that the leading families played a dominant role.

The various communities that went into the making of the Athenian polis were often very different from each other at the most basic level, such as, for example, in the differences between very small and larger communities, poor insignificant communities and wealthy and powerful communities with wealthy and powerful leading families; or in the differences between communities that may have been near, and closely interacted with, other communities and more isolated villages; or the community or communities that were located at the centre of what was to become the *asty*, and communities in the periphery of what was to become the polis. These circumstances would be conducive to significant diversities in the allocation of cultic roles to the different *genē* in the different whole polis cults. Clearly, then, one parameter shaping the creation of these earliest *genē* would have been the diverse circumstances, which were conducive to non-uniformity and even messiness; but another parameter would have been the desire to systematize and create some relative homogeneity, though not necessarily equality, since powerful families in powerful communities may have made claims to greater power and influence—also in the religious sphere.

The Athenian *genē* can be said to have participated in cults and festivals in two main ways: first, ritually (the *gennetai*, or some of them, performed ritual roles in the cult); and second, managerially (the *genos* participated in the administration (a concept which includes the financing) of the festivals and cults). This distinction is heuristic, since the two aspects sometimes merge (as, for example, when sending and taking part in a procession), and both functions were performed by the gentilicially appointed priests and priestesses. These gentilicial priests and priestesses provided an irreducible minimum *genos* involvement in the cults which were served by such priesthoods.[10]

One of the themes of the book, then, is the exploration of the extent and the nature of gentilicial participation in different

---

[10] [On the mode of appointment to such priesthoods, see Blok and Lambert 2009.]

Athenian festivals, and the attempt to determine whether or not there were any significant differences in the extent to which different *genē* participated in the different festivals and cults. I must stress that this is not a systematic investigation of the relationship between *genē* and Athenian festivals; I am proposing the reconstruction of some general trends on the basis of a set of in-depth explorations of a few festivals, though the conclusions are not, to my knowledge, invalidated by any extant evidence pertaining to the relationships between *genē* and other festivals, some of which I shall also discuss briefly.

The in-depth explorations I set out involve the investigation of gentilicial participation in festivals of two different kinds: on the one hand the festival nexus of the Plynteria and Kallynteria and on the other the Panathenaia and the City Dionysia, two festivals that I characterize as 'panathenaic', a term on which I shall elaborate below. My investigation began with the detailed exploration of the question of what gentilicial participation, if any, there had been in the City Dionysia. This subsequently led me, for purposes of comparison, to the investigation of gentilicial participation in the Panathenaia, a festival which, on my reading, is significantly comparable to the City Dionysia in some very important aspects, which, it will emerge, are aspects that directly concern the issue of *genē* involvement in cult.

Some of the Problematik concerning gentilicial participation in the Panathenaia also involves the Plynteria. The Plynteria and the Kallynteria (a festival associated with the Plynteria in ways that need to be further determined) belong to the same cult as the Panathenaia, the cult of Athena Polias, and both the Plynteria and the Panathenaia were concerned with the *peplos* of Athena. There is evidence to suggest that the Plynteria involved a significant gentilicial participation, above all by the *genos* of the Praxiergidai. In the course of the exploration of the involvement of the Praxiergidai in the Plynteria it became apparent to me that the festival nexus of the Plynteria and the Kallynteria was in need of a detailed investigation in its own right. Thus, I set out here a detailed attempt to reconstruct, as much as possible, the ritual acts that made up this festival nexus, its ritual structure, and the Athenian perceptions, the representations and perceived meanings and functions, connected with this nexus of festivals, and also the ways in which this nexus relates to the Panathenaia.

The attempted reconstruction of a segment of the nexus of the Plynteria and Kallynteria, the procession to Phaleron, necessitated the detailed investigation of another cult, that of Athena at the Palladion. For it has been argued, by no less eminent a scholar than Walter Burkert,[11] that the procession to Phaleron reflected in the sources was not, as had been thought, part of the Plynteria; that it belonged to the cult of Athena at the Palladion and took the Palladion for a ritual bath at Phaleron. In my attempted reconstruction of the Plynteria I set out a series of independent and converging arguments that lead to the conclusion that the procession was indeed part of the Plynteria. But a rigorous methodology demands that the case for the view that this procession was part of the cult of Athena at the Palladion should also be seriously considered; specifically, that I should investigate the one important argument for the view that the Phaleron procession involved the Palladion that has not yet been challenged by the other scholars who have criticized that hypothesis: the notion that a particular mytheme, a unique account attested in a scholion, was the *aition* for a ritual bath of the Palladion at Phaleron. I have therefore set out an exploration of the cult of Athena at the Palladion, and especially an investigation of the myths of the acquisition by the Athenians of the Trojan Palladion, conducted in the context of an exploration of the Palladion myths as a whole.

Though its starting point was the exploration of the mytheme mentioned above, the investigation of the myths of the Palladion is conducted in its own right, and, I hope, may throw some new light on the development of those myths. As regards the mytheme that was the starting point of this set of explorations, its investigation within the wider mythological nexus of which it was part shows that it was a very late construct and that it was not an *aition* in the cult of Athena at the Palladion, and that therefore it does not support the hypothesis that the statue of Athena at the Palladion was bathed at Phaleron. This conclusion, then, converges with the conclusion that the Phaleron procession was part of the Plynteria.

---

[11] Burkert 1970a: 356–68 = Burkert 1990: 77–85.

I shall discuss the methodological issues raised by the reconstruction of Athenian festivals in a moment. First, I shall consider an objection to the notion of a reconstruction of general trends that may govern the associations between polis festivals and *genē*: our knowledge concerning gentilicial involvements in Athenian cults is both extremely fragmentary and dependent on random survival; therefore, while greater gentilicial participation may be unproblematically detected, the determination of an absence of participation, or of lesser, or minimal, participation, would need to rely, even more than in better documented circumstances, on *argumenta ex silentio*. I hope to show that this is not the case. Some arguments are not *ex silentio*. Thus, for example, if we know that one procession was sent out jointly by a unit representative of the whole polis and a *genos* (as was the case at the Plynteria), while another procession in the same cult, in a different festival (the Panathenaia), was sent out only by units representative of the whole polis, it is clear beyond doubt that gentilicial participation in the first festival was much more significant than in the second. Of course, the *genē* also represented the whole polis when they administered a festival. But this was one facet of their persona; the other was that they were a restricted exclusive group located at the opposite end of the symbolic spectrum from a whole polis representative like, for example, the archon.

I will now suggest that an extension of this argument, which exemplifies a whole category of comparable arguments, appears superficially to be *ex silentio*, but in reality it is not; nor are the comparable arguments in this category. For such arguments rely not on a simple absence of evidence, but on reconstructions of structures of presences and absences drawn on a wider canvas: if we have a respectable amount of evidence concerning the administration of a particular festival in the overall context of the cult, and this evidence not only does not include any mention of any gentilicial involvement, but also shows that the administration was conducted by units representing the whole polis, such as boards of *hieropoioi* or Treasurers of Athena, which are clearly alternatives to gentilicial involvements,[12] or of *epimeletai* which at least once explicitly incorporated gentilicial involvement,[13]

---

[12] See, on this nature of these boards, Parker 1996: 127.
[13] See pp. 328–9 below.

the conclusion that there was no (or, at the very least, extremely minimal) gentilicial involvement in the administration of that particular festival is not based simply on the absence of evidence for the involvement of *genē*, but on the combination of this absence and the presence of alternatives to gentilicial participations. It is therefore not, I submit, an *argumentum ex silentio.*

I will not repeat here the methodological critique of post-modernism that I have set out elsewhere,[14] but I will say that it is more rigorous to try to reconstruct possibilities on the basis of detailed analyses in which the argument is open to scrutiny, than choose the apparently puritanical option of allowing blanks; for such blanks in the scholarly discourse are inevitably, and implicitly, filled, either with commonsense assumptions, or, through seepage, with notions and hypotheses derived from earlier discourses, even when those discourses have been questioned or even invalidated, because the connections between those discourses and the assumptions they had generated may be hidden or forgotten. This is indeed the default alternative: if we do not try to set out tentative reconstructions constructed as rigorously and systematically as possible, the vacuum is uncritically and implicitly saturated by assumptions, often unconscious and unquestioned assumptions, the ultimate origins of which lie in the speculations of earlier scholarship, in which awareness of methodological difficulties may have been less acute.

Thus, in the case of gentilicial involvements in Athenian festivals it may be implicitly assumed that all *genē* involvements were more or less the same in the different festivals—and whether or not the assumption is explicitly articulated it may govern the readers' perception and manipulation of the available evidence; or it may be implicitly assumed that the greater or lesser densities of gentilicial involvement in the different festivals were simply random, and that may colour the perception of the role of the *genē* in Athenian cult. These assumptions may or may not be right—I will try to show that they are not—but the point is that they need to be examined, not implicitly absorbed and allowed unconsciously to shape the discourse.

---

[14] Sourvinou-Inwood 2005: 15–17.

I will now discuss the methodological issues raised by the reconstruction of Athenian festivals. Given 'the randomness of the evidence that is available to us for Attic festivals',[15] any attempted reconstruction of a festival is especially vulnerable to cultural determination. I will now suggest a strategy that is, in my view, conducive to minimizing the danger of cultural determination in the attempted reconstructions of festivals.

I begin with a principle that should govern not only the attempted reconstruction of festivals, but also any attempted reconstruction of ancient realities, for it is conducive to at least not maximizing cultural determination: exhaustiveness; it is, I suggest, advisable to set out exhaustive investigations of all available data in their full context, such as, for example, the mythological nexus of which a mytheme is part—as I am doing, for example, with the mytheme concerning the bath of the Palladion. I include mythological realities in the term 'ancient realities', first because the term expresses the fact that the location of particular myths in particular nexuses at particular times was a reality, a theoretically determinable fact—though it may be open to argument whether or not it can be determined by us, given our limited access—and, second, because it is a reality that the meanings of particular myths were constructed by the ancient Greeks within certain parameters shaped by cultural assumptions that are different from those that shape the parameters within which modern readers (when not trying to reproduce the ancient processes of meaning creation) would construct such meanings—even if the reconstruction of the relevant parameters may be a matter of controversy in the individual cases. Of course, though the elements that make up the festivals (and the problems concerning them) should be placed in as exhaustively reconstructed a framework as possible, it should be acknowledged that exhaustiveness is an ideal, and that practical considerations dictate compromises.

Each element in any nexus under investigation should be placed, and assessed, in the context of that whole nexus, since meanings are constructed also through interactions between the elements of a nexus and with the nexus as a whole. For example, the semantic

---

[15] Parker 2005a: 156.

field of the cake of dried figs called *hegeteria*, which was carried in the
procession of the Plynteria, included associations with purification
and with primordial times and autochthony; the fact that, as we shall
see, other elements in the Plynteria are also connected with primordiality, and that the movement from pollution to purification is
important in the festival, entails, first, that these aspects of the
semantic field of *hegeteria* were indeed activated in the Plynteria
procession, and, second, that the *hegeteria* was part of the construction of primordiality and autochthony at the Plynteria, and also an
element in the complex process of purification in that festival; finally,
it confirms that this particular part of the ritual nexus, the procession, was associated with primordiality and autochthony.

Meanings are also constructed through (and thus can also, up to a
point, be reconstructed through the reconstructions of) sets of relationships of similarities with, and differences from, other, semantically related elements that can be seen as alternatives that might have
been part of the nexus but were not.[16] For example, the fact that
Aglauros was honoured at the Plynteria and Kallynteria on her own,
the fact that Aglauros' sisters Pandrosos and Herse do not appear to
have a place in these particular festivals, and certainly did not have a
significant role, helps define the meaning of Aglauros' place and role
in these festivals as one involving her specifically, and not the Kekropidai as a group. This, we shall see, converges with the fact that other
evidence shows that the dominant aspect of Aglauros in this nexus of
festivals was her persona as the first priestess of Athena.

To refocus the strategy on the specific enterprise of attempting to
reconstruct a festival: one further stage, one outcome of these exhaustive investigations advocated here, will be the reconstruction of
'stable points' reflecting clearly established ancient realities concerning the festival nexus under investigation. Some of these involve
ritual acts, others involve associated perceptions and representations.
At the most concrete end of the spectrum such elements would
be unambiguously attested facts, for example, the unambiguously
attested nexus of ritual acts and associated perceptions of 25 Thargelion, about which we know, for example, that the day was *apophras*,

---

[16] I have discussed these constructions of meanings through sets of relationships
and their methodological implications in Sourvinou-Inwood 1991: 11–16.

'ill-omened', and that members of the *genos* Praxiergidai performed secret rites. At the least concrete end will be reconstructed representations, such as the perception that (at least in certain circumstances in Athenian cult) the return of a statue to its sanctuary was correlative with a representation of the deity's advent.

A second stage should involve the reconstruction of as many as possible of the manifold relationships between these stable points: relationships concerning sequence, relationships of association, of incompatibilities, of symbolic correlations. In other words, it is necessary to try to structure these reconstructed stable elements into a basic skeleton that should, if correctly [re]constructed, roughly reflect the basic structure of the festival in terms of sequences of ritual acts and also associated representations and perceived ritual outcomes. Some information necessary for this structuring of the stable points is part of the stable points themselves, such as sequences established on the basis of known dates, for example, that 25 Thargelion was part of the Plynteria, and the 28th was the date on which the archon unsealed the temple and the Praxiergidai returned the keys and control of the temple to the archon and though him the priestess; or associations, for example the association of the Plynteria procession with the *hegeteria* cake, and of the *hegeteria* cake with primordiality, autochthony, and purification.

In order to minimize cultural determination, these individual structurings, and, even more so, the proposed structurings for which the available evidence is deficient, should be constructed with the help of the parameters that shaped the structure of the festival nexus. Let me elaborate.

A festival is structured through the interactions between its constituent elements, indeed, it can be seen as an image of the outcomes of those interactions. While all the interacting elements of the ritual nexus had functioned as shaping parameters, some were more intensively and dominantly interactive than others and functioned as especially significant parameters shaping that nexus and the ways in which participants in the culture made sense of it. For example, at the Plynteria and Kallynteria, one of the stable points that can be established is that the notions of pollution and purification were central to the ritual acts and their outcome. We should therefore try to set such parameters into place when we try to structure the stable points into a skeleton—as near as possible to the skeleton that articulated the festival being investigated; for example, when trying to structure the elements that made up the Plynteria and Kallynteria into an articulated nexus, one shaping parameter, at a very elementary level, should be the fact that in a Greek ritual nexus involving pollution the eventual outcome will be purification. This brings us to another important methodological issue.

This sequence pollution-to-purification is a well-known established sequence reconstructed on the basis of other Greek rituals. It is a very small segment of what we may call Greek ritual logic, the system of structuring principles and modalities that articulates Greek rituals, which is itself articulated by, and expresses, important Greek religious perceptions. Greek ritual logic governs the interactions of ritual elements, their structuring into nexuses. For example, Greek ritual logic structured ritual elements, such as prayers or libations, into ritual schemata, such as sacrifice. One way of defining ritual schemata is as structured combinations of ritual acts that always occur in a certain order because they are articulated by, and articulate, this Greek ritual logic—which in its turn is articulated by important religious perceptions. These schemata both structured rituals and also helped shape Greek perceptions of the rituals. Festivals are structured through combinations of ritual schemata, combinations that are themselves structured through what we may call 'festival schemata', configurations that articulate the festival's main thematic concerns, for example, the 'New Year/renewal' schema (not limited to New Year festivals, there were also 'New Year type' festivals involving other forms of renewal).[17] A festival may be dominantly structured by one dominant festival schema, or through the interaction of more than one, for example, a 'New Year/renewal' schema and 'an advent festival' schema, expressing 'divine arrival'.

In these circumstances, I suggest that, despite the fact that there are, of course, large gaps in our knowledge, missing elements in the reconstructed skeleton, it is possible that at least some of the interactions that shaped the nexus of festivals we are trying to reconstruct may be recovered with the help of the reconstructed

---

[17] On New Year festivals, see esp. Burkert 1985: 227–34; cf. also Burkert 1983: 142, 154, 164.

relevant segments of Greek ritual logic. I suggest that the interactions between the visible elements can sometimes allow us to trace fluid contours of the missing elements and their place in the nexus, in a rough approximation of the process of triangulation that pinpoints the location of a radio transmission, with the big difference that the nature of the phenomena being investigated, as well as our limitations of access, entail that what we are trying to do is recreate fluid contours; we cannot recover the actual missing elements (the equivalent of accurately locating definite positions), unless there is other evidence. I shall illustrate this with one simple example involving fluid contours and one more complex one in which the process of reconstruction can be taken a little further.

First the simple example. One of the 'stable points' for the reconstruction of the Plynteria, the fact that it included a procession, shows that the festival had a public part; another 'stable point', the fact that the Praxiergidai performed secret rites, shows that it also had a restricted one; the interaction between these two stable points shaped the nature of the festival, and, looking at it from the point of view of our reconstruction, tells us that this was a particular type of festival.

In the more complex example, the interaction between the absence of the statue from its sanctuary as an expression of abnormality and the return of a statue to its sanctuary as a representation of the deity's advent suggests that certain types of rites, such as sacrifices, are likely to have been associated with the return of Athena's statue to the Acropolis in the nexus of the Plynteria and Kallynteria. If in addition (as, I will argue, is the case here) there is also other, independent, evidence that indicates the possibility that sacrifices may have been performed at the statue's return, the convergence with the reconstructed fluid contours would, I submit, constitute a very good argument for concluding that such sacrifices were indeed performed on that occasion.

These operations, then, can allow us to reconstruct the nexus of festivals in the form of an articulated skeleton of ritual acts, representations, and outcomes, with (of course) some blanks and some parts consisting of fluid contours of actions and representations that we do not know about but the placements of which we can roughly reconstruct.

The notion of Greek ritual logic and of ritual schemata takes us to the general methodological issue of the use of comparative material. In Chapter 3, section 3.iv I will consider some ritual material from other cults, mostly (by necessity) from places other than Athens, for the purposes of comparison. I will therefore now consider the question of the methodological legitimacy of such comparisons. This question becomes more acute when it is considered that in this case the comparative material involves different festivals, different goddesses, and mostly different cities, and they were therefore part of multiply different nexuses.

In these circumstances, to what extent, and how, is it legitimate to use comparative material in the attempted reconstruction and study of a ritual? Clearly, it is legitimate to use comparative material from Greek religion in ways comparable to that involved in the deployment of anthropological models from other cultures, that is, as eye-openers, to disrupt the default operation of culturally determined commonsense assumptions. But is it legitimate to use comparative material from the Greek world in any other way? I suggest that it is, but that the deployment of such comparative material should be done very carefully and in very circumscribed ways.

I suggest that it is legitimate to deploy such material as culturally specific eye-openers. This allows, first, a heightened version of the ordinary eye-opener function to disrupt cultural determination; a version which allows the possibility of direct parallels, the possibility that the ritual under investigation may not be vastly different from the one about which more knowledge is available, because similar rituals belonging to the same culture are shaped by closely comparable parameters. Once such possibilities are formulated, it is possible to explore them, perhaps to ask new questions of the data—provided that these questions and possibilities are not allowed to structure the evidence, to function as 'organizing centres' which, like pre-constructed models, may falsify the evidence to construct reflections of preconceived expectations.[18]

Second, such a deployment of comparative material also allows the reconstruction of fragments of charts of ritual relationships, such as,

---

[18] I have discussed these methodological questions in Sourvinou-Inwood 1995: 413–15.

for example, as we shall see in Chapter 3, section 3.iv, the association between activities involving cleaning the temple, physically renewing some of its elements on the one hand, and on the other the washing of the statues. In other words, such deployment allows the reconstruction of small and disparate fragments of Greek ritual logic. It is through such comparisons that Greek ritual logic can be, up to a point, reconstructed.

I briefly considered above ritual schemata and festival schemata. The 'advent festival schema', which is focused on the deity's arrival, sometimes dominates a festival, and sometimes is part of a more complex festival nexus.[19] In Greek advent festivals the deity's statue was moved from its usual place in order to allow the enactment of its return to represent in a concrete way the arrival of the deity; but there was no ritual enactment of, or belief in, the deity departing, and the place to which the statue was taken was within the polis; not only is there no reference to the deity departing from the city, but even the statue does not leave the polis. Greek advent festivals enacted and celebrated an arrival of the deity that had not been preceded by that deity's departure. This does not appear 'logical' to those who, like us, do not share in the ritual assumptions and ritual logic of Greek religion, but it is correlative with the notion that while the deity is emphatically present at the advent festival, she is not really continuously absent between advent festivals. The various ritual enactments of the arrival of the deity in advent festivals, which gave concrete expression to the deity's actual advent, often presented themselves as commemorations of a mythological arrival of the deity or of the cult.

Of course, ritual schemata must not be imported into the attempted reconstruction of a festival on the basis of plausibility or apparent similarities to a comparable ritual. It is only after the attempted reconstruction of the festival under investigation has taken place on the basis of the stable elements, and after the structurings indicated by the visible interactions have been identified, that it may be recognized that a particular schema is part of the festival. Then it is legitimate to consider, with caution, whether a consideration of other articulations of that schema may help the

---

[19] On advent festivals, see below, Chapter 3, section 4.

reconstruction. But this must be done with caution, because, even when it is clear that a ritual schema is articulating a festival, it is not legitimate to fill in blanks on the basis of manifestations of that schema that structure other festivals, not least because interactions create different variants, the interaction between different festival schemata produces different configurations of those schemata in the different festivals. In addition, the perception of comparabilities, and of the extent to which these allow assumptions about similarities, is inevitably culturally determined. Thus, using parallels to fill in gaps in ritual schemata structuring less well-attested ritual nexuses is a less rigorous strategy; if circumstances make such a strategy inevitable, as is sometimes the case, it should be deployed in a careful and controlled way, not implicitly and by default.

However, comparative material can legitimately be used in another way. If (as will be the case here) the attempted reconstructions are conducted without input from a particular nexus of comparative material, this nexus can help test their validity. Thus, if a reconstructed ritual schema corresponds to an attested schema structuring a ritual nexus that is comparable to the one investigated (for example one involving the washing of a cult statue), this would offer some support for that reconstruction—provided that the latter has not used material from that attested schema. In general, if the reconstructed rites have close parallels in other Greek rituals (not implicated in the reconstructions), this would indicate that the reconstructed rites fit Greek ritual logic and ritual modalities. Besides the shared ritual logic that can be seen to structure Greek rituals, the festivals of different cities were not impermeable to influence from festivals of other cities—though it was, above all, Panhellenic festivals celebrated in the major Panhellenic sanctuaries (as well as exceptionally prestigious and well-known festivals such as the Athenian City Dionysia) that exerted significant influence.

Finally, relationships of similarities to, and differences from, other comparable but unrelated nexuses should also be considered in order to minimize culturally determined judgements; that is, assessments should take place with the help of such comparisons. For example, the involvement of *genē* at the Panathenaia (whether it is large or less significant) should be assessed not through the filters of common sense but with the help of comparisons with the involvement of *genē* at, for example, the Eleusinian Mysteries.

I shall be using the term 'panathenaic' to bring out and emphasize an important characteristic shared by the Panathenaia and the City Dionysia, their 'whole polis' emphasis and their correlative nature as loci in which the Athenian polis articulated itself. I will now try to justify the construction of this category, and the fact that I consider the City Dionysia to be a 'panathenaic' festival.

The Panathenaia was the major festival of the poliadic deity, Athena Polias, and therefore it inevitably had a close symbolic con- nection with the Athenian polis as a whole.[20] Therefore the festival also became a locus for the articulation, and so symbolic validation, of the subdivisions constituting the polis created by the Kleisthenic reforms: some of the competitions were organized by tribes, the demarchs mustered the procession, and the meat of the sacrificial victims was distributed deme by deme, among the participants sent by each deme. To put it differently, the new articulation of the polis was symbolically strengthened by the restructuring of parts of the Panathenaia through its constituent parts. The polis articulated in this festival presents itself as a wide and open system: besides the resident foreigners, the metics, Athens's colonists also participated, in that they were required to send a cow and a panoply to the Panathe- naia.[21] Because this festival was a locus for the symbolic articulation of the polis, it also became a locus for the articulation of the new configuration, the Athenian Empire—for this was one of the results achieved by the fact that at the Great Panathenaia the Athenian allies were required to bring a cow and a panoply like colonists.[22] The festival also had a Panhellenic facet, since the musical, rhapsodic, and athletic games were Panhellenic. This helped place Athens within

---

[20] On the Panathenaia, see now Parker 2005a: 252–69; specifically on the proces- sion, 258–64.

[21] When the colony of Brea was sent out in the 440s the colonists were required to send a phallos to the Dionysia and a cow and a panoply to the Panathenaia (Meiggs and Lewis 1988: no. 49.11–13, cf. p. 131). According to a fourth-century decree the Parians, as colonists of the Athenians, also had to bring a phallos to the Dionysia and a cow and a panoply to the Panathenaia (see the text in Accame 1941: 230 (ll. 3–5) = *SEG* XXXI 67; cf. Hornblower 1991: 69–70).

[22] See Meiggs and Lewis 1988: no. 46. 41–2; cf. pp. 120, 121.

the wider system of Panhellenic religion: it was one of the places that held Panhellenic games.

In the procession of the Panathenaia[23] the citizens of Athens were articulated into different segments, not only on the basis of gender but also in other ways: male citizens, the hierarchically superior category, were articulated into different groups, such as the military component, or elderly citizens, a group of the most beautiful old Athenian men, who processed carrying olive twigs. Metics, colonists, and allies were visibly differentiated, by clothes and by what they carried; freedmen and other barbarians were included in an outer circle, for they carried an oak branch through the Agora. In this procession, then, the polis articulated itself as an open system.

The City Dionysia is not a festival of the poliadic deity, so I will now explain in what way I consider it to be a 'panathenaic' festival. To summarize before elaborating: first, the City Dionysia shared with the Panathenaia characteristics that in the Panathenaia were manifestations of that festival's panathenaic nature; second the festival (and the cult), though of course not poliadic, constructed, and depended on, a very strong whole polis emphasis.

First, the polis articulated itself at the City Dionysia as it did at the Panathenaia. Like the Panathenaia, this was a pre-Kleisthenic whole polis festival with a whole polis focus that was reorganized to include articulations through the new polis subdivisions.[24] The theatrical competitions had a whole polis articulation, in that both the selection of the poets and of the *choregoi* by the archon was personal, and not by polis subdivision; the archon appointed three *choregoi* for tragedy from all the Athenians;[25] so it is the whole polis that constitutes the selection unit; only the selection of the judges involved a tribal articulation.[26] The fact that the dithyrambic competitions had a tribal articulation that reflected the Kleisthenic subdivisions shows that they had been reorganized in the context of the Kleisthenic

---

[23] On inclusion and ranking at the Panathenaia procession, see Parker 2005a: 258–64.

[24] For the discussion of, and evidence and arguments for, the statements in this section, see Sourvinou-Inwood 2003a: 67–140.

[25] Arist. *Ath. Pol* 56.iii. On *choregoi* at the City Dionysia, see Wilson 2000: 21–3; cf. also MacDowell 1989: 65–9.

[26] On this selection, see Pickard-Cambridge 1968: 95–8.

reforms. Thus, like the Panathenaia, the City Dionysia was a locus for the articulation and symbolic validation of the polis subdivisions created by the Kleisthenic reforms. The fact that in the City Dionysia a non-Athenian poet could be given a chorus and the flute player could also be a foreigner may be considered as partially comparable to the Panhellenic facet of the Panathenaia.

As in the procession of the Panathenaia, so also in that of the City Dionysia the polis articulated itself as an open system, with male citizens at the hierarchical centre. I have argued that women participated in the Dionysia procession,[27] in which, again, citizens and non-citizens were clearly differentiated. Citizens processed wearing whatever they liked and carrying wineskins. Metics processed in purple garments and carrying *skaphai*, small tubs or basins. The *choregoi* wore magnificent clothes and golden crowns. There was, then, in this procession also a differentiation between the different elements that made up the polis, an articulation of the polis into its constituent parts. Athenian colonists also took part in the procession of the Great Dionysia; they were sometimes required to send a phallos to the Dionysia and sometimes a cow and a phallos.[28] The tribute of the Athenian allies was brought to Athens at this festival and displayed in the theatre.[29] People were also displayed in the theatre as part of Athenian ideological construction: the orphan sons of the war dead who had been raised at the polis's expense and had come of age were paraded in the full armour given them by the polis before the performances.[30] Furthermore, before the performances, the honours given to citizens and foreigners for great services to the polis were proclaimed.[31] This was also an act of positive self-presentation and part of the ideological construction of the democratic Athenian polis.

Clearly, then, in the fifth century the Dionysia were a locus for the polis's articulation and self-definition. This may appear to be simply motivated by pragmatic considerations, that is, to be the result of the

---

[27] On the participation of women at the City Dionysia, see Sourvinou-Inwood 2003a: 177–84.

[28] See n. 21 above.

[29] See e.g. Isocr. *De pace* 82; Schol. Ar. *Ach.* 504.

[30] See e.g. Isocr. *De pace* 82.

[31] See e.g. Dem. 18. 120; Aeschin. 3. 41.

fact that the theatre offered the appropriate stage for the display of tribute as well as of the orphans and the Athenian honours list and for the announcement of honours. But such a monocausal 'rational' explanation can only be a partial one; I will now try to show that the festival was focused on the fundamental relationship between the whole polis and Dionysos, which generated a very strong whole polis emphasis, conducive to the creation and strengthening of this 'panathenaic' aspect.

I hope to have shown elsewhere that the festival of the City Dionysia, which was an advent festival (as we saw, a common type of Greek festival celebrating the deity's arrival), was a simple (that is, not complex, albeit lavish) festival focused on the reception of Dionysos.[32] Unlike Dionysos' older festivals, which were structured by complex mythicoritual nexuses, the City Dionysia, created as a new festival around the 530s, has a simple mythicoritual core, focused on the introduction of the god's cult. According to the festival myth,[33] Pegasos of Eleutherai brought Dionysos' statue to Athens, but the Athenians did not receive the god with honour. Dionysos was enraged and struck the male sexual organs with an incurable disease. They consulted the oracle who told them to bring in the god with every honour; they manufactured phalloi, both privately and publicly, and with these they honoured the god, commemorating their misfortune.

In the City Dionysia the Athenians re-enacted their reception of the god with honour after they had spurned him and aroused his wrath. This was especially marked by the carrying of phalloi, which re-enacted the first phallos-carrying in the festival myth, when they first received the god and established his cult. The procession would have been perceived both as a procession in the present and as a re-enactment of the first procession that had established the cult. The dramatic and dithyrambic competitions were ritually connected with the reception of Dionysos: the presence of the god's statue in the theatre during the performances shows that a strong dimension in the perception of the festival was that the dramatic and dithyrambic

---

[32] Sourvinou-Inwood 2003a: 67–100; cf. 100–21.
[33] I discuss the festival myth in detail in ibid.: 72–81, 105–6, 150–4.

competitions were entertainment for Dionysos, part of the god's ritual reception in which he was honoured and propitiated, as he had been when, in the mythological past, his cult was first introduced after the initial offence against him.[34]

Thus, in a way, this festival, and the cult of which it is part, encompassed and enabled all other cults of Dionysos. Therefore the nature of the City Dionysia can be seen as (very) partially comparable to that of the Panathenaia. Consequently it set out and celebrated the relationship between Dionysos and his cult and the Athenian polis. Correlatively, like the Panathenaia, it also functioned as a locus for the articulation of the Athenian polis as a whole polis—a function further developed with the help of the fact that its nature and settings created a context and an arena that offered an effective and 'cosmopolitan' stage for this self-display.

In the investigations concerning these two 'panathenaic' festivals set out here, I will consider, among other issues, also a set of recent and relatively recent suggestions all of which imply a significant gentilicial involvement in the Panathenaia and the City Dionysia. Two of the suggestions I will be investigating pertain to the Panathenaia and two to the City Dionysia. The suggestions pertaining to the Panathenaia concern the *peplos* of Athena. The first claims that it was not the priestess of Athena Polias who dressed the statue with the new *peplos*, as has always been assumed,[35] but the Praxiergidai, the *genos* who put the *peplos* around the statue at the Plynteria. The second claims that the new *peplos* was not wrapped around Athena's statue at the Panathenaia, when it was presented to her, but at the Plynteria or the Kallynteria, many months later. The first hypothesis ascribes to the *genos* of the Praxiergidai a symbolically significant role involving the *peplos* at the Panathenaia. The second hypothesis, if correct, would alter the nature not only of the Plynteria but also of the Panathenaia, and especially of the *peplos* offering to the poliadic deity.

I will argue that all these suggestions concerning the Panathenaia and the City Dionysia are mistaken; and that gentilicial participation in both the Panathenaia and the City Dionysia is different from

---

[34] See esp. Sourvinou-Inwood 2003a: 108 and cf. 141–72 passim.
[35] See e.g. Rhodes 1981: 568–9 ad 49.iii.

gentilicial participation in the Plynteria and Kallynteria, and also different from that in another major polis festival and cult, the Eleusinian Mysteries. For in Chapter 7, I will compare gentilicial participation in the Panathenaia, the City Dionysia, and the Plynteria to that in the Eleusinian Mysteries in order to avoid the danger of culturally determined judgements in assessing what counts as significant, or different, or limited, gentilicial involvement. Gentilicial involvement in the Eleusinian Mysteries was very great and constitutes the maximum end of the spectrum of what, on this reconstruction, is a spectrum of differential involvement of different *genē* in different festivals; this differential involvement, I will argue, is (at least to a significant extent) correlative with the nature of the festivals.

2

Cultic Myths and Others

Aglauros, Erichthonios, Erechtheus, Praxithea

1. READING CULTIC MYTHS

My attempted reconstructions of the Plynteria and Kallynteria in Chapter 3, and the explorations of the Panathenaia in Chapter 5, include readings of the cultic myths associated with those festivals. As we shall see, Aglauros[1] was the second cult recipient, after Athena Polias, at the Plynteria and the related and connected festival Kallynteria and she was also the central figure in the *aitia* of both festivals.[2] Erichthonios was the founder of the Panathenaia in one of the myths about that festival, which, I will argue, was an important cultic myth. In this section I will set out the main lines of the mythicoritual personae of Aglauros and Erichthonios, and try to reconstruct their place in the wider framework of Athenian mythology, as part of an attempt to set in place the main parameters within which the ancient Athenians made sense of the cultic myths of all three festivals, the Plynteria, the Kallynteria, and the Panathenaia. Inevitably, this enterprise needs to include an attempt to reconstruct the relationship

---

[1] I use the form 'Aglauros' rather than 'Agraulos' throughout. I should explain at this early stage that I do not use Roman sources, since they belong to a different culture and, I hope to have shown (Sourvinou-Inwood 2004), construct different myths. I do not use Nonnos either, because, as I argued elsewhere (Sourvinou-Inwood 2005: 191, 202), the filters through which he handled earlier material were different from those governing the Greek mythopoeic construction with which we are concerned here.

[2] See Chapter 3, section 2.

between Erechtheus and Erichthonios and therefore also an exploration of the figure of Erechtheus—investigations which, we shall see, are also crucial for the placing of Aglauros.

As is widely accepted, Erechtheus and Erichthonios were eventually constructed as separate figures out of mythicoritual material that had in earlier periods been part of, had belonged to, and defined, one figure, a figure called Erechtheus. For Erechtheus is attested first, long before Erichthonios. I will try to reconstruct the parameters of the complex mythological processes that eventually led to the construction of these two different Athenian kings, Erichthonios and the figure I shall (conventionally) call 'post-split'[3] Erechtheus.

A general modality that governs cultic myths should guide any attempted reconstruction of the ways in which these figures were perceived by the Athenians as part of their past history and ritual present: cultic myths, the *aitia* of rituals and the aspects of mythological figures that are directly relevant to their persona as cult recipients, focus on particular segments of those figures' mythological nexuses and also particular segments of the polis's history; they are not usually, and certainly not necessarily, placed precisely inside a coherent chronological system of linearly perceived history. When mythographers, above all, as far as Athenian history was concerned, the Atthidographers, chose to write systematic histories, involving a coherent chronological framework, various difficulties, incongruities, and apparent contradictions emerged, and various strategies were adopted for coping with these difficulties, such as, for example, the creation of a second king called Kekrops or a second king called Pandion.[4]

The many and diverse mythopoeic processes that took place over many centuries, and the limited and erratic access that we have to those myths, result in Athenian myths about early Athens appearing to be very messy, which may lead to the belief that any attempt to

---

[3] I use the word 'post-split' as a conventional shorthand for the much more complex processes that generated the two figures.

[4] See Kearns (1989: 110): 'Kekrops, Erichthonios and Erechtheus, Pandion are cult figures whose origins lie in religious practices on the Acropolis. The order of their reign and their mutual relationships is of no significance—the difficulties in applying chronological criteria to such figures are seen in the somewhat desperate atthidographic hypothesis of a second Pandion and a second Kekrops.'

reconstruct those processes is highly problematic. But I will try to show that it does not follow that we cannot reconstruct some of the parameters governing the messiness, some of the parameters governing the developments that led to some of the complexities and ambiguities in the extant myths. For example, while in modern perceptions Aglauros is defined by her most famous myth, in which she is the daughter of Kekrops whose disobedience towards Athena over the matter of Erichthonios in the basket led to her death, in the cultic myths of Athens, we shall see, she was, above all, the first priestess of Athena who gave her life to save the city. Her involvement in the myth of Erichthonios was a fifth-century construction, and it is possible to set some of the parameters of the interactions between these two sides of her mythological persona.

I will begin the discussion of these myths with the main lines of the nexus of Aglauros, then I will consider Erechtheus and Erichthonios in detail, and finally I shall return to Aglauros and her father Kekrops and consider their relationship to Erechtheus and Erichthonios in the Athenian mythologies of the different periods.

2. AGLAUROS

i. Life, cults, paradigmatic roles, early images

Aglauros[5] was the daughter of Kekrops and the sister of Pandrosos and Herse. In the extant myths her mother was a shadowy figure. As we shall see when we come back to this shadowy figure in section 3.iv of this chapter, Aglauros' mother was either nameless or she was called Aglauros like her daughter.[6]

The mythicoritual nexus of Aglauros is very complex and its constituent facets contain apparently conflicting elements that seem to construct apparently conflicting meanings. One aspect of Aglauros'

---

[5] On Aglauros: Parker 1987a: 195–7; Kearns 1989: 24–7, 60–1, 139–40; Burkert 1990: 40–59 passim; Parker 2005a: 216–17, 221–2, 427, 434, 449; see also Kearns 1990: 330; Christopoulos 1992: 28–31; Larson 1995: 39–41; Lupu 2005: 146–7 with bib.; Gourmelen 2005: 69–70, 151–9, 162–71 with bib.

[6] Paus. 1.2.6; Apollod. 3.14.2.

persona is very positive, another is negative. She has a mythological and cultic persona as a single figure, and also a persona as a member of the 'three daughters of Kekrops' group, together with Pandrosos and Herse. Her sisters also received cult,[7] but while Pandrosos, like Aglauros, was cultically embedded in Athenian religion Herse was not and was clearly a later addition that turned the pair into a triad. I shall return to this. Aglauros and Pandrosos both appear, identified by name, on separate fragments of early sixth-century vases found on the Acropolis. The scenes depicted cannot be recovered with certainty, but I suggest elsewhere that one of the vases (by Sophilos) shows Aglauros, Pandrosos, and their father Kekrops arriving as witnesses of the contest between Athena and Poseidon (a myth to which the vase would in turn become the first witness).[8]

The nexus of Aglauros that can be reconstructed on the basis of the elements reflected in our sources may well be a composite one; that is, the different elements that make it up may not have been part of one system that operated simultaneously in all contexts; the possibility exists that different elements may have been part of different nexuses: for example one or more nexuses may have been associated with particular cultic contexts, others may never have been cultic myths, and yet others may have been created by systematizing mythographers as part of an attempt to reconcile apparent difficulties and contradictions. We therefore need to try to reconstruct as much as possible these different contexts and the ways in which the different myths associated with Aglauros functioned in the Athenian conceptual universe.

The myth of the birth of Erichthonios, in which Aglauros was involved together with her sisters, will be discussed later on; I will begin with the cultically embedded myths involving Aglauros on her own.

I will discuss and explore the cult of Aglauros in more detail in Chapter 3. Here I will mention its main facets, starting with two

---

[7] On Pandrosos, see esp. Kearns 1989: 192–3 with bib.; Parker 2005a: 219, 221–2, 434, 449; see also Gourmelen 2005: 151–7, 159–71 with bib. Herse is less rooted in cult than Aglauros and Pandrosos (see e.g. Burkert 1990: 47; Parker 2005a: 434 n. 63; see also Shapiro 1995: 42).

[8] Sourvinou-Inwood 2008.

incontrovertible facts of ritual reality:[9] Aglauros had a sanctuary, on the east slope of the Acropolis, which was associated with a cave,[10] and she also had a priestess, whose office is involved in a set of problems that will be discussed in Chapter 3. Then, as I mentioned, Aglauros was the second cult recipient, after Athena Polias, at both the Plynteria and the Kallynteria. Aglauros' name was said to be also a cult name of Athena.[11] Also, women swore in Aglauros' name.[12]

A very important aspect of Aglauros' cultic persona is that she "was the chief divine patroness of the ephebes".[13] It was in her sanctuary, on the east slope of the Acropolis, that the ephebes swore their oath, and Aglauros was the first deity invoked as a witness in the ephebic oath.[14] I should mention that I do not believe that the ephebeia began for the first time (as opposed to becoming crystallized and systematized) in the fourth century, but whether or not this is right, in any case, what is important here is that the oath itself is

[9] On Aglauros in Athenian cult, see also Kearns 1989: 25–7, 139–40; Parker 2005a: 216–17, 427, 434, and n. 64.

[10] On Aglauros' sanctuary, see Hdt 8.53.2; Paus. 1.18.2; Polyaenus, *Strat.* 1.21.2 (he mentions Aglauros' sanctuary in connection with Peisistratos). See Dontas 1983: 48–63; Hurwit 1999: 10 fig. 8, 101, 136, 204; Schmalz 2006: 40–2. Aglauros' sanctuary was associated with a cave (Dontas 1983: 63) just above it: we can only conjecture the relationship between the sanctuary and the cave, but that there was some relationship seemed to Dontas very probable. See Hurwit 1999: 10 fig. 8.

[11] Bion of Prokonnesos *FGrH* 332 F 1; Harp. s.v. Aglauros. See now on this, Parker 2005a: 449 (sceptical).

[12] Bion of Prokonnesos *FGrH* 332 F 1; see e.g. Ar. *Thesm* 533, and cf. a scholion on Ar. *Thesm.* 533: 'For they would swear by Aglauros; and by Pandrosos more rarely. But I have not found that they swear by Herse.' Bion of Prokonnesos is a problematic figure who may have been writing in the last third of the fourth century BC (Jacoby 1954: i. 611). He writes that 'woman honour and swear by her; for the goddess assigned some privileges to Agraulos to honour her father Kekrops.' Jacoby (1954: i. 612 ad 332 F1) suggests that perhaps 'to honour her father Kekrops' solved the problem as to how the offender could enjoy worship. If this is right, if it was later thought incongruous that she should be honoured in cult, it strengthens the notion that the mythicoritual status of Aglauros that was cultically embedded was felt to be incongruous with the Ericthonios myth, and this, I submit, supports my reconstruction that the persona of Aglauros as a cult recipient on her own was that of a priestess of Athena and a woman who sacrificed herself to save the city.

[13] Parker 2005a: 434.

[14] RO 88. 5–20; Dem. 19.303; Philoch. *FGrH* 328 F 105; Plut. *Alc.* 15.7–8; Poll. *Onom.* 8. 105–6 s.v. *peripoloi.*

clearly of archaic date,[15] and so it must have been sworn by groups of young males whose patroness Aglauros was.

Before I discuss the myth associated with this aspect of Aglauros' cultic persona I should say something further about this cultic aspect: her involvement with the ephebes was correlative with a role as *kourotrophos*, 'rearer of young men/women',[16] as was her sister's Pandrosos' cultic association with the *arrhephoroi*. The relationship of the Kekropidai with the *arrhephoroi*, whose mythological prototype they were, will be discussed below. What is important here is that two inscriptions make it clear that Pandrosos was the second honorand of the *Arrhephoria*, for they are dedications on the occasion of girls having been *arrhephoroi* and they are dedications to Athena and Pandrosos.[17] Clearly then, before the pair Aglauros and Pandrosos became a triad (with the addition of Herse), each of the two sisters was the main patroness of a maturation rite of one or the other gender, male in the case of Aglauros, female in the case of Pandrosos. This is reflected in, or, to put it differently, another manifestation of, the fact that the kourotrophic function of both Aglauros and Pandrosos is rooted in cult and shaped the cults' priesthoods.

The institution of the priesthood of Aglauros and the problems associated with it will be discussed in Chapter 3, section 2. Here I will mention that when it first becomes visible to us there was a joint priesthood of Aglauros and Pandrosos and Kourotrophos, while in later documents the priesthoods were distinct.[18] The fact that these three figures were connected[19] is correlative with Aglauros' and Pandrosos' kourotrophic functions. Furthermore, the inscribed seat in the theater of Dionysos from the Roman period: Κουροτρόφου ἐξ Ἀγλαύρου. Δήμη<τ>ρος, apparently '(For the priestess) of Kourotrophos, the one from the shrine of Aglauros, and of

---

[15] See Siewert 1977. On the Lykourgan organization of the ephebeia, see now Humphreys 2004: 82–4, 88–93, 114, and n. 12. For a discussion of the religious figures involved in the ephebic oath, see Parker 2005a: 397–8, 434–7.

[16] On *kourotrophia* in Athens in general, see Parker 2005a: 426–39.

[17] *IG* II² 3472 (of the first half of the second century BC) and *IG* II² 3515 of the Augustan period.

[18] See pp. 152–3.

[19] See also Parker 2005a: 222 and n. 19.

Demeter', suggests that there was a cult of Kourotrophos at the Aglaureion.[20]

Aglauros and Pandrosos were ideally suited to be kourotrophic figures. First, as the daughters of an earthborn king they were the granddaughters of Gaia who was certainly *kourotrophos*.[21] Then, as we shall see, on the reconstruction set out here, in the earlier Athenian mythologies they had also been the granddaughters of Kephisos, the most important river in Attica, and a kourotrophic deity himself.[22]

To return to the discussion of the cultic myths, since two very significant pieces of information on the cultically embedded myths of Aglauros are given by Philochoros, I should stress that Philochoros, who was the last, and a very important, Atthidographer, was not simply an Athenian who shared in the mythicoritual assumptions of late classical and early Hellenistic Athens; he was actually an Athenian religious expert.[23] Consequently, his testimony must be given due weight.

According to Philochoros, Aglauros was a priestess of Athena—apparently the first such.[24] The mytheme that Aglauros had been a priestess of Athena also underlies the *aitia* associated with the Plynteria and Kallynteria, as we shall see in Chapter 3. Aglauros' persona as the first priestess of Athena was embedded in Athenian cult and was therefore a significant part of the Athenian representations of Aglauros.

Aglauros' cultic persona as the chief divine patroness of the ephebes was associated with an important facet of her mythological persona attested to by Philochoros: according to Philochoros,[25] when Eumolpos attacked the Athenians under Erechtheus, that is, in the

---

[20] *IG* II² 5152, as translated by Hadzisteliou Price 1978: 113.

[21] On the relationship between Gaia and Kourotrophos in Athens, see Parker 2005a: 426–7.

[22] On Kephisos as *kourotrophos*, see Parker 2005a: 430–2.

[23] *FGrH* 328 T 1, 2; see the discussion in Jacoby 1954: i. 256–61; see also K. Meister in *Neue Pauly* s.v. Philochoros, 821–2; Parker 2005a: 117.

[24] Philochoros *FGrH* 328 F 106; cf. Hesych. s.v. Aglauros; Phot. s.v. Kallynteria kai Plynteria; *Anecd. Bekk.* 1.270.2, s.v. Kallion.

[25] Philochoros *FGrH* 328 F 105. On her voluntary death to save Athens, see also Redfield 2003: 94, 126–7. But was the whole passage part of Philochoros' text? Jacoby notes the difficulties that would be involved, but in the end considers it likely that it

war between Athens and the Eleusinians, the oracle said that Athens would be saved if someone killed themselves for the city, and Aglauros threw herself from the wall and Athens erected a sanctuary to her. Clearly, both the position and the function of her sanctuary reflected, and were reflected in, this myth of Aglauros' self-sacrifice and the manner of her death. I will discuss the complex and apparently problematic relationship between Aglauros and Erechtheus below, after I have discussed the relationships between the figures of Erichthonios and Erechtheus. I will also discuss below the partial replacement of Aglauros by the daughters of Erechtheus in the role of female lives offered for the city's salvation in the war between Athens and the Eleusinians. Here I will continue with the main lines of Aglauros' mythicoritual persona.

In this myth as it is reflected in Philochoros, in which Aglauros was both the priestess of Athena and the woman who sacrificed herself to save the polis and received the reward of a sanctuary, Aglauros was a

reflects Philochoros. The first difficulty involves chronology and I will discuss it in a moment. The second difficulty he mentions (Jacoby 1954: i. 424 ad loc.), that kings sacrificed their own daughters, not those of their predecessors, is not in fact a difficulty; for it was Aglauros herself who chose to sacrifice her life for the city and she killed herself. This is a different mythological schema from 'father sacrifices his daughter at the altar' that structures the myth of the daughters of Erechtheus and of Iphigeneia. This schema is closer to that of the one self-sacrificing virgin youth in a surviving Euripidean tragedy, Menoikeus in Eur. *Phoen.* (see 997–1005). I will be suggesting below that in an earlier version of her myth Aglauros had been sacrificed by her father, who in that version was Erechtheus, before the figure of Kekrops was constructed. The real difficulty is the chronological discrepancy, since Aglauros' sacrifice in the reign of Erechtheus would only be possible if Erechtheus succeeded Kekrops immediately, or at a very short interval as he does in Hdt 8.44, while Philochoros assigned Kekrops to the sixth generation before Erechtheus. Thus, Jacoby comments [1954: i. 426], the accepted tradition is impossible for Philochoros if the whole scholion belongs to him. But he then continues that if he knew an old legend about the sacrificial death of Aglauros, and if he thought that he must keep to this tradition, only one form is possible: at the end of each reign Philochoros gave the descendants of each, supplying short notes about them, e.g. that Aglauros was the first priestess of Athena and sacrificed herself for her country. By this expedient the question of chronology lost its primary importance, or at least the incompatibility would not be so glaring. 'Even if a reader did feel doubts, the λέγουσι, by which Philochoros shifted the responsibility from himself, would appease him' (p. 427). According to Jacoby this is the simplest and most likely solution. In my view, the reason why Philochorus thought that he must keep to this tradition is that it was cultically embedded.

partial mirror image of the version of the myth of Iphigeneia reflected in Euripides' *Iphigeneia in Tauris*. In that tragedy Iphigeneia
was sacrificed by her father at the altar, it was not her own choice; but
she did not die and eventually she became a priestess. Aglauros was a
priestess, and she herself chose to sacrifice her life for the city and
killed herself, not at the altar, and her life did come to an end; she was
therefore rewarded with a sanctuary, not a priesthood. Aglauros'
double persona of priestess of Athena and female who sacrificed
herself to save the city is split between different figures in Euripides'
Erechtheus, on the one hand the daughters of Erechtheus, one of
whom was sacrificed and the others killed themselves (because of an
oath they had taken with their sister), and on the other their mother
Praxithea, who was willing to offer a daughter as sacrifice to save the
polis, and who became Athena's priestess. I shall return to the figure
of Praxithea below.

In one version of her myth[26] Aglauros had a daughter by Ares,
Alkippe, reflecting her connection with war.[27] According to Pausanias, the Kerykes, the *genos* which, together with the Eumolpids,
administered, and had a most important place in, the Eleusinian
cult, claimed that Aglauros was the mother of their ancestor Keryx by
Hermes.[28] In other versions other daughters of Kekrops were mentioned in the role of Keryx's mother.[29] According to Androtion Keryx
was the son of Pandrosos and Hermes.[30] Jacoby believes that this
was the official tradition of the *genos* of the Kerykes in the fourth
century.[31] It is therefore possible that the myth that Aglauros was the
mother of Keryx may have been generated by the gentilicial mythopoeia of the Kerykes, which aimed at enhancing the prestige of the

---

[26] Hellanikos of Lesbos *FGrH* 4F 38 = 323a F1; Apollod. 3.14.2.
[27] Kearns 1990: 330.
[28] Paus. 1.38.3.
[29] See Jacoby 1954: i. 108–9 ad 324 F1.
[30] Androtion *FGrH* 324 F1.
[31] Jacoby 1954: i. 109 ad 324 F1. Jacoby also says that the Kerykes themselves seem
to have named different daughters of Kekrops at different times as Keryx's mother, for
we have sound attestations for all three. But there is no evidence to suggest that those
other versions of the myth were told by the Kerykes, for, given the importance of the
genos in Athenian cult and life (Parker 1996: 300–2), alternative versions of their
genealogy may have been constructed in other contexts than that of their own
gentilicial genealogy.

genos, and also its connections to the centre of the Athenian polis, by associating it with the woman who had ensured Athenian victory over Eleusis, a victory that led to the salvation of the city and its crystallization in the present form that included Eleusis, a woman who had also been an Athenian princess and the priestess of Athena. If this is right, the myth that Aglauros was the mother of Keryx was a by-product of the myth of Aglauros' self-sacrifice in the war against the Eleusinians. If so, it would follow that the notion of Aglauros being a mother was not perceived as being in conflict with the myth of her self-sacrifice to save the city—since otherwise such a mythopoeic construction would have been blocked. Perhaps further mythopoeic activity, not necessarily by the Kerykes themselves, had constructed versions in which Aglauros was replaced by one of her sisters in the role of Keryx's mother—possibly because the representations that had shaped the construction of a connection between one of the *genē* that were central in the Eleusinian cult and the woman who ensured Athenian victory had become less significant.

The myths of Aglauros' self-sacrifice and the myth that she was the mother of Keryx would not necessarily have been perceived as 'incompatible'; *pace* Jacoby,[32] it is not the case that in Philochoros Aglauros sacrifices herself as a virgin. This is how modern readers are inclined to make sense of her sacrifice, because it is automatically assimilated, in modern perceptions, to the common Greek schema 'sacrifice of a virgin in war'. However, Aglauros' was a self-killing, she was not killed at the altar by her father, and since apparently small differences are more significant for the participants in a culture, and meanings are created also through relationships of differences,[33] I suggest that the possibility cannot be excluded that she may have been perceived to have killed herself as a woman who, though unmarried, was not a virgin. But I must make clear that the fact that she was a priestess of Athena, and that, in the cult of the present, priestesses of Athena were not virgins (nor was Praxithea, the other iconic priestess), cannot necessarily be taken to show that this was indeed the case. For there are other myths, in other cults, in which the first priestess was a virgin, though in the actual practice of the

---

[32] Jacoby 1954: i. 109 ad 324 F1.
[33] See Sourvinou-Inwood 1991: 11.

present the priestess was not a virgin, as was the case with Iphigeneia
and the cult of Artemis Brauronia, and also other myths that say that
a change from a virgin priestess to a non-virgin one had taken place,
for some reason, in the past, as was the case with the Pythia.[34]

There is, then, a certain ambiguity as to her perceived biological
(and corresponding social) status; on the one hand, the schema of the
female death to save the city is intimately connected with maidens,
through the schema 'a maiden dies to save the city', on the other
Aglauros in different myths is said to have had children by two
different gods.[35] As Parker noted, as the most prominent Athenian
females of the earliest times the daughters of Kekrops were ascribed
descendants.[36] Let me put all this differently. Did the Athenians have
a clear picture as to whether or not Aglauros was a virgin when she
died? We cannot answer this question, for we do not know what the
various versions of her myth may or may not have stated. On the
other hand, on the basis of the fragments of her various myths that are
extant, we can set out some of the main parameters within which such
an answer would be located. The schema 'virgin sacrifice to save the
city' may have directed the Athenians to perceive that Aglauros was a
virgin when she died to save Athens but it need not necessarily have
done so. For the fact that in the extant version Aglauros' death to save
the city was her own, not her father's choice, and, secondly, occurred
through suicide from the Acropolis wall, not an actual sacrifice at the
altar, would have distanced that version from the common form of
the schema; and this may well have left it ambiguous whether or not
that schema had structured her myth. If the possibility that she
died a virgin was constructed, explicitly or implicitly, by the myth
of her self-sacrifice, the myths that she was the mother of Alkippe,

---

[34] Diod. Sic. 16.26.6.

[35] Redfield suggested that this and associated variations are also connected with
the instability of the mythological personalities of the Kekropids, and of the representations of primordial Athens in general (Redfield 2003: 121).

[36] Parker 1987a and 210 n. 43. He thinks that in their main myth they died virgins.
Gourmelen (2005: 59–60) thinks that the fact that Aglauros was the name both of
Kekrops' wife and of one of his daughters means that Aglauros was both his wife and
daughter—and that therefore he was surrounded by feminine powers, the mother
(Ge) and the wife-daughter.

or Keryx, or both would have been perceived as alternative representations which the Athenians may or may not have perceived to be 'true'.

There is a nexus of associations between the war against the Eleusinians, Aglauros, and the Skir- element in Athenian myth and cult that may testify to the deep rootedness of Aglauros' role in that war. As we shall see in Chapter 3, section 2, Aglauros and her priestess were involved in the sanctuary of Athena Skiras at Phaleron. According to Philochoros, Athena Skiras took her name from Skiros who was a seer from Eleusis;[37] according to Pausanias,[38] the sanctuary of Athena Skiras at Phaleron was founded by a seer called Skiros, who had come from Dodona but was also associated with Eleusis, since, after he was killed in the war between the Eleusinians and the Athenians under Erechtheus, the Eleusinians buried him near a torrent, and he gave his name both to the place and to the torrent. Since, we saw, in Philochoros' version of her myth, Aglauros killed herself to save the city during this same war, Skiros and Aglauros are, in some ways, partial mirror images, in that both died in that war, though on opposite sides, and subsequently both receive cult in the 'new' Athenian polis which after the war became as it is 'now'.[39] Aglauros' cult was located at the centre, on the slope of the Acropolis; in addition, besides having deme cults, she was also connected—at the very least through the involvement of her priestess[40]—with the sanctuary of the polis cult of Athena Skiras at Phaleron which had been founded by Skiros. Skiros had a cult at Phaleron and he was also strongly associated with the locality called Skiron, where his grave was and where

---

[37] *FGrH* 328 F 14. According to Praxion the Megarian she took her name from Skiron (*FGrH* 484 F1). See also Strabo 9.393. On the different derivations of Athena Skiras, see Jacoby 1954: ii. 200–4 (n. 77). On Skiros and Athena Skiras, see Jacoby 1954: i. 285–305; on Skiros, see Ferguson 1938: 18–20; Kearns 1989: 197–8 (though I do not think the various Skiros figures can be unproblematically separated); Parker 1996: 313, 315–16.

[38] Pausanias 1.36. 4.

[39] All this is simple myth, since the notion that Eleusis had been independent of the Athenian polis does not correspond to historical reality (Sourvinou-Inwood 1997a and 2003b).

[40] Salaminioi inscr. (*LSCG* 19) 41–5.

he may have received cult.[41] The locality Skiron had a significant symbolic place in the mythology concerning the relationship between Athens and Eleusis[42] and, as we shall see in Chapter 3, it was in some ways symbolically correlative with Phaleron.[43]

Another, apparently cultically embedded, minor myth involves Aglauros in association with her sisters, of whom Pandrosos has the leading role. This myth says that Pandrosos and her sisters were the first to weave woollen clothes for mortals.[44] As Kearns noted, this mythological fact can hardly be unrelated to the weaving of Athena's *peplos* by the *arrhephoroi*.[45] The *arrhephoroi* were specifically associated with Pandrosos.[46] This mytheme would appear to entail that the *peplos* as the normal dress of the statue of Athena Polias was introduced by Aglauros, who was Athena's priestess—after she and her sisters had first woven woollen clothes. Pandrosos would seem to have been perceived as having had the leading role in the 'invention' of the weaving of such clothes, correlatively with her closer cultic association with the *arrhephoroi*, while Aglauros, as Athena's priestess, would have been perceived as having dressed the statue in the woollen *peplos* for the first time.

ii. Aglauros and her sisters in the myth of Erichthonios

The myth of the birth of Erichthonios and the Kekropidai is widely thought to be the mythological prototype and correlative of the rite

---

[41] Phaleron: Philochoros *FGrH* 328 F 111; Salaminioi inscr. (*LSCG* 19) 93 (cf. Ferguson 1938: 28, 33). Skiron: Pausanias 1.36. 4; see Kearns 1989: 198; Jacoby 1954: ii. 290–1, 206–7 (n. 82).

[42] See Sourvinou-Inwood 1997a: 147–9.

[43] See also Calame 1990: 341–3.

[44] Phot. s.v. *protonion*; cf. Suda s.v. *protonion* which gives the variant Pandora. See also Gourmelen 2005: 161. The fact that we are told that the daughters of Kekrops were the first to weave woollen clothes for mortals should not be taken to entail that woollen clothes had been woven before, but only for statues; rather, if there is a differentiation underlying the expression, it would be between woollen clothes available to mortals and woollen clothes that were always available to the gods.

[45] Kearns 1989: 24. On the *arrhephoroi* and the daughters of Kekrops, see Burkert 1990: 40–59.

[46] See e.g. Kearns 1989, 24, 192. On the association with Herse, see Istros *FGrH* 334 F27 and Jacoby 1954: i. 643–4; Burkert 1990: 42–3; Kearns 1989: 161.

of the *arrhephoroi*. Does this mean it was a cultically embedded myth? I shall consider this relationship below. First, let us consider this myth, which, among other things, expresses very strongly the representation 'Athenian autochthony'.[47] According to Apollodoros,[48] there was a version of his myth in which Erichthonios was a son of Hephaistos by Atthis, daughter of the early king Kranaos; in the other version "he was the son of Hephaistos and Athena", a statement which he explains by telling the story in which Athena was being pursued by an amorous Hephaistos, who spilled his seed on her leg; she was disgusted, wiped off the seed with wool, and threw it on the earth, and in this way Erichthonios was produced. The main lines of the story are the same in Euripides *TrGF* 5 F 925, as reported in Hyginus *Poetica Astronomica* 2.13 and Eratosthenes [*Cat.*] 13 *Heniochou*. Hyginus calls Erichthonius a snake, but Eratosthenes says that a boy was born. It is undoubtedly the latter version, which corresponds to Erichthonios' human form in the images, that reflects Euripides.

To continue with the account in Apollodoros,[49] Athena brought Erichthonios up in secret from the other gods, and put him in a chest, which on this version she entrusted to Pandrosos, daughter of Kekrops, forbidding her to open it; but her sisters did open it and saw a snake coiled around Erichthonios; in some versions there were two snakes.[50] In some versions the Kekropidai were destroyed by the snake, but according to others Athena's wrath drove them mad and they threw themselves down from the Acropolis.[51] This myth is spoken of in two passages in Euripides' *Ion*. In the first,[52] Athena is

---

[47] I will discuss the figure of Erichthonios in detail below. Here I will only mention the myth of his birth, because it impinges on the figure of Aglauros. On this myth see esp. Parker 1987a: 195–7; Parker 2005a: 221–2 with bib.; see also Brulé 1987: 28–62; Gantz 1993: 235–9; Shapiro 1995: 39–48 esp. 40–1; Redfield 2003: 119–20. See Frazer 1921: ii. 90–1 ad loc. and *LIMC* IV.i s.v. Erechtheus, 925 for further refs.

[48] Apollod. 3.14.6.

[49] Ibid.

[50] There are two snakes in Euripides' *Ion* (see below) and Amelesagoras *FGrH* 330 F1. The version in Callim. *Hekale* fr. 70 Hollis is partly based on Amelesagoras (see Jacoby 1954: i. 602 ad loc; Hollis 1990: 227). On the fr. of Callim., see Hollis 1990: 226–37.

[51] Apollod. 3.14.6. According to Paus. 1.18.2, when they saw Erichthonios they were driven mad and hurled themselves off the Acropolis. In Euripides' *Ion* 267–74 also they threw themselves to their death from the cliffs of the Acropolis.

[52] Eur. *Ion* 20–6.

said to have set beside Erichthonios two snakes to guard him, before
she entrusted him to the daughters of Kekrops (here referred to as
'Aglaurid maidens'), and for that reason the Erechtheidae 'rear their
children in chased-gold snakes' (i.e. gold snake bracelets or armlets).
In the second,[53] Erichthonios was said to be earthborn, and Athena
took him up, but was not his mother, and she gave him to the
daughters of Kekrops, and they opened the container and threw
themselves to their death from the cliffs of the Acropolis. In Euripides' *Ion* all three sisters jump off the Acropolis,[54] while in some
versions it is only two, Aglauros and one of her sisters, sometimes
Pandrosos, sometimes Herse, because the other had obeyed Athena's
injunction and is not said to have died.[55] In Kallimachos also, as in
Euripides' *Ion*, all three sisters were guilty of disobedience.[56]

The account in Apollodoros continues by saying that Athena
herself brought up Erichthonios in her sanctuary; when he grew up
he expelled Amphiktyon and became king, set up Athena's wooden
statue which is on the Acropolis, founded the Panathenaia, and
married the Naiad Nymph Praxithea by whom he had a son, Pandion.[57] When he died he was buried in the sanctuary of Athena.[58]

Leaving aside all the issues concerning the appearance of
Erichthonios and his relationship with Erechtheus, which will be
discussed below, it is clearly important to try to establish the date
of the myth of the disobedience of Aglauros and her sister or sisters
and subsequent death. The mytheme of Hephaistos' pursuit of
Athena appears early: according to Pausanias, on the throne at
Amyklai, Athena is represented running away from Hephaistos who

---

[53] Eur. *Ion* 267–74; after this follows a reference to Erechtheus sacrificing his
daughters.

[54] See e.g. Eur. *Ion* 273–4.

[55] Euphorion, fr. 9 Powell seems to single out Herse as the sister who opened the
basket and was thereafter driven to suicide. Paus. (1.18.2 and 1.27.2) speaks of
Pandrosos as the only innocent one of the sisters; the same may be implied by
Apollod. (3.14.6) where Pandrosos receives the basket and her sisters open it. In
Amelesagoras (*FGrH* 330 F1) Aglauros and Pandrosos opened the basket.

[56] Callim. *Hekale* fr. 70.12–13 Hollis; see Hollis 1990: 230.

[57] Apollod. 3.14.6.

[58] Kearns (1992: 84 n. 23) cautions that the modern notion that Erechtheus had a
tomb in the Erechtheion is not what the sources say.

is pursuing her,[59] and this representation should probably be dated in the late sixth century.[60] Since myths develop and are shaped and reshaped through a process of bricolage, in which mythological material is deployed and redeployed in different myths in different forms, with mythemes combined in different combinations in the different myths, the presence of one mytheme known to us from a particular myth cannot be legitimately assumed to be an index for, a manifestation of, the particular form of that myth that is known to us. Therefore, the representation of Hephaistos' erotic pursuit of Athena does not necessarily entail that it reflects a myth in which this pursuit was combined with all the mythemes that were combined with it in the myth of the birth of Erichthonios; this mytheme does not necessarily entail a story about a baby being born of the god's seed, let alone the myth of the disobedience of the Kekropidai. It is at least equally possible that the myth of the birth of Erichthonios was generated with the help of the deployment (and, of course, transformation) of an established myth of a simpler erotic pursuit of Athena by Hephaistos.[61]

Let us now consider the early images of the Kekropidai and the birth of Erichthonios on Athenian vases and try to determine what if anything they can tell us about the development of this myth. As Shapiro rightly states, in an important paper on the Kekropidai,[62] in the archaic period the daughters of Kekrops are never explicitly associated with Erichthonios' story: "it is only after the Persian Wars that this part of the myth is developed and then in such different ways as to suggest that this charter myth of Athens was still evolving through the fifth century and into the fourth."[63]

---

[59] Paus. 3.18.13.

[60] On the date of the throne, see now the exhaustive discussion with bib. in Faustoferri 1996: 297–358 (cf. 292–5, where she argues for a date in the middle of the sixth century; see also Faustoferri 1993: 159–66).

[61] The association of the schema erotic pursuit with marriage in the Greek collective representations (Sourvinou-Inwood 1987a = 1991: 58–98) may be one parameter that helped shape the variant in Amelesagoras (*FGrH* 330 F1), in which Athena is given to Hephaistos but disappears miraculously (see on this Jacoby 1954: ii. 491–2 n. 4; Hollis 1990: 227–8).

[62] Shapiro 1995: 39–48.

[63] Ibid.: 44. He began by saying that it seems likely that the story of Erechtheus' origin on the Acropolis, his 'stepmother' Athena, and her entrusting him to the

The earliest representation of Gaia handing a child to Athena is on a black figure lekythos of *c.*490, which shows Gaia emerging from the earth and handing a child to Athena in the presence of Kekrops and a male with a phiale, but not the Kekropidai.[64] The earliest image that can be associated with a version of the story that involved the Kekropidai, though Erichthonios is not present, is the scene on side B of the red figure cup Frankfurt, Liebieghaus, St.V.7,[65] of *c.*470, on which two terrified girls flee from a large snake towards a palace, in which a bearded man and a youth are sitting, while a third girl, also still in the palace, rushes to meet them. The large snake is emerging from foliage on the right, around the area of the handle; the chest has been displaced to the other side of the handle, on the left of the scene on A. The terrified girls have been identified as the two disobedient daughters of Kekrops, the girl in the palace as the obedient sister and the man and boy as Kekrops and his son Erysichthon.

In the tondo of this cup a woman is pursued by Poseidon; it is thought that she may be Aithra, Theseus' mother. Side A of the cup depicts Triptolemos in his winged chariot about to leave on his mission to give to the world the gift of corn that Demeter had given him. The association between autochthony, the Athenians being the earth's children, and a transformation of the myth of Demeter's gift of corn to the Eleusinians, presented as the gift of the earth and a proof of the Athenians' autochthony, was part of the ideologies expressed in the Funeral Speeches, in which the focus is not on individual heroic figures but on the Athenians en masse.[66] The two heroic figures involved are associated in a much later source: Erichthonios is associated with Triptolemos in Aristides, in a context

Kekropidai was also known in the archaic period, as hinted by meagre but suggestive iconographical evidence: what this evidence shows is that the daughters of Kekrops were established figures associated with the Acropolis, not that they were involved in the story of Erichthonios' birth. On the iconography of Erichthonios in the basket and the Kekropidai, see also Oakley 1982: 220–2 (esp. 221 on basket shapes); Kokkorou-Aleura 1988: 103–14.

[64] Mormino Collection (Palermo) 769; *LIMC* s.v. Ge no. 13; *LIMC* s.v. Erechtheus 928 no. 1 (see Gantz 1993: 236).

[65] *ARV* 386, 398.7, 1649; *Add* 229; *LIMC* s.v. Aglauros, Herse, Pandrosos no. 15; Shapiro 1995: 43 figs. 9–10; 44.

[66] Pl. *Menex.* 238E- 238B; Dem. 50.5; cf. Parker 1996: 138. In Plato the earth also gave the gift of the olive and introduced gods.

about culture heroes, where he says that Athena gave Erichthonios the chariot and Demeter gave Triptolemos the seeds.[67] If the same association of ideas helped shape this vase painter's selection to juxtapose these two scenes on the outside of the cup, it would follow that the myth that Erichthonios invented the chariot was extant at that time. But of course we cannot be certain that this was the case; we cannot even be certain that there was a connection between the three sides of the vase. Therefore this vase is not evidence that the myth that Erichthonios invented the chariot was extant in the 470s, though it does point in that direction. But if it was extant, and if the juxtaposition was shaped by this association of ideas, Athenian viewers would indeed have identified the woman pursued by Poseidon in the tondo as Aithra, Theseus' mother, and so the scene as one representing the origin of the greatest Athenian king of all.[68]

The vase certainly shows that some form of the myth of Erichthonios involving a snake and three girls who are almost certainly the Kekropidai was known in Athens at that time. Shapiro suggested that the early images do not indicate that the Kekropidai were about to be punished with death for their disobedience.[69] He notes that it looks as though on the cup Frankfurt, Liebieghaus, ST V 7 the girls escape to safety, and also that in the next generation of the representations showing Athena chastising the girls there is no indication that they will pay with their lives. He wonders whether this may have been a fifth-century elaboration or an early variant never fully accepted; he notes that in the earliest extant reference to this death, in Euripides' *Ion*, the story's veracity is questioned by Ion and he receives no reply. Whether or not this is right, it is certainly right that on the cup Frankfurt, Liebieghaus, ST V 7 the girls do seem to escape to safety. If, as seems to be the case, Shapiro is right that the early images do not indicate that the Kekropidai were about to be punished with death for their disobedience, it would follow that the earliest versions of the myth were in less radical conflict with the persona of Pandrosos, and especially Aglauros, embedded in the cult and the associated

---

[67] Aristid. *Or.* 37 Keil (*Athena*) 14.
[68] *ARV* 386; Shapiro 1995: 48 n. 51.
[69] Shapiro 1995: 44–5.

cultic myths than the versions in, for example, Euripides' *Ion* and Apollodoros.[70]

Later I shall contrast inconsistencies that were not necessarily perceived as problematic with radical conflict in narrowly focused cultic myths. Here I will simply suggest that the pattern of the myth's appearance on vases suggests a development in the course of the fifth century which eventually led to the version in which a disobedient Aglauros is punished with death. This is one indication that the myth of the birth of Erichthonios leading to the death of Aglauros was not a long-established cultic myth. There are, we shall see, also some others.

But if this is true, how do we explain the widely accepted view that the story of Erichthonios and the Kekropidai is the mythological prototype and correlative of the ritual of the *arrhephoroi*?[71] Does this correlation not mean that the myth of the disobedient Kekropidai was cultically embedded from an early age? Let us consider this question.

The *arrhephoroi*[72] were two or four girls—the evidence is contradictory[73]—between the ages of 7 and 11 chosen by the *archon basileus* to serve Athena Polias. They lived on the Acropolis for a year, they played a ritual game of ball, and they participated in the weaving of the robe offered to Athena at the Panathenaia—a ritual weaving, to which I shall return, which relates to the girls' gender roles as well as to Athena.

First, whatever the complex relationship between the myth of the Kekropidai and the rite of the *Arrhephoria*, Pandrosos was clearly, as we saw above,[74] the second honorand of the *Arrephoria* beside Athena. Then, it is clearly right that the Kekropidai are the mythological prototype of the *arrhephoroi*. The weaving of the *peplos* of Athena,[75] the living and playing on the Acropolis, and the relationship on the one hand of the Kekropidai with the king who was their

---

[70] Eur. *Ion* 267–74; Apollod. 3.14.6.

[71] Burkert 1966: 1–25 = Burkert 1990: 40–59; Burkert 1983: 150–4.

[72] See now Parker 2005a: 219–23, with earlier bib.

[73] Parker 2005a: 220.

[74] See n. 17.

[75] On the role of the *arrhephoroi* in the weaving of the *peplos* of Athena, see p. 268. On weaving and the Kekropidai, see below.

father and on the other of the *arrhephoroi* with the *archon basileus*, who elected them,[76] are significant common elements.

It is the relationship between the myth of the birth of Erichthonios and the nocturnal rite performed by the *arrhephoroi* that marks the completion of their office that is the crux of the matter, the part of the ritual nexus of the *arrhephoroi* that would be equivalent to the myth of the disobedience of the Kekropidai in the myth of Erichthonios. Let us consider this rite, which marks the completion of office of one crop of *arrhephoroi* and the beginning of that of the next.

Pausanias says the following about the ritual office of the *arrhephoroi*:[77]

Two maidens, whom the Athenians call *arrhephoroi*, live not far from the temple of Athena Polias. They stay with the goddess for a time, but when the festival comes round they do the following in the night. They place on their heads what the priestess of Athena gives them to carry and neither she who gives knows what she is giving nor they who carry; there is an enclosure in the city (*or*, 'on the Acropolis') not far from the sanctuary of Aphrodite called in the Gardens[78] and through it a natural underground descending passage—it is through this that the girls descend. They leave what they carry below and having received something else they bring it back covered up. Then they are let go and other maidens are brought to the Acropolis in their place.

First, and most importantly, as Parker remarked, the myth and the rite are never aitiologically (or otherwise) connected in an ancient source.[79] Second, the correlations between the myth and the rite are far from close. As Parker remarked, "the ritual moves to an ending—the bringing back to the acropolis of new sacred objects—quite absent from the story".[80] He cites Redfield's notion[81] that the *arrephoroi* pass the test that the Kekropidai failed but notes that nothing

---

[76] On the *basileus* and the *arrhephoroi*, see below p. 296; also Brelich 1969: 234; and esp. Parker 2005a: 220.

[77] Paus.1.27.3.

[78] I follow Parker 2005a: 221 on the topography.

[79] Ibid.: 222 n. 17.

[80] Ibid.: 222.

[81] Redfield (2003: 120) admits that the story is not a true *aition*, but nevertheless claims that myth related to the ritual in the manner characteristic of an *aition*: the *arrephoroi* pass the test that the Kekropidai failed and the rite normalizes danger.

in the attested ritual actions of the *arrhephoroi* evokes the notion that they anticipated the function of child-rearing that they would perform in later life with regard to their own children.

In Apollodoros the schema of 'child in a chest/basket' is associated with Athena raising Erichthonios 'secretly from the other gods' and placing him in a basket which she gave to Pandrosos and told her not to open.[82] Again in Apollodoros, shortly before this passage, another divine child who was taken to be reared by a goddess had also been hidden in such a container: Aphrodite hid Adonis in a chest 'in secret from the gods' and handed him over to Persephone.[83] I have argued elsewhere that this schema 'child in a basket' also helped shape the form of the ritual presentation of children to a kourotrophic deity, Persephone, at Locri Epizephyrii.[84]

Clearly, then, the myth of Erichthonios' babyhood is structured by a transformation of the schema 'child in a chest/basket hidden and reared by a goddess'; for the version in which the 'chest/basket' is opened by the recipient figure, as in the myth of Adonis (and, on my reading, the Locrian ritual schema), is consistent with the mythico-ritual schema of 'child-rearing', of which these are versions, while the form of the schema in which the recipient figure is forbidden from opening the container with the child is very much less so.

This transformation of the schema 'child in a chest/basket hidden and reared by a goddess' in the myth of Erichthonios was constructed through the interaction of this schema with an element 'forbidden to open the container'. The latter element also helps structure the rite of the *arrhephoroi*, indeed it is the only element that the myth of the involvement of the Kekropidai in Erichthonios' babyhood has in common with the rite of the *arrhephoroi*, as becomes clear when the two are compared closely. For though there appears to be a general similarity between myth and rite a closer comparison brings out the very significant differences. Both groups, the Kekropidai and the *arrhephoroi*, were given, the first by Athena, the second by the priestess of Athena, covered containers which they were not allowed to open; however, the *arrhephoroi* received covered containers twice. We do not know who, if anyone, gave them the second load to carry

---

[82] Apollod. 3.14.6.   [83] Apollod. 3.14.4.
[84] Sourvinou-Inwood 1991: 174. See also Redfield 2003: 384.

to the Acropolis, but whoever that may have been, there was a second load and, as Parker noted, this entailed a fundamental difference between the rite of the *arrhephoroi* and the myth of the involvement of the Kekropidai with Erichthonios, the bringing of new sacred objects to the Acropolis.[85]

Even in the more comparable part there are significant differences. Athena knew what was in the container and ordered the girls not to open it. The priestess of Athena did not (according to Pausanias) know what the objects she handed over were, and there is no explicit mention of forbidding the girls to look—it is taken for granted that they will not. Furthermore, the something hidden in a basket that should not be opened was radically different in the two cases, and, most importantly, of the two different loads involved in the ritual it was the first that would have been correlative with Athena handing over Erichthonios in the basket, since it was handed over by Athena's correlative, her priestess; and that first load in the rite was discarded, replaced by another, which makes it clear that the apparent similarities are to a large extent illusory.

The only common element between myth and rite, then, was the element 'forbidden to open the container'.[86] Since, we saw, the myth of Erichthonios was structured by a transformation of the schema 'child in a chest/basket hidden and reared by a goddess' that was constructed through its interaction with the element 'forbidden to open the container', a transformation that was less appropriate for structuring the schema 'child-rearing' than the other forms of this schema, I submit that this common element originated in the rite: that in the mythopoeic process which created (through bricolage) a myth involving the Kekropidai (or one of them) being given a closed

---

[85] Parker 2005a: 222.

[86] Any notion that the death of the Kekropidai was an early, cultically embedded element, an ancient mythological reflection of the element of the descent of the *arrhephoroi*, or the termination of their term of office, is not really tenable. First, the 'descent' of the Kekropidai to their death was structurally different from that of the *arrhephoroi*, who returned to the Acropolis; the handover of the office followed their return, and the same girls ascended as had descended. Second, as we saw, there are reasons for thinking that the early versions of the myth of the Kekropidai did not involve their death as a result of their opening of the basket. Therefore, such a notion does not appear to be consistent with the (admittedly fragmentary) picture we have of the myth's pattern of appearance.

container, the element 'forbidden to open it', that had been part of the rite of the *arrhephoroi*, became attracted to the myth, to the Kekropidai who (and because they) were the mythological proto-types of the *arrhephoroi*. This occurred in the course of the creation, and grafting into earlier established Athenian mythology, of the figure of Erichthonios which was generated out of an earlier figure of Erechtheus, a process that I will discuss in a moment. Of course, the possibility cannot be excluded that, once the new myth was established in this form, the perception may have arisen that there was some relationship between the ritual actions of the *arrhephoroi* and the past actions of the Kekropidai who were otherwise their mythological prototypes. However, as we saw, the myth and the rite are never aitiologically (or otherwise) connected in the ancient sources.

The conclusion that the myth of the birth of Erichthonios was not a refraction of the rite of the *arrhephoria* converges with the conclusion of another argument I will now set out. The myth of Aglauros' self-sacrifice on the one hand, and on the other the myth of the death of Aglauros and her sister[s] as a punishment for their disobedience, have one important element in common: the manner of Aglauros' death. For in the myth of her self-sacrifice, according to Philochoros, Aglauros threw herself from the wall and the Athenian polis erected a sanctuary to her. This death was reflected in the position of her sanctuary as it was in its function. This manner of death is the same as that of the 'death as punishment for their disobedience' of Aglauros and her sister[s] in some, though not all, versions of the myth of the birth of Erichthonios.[87] In the latter myth, as we saw, Aglauros does not jump off the wall alone, but sometimes with both her sisters and sometimes with only one, because the other had obeyed Athena's injunction and is not said to have died.[88] But the fact that it is always Aglauros and one other coincides with the fact that this manner of death was associated with Aglauros in an entirely different myth, and this suggests various possibilities with regard to the mytheme 'Aglauros died by jumping off the Acropolis wall', which was deployed in these two very different myths.

---

[87] See e.g. Eur. *Ion* 273–4; Paus. 1.18.2; cf. Apollod. 3.14.6.
[88] See p. 38 above.

One possibility is that one of the myths took over (and trans-formed) the mytheme from the other; another is that both forms of the mytheme in the two myths were reflections of a ritual element, which either generated these different forms of the mytheme inde-pendently, or generated one mytheme that was a (more or less) direct reflection of the cultic feature in one myth, while the other mytheme in the other myth was constructed as a transformation of the already established mytheme, with a pseudo-anchoring in the cultic reality. This latter possibility, in other words, converges with the possibility mentioned first, that one of the myths 'took over' the mytheme from the other.

Since, we have seen, the myth that Aglauros saved the city by throwing herself from the wall was reflected in, and reflected, her sanctuary, which Athens gave her in honour of her self-sacrifice, and specifically in both the sanctuary's function and its position, this myth was clearly cultically embedded, closely intertwined with the cult of Aglauros. This converges with the conclusion on other grounds that the myth of the birth of Erichthonios leading to the death of Aglauros and her sister[s] as punishment for their disobe-dience was not an early cultic myth. In these circumstances, I suggest that the mytheme 'Aglauros and her sister[s] jumped off the Acro-polis as a punishment for their disobedience', which, in contrast to that of Aglauros' self-sacrifice, appears to be in what we may call mythicoritual disharmony with the cultic reality of her sanctuary, was less a direct reflection of that reality than a transformation of the mytheme of her self-sacrifice, a secondary, later construction that became attached to some versions of the myth of the birth of Erichthonios in the course of the fifth century, when the shaping of that myth is, up to a point, visible to us.

Though, we saw, inconsistencies were not necessarily perceived as problematic, since cultic myths focus on particular segments of each figure's mythological nexus and of the polis' history, and are not necessarily placed precisely inside a coherent chronological frame-work, significant inconsistencies are unlikely to have been unproble-matic within a narrowly focused segment of cultic myths, such as this which is focused on the figure of Aglauros, the first priestess—and the cults and festivals associated with her. For while uncertainties, ambiguities, and multivocalities may have been part of the fabric of the myths, radical conflict in such a narrowly focused context would have blocked the functioning of those cultic myths. I therefore submit that it is unlikely that significant conflicts would have involved segments that inhabited such a narrowly focused context. Aglauros' cultic persona, we saw, included the mytheme that she killed herself to save the city. Therefore, it is unlikely that the myth of the birth of Erichthonios leading to the death of Aglauros was a long-established part of Aglauros' cultic persona, since it is inconsistent with her important cultic myth.

Thus, and especially, in the case of the ephebes (and their predecessors), when they swore their oath in Aglauros' sanctuary and invoked Aglauros as their first witness, they were aware of, and had undoubtedly been formally instructed about, the story of her self-sacrifice which was correlative with their own association with Aglauros, whose example they were expected to follow. It is that aspect of Aglauros, and perhaps also her persona as the first priestess of Athena, that would have dominated the perceptions of the participants in the ritual—and, as a result, probably also the wider perceptions of the ritual itself. That is, they focalized the ritual through this representation of Aglauros as the saviour of the city. The representation 'Aglauros the foolish girl who disobeyed Athena and died as a result' would have been narcotized, except in reflective discourses in which her role in the cult was consciously examined in the light of her negative representation.

In the case of the Plynteria and Kallynteria the stories told (by, one would suppose, among others, the Praxiergidai and perhaps also the priestess of Athena) would have focalized the perception of Aglauros through her persona as the first priestess of Athena who had, for example, been the first who 'adorned the gods'. And when eventually (as we shall see) the ephebes became involved in the procession of the Plynteria, their dominant perception of Aglauros' role resulting from her self-sacrifice would also have come into play—and the negative representation would have been narcotized.

iii. Aglauros as a whole

I am arguing, then, that the aspects of Aglauros' persona that were deeply rooted in the cultic myths of Athens were, first, those that pertained to her role as the first priestess of Athena (and associated elements); second, those that pertained to her role as a female heroine who gave her life to save the city in time of war, which are associated with her third cultically rooted facet, her kourotrophic function, which was focused on males, while her sister Pandrosos' was focused on females. I am also arguing that her persona as foolish girl who disobeyed Athena by opening Erichthonios' basket and died as a result was the result of a fifth-century process of mythopoeic construction which was perceptually marginalized in the rituals, such as the ephebic oath, the Plynteria, and the Kallynteria, in which the other, older, aspects of her persona were implicated and played a significant role.

In the wider mythologies of Athens the conflict between the Erichthonios myth (in the version in which Aglauros died) and the cultic myth of Aglauros' self sacrifice may have been perceived in a variety of possible ways; for example, it may have supported, at least as a minor voice, the notion of unknowability, the ultimate unknowability of the divine world seeping into the perception of the myths of cult recipients. As for the conflict between on the one hand the kourotrophic aspect of Aglauros, which is, we saw, deeply rooted in cult, and on the other her failure in the 'child-rearing' of Erichthonios, it may have been perceived as a constructive contrast: while she failed in the case of a heroic age earthborn baby of divine parentage, she succeeds when it comes to present-day woman-born human youths. The modality shaping such a perception would be at least partly comparable to the modality (and the mythicoritual mentality that articulated it) that structures mythicortual nexuses in which an 'initiatory rite' is founded as a result of the death of a 'failed ephebe'.[89]

---

[89] See on this and on the definition of 'initiatory rite', Sourvinou-Inwood 2005: 252–61.

In the wider Athenian mythological universe taken as a whole the juxtaposition of Aglauros' positive and paradigmatic mythological persona as both the saviour of the city and first priestess of Athena with the representation 'Aglauros the foolish girl who disobeyed Athena and died as a result' made her into an ambivalent figure. In this wider mythological universe taken as a whole Aglauros' mythological persona also involved a further ambivalence. As we saw, there is a certain ambiguity and ambivalence as to her biological (and corresponding social) status, in that the schema of the death to save the city is intimately connected with maidens, while Aglauros is said to have had a daughter by Ares, Alkippe, and, according to the genealogy of the Kerykes, she was the mother of Keryx by Hermes. The fact that in the wider mythologies of Athens Aglauros is characterized by ambivalence is not problematic, since certain types of ambivalence are characteristic of heroic figures in the Greek mythological mentality.[90]

A fundamentally important aspect of Aglauros' persona is that she was associated with primordial times and autochthony; for she was the daughter of the half-snake Kekrops, one figure of autochthony, and was also involved in the other important myth of Athenian autochthony, that of Erichthonios.[91] At the same time, she was associated with a movement away from primordiality, for she was connected with the establishment of some aspects of the present, of things as they are now: she was the first priestess of Athena, the first to have adorned the gods, the first, with her sisters, to have woven woollen cloth, and also presumably the first to have dressed the statue of Athena in a woollen *peplos*, and finally, through her sacrifice that saved the city in the war against the Eleusinians, she was associated with the crystallization of the Athenian polis that includes Eleusis. I shall return to Aglauros after I have discussed the two other figures that are especially important in our investigation, Erechtheus and Erichthonios—as well as some other figures associated with them.

---

[90] [A footnote was indicated but not written here.]
[91] On Aglauros' association with autochthony, see also Redfield 2003: 121–4.

3. ERECHTHEUS, ERICHTHONIOS, AND OTHERS

i. Erechtheus, 'complex' Erechtheus, and Erichthonios

In this section I will investigate Erechtheus, Erichthonios, and the complex relationship between them.[92] I will try to reconstruct at least the main parameters of the complex mythological processes that eventually led to the construction of Erichthonios, and, as a result, to a transformation of the nexus of Erechtheus and the eventual construction of the figure I call 'post-split' Erechtheus. Erichthonios was constructed above all, albeit not exclusively, through the deployment of material that had been part of the mythicoritual nexus of Erechtheus, attested long before the first appearance of Erichthonios. I shall call this early Erechtheus 'complex Erechtheus', to mark the fact that his material eventually helped construct two new mythico-ritual nexuses, each crystallizing into two different figures, Erichthonios and the 'post-split' Erechtheus. That is, in a mythopoeic process that constructed new, and new forms of, myths, the elements that made up the 'complex' Erechtheus nexus eventually became attached to one or other, or sometimes both, of the two figures constructed out of that material, Erechtheus and Erichthonios, and in the process those elements were transformed, not least through their belonging to a different figure, a different mythicoritual system.

Let us now consider the early appearances of a hero called Erechtheus. In the Homeric poems, in a passage in the *Iliad* that is a segment of the Athenian part of the Catalogue, Athens is characterized as the land of Erechtheus, who is said to have been born from the earth, and to have been the nursling of Athena; he is also said to

---

[92] See Mikalson 1976; Parker 1987a: 200–1; on the two figures, see also Kearns 1989: 110–15, 160–1; and for bib. Kron *LIMC* s.v. Erechtheus 927–8 and notes below. For some views on the relation of the two names, see Mikalson 1976: 141 n. 1 (Erechtheus original, Erichthonios a secondary formation); Parker 1987a: 201 'It has often been inferred that they were simply alternative forms of the same name and that this single figure with two names came to be divided into two figures. The actual development was perhaps more complex (Footnote: Assimilation followed by re-division of two distinct figures with different names is perhaps more plausible) but it seems true that they are joint heirs to a single mythological inheritance.'

receive cult involving youths sacrificing bulls and rams.[93] Whether they did so in Athena's temple or in Erechtheus' own temple is not certain.[94] In a much discussed passage in the *Odyssey* Athena is said to enter Erechtheus' 'sturdy house' in Athens.[95] I take this to be referring to the present (the *Odyssey*'s present) day king's palace, which is referred to as the palace of Erechtheus in the same way that Athens is characterized as the land of Erechtheus, in the *Iliad*. If this is right, it does not follow that the passage is locating Athena's place of worship inside the palace, whatever the situation may or may not have been in the Mycenaean period, which does not concern us here; what concerns us is that this passage also presents Erechtheus as a defining early Athenian king.

Mythicoritual nexuses in the Homeric poems do not necessarily always reflect actual mythicoritual nexuses; for they may be composite constructs deploying material from different cults that had not in reality belonged together in an actual cult—albeit deploying such material in ways that 'made sense' to the poet who perceived and manipulated the material through the filters of eighth-century Ionia, and therefore in ways that were compatible with Greek religious mentality. But in this case (and leaving aside the question of the locus of Erechtheus' cult, to avoid circularity) it is clear that the nexus in the *Iliad* (as well as the passage in the *Odyssey* since—insofar as we can see—it is consistent with it) does appear to reflect cultic reality, at least as far as its skeleton is concerned, whether or not the specific form of the cult (youths sacrificing bulls and rams) accurately reflects Athenian practice. For the elements 'Erechtheus' 'primordial king' 'earthborn' 'nursling of Athena' 'cult recipient' 'cattle sacrifices' structure the Athenian mythicoritual nexus of Erechtheus, as will become clear in the discussion below. What the Homeric poems tell us is that this nexus was attached to the name 'Erechtheus' in the representations reflected in the Homeric poems.

---

[93] Hom. *Il.* 2.546–51.

[94] The usual reading of Hom. *Il.* 2.549 is that Athena made Erechtheus dwell in her own rich temple (see e.g. the commentary of G. S. Kirk ad loc.) Recently it has been argued (Ferrari 2002: 16 n. 29) that the formulation is to be read as meaning "in his own rich temple".

[95] Hom. *Od.* 7.80–1; see the commentary of J. B. Hainsworth, pp. 325–6, ad loc. On both Homeric passages, see Parker 1996: 19–20.

At the end of the sixth century Erechtheus was one of the heroes selected to be an eponymous tribal hero: when the Kleisthenic tribes were created,[96] his name was selected by the Pythia from the preliminary list submitted to her.[97] Thus, then, Erechtheus acquired a tribal cult.[98] But he also continued to have a whole polis cult; this becomes clear when we consider Herodotos' reference to Erechtheus' sanctuary. According to Herodotos, Erechtheus was earthborn and he had a sanctuary on the Acropolis which contained the *martyria*, 'tokens, evidence', of the contest between Athena and Poseidon over the sovereignty of Athens, the olive tree of Athena and the 'sea' created by Poseidon.[99] If nothing else, the fact that the *martyria* of the contest that decided the poliadic deity of Athens were in his sanctuary proves beyond doubt that this was a whole polis cult, not simply a tribal one. I shall return to this sanctuary below. Also in Herodotos Erechtheus succeeded Kekrops.[100] He is therefore an earthborn primordial king.

I shall return below to the space in which Erechtheus received cult. Here I will open a brief parenthesis to help clear the ground by considering a problematic reference to that space that concerns the nature of Erechtheus and his relationship to Erichthonios. It is a reference to Athena's guardian snake, the guardian snake of the Acropolis. According to Hesychios, this snake was believed to have been housed in the sanctuary of Erechtheus.[101] But is this reporting true Athenian belief? Eustathios' statement that this snake was

---

[96] On which, see esp. Parker 1996: 117–21.

[97] On this process involving the oracle, in which a preliminary list of heroes is said to have been submitted to the Pythia for the final selection, see Parker (1996: 118); and most recently Bowden (2005: 95–100).

[98] On which, see Kron 1976: 52–5; Kearns 1989: 210–11.

[99] Hdt. 8.55: on the Acropolis there is a 'temple' (νηός, *sic*) of Erechtheus the earthborn (more precisely, τοῦ γηγενέος λεγομένου). On the sanctuary referred to in Herodotos, see Hurwit 1999: 144–5, 202. See also below. It would appear that Herodotos used the word 'temple' loosely here (see also Ferrari 2002: 16 n. 30). The formulation suggests that there is a sanctuary there now, and perhaps implies that there was one there also before the Persian invasion.

[100] Hdt. 8.44.

[101] Hesych. s.v. οἰκουρὸν ὄφιν: 'the snake which guards the Polias; some say there was one, others say there were two, in the sanctuary (ἱερόν) of Erechtheus.' Ar. *Lys.* 759 speaks of ὄφιν . . . οἰκουρόν.

housed in the temple of Athena is probably not trustworthy,[102] but it is not impossible that Herodotos may be saying that the snake was believed to live in the sanctuary of Athena; he certainly makes clear that it was the priestess of Athena who had ultimate jurisdiction over the snake.[103] Herodotos reports, in the context of their reactions to Xerxes' invasion, that the Athenians say that 'a large snake, guardian of the acropolis, lives in the sanctuary', and that when the priestess made it known that the snake had not eaten the monthly offering of the honeycake they considered that Athena had left the Acropolis.[104] The sanctuary referred to here is probably the whole Acropolis; but if not, then it would have had to have been the most important sanctuary on the Acropolis, that of Athena Polias. I suggest that, since that snake was not real, the most likely interpretation of these data is that its dwelling was not necessarily believed to have been a precise spot, and that therefore there had probably been more than one story about this dwelling. These stories may have included the representation that the snake dwelt on the Acropolis which it guarded and one in which it was believed to live in the Athena Polias focused segment of the Acropolis; but there may well have been another representation in which, under the influence of a perceived association between Erechtheus and snakes, the snake could have been believed to have lived in the sanctuary of Erechtheus, as Hesychios claims.

The Erechtheus associated with snakes was the 'complex' Erechtheus, for it is earthborn heroes who are associated, and symbolically correlative, with snakes; after the 'split' that association drifted to Erichthonios.[105] Therefore, the representation that

---

[102] Eustathios ad *Od.* 1.357 p. 1423.8; as Ferrari remarks (2002: 16) he is clearly extrapolating.

[103] Hdt. 8.41.3.

[104] Hdt. 8. 41.2. In commenting on this passage Harrison 2000: 86–7 states that "the Athenians believed that Athena in some sense took the form of a snake on the Acropolis". But in my view things were rather more complex; as is made clear by the formulations that refer to it such as 'watching the house', οἰκουρός (see n. 101) and 'guardian' (Hdt. 8.41), the snake was a sign of the divine presence, not the embodiment of it.

[105] The actual identification of Erichthonios with a snake (I cannot see that it is the οἰκουρὸς ὄφις, as is sometimes claimed in modern scholarship) is clearly late: Paus 1.24.7 in describing the statue of Athena Parthenos says that the snake (δράκων) near

Athena's snake lived in the sanctuary of Erechtheus is likely to have been constructed before that 'split', and so also before the construction of the Erechtheion, and to have been associated with an independent sanctuary of Erechtheus, such as that mentioned in Herodotos—or an earlier version of it.[106]

Xenophon speaks synoptically of Erechtheus' nurture (*trophe*) and birth and the war that took place in his reign.[107] This was the war against the Eleusinians that was mentioned above in connection with Aglauros. Xenophon's reference to Erechtheus' *trophe* and birth is rightly taken to refer to an Erechtheus whose persona was nearer that of the figure I call the 'complex' Erechtheus; for in other configurations some of the elements that are here combined belonged to the 'post-split' Erechtheus (the war) and others to Erichthonios (nurture and birth, for in this context they signify exceptional ones, autochthony and being nursed by Athena).[108]

In these circumstances, it is clear that in the earlier sources Erechtheus was characterized by elements, above all the traits 'earthborn' and 'nursling of Athena', which eventually became attached to Erichthonios. This, then, is the 'complex' Erechtheus, who was a primordial figure who succeeded Aglauros' earthborn father Kekrops. Of the reconstructed nexus of the 'complex' Erechtheus, one set of elements, 'earthborn king' and 'a nursling of Athena', intrinsically belonged to the earliest, primordial, segment of the history of Athens. Therefore these elements became attached to, were 'inherited' by, Erichthonios, for it was he who became located at the primordial

---

Athena's spear should be Erichthonios. Incidentally, Philostr. (*VA* 7.24) does not testify to an Athenian identification of Erichthonios with the guardian snake. The text claims that Athena gave birth to a snake for the Athenians—a representation so distant from classical (and Hellenistic) Athenian ones that it need not concern us.

[106] Since we know that in his time the cult of Erechtheus was housed in the Erechtheion, Cicero's reference (*Nat. D.* 3.49 cf. also 3.50) to the shrine (*delubrum*) (and priest) of Erechtheus in Athens clearly does not refer to a separate sanctuary.

[107] Xen. *Mem.* 3.5.10.

[108] Mikalson 1976: 142 considers that Xen. *Mem.* 3.5.10 refers to the birth and nursing of Erechtheus in such a way as to exclude the figure of Erichthonios. But this is too schematic. Clearly, for some time, mythemes that had been part of the 'complex' Erechtheus and had subsequently gone into the making of the figure of Erichthonios, had not been 'shed' from the figure of Erechtheus that was morphing into the 'post-split' Erechtheus; see the discussion below.

segment after the 'splitting' process; it was Erichthonios, rather than Erechtheus, who was located early in the royal succession, just as autochthony came to be attached to Erichthonios and not to the 'post-split' Erechtheus. In his earlier myths, Erichthonios probably succeeded Kekrops immediately,[109] as the 'complex' Erechtheus had previously done, since, we saw, in Herodotos Erechtheus succeeded Kekrops.[110] That this had been the case for Erichthonios is also suggested by the relationship between Erichthonios and the daughters of Kekrops in the myth of the former's babyhood. In later myths there is an interval: in Apollodoros' version[111] Kekrops was succeeded by Kranaos, who was expelled by Amphictyon, who was expelled by Erichthonios.

In the sequence 'Kekrops is succeeded by Erichthonios' a strongly 'earthborn' king, Kekrops, would be succeeded by another strongly 'earthborn' king, Erichthonios, and this, I submit, constitutes an argument in favour of the validity of that reconstructed sequence, since in the alternative just mentioned the earthborn dimension is weakened: Kranaos was said to be an *autochthon*, 'of the earth, land', in Apollodoros[112] but not in Pausanias,[113] where his parentage is not mentioned. Amphictyon is even more ambivalent from the point of view of autochthony: in one version he is said to have been earthborn but in another he was a son of Deucalion.[114] So at the very least neither is very strongly earthborn.

Erichthonios is an 'earthborn king' with an elaborate and more specifically focused divine parentage than Kekrops (we do not know what was the case with the 'complex' Erechtheus), and also a 'nursling of Athena', again with an elaborate myth embodying this

---

[109] For the view that in earlier genealogies Erichthonios had probably succeeded Kekrops, see also Parker (1987a: 200). In the fourth-century king-lists what Parker (1987a: 200) calls "two shadowy kings" came in between Kekrops and Erichthonios: first Kranaos, and then Amphictyon (see e.g. Paus. 1.2.6). Kranaos, and in some versions also Amphictyon, was autochthonous (Apollod. 3.14.5; see also, with further references, on Kranaos, Kearns 1989: 179; on Amphictyon, Kearns 1989: 147. See also below).

[110] Hdt. 8.44.
[111] Apollod. 3.14.5–6. See also Paus. 1.2.6.
[112] Apollod. 3.14.5–6.
[113] Paus. 1.2.6.
[114] Apollod. 3.14.6.

representation. Erichthonios played a significant role in the poliadic cult. In the extant myths Erichthonios is said to have set up the statue of Athena and to have founded the Panathenaia.[115] Before the construction of Erichthonios these elements had clearly belonged to the 'complex' Erechtheus, since the 'complex' Erechtheus was the successor of Kekrops, in whose reign the poliadic cult was established; for through those acts, especially the setting up of the statue, the establishment of the poliadic cult was completed. Indeed, we shall see, in the common Greek schemata the establishment of a cult and the setting up of the statue belong together in one nexus. I will be arguing that they may have belonged together in an earlier nexus in which the 'complex' Erechtheus was the first king of Athens. In any case, the elements 'installer of Athena's statue', 'founder of the Panathenaia' (and the associated mytheme 'inventor of the chariot'), also drifted, and became attached, to Erichthonios. With regard to the mytheme 'invention of the chariot', which, we shall see, is associated with the foundation of the Panathenaia, we will find some additional reasons for concluding that it had originally been part of the nexus of the 'complex' Erechtheus.

Unlike the elements concerning primordiality, the war against the Eleusinians was potentially mobile; when this myth was located in the reign of the complex Erechtheus (who was, I shall be arguing, the first king in the early versions of Athenian history) it had represented the crystallization of the just-born polis of Athens; but it was also capable of representing a more generalized threat to the polis that could be situated at any time in its history—a threat which eventually led to victory and the crystallization of the polis as it now is, which includes Eleusis. Thus, the mythemes associated with the war with the Eleusinians became attached to the figure of the 'post-split' Erechtheus. Hence, the main myth associated with Erechtheus after the 'split' was the myth involving the war against the Eleusinians; in the Athenian perceptions that are visible to us, this war led to the final confirmation of Athena's poliadic status, the crystallization of the polis in its present form, in which Eleusis and the Eleusinian cult are part of it. Of course, in Euripides' *Erechtheus* the Thracian

---

[115] See e.g. Apollod. 3.14.6.

ethnicity of Eumolpos and his army also brought in the semantic dimension of the barbarian threat and defeat,[116] but this does not concern us here. In any case, in Euripides' *Erechtheus* a very important semantic representation of the war is also as a human replay of the contest between Athena and Poseidon, an attempt to reverse Athena's victory and replace her by Poseidon. The failure of the attempt leads to the 'final establishment' and crystallization of the poliadic cult.

'Post-split' Erechtheus, then, inherited the mytheme 'the war against the Eleusinians' from 'complex' Erechtheus. Aglauros had killed herself to save the city in the nexus of the 'complex' Erechtheus. For since the primordial earthborn 'complex' Erechtheus had succeeded Aglauros' earthborn father Kekrops, a succession reflected in Herodotos,[117] this mytheme of Aglauros' self-sacrifice during the war with the Eleusinians in the reign of Erechtheus had belonged in the mythocoritual nexus of the primordial earthborn 'complex' Erechtheus.

We cannot be certain that the early versions of the myth of the war against the Eleusinians, which placed it in the reign of the 'complex' Erechtheus, had included the mytheme that the Eleusinians were trying to reverse the result of the contest for the sovereignty of Attica and make Poseidon the poliadic deity. However, there are good reasons for thinking that they had indeed included that mytheme. First, in the earlier forms of the extant myths the war against the Eleusinians took place in the reign that immediately followed the reign of Kekrops, in which the poliadic cult of Athena was established; indeed, on my reconstruction, in earlier myths the establishment of the poliadic cult of Athena and the war against the Eleusinians had both taken place in the reign of the complex Erechtheus. It is in this context of primordiality, in the period immediately (or virtually immediately) following the divine contest and establishment of the poliadic deity, that such a mytheme organically belongs, not in the period of the 'post-split' Erechtheus so long after those events, when Athena had been long established as the

---

[116] On Eumolpos' complex ethnicity, and the semantic dimension of the barbarian threat and defeat, see Parker 1987a: 202–4.
[117] Hdt 8.44.

poliadic deity. This is not to say that the mytheme could not function adequately in the latter case, for, clearly, it did. However, I submit, the notion of overthrowing the result of the contest, and thus the generation of this mytheme, organically belongs to the immediate aftermath of that contest. This suggests that this mytheme had been part of the nexus of the complex Erechtheus, and that therefore the myth of the war against the Eleusinians had included the mytheme that the Eleusinians were trying to reverse the result of the contest for the sovereignty of Attica and make Poseidon the poliadic deity.

This conclusion is inevitably based on a culturally determined judgement: the question is whether this judgement corrupts, or helps reconstruct, the ancient realities. I believe that it does the latter. Indeed, the conclusion gains some support from a different consideration: the fact that in the procession from the Acropolis to Skiron, a place that was implicated in the myths of the war,[118] the priestess of Athena Polias and the priest of Poseidon Erechtheus walked out under a canopy called *skiron*, carried by Eteoboutadai.[119] This suggests that Poseidon's association with the nexus of the war between Athens and the Eleusinians was cultically embedded from an early period.[120]

Another consideration that may point in the same direction is that Eumolpos' status as the son of Poseidon, which is intimately connected with the mytheme under consideration, pre-dates Euripides' *Erechtheus*.[121] Poseidon was worshipped at Eleusis under the title 'Father', which fits the notion that he was the father of an Eleusinian, not, as he is in Euripides' *Erechtheus*, Thracian, Eumolpos.[122] Finally, it is possible to argue that the double identity of Aglauros in her cultically embedded myths, as both the first priestess of Athena and the person who killed herself in order to ensure victory in this war, may be correlative with the representation that the cult she served, as well as the polis, was being threatened, and that therefore she, more

---

[118] See p. 35 above.

[119] Lysimachides *FGrH* 366 F 3.

[120] For the nexus concerning the relationship between Athens and Eleusis was shaped at an early period (see Sourvinou-Inwood 1997a).

[121] See Richardson 1974: 197 ad 154.

[122] As Parker 1987a: 203 points out. See Paus. 1.38.6. On Poseidon Pater, see also Parker 2005a: 417.

than anyone else, a princess of the polis and the priestess of the cult, had an obligation to serve it in the ultimate way, by sacrificing her life.

Before considering further Erichthonios and the 'post-split' Erechtheus, I will try to place all these figures in the wider framework of the ancient perceptions of heroic-age Athenian history. In the Athenian myths about the polis's past the transition from the beginning of the polis to things as they are now went through many stages, which varied in the different versions; the ideologically significant aspects of that transition were perceived to have taken place in the heroic age. It is possible to argue that this transition involved three conceptual stages, focused on three different kings. By this I mean that, whether or not Athenian mythopoeia about the polis's early history began with these (or another form of) three conceptually focal kings, or whether it began with fewer conceptual foci, those three stages appear to form the conceptual skeleton of the mythology of heroic-age Athens that is visible to us.

The first stage, the beginnings, is symbolically focused on Kekrops, who was strongly associated with autochthony and with the establishment of Athena as the poliadic deity of Athens.[123] The second stage represents the consolidation, development, and crystallization of both polis and cult and was associated with Erechtheus; it was associated with the 'complex' Erechtheus and appears also to have remained attached to the 'post-split' Erechtheus. The third stage is represented by Theseus, the greatest Athenian king who refounded Athens—and the Panathenaia; he eventually came to be represented as a democratic king, and so a founder of democracy.[124]

---

[123] In some versions (see e.g. Paus. 1.2.6 where the first king is Aktaios) Kekrops is not the first king. The notion that Kekrops was not the first king of Athens is a further elaboration of the beginnings, known to, and rejected by, Philochoros (see Philochoros *FGrH* 328 F 92 and see Jacoby 1954: i. 386–9 ad F 92–8). On these myths, see Parker (1987a: 193–5). On Kekrops, see now Gourmelen (2005). On the autochthony of Kekrops and Erichthonios, Gourmelen (2005: 24–40, 47–9, 70, 73, 96–7, 123–41, 143, 207, 329–41, 369–73; cf. 351–66 and passim).

[124] Some may argue that another stage is represented by Kodros, in those versions of the myth in which he was the last king of Athens (see Jacoby 1954: i. 43–51 ad Hellanikos 323a F23; see also Arist. *Ath. Pol.* 3.3 and Rhodes 1981: 100 ad loc. On Kodros, see also Kearns 1989: 56–7, 178); that he represents the end of the heroic age and of Athenian kingship, and the transition to the 'present-day' world. But,

Interestingly, Kekrops, Erechtheus, and Theseus are the three kings mentioned by Thucydides in his digression on the history of heroic-age Athens, which is structured around Theseus' synoecism.[125] The first two stages, represented by Kekrops and Erechtheus, can be considered an elaboration of one stage, for both kings were associated, first, with autochthony, and second, with the establishment and crystallization of Athena's poliadic cult and of the polis, that is, with the establishment of the main, most important, lines of things as they are now as far as the polis and the poliadic cult are concerned. I shall be returning to this.

Be that as it may, it cannot be doubted that in the Athenian perceptions of the classical period Kekrops, Erechtheus, and Theseus represent significant stages in the movement from primordiality to things as they are now. Kekrops and Erechtheus were eponymous tribal heroes; Theseus was not, for he was the greatest Athenian king, refounder of the polis, and represented the whole of Athens, and could not be associated with only one tribe. Therefore his name would not have been part of the preliminary list submitted to the Pythia.[126] If this is right, it suggests that by the time of the Kleisthenic reforms Theseus was the defining Athenian king, and not, as we shall see was the case in the Homeric poems, Erechtheus.

In the cultic myths of Athens Aglauros was the first priestess of Athena and the daughter of Kekrops, and she was also active in the reign of Erechtheus, when she killed herself to save the city. Therefore Aglauros was located at the transition between stage one and stage two, bridged, as it were, the reign of her father Kekrops and that of Erechtheus.

Various mythopoeic constructions, sometimes in interaction with the conceptual 'needs' generated by cultic myths and their interactions with the rituals in action, elaborated both the three stages and the transitions between them; both foci and transitions were clearly

---

whenever the figure of Kodros was first constructed, this stage did not mark itself anywhere near as strongly in Athenian consciousness—as is also testified by the fact that Kodros is not always presented as the last king.

[125] Thuc. 2.15.1–2; see also Hornblower 1991: 259–65 ad loc.

[126] On this process involving the oracle, in which a preliminary list of heroes is said to have been submitted to the Pythia for the final selection, see n. 97 above.

perceived as elastic, and could be expanded or condensed. The splitting of 'complex' Erechtheus into two figures was a most significant manifestation of such elaboration.

The figure of Erichthonios, and the tradition that Erechtheus and Erichthonios were distinct figures, first appears in the fifth century.[127] Erichthonios is part of the chronological sequence of Athenian kings in the Atthidographers.[128] The main sets of mythemes that made up the Erichthonios myth are those concerning his birth and babyhood, including his persona as nursling of Athena, and those concerning his adulthood. The myth of Erichthonios' birth and babyhood has already been discussed. The mythemes concerning his adulthood are the following: 'Erichthonios set up the wooden image of Athena in the acropolis', 'Erichthonios founded the Panathenaia', which is associated with 'Erichthonios invented the chariot', and finally 'Erichthonios was buried in the sanctuary of Athena Polias'.[129]

The mytheme that Erichthonios founded the Panathenaia will be considered in more detail in the discussion of the Panathenaia.[130] Here I will mention that this foundation is associated with the mytheme that Erichthonios invented the chariot. As part of placing the myth of the foundation of the Panathenaia I will now consider the question whether Erichthonios inherited these two associated mythemes from the nexus of the 'complex' Erechtheus.

Aristides says in the *Panathenaikos* that the 'companion' (*paredros*) of Athena, which is, we shall see, what he calls Erechtheus, 'was the first of men to yoke a complete chariot (ἄρμα τέλειον) with the goddess' and revealed to all 'complete horsemanship'.[131] Elsewhere[132]

---

[127] See the discussion in Parker (1987a: 200–1 and 211–12 n. 60), where he notes that references to Erichthonios before the 430s are either not verbatim (*Danais, EGF* 141 F2 Davies, and Pindar fr. 253) or may refer to someone else (Soph. *TrGF* 4 F 242). The relevant images have already been discussed in Chapter 2, section 2.ii.

[128] Jacoby 1954: i. 55 ad *FGrH* 323a F 27 (cf. Jacoby (1954: ii. 11–12) where he asserts that Erechtheus and Erichthonios were separate figures in Hellanikos of Lesbos, though the argument does not seem to me be as watertight as it might have been).

[129] See n. 58 above.

[130] In Chapter 5.

[131] Aristid. *Or.* 1 Behr (*Panathenaikos*) 43–4.

[132] Aristid. *Or.* 37 Keil (*Athena*) 14.

he says that it is said that Erichthonios, the nursling, *trophimos*, of Athena, was the first among men 'to yoke a chariot of horses'. This, the myth that Erichthonios invented the chariot, is the cultic myth of the Panathenaia,[133] as it developed after the figures of Erichthonios and the 'post-split' Erechtheus were generated with the help of material from the nexus of the 'complex' Erechtheus.

A scholion on the *Panathenaikos* passage[134] claims that Aristides 'calls Erechtheus the *paredros* of Athena because on the Acropolis behind Athena (*that is, behind her statue in the temple of Athena Polias*), there was a painting of Erechtheus driving a chariot, because he was the first to have yoked a complete chariot, which is a four horse chariot'. It would be easy to dismiss the scholion as unreliable, assuming that it is mistaking Erechtheus for Erichthonios.[135] However, Aristides makes a distinction between the invention he ascribes to Erichthonios, Athena's nursling, on the one hand and what he says about Athena's *paredros* on the other. While he says that Erichthonios is said to have been the first simply 'to yoke a chariot of horses', in the passage in the *Panathenaikos* it is a 'complete chariot' that the *paredros* of Athena yoked with the goddess, and he also revealed to all 'complete' horsemanship.[136] This differentiation may have been constructed as an accommodation to reconcile the conflicting representations on the one hand that Erichthonios invented the chariot, which had become the cultic myth of the Panathenaia, and on the other an association that Aristides was aware of between the chariot and Erechtheus, the 'complex' Erechtheus, an association that was also reflected in the painting inside the temple, which, if this is right, would have been reflecting the earlier tradition.[137]

The mytheme of Erichthonios' invention of the chariot is associated with the mytheme that he first drove his invention at the first

---

[133] See on this myth, Chapter 5 below.
[134] Schol. in Aristid. *Or.* 1 Behr (*Panathenaikos*) 43, Dindorf iii. 62.
[135] Cf. Mansfield 1985: 210, 232–3.
[136] Aristid. *Or.* 1 Behr (*Panathenaikos*) 43.
[137] Schol. in Aristid. *Or.* 1 Behr (*Panathenaikos*) 350, Dindorf (iii. 317.34–5) claims that Erechtheus was the first to receive the chariot from Athena, but others say that it was Pelops, who received it from Poseidon. If this scholion is reliable, if it reflects information rather than confusion, it also reflects a tradition that associated the invention of the chariot with Erechtheus.

Panathenaia and this is connected with the *apobates* competition, and so with the myth that Erichthonios founded the Panathenaia, which will be discussed in Chapter 5, section 2. Here I want to say that if the above readings are right, the nexus 'invention of the chariot, *apobates* competition, foundation of the Panathenaia' had been part of the nexus of the 'complex' Erechtheus and became attached to that of Erichthonios when the latter was constructed, because it is now Erichthonios who belongs to the period of the establishment of the cult of Athena Polias, after that cult had become the poliadic cult in the reign of Kekrops, who, in the versions from which this nexus was generated, had immediately preceded Erichthonios.

What, then, of the mythemes concerning Erichthonios' birth and babyhood? Was the myth of Erichthonios' birth as we know it in its main lines an adaptation of a comparable earlier myth concerning the birth of the 'complex Erechtheus'? As we saw, there are reasons for thinking that the myth had been shaped, and was developing, in the course of the fifth century. Since myths are shaped and reshaped through bricolage, the presence in a mythological nexus of one mytheme that is also present in another, better attested and related, nexus, does not entail that all, or most, of the elements in the latter nexus may be presumed to have also been part of the former. Therefore, the fact that Erechtheus was the earthborn nursling of Athena in the mythicoritual nexus reflected in the Homeric poems does not entail that there was a myth in which the birth of Erichthonios involving Hephaistos' seed and the disobedience of the Kekropidai had been attached to Erechtheus.

Clearly, then, we cannot give a definitive answer to the question whether before the 'split' the myths now attached to the conception, birth, and involvement of the Kekropidai with Erichthonios had been part of the nexus of Erechtheus. However, the fact that the involvement of the Kekropidai appears to be developing in the course of the fifth century, and, I have argued, was not an early cultic myth, suggests, I submit, that, at the very least, it is extremely unlikely that they had been involved with the babyhood of the complex Erechtheus and still more that such an involvement would have resulted in their death. I will argue below that there is some reason for thinking that Aglauros, Pandrosos (and Herse, if she was their sister at the time) were not involved with the babyhood of Erechtheus in the earliest forms of his myth.

I will now try to place the construction of Erichthonios in some kind of conceptual framework by attempting to reconstruct what meanings, if any, his myth added to, or changed in, the history of early Athens, when it is compared to versions of that mythological history from which it is absent. First, clearly, the version that includes Erichthonios elaborates further, and strongly reinforces, the representation 'autochthony', and so the Athenians' claim to autochthony. Then, if the myths of his conception and birth were not part of the myth of the 'complex' Erechtheus, if they were constructed in this form in connection with the construction of Erichthonios, this construction would have added to the mythological history of early Athens a story of doubly divine descent; it would also have created an even closer association between Athena and the city through this early king who was not just her nursling but also as near to a son as she, a virgin, could have. Erichthonios thus was constructed through material from the 'complex' Erechtheus nexus, transformed through the ideological importance of autochthony.

Erichthonios also shared some traits, above all the association with snakes,[138] with the half-snake *autochthon* Kekrops.[139] These relationships between Kekrops, Erechtheus, and Erichthonios suggest that the construction of Erichthonios was also shaped by interactions between Kekrops and Erechtheus, the two kings who in earlier versions of their myths had suceeded each other, but who in later ones are separated by (among others) Erichthonios.

The 'post-split' Erechtheus appears in Euripides' *Erechtheus*. As we saw, the main myth associated with Erechtheus after the 'split' was that of the war against the Eleusinians, which led to the crystallization of the polis in its present form and was also associated with the cult of Poseidon. In the version in Euripides' *Erechtheus*, the names Poseidon and Erechtheus are coupled in one cult. I will discuss

[138] Erichthonios is usually (and certainly early) represented as fully human. The image of a snake lower body emerges later. But he was associated with the snakes who guarded him, as e.g. in Eur. *Ion* 20–6.

[139] See Kearns (1989: 111), on Kekrops and Erichthonios as figures of essentially the same type, both related to the guardian snake of the Acropolis. See e.g. Eur. *Ion* 1165.

this particular coupling below. First I will discuss the relationship between Poseidon and Erechtheus in general.

ii. Erechtheus and Poseidon, Poseidon Erechtheus

The relationship between Poseidon and Erechtheus is clearly complex.[140] I will begin by setting out the parameters within which the figure of Erechtheus was perceived. First, we saw, Erechtheus received cult as an independent figure on the Acropolis; not only as a tribal hero, but also, and very importantly, as a whole polis cult recipient. In Pausanias' time there were three altars inside the Erechtheion: the altar of Poseidon, on which they also sacrifice to Erechtheus as a result of an oracle, Pausanias tell us, the altar of the hero Boutes, and the altar of Hephaistos.[141] This arrangement indicates a figure of Erechtheus that is separate from Poseidon. In addition, I submit, the notion that the shared altar resulted from an oracle may indicate a perception that this shared altar was the result of a change from earlier practice, instigated by an (undoubtedly solicited) oracle.

To put it differently. Both the Homeric passage and Herodotos' testimony about a sanctuary of Erechtheus the earthborn[142] lead us to the conclusion that, at least in the periods reflected in these two texts, Erechtheus was worshipped separately from Poseidon, and not only as a tribal hero, but in a whole polis cult. For Herodotos speaks of the sanctuary of Erechtheus the earthborn, which cannot be imagined to denote the god Poseidon Erechtheus. (As to whether the cult of Poseidon Erechtheus could also have been housed in this sanctuary, I shall return to the question below, after I have considered

---

[140] The most recent discussion of the problem known to me is that by Christopoulos 1994, which sets out the evidence. Christopoulos believes that Erechtheus and Poseidon are completely separate beings, and that even when the names Poseidon and Erechtheus were connected, they were never perceived as one person; he thinks the names were combined to express in cult a collective ideal that Athens claimed for itself involving autochthony and a close connection with the sea. See too Kearns 1992: 83–4.

[141] Paus. 1.26.5.

[142] Hom. *Il.* 2. 546–51; Hdt. 8.55.

the figure of Poseidon Erechtheus.[143]) This reconstructed persona of Erechtheus, in which he was separate from Poseidon and the recipient of a whole polis, as well as a tribal hero, cult, coincides with the state of affairs described by Pausanias as obtaining in his own time. Furthermore, it also coincides with the representation of Erechtheus in Aristides. Aristides presents Erechtheus as a hero, a culture hero and a patriotic hero, certainly a mortal,[144] whose sacrifice of his daughters was rewarded by the polis, who made him *paredros* of the gods on the Acropolis.[145] Therefore, in Aristides' perceptions Erechtheus had an independent whole polis cult, which was unequivocally distinct from the cult of Poseidon Erechtheus. These statements were part of the *Panathenaikos*; if it is right that the *Panathenaikos* was performed at the Panathenaia,[146] this context of performance would have inevitably imposed certain parameters concerning cultic myths and cultic realities. Whether or not it is right, his representation of Erechtheus as an originally human hero, with a whole polis cult entirely separate from Poseidon, is likely to have corresponded to the cultic realities of the time. I suggest that there is no reason whatsoever to support a hypothesis that things were different in earlier times. On the contrary, as we saw, Herodotos' mention of Erechtheus' sanctuary represents the same persona of Erechtheus as separate from Poseidon and as whole polis cult recipient.

The cult of Poseidon Erechtheus, by contrast, was clearly perceived as a cult of the god Poseidon. This is illustrated most strikingly by the fact that the trident symbolized and signified the priesthood of Poseidon Erechtheus in the eyes of the family that held that priesthood. The family of the orator Lykourgos was entitled to, and held,

---

[143] It could be argued that Erechtheus' very selection as one of the ten eponymous tribal heroes also suggests that before that he had been a separate cult recipient. For though it could be countered that in theory, before the Kleisthenic selection, he may have been perceived as an independent figure in myth, but not in cult, the correspondence between the Homeric passage and Herodotos' testimony about a whole polis sanctuary of Erechtheus the earthborn suggests, I submit, that this had not been the case.

[144] Aristid. *Or.* 1 Behr (*Panathenaikos*) 43.

[145] Ibid. 87–8.

[146] Cf. *Neue Pauly* 1 s.v. Aristeides, 1097′–8.

the priesthood of Poseidon Erechtheus; Lykourgos' son Habron dedicated a pinax that was placed inside the Erechtheion, representing the genealogy of all those who had held the priesthood of Poseidon Erechtheus; because Habron was entitled to the priesthood but conceded it to his brother Lykophron, Habron was represented giving Lykophron a trident.[147]

Let us now consider the epigraphical record. Some of the extant inscriptions refer to Poseidon Erechtheus. Thus a dedication to Poseidon Erechtheus from the Acropolis dating to the mid-fifth century (460–450 BC) is dedicated 'to Poseidon Erechtheus', and a Neronian base is inscribed 'the priest of Poseidon Erechtheus Gaieochos'.[148] An inscription on a base from Eleusis dating to the middle of the second century BC refers to '[priest] of Erechtheus Poseidon',[149] which is surely a 'stylistic' variation of Poseidon Erechtheus.[150]

A priest's seat in the theatre of Dionysos was inscribed in the second century BC 'for the priest of Poseidon Gaieochos and Erechtheus'.[151] Though the Neronian inscription may lead us to think that this signifies the priest of Poseidon with the epithets Gaieochos and Erechtheus, the formulations in the other seats make it more likely that this inscription would have been composed, and read, as signifying the priest of Poseidon with the epithet Gaieochos who was also at the same time the priest of Erechtheus.[152]

Finally, in a fragmentary inscription from the first half of the fourth century BC, which appears to be a tribal decree, and certainly

---

[147] [Plut.] *XOrat.* 843F. Christopoulos 1994: 121 suggests that the trident was not simply a pictorial symbol, but the religious emblem of the priestly office of Poseidon Erechtheus. Whether or not this is right, the fact that, in whatever way, the trident represents the priesthood leaves no doubt about the perceived identity of the cult recipient being the god Poseidon with the epithet Erechtheus. The perception that the cult of Poseidon Erechtheus was a cult of the god Poseidon is also reflected in the entry in Hesychios s.v. Erechtheus, in which Erechtheus is said to be 'Poseidon at Athens'.

[148] *IG* I³ 873; *IG* II² 3538; Christopoulos 1994: 123 nos. 1–2. See the discussion by Christopoulos 1994: 123–4.

[149] *IG* II² 4071; Christopoulos 1994: 123 no. 3.

[150] Christopoulos' comment (1994: 124) is that it very probably refers to one deity.

[151] *IG* II² 5058; Christopoulos 1994: 123 no. 4.

[152] This is the reading that Christopoulos (1994: 124) also appears to prefer, though he mentions the alternative without comment.

involves the Erechtheis tribe, the formulation is: 'the priest shall serve as priest for Poseidon and Erechtheus.'[153] As Kearns has pointed out, the same priest served the tribal cult as the central polis cult.[154] But I do not think that there is any evidence for thinking that the perceptions of the recipients were radically different in the two cults. In both cults the priest served both Poseidon and Erechtheus; in the central polis cult the god was Poseidon Erechtheus, and so he served both Poseidon Erechtheus and the associated hero Erechtheus; in the tribal cult this priest served the eponymous tribal hero Erechtheus and also Poseidon, perhaps Poseidon in a wider persona.

I would argue that this pattern of appearance of the two names in these inscriptions can be unproblematically read as reflecting a state of affairs in which there existed distinct but associated polis cults of Erechtheus and of Poseidon Erechtheus, the god. The attachment of the name of a hero to a deity as a cultic epithet is a known Greek modality.[155] The cult of Poseidon Erechtheus, in which 'Erechtheus' was a cult title of Poseidon, involved Poseidon in the aspect of his persona that was associated with Erechtheus, comparably to divine epithets based on the names of other deities, such as Zeus Heraios and Athena Areia.[156] Let us consider whether it is possible to try to reconstruct the main lines of what that aspect may have been.

I will begin with another epithet. It is clear from the evidence cited above that in this cult of Poseidon the epithet Erechtheus was associated with the epithet Gaieochos. Let us consider what, if any, aspects of the persona of Poseidon Gaieochos we can reconstruct from the epithet. Gaieochos means earth-moving and it applies above all to Poseidon who shakes the earth with earthquakes.[157] It also means protector of the country and in this capacity it is also

---

[153] *IG* II² 1146; Christopoulos 1994: 123 no. 5; see the discussion by Christopoulos 1994: 124. See also Kearns 1989: 210–11.

[154] Kearns 1989: 210–11.

[155] On epithets in which the name of a hero is coupled with that of a god, see Parker 2005b: 223–4. Specifically on Poseidon Erechtheus, Parker 2005b: 224.

[156] On such epithets, see Parker 2003: 180 and 2005b: 219–26.

[157] On Poseidon the Earth-shaker, see Burkert (1985: 137–8). [The *meaning* of Gaieochos is merely 'earth-holding', but it is applied to Poseidon in a propitiatory way because he can also shake the earth. R.P.]

applied to other deities, such as Zeus and Artemis.[158] Both meanings, I suggest, were relevant to Poseidon's persona in the contest and its aftermath, including the installation of his cult in Athens. On the one hand, in one version of the myth at least, Poseidon, enraged at the Athenians' victory in the war and the death of his son Eumolpos, shook the earth with earthquakes.[159] On the other hand, after he was accommodated in the Athenian pantheon, he became a protector;[160] not the 'city-holding' (*poliouchos*) deity, but a deity protecting the land, Poseidon Gaieochos. The epithet Gaieochos, then, is ambivalent; it brings up both the dangerous and threatening aspect of the god, and the protective one, and so it is closely symbolically correlative with the god—the specifically protective aspect of Poseidon with regard to earthquakes was invoked by the function-specifying epithets Asphaleios, 'Immovable', and Themeliouchos, 'Foundation-holding'.[161]

How, then, does the epithet 'Erechtheus' relate to all this, and what can we reconstruct of the persona of Poseidon Erechtheus Gaieochos? One clear connection of the epithet 'Erechtheus' with Poseidon, especially Poseidon Gaieochos as understood here, lies in the mythological fact that the hero Erechtheus played a crucial role in the events that led to the crystallization of things as they are now, presumably including the accommodation of the cult of Poseidon in Athenian polis religion. This 'historical' association, and specifically the mytheme that Poseidon killed Erechtheus, is offered as an explanation of the combination of the names Poseidon and Erechtheus in Euripides' *Erechtheus*, though this explanation, we shall see below, does not necessarily involve a straightforward reflection of the cult as it was practised in the fifth-century 'present'. In any case, the fact that the name 'Erechtheus' evoked the circumstances in which Athena's victory, and so also her poliadic identity, were confirmed

---

[158] E.g. to Zeus: Aesch. *Supp.* 816; to Artemis: Soph. *OT* 160.

[159] See Eur. *Erechtheus* F 370. 45–57. After his defeat by Athena in one version of the myth Poseidon flooded the Thriasian plain (Apollod. 3.14.1).

[160] On the relationship between Poseidon and Athens expressed in the myth of the contest for the sovereignty of Athens and its aftermath, see Parker 1987a: 199–200; cf. Parker 2005a: 476–7.

[161] See Parker 2005a: 411. On Poseidon Asphaleios, see also Burkert 1985: 138. On some function-specifying epithets of Poseidon, see Parker 2003: 176.

and crystallized, through the defeat of the Eleusinian invasion, entails that it helped 'place' Poseidon Gaieochos in the pantheon of the polis, as hierarchically inferior to Athena, but nevertheless a god whose protection was desirable for the polis. Poseidon Gaieochos Erechtheus was also Poseidon with all the multiple meanings expressed through the myth of the contest and its aftermath. This would make Poseidon (Gaieochos) Erechtheus an appropriate *paredros* of the poliouchos goddess, Athena Polias.

It has also been argued that another association between Gaieochos and Erechtheus may have been a perception that the name Erechtheus was connected with ἐρέχθω, push, break, which recalls epithets of Poseidon such as Gaieochos, *enosichthon*, *elelichthon*, and *seisichthon*, all roughly meaning 'Earth-shaker'.[162] It is interesting in this connection that in Hesychius the entry 'Erechtheus. Poseidon at Athens' is followed by the entry ἐρεχθομένη, the first meaning of which is given as σαλευομένη, made to shake. If this is right, if a meaning connected with earthquakes was heard by the Athenians in the epithet Erechtheus, Poseidon's association with earthquakes would have been more strongly felt. In fact, though it is probable that such a meaning had not been heard in the name of the hero Erechtheus, it is difficult to see how it could not have been activated by the combination 'Poseidon Erechtheus', and even more in the combination Poseidon Gaieochos Erechtheus. If this is right, it would have reinforced further the ambivalent, threatening, and (it was hoped) protective facet of the god—in combination with his persona concerning the contest and its aftermath.

The possibility cannot be excluded that the use of the name 'Erechtheus' as an epithet for Poseidon may have been a subsequent development; that the name 'Erechtheus' became attracted and attached as an epithet to a nexus 'Poseidon Gaieochos' sometime before the 450s when Poseidon Erechtheus is first attested. For this to be in any way plausible, we need to consider whether there were any circumstances conducive to such a process. Clearly, one result of the addition of the epithet 'Erechtheus' to the name 'Poseidon Gaieochos' would have been to bring to the fore the representations

---

[162] See the discussion in Christopoulos 1994: 124.

concerning the circumstances in which Poseidon killed Erechtheus and the Athenian polis was crystallized; another result would have been the reinforcement of the notion of protection from earthquakes, which is included in the epithet Gaieochos. Might the catastrophic Spartan earthquake of 464 BC have been at least one factor in such a creation? And might the (earlier) generation of a 'post-split', 'not complex' Erechtheus have facilitated such a process? These are possibilities, but we cannot take them further.

Let me sum up the results of the investigations so far. Erechtheus was an independent figure, who in Herodotos' time had his own sanctuary and was a recipient of a whole polis cult, as well as a cult recipient in his persona as a tribal hero. The cult of Poseidon Erechtheus was unambiguously perceived as a cult of the god Poseidon with the epithet Erechtheus, which was sometimes associated with the epithet Gaieochos. Poseidon Gaieochos and a city-holding Athena, Athena Polias, can be seen as a complementary pair. The cults of Athena Polias and Poseidon Erechtheus were connected through their mythology (one physical manifestation of which was the *martyria* of the contest), through the fact that the priesthoods of both cults belonged to the same *genos*, the Eteoboutadai, and that, in at least one ritual that was not part of either of their cults, these two priests acted together and also in association with other members of their *genos*;[163] finally they were also connected through the fact that (at least) after the Erechtheion was built, the two cults were housed in the same temple. I will be calling this cult building by the established name Erechtheion for the sake of convenience, even though only two (late) ancient sources use the name.[164] I note in passing that I believe the 'orthodox' interpretation of the Erechtheion to be right;[165] that

---

[163] At the Skira: Lysimachides *FGrH* 366 F 3.

[164] [Plut.] *XOrat.* 843 E, referring to the part of the temple that belonged to Poseidon Erechtheus, in which the cult of Erechtheus was also housed; Paus. (1. 26. 5), apparently with reference to the whole building, for he speaks of a building, οἴκημα (on the name, see also Hurwit 1999: 200).

[165] A small minority of scholars disagree in different ways and have proposed different hypotheses concerning different aspects of the building and cults. On the views of Jeppesen and of Mansfield, see the brief discussion in Hurwit (1999: 200–2). Ferrari (2002: 11–35) argued that the archaic temple of Athena Polias was not destroyed in the Persian Sack but remained standing into the Roman period and that the building we call Erechtheion was simply that, the Erechtheion, housing the

is, I believe that the Erechtheion was the combined temple of Athena Polias and Poseidon Erechtheus (and the other cults associated with it, including that of Erechtheus) and that the cult of Athena Polias was housed in the eastern part of the building. I do not know if, after the Persian Sack and until the Erechtheion was built, the temple of Athena Polias had continued to be used (after some repairs) and had housed the statue,[166] or if the statue had been housed in the small building underneath the Erechtheion.[167] But this does not concern me here.

Let us sum up the relationships between the three cult recipients involved in this cultic nexus. Clearly, each of the three was paired with the other two, and the three pairs represent three different types of relationship:[168] first, Athena and Erechtheus, goddess and hero, are in a relationship of (an obviously asymmetrical) friendship, as reflected in the Homeric poems; second, Athena and Poseidon, a quasi but not quite poliadic pair, are presented as antagonistic in the mythological past, but are complementary in the cultic present, with Athena in the hierarchically superior position; finally, Poseidon and Erechtheus, a god and a hero, are also presented as antagonistic in the mythological past but are complementary in the cultic present. Among the aspects of this complementarity, the sharing of an altar, I will now argue, must not be assumed to have been an early aspect of their relationship.

Pausanias tells us that in his time the two cults shared an altar in the Erechtheion, but, I suggested above, his formulation suggests, first, that this sharing was not self-evident, and second, that there was a story that it resulted from a change inspired by an oracle. I will now

cult of Poseidon Erechtheus, Erechtheus, and the other associated cults, but not of Athena Polias. This is an intelligent, well-argued paper that cleverly unpicks some established presumptions and weaknesses in the established positions. However, in my view, it does not demonstrate that the two cults did not share space in the Erechtheion after the latter's completion. I should note, because it pertains to our direct concerns, that Ferrari (2002: 16) implicitly assumes that the situation that had obtained in Herodotos' time also obtained later.

[166] Korres (1994b: 42, 56–7) allows for the survival of the cella until the completion of the Erechtheion.

[167] See Hurwit 1999: 145.

[168] See also, briefly, on these relationships, Kearns 1992: 83–4.

set out some other arguments in favour of the view that the two cults did not share the same space before the building of the Erechtheion. I begin with an argument based on the reading of Aristides. The knowledge and assumptions of Aristides, who had studied in Athens, and had a deep knowledge of classical literature, led him to choose in the significantly named *Panathenaikos* to call Erechtheus, first, a *paredros* of the gods on the Acropolis and, second, a *paredros* of Athena, but not a *paredros* of Poseidon.[169] This, I suggest, adds support to the notion that the spatial association between the cult of Poseidon Erechtheus and of the hero Erechtheus after the building of the Erechtheion did not reflect a deeply rooted cultic connection between Poseidon and the hero Erechtheus that can be projected back to the time when Erechtheus had an independent sanctuary.

Another reason for thinking that it is less likely that the two cults shared a space before the Erechtheion was built is the following. If, as I tried to show, it is right that the two figures were distinct, the cult of Poseidon Erechtheus was unlikely to have been housed in the sanctuary of Erechtheus the earthborn mentioned by Herodotos. For if that had been the case, Poseidon Erechtheus would have been housed in the sanctuary of the hero Erechtheus, that is, a god would have had a subordinate position in a hero's sanctuary, which is an extremely rare, almost unprecedented modality in Greek cult.[170] Herodotos in fact does not mention Poseidon as being worshipped in that sanctuary, though the context, his reference to the contest and the *martyria*, would have been most conducive.

---

[169] Aristid. *Or.* 1 Behr (*Panathenaikos*) 43.

[170] Kearns, who discussed the relationships between hero sanctuaries and divine sanctuaries (1992: 78–93) and who believes that in the fifth century "no separation was made in cult" between Poseidon and Erechtheus (1992: 83), only cites one instance of an apparent subordination of the divine to the heroic (1992: 85–6), the sanctuary of Hippolytos at Troizen, which contained temples of more than one deity, and perhaps also the sanctuary of Hippolytos in Athens where in *IG* I³369.66 there is reference to Aphrodite ἐν Ἱππολυτ[είωι (see on these sanctuaries, Pirenne-Delforge 1994: 178–81, 40–6). Hippolytos' heroic, rather than divine, status at Troezen is not unambiguous (Kearns 1992: 85–6; Pirenne-Delforge 1994: 180–1), or rather, his persona is not unaffected by divine personality elements. Kearns (1992: 83) suggests that Erechtheus belongs to a "pre-heroic class of beings"; but in the fifth century he was an earthborn king of the heroic age who was a recipient of cult, both tribal and whole polis cult.

There are some further arguments in support of this conclusion. First, the topographical argument. If Herodotos accurately reflects cultic reality, and this was a sanctuary of the earthborn Erechtheus, the *martyria* produced by Athena and Poseidon during the contest were contained in the sanctuary of Erechtheus, the hero whose lifetime and death were associated with the aftermath of the contest, which included the accommodation of the defeated god in the city's pantheon and so also the new state of affairs in which both *martyria* were valid symbols of divine protection. These *martyria* would not have been moved; since, after the Erechtheion was built, Poseidon's 'sea' was in the part of the Erechtheion in which Poseidon Erechtheus and Erechtheus were worshipped,[171] while Athena's olive tree was in the Pandroseion,[172] two conclusions may be drawn. First, the sanctuary of Erechtheus described by Herodotos had occupied part of the western part of the extant Erechtheion and part of the Pandroseion; that is, the space that had previously been occupied by the sanctuary of Erechtheus was partly incorporated in the western part of the extant Erechtheion and partly became part of the (now presumably expanded) Pandroseion.[173] Second, the *martyria* were consciously separated in the new arrangement, though not moved: the one connected with Poseidon was in space now assigned to Poseidon Erechtheus and Erechtheus; the *martyrion* concerning Athena was now in a cultic space belonging to Pandrosos, a figure associated with Athena but not Poseidon. The fact that in the Erechtheion each *martyrion* was in a space belonging to either the appropriate deity or to a figure associated with the appropriate deity makes it very unlikely that before the Erechtheion was built both *martyria* had been in a space belonging to one of the contesting deities, especially that of Poseidon, the defeated contestant. It is much more likely that they had been in a space that belonged exclusively to the hero Erechtheus who was associated with both deities—in different ways.

What of the joint priesthood of Erechtheus and Poseidon Erechtheus? It may have followed the development that (on the argument above) led to their sharing an altar, especially if, as is likely,

---

[171] Paus. 1.26.5.
[172] Philoch. *FGrH* 328 F 67; Apollod. 3.14.1.
[173] Hurwit 1999: 144–5, citing earlier work.

any independent priesthood of Erechtheus there may have been belonged to the *genos* of the Eteoboutadai, as did the priesthoods of the other two members of the triad. Altar-sharing and priesthood-sharing may both have been a secondary development connected with the building of the Erechtheion.

If all this is right, the question arises where the cult of Poseidon Erechtheus had been located before the building of the Erechtheion. I suggest that the cults of Athena Polias and Poseidon Erechtheus had been housed in the same temple even before the building of the Erechtheion, more specifically, that before that building Poseidon Erechtheus had an altar in the temple of Athena Polias; that he did not share in the sanctuary of Erechtheus. If it is right, as I will argue, that this cohabitation went back further in time, in its earlier manifestation Athena's hierarchical superiority had been more strikingly visible, for (on my reconstruction) the earlier temple was a temple of Athena, and Poseidon would only have had an altar in that old temple of Athena. The notion that the archaic temple of Athena may also have contained the altar of Poseidon fits established Greek cultic modalities; for at Delphi Poseidon, who in one version of the myth had been a Previous Owner of the oracle, had an altar in the temple of Apollo.[174] Then, the cults of Athena Polias and Poseidon Erechtheus were complementary, a quasi but not quite poliadic pair, presented as antagonistic in the mythological past, who are complementary in the cultic present, with Athena in the hierarchically superior position.[175]

If we compare the situation before the building of the Erechtheion as reconstructed here (on the hypothesis that Poseidon had an altar in the temple of Athena) with that following that building, what would emerge is that Poseidon has a much greater share of cultic space in the Erechtheion than he had before. This may be correlative not only with an increased importance of the sea, but also with the earthquakes that afflicted Athens in the 420s.[176]

---

[174] Paus. 10.24.4; Sourvinou-Inwood 1987b: 232.

[175] Another aspect of the well-established complementarity of these two gods: Detienne and Vernant 1974/1991: 176–200 (187–213).

[176] See Thuc. 1.23.3; 3.87.4; 4.52.1.

But if the conclusions about Erechtheus and the cult of Poseidon Erechtheus reached here are right, what are we to make of Athena's words in Euripides' *Erechtheus?*[177] For she seems to say something different. I shall consider this question after I say something very briefly about this tragedy.

The action in this tragedy takes place in Athens while Erechtheus, married to Praxithea, was king, and the Eleusinians with an army of Thracians led by the Thracian Eumolpos, son of Poseidon, were threatening Athens. Eumolpos wanted to replace Athena with his father Poseidon as the poliad divinity of Athens, though Poseidon had been the loser in the contest. After the Delphic oracle told Erechtheus that he would be victorious if he sacrificed his eldest daughter to Persephone he did so, and two more daughters sacrificed themselves of their own volition because of an oath they had taken with their sister.[178] The enemy was defeated and Eumolpos was killed by Erechtheus but Erechtheus was himself killed by Poseidon. At the end Athena appears and gives instructions to Praxithea which for convenience I print and translate here:

> σὺ δ᾽,] ὦ χθονὸς [σώτειρα Κηφισοῦ] κόρη,
> ἄκου᾽ Ἀθάνας τῆς ἀμήτορο[ς λό]γους.
> 65 καὶ πρῶτα μέν σοι σημανῶ παι[δὸς] πέρι
> ἣν τῆσδε χώρας σὸς προθύεται [πόσι]ς.
> θάψον νιν οὗπερ ἐξέπνευσ᾽ ο[ἰκτ]ρὸν βίον,
> καὶ τάσδ᾽ ἀδελφὰς ἐν τάφωι τ[αὐτ]ῶι χθονὸς
> γενναιότητος οὕνεχ᾽, αἵτιν[ες φί]λης
> 70 ὅρκους ἀδελφῆς οὐκ ἐτόλμησα[ν λι]πεῖν.
> ψυχαὶ μὲν οὖν τῶνδ᾽ οὐ βεβᾶσ᾽ [Ἄιδ]ην πάρα,
> εἰς δ᾽ αἰθέρ᾽ αὐτῶν πνεῦμ᾽ ἐγὼ [κ]ατώικισα.
> ὄνομα δὲ κλεινὸν θήσομαι κα[θ᾽ Ἑλλ]άδα
> Ὑακινθίδας βροτοῖσι κικλή[σκε]ιν θεάς.
> 75 ἐπεὶ c. 10 κα..οιχετητ[. . . .]μένη
> τοῦ συ c. 12 ὑακίν[θου γ]άνος
> καὶ γῆν ἔσωισε, τοῖς ἐμοῖς ἀστο[ῖς λέγ]ω
> ἐνιαυσίαις σφας μὴ λελησμ[ένους] χρόνωι
> θυσίαισι τιμᾶν καὶ σφαγαῖσι [βουκ]τόνοις

---

[177] I have discussed this tragedy in Sourvinou-Inwood 2003a: 25–30. See now *TrGF* 5 (24).

[178] See on this, Collard, Cropp, and Lee 1995: 151.

80   κοσμοῦ[ντας ἱ]εροῖς παρθένων [χορεύ]μασιν.
          γνον[. . . . . .]χθρ εἰς μάχη[ν
          κιν[η . . . . . .]ας ἀσπίδα στρατ[
          πρώταισι θύειν πρότομα πολεμίου δορὸς
          τῆς οἰνοποιοῦ μὴ θιγόντας ἀμπέλου
85   μηδ᾽ εἰς πυρὰν σπένδοντας ἀλλὰ πολυπόνου
          καρπὸν μελίσσης ποταμίαις πηγαῖς ὁμοῦ.
          ἄβατον δὲ τέμενος παισὶ ταῖσδ᾽ εἶναι χρεών,
          εἴργειν τε μή τις πολεμίων θύσηι λαθὼν
          νίκην μὲν αὐτοῖς γῆι δὲ τῆιδε πημονήν.[179]

Daughter of Kephisos, saviour of this land. Hear the words of motherless
Athena. (65) First I shall give indications about your daughter, whom your
husband sacrificed in defence of this land. Bury her where she breathed out
her sad life, and these sisters of hers in the same tomb in the soil, for their
nobility, (70) since they refused to abandon their oath to their dear
sister. The souls of these girls have not gone to Hades; rather, I have housed
their spirit (*pneuma*) in the *aither*. I shall make their name famous in Greece,
to be called the divine Hyakinthides by mortals. (75) . . . brightness of
hyacinth, and saved the land. I instruct my citizens to honour them with
annual sacrifices, not forgotten through the passage of time, and slaughter
of oxen, (80) glorifying them with sacred maiden dances . . . enemy . . . to
battle . . . spear army . . . to sacrifice first to them pre-offerings against the
enemy spear, not touching the wine-producing vine, (85) nor pouring libations onto the pyre, but only the fruit of the labouring bee with river waters.
The precinct for these children must be unentered, and you must prevent
any enemy sacrificing secretly there, to bring victory to them and grief to
this land.

So Athena instructs Praxithea to bury her daughters and informs her
that their souls did not go to Hades, but that she, Athena, installed
their breath/spirit (*pneuma*) in the *aither* and made them into the
goddesses Hyakinthides, whose cult she is now instituting, with
specific instructions about the sacrifices and other rites that should
in future be performed in their honour. She says that they will be
called goddesses, 'divine Hyacinthids', throughout Greece; but it is
also clear that they have died, and they will be buried, and that their

---

[179] *TrGF* 5 F 370. 63–89.

grave would be a site for cult; it seems likely that their grave would have been the focus of the 'unentered precinct', where Athena says enemies must never be allowed to sacrifice, for if they did, they would achieve victory at Athens's expense. This interdiction places the Hyakinthides in the same category as certain other heroes protecting Athens,[180] and their persona of maiden saviours of the city also belongs to a general category characterized by heroization.[181]

The mythicoritual nexus of the Hyakinthides as it is presented in Euripides' *Erechtheus*[182] combines elements of heroic and divine cult, heroic and divine personae.[183] They are both goddesses and heroines, in the sense that they belong to the category of immortalized mortals who had begun their cult recipients life as heroes[184]—at least, this is how they are presented in *Erechtheus*. The very nature of their celestial immortality, the fact that their *pneuma* was installed in the *aither*, shows the strength of the heroic element in their persona, at the same time as we hear that they will be called goddesses and receive sacrifices.[185] For the expression in lines 71–2 would have recalled, for the Athenian audience, line 5 of the public epitaph for the men who died in the battle of Poteidaia:[186] 'the *aither* has received their souls, the earth their bodies.' This would have zoomed the world of the tragedy to the world of the audience,[187] in which the Athenian war dead were heroized, and in this case presented as

---

[180] See Wilkins 1993: 190–1 ad 1040–2; Collard, Cropp, and Lee 1995: 192 ad 88.

[181] See Kearns (1990: 323–44, esp. 327–32, 338–42) for heroized saviours, especially maidens; see also Kearns 1989: 57–63; Kron 1999.

[182] On the cult of the daughters of Erechtheus, see also Philochoros *FGrH* 328 F 12.

[183] See also Larson 1995: 20. The ambivalent nature of this cult may be illustrated by the fact that two recent short treatments of the Hyakinthides, both excellent, sum up their persona in different ways, one as heroines (Kearns in *OCD*³, 733; cf. Kron 1999: 78–9), the other as goddesses (Graf in *Neue Pauly* s.v. Hyakinthides). Both polarizations are right.

[184] I have discussed the category of deified mortals in Sourvinou-Inwood (2005: 329–45 and passim) (see index s.v. deification).

[185] See the Appendix (b) to this chapter for argument against the view that Euripides in *Erechtheus* identified the Hyakinthides with the Hyades.

[186] *CEG* 10.

[187] On this notion of zooming, see Sourvinou-Inwood 1989: 136–7 and passim; Pelling 1997: 218, 228–9, 233–4.

achieving celestial immortality;[188] this correlation between the fate of the Hyakinthides and the fate of the war dead would have made the Hyakinthides be perceived as—among other things—mythological models for the Athenian war dead and their achievement of higher status in the afterlife, which usually took the form of heroization.

I will return to the daughters of Erechtheus and their cult, and also to the beliefs concerning celestial immortality, below. Here I will continue with Athena's speech.

90   πόσει δὲ τῶι σῶι σηκὸν ἐμ μέσηι πόλει
        τεῦξαι κελεύω περιβόλοισι λαΐνοις,
        κεκλήσεται δὲ τοῦ κτανόντος οὕνεκα
        σεμνὸς Ποσειδῶν ὄνομ' ἐπωνομασμένος
        ἀστοῖς Ἐρεχθεὺς ἐμ φοναῖσι βουθύτοις.
95   σοὶ δ', ἣ πόλεως τῆσδ' ἐξανώρθωσας βάθρα,
        δίδωμι βωμοῖς τοῖς ἐμοῖσιν ἔμπυρα
        πόλει προθύειν ἱερέαν κεκλημένην.
        ἃ μὲν κατ' αἶαν τήνδε <δεῖ> 'κπονεῖν κλύεις,

(90) But for your husband I order you to build a precinct in the middle of the Acropolis (*or*, 'city') with a stone enclosure. And because of his killer, he will be called, by the citizens slaughtering sacrificial oxen, revered Erechtheus with the added name Poseidon. (95) And to you, who raised up again the foundations of this city, I grant to make burnt offerings for the city on my altars, being called my priestess. You have heard the tasks you must undertake in this land.

The lines concerning Erechtheus' fate, 92–4, are very difficult. One thing that is beyond doubt is that it is not a divine cult, it is a cult of Praxithea's husband Erechtheus, the hero who was killed by Poseidon during the war with the Eleusinians. I now believe[189] that the reading according to which Athena is referring to the cult of Poseidon Erechtheus practised in the polis in the present was not open to the Athenian audience. For Athena makes clear that the cult being instituted is a cult of Erechtheus, the husband of Praxithea, which

---

[188] On the heroization and immortality of the Athenian war dead and the epitaph for the men who died in the battle of Poteidaia, see Sourvinou-Inwood 1995: 194, 202.

[189] I did not see this in Sourvinou-Inwood 2003a.

means that if the cult being founded had been the cult of Poseidon Erechtheus, this tragedy would be representing the cult of Poseidon Erechtheus as being a cult of Erechtheus, the husband of Praxithea, not of the god Poseidon, while in reality, we saw, there can be no doubt that the cult of Poseidon Erechtheus was a cult of Poseidon with the epithet Erechtheus. I shall return to this after I have considered the sanctuary.

I should stress that, in my view, Athena's formulation of the command concerning the sanctuary to be built for Erechtheus is not, as has been claimed, deliberately vague, "evoking the new building while not ignoring its predecessors".[190] Though the formulation a 'precinct in the middle of the Acropolis (or the city) with a stone enclosure' may have been capable of describing "the marble cladding of the newly designed Erechtheum",[191] I suggest that the Athenian audience would have made sense of this through filters shaped by the expectation that the sanctuary ordered by Athena in the heroic age would have been referring to an earlier sanctuary, not to the one which was being, or was about to be, built,[192] and that expectation would have been confirmed by the description, which they would have understood as describing a stone enclosure. Of course the new building would inevitably have also been evoked, but not as the primary reference, it would have been evoked as something that lay in direct continuity from the sanctuary whose foundation relied on the authority of Athena.

If any particular sanctuary had been visualized by the audience as a representation of what that heroic-age sanctuary had been like, it would have been that mentioned by Herodotos. First, because that sanctuary had been established at an earlier time, it was more distanced from the present and symbolically closer to the heroic-age one the construction of which Athena is ordering. Second, in the assumptions that shaped the Athenian audience's perceptions, there would have been less disjunction between Athena's words and the sanctuary mentioned by Herodotos, which would have involved an

---

[190] As Collard, Cropp, and Lee (1995: 193 ad 91) believe.

[191] Collard, Cropp, and Lee 1995: 193 ad 91.

[192] On the problems of dating the play precisely, see Collard, Cropp, and Lee 1995: 155; see also ibid. 193 ad 90.

enclosure within which were contained the *martyria*, than between her words and a segment of a section of the built temple that was the Erechtheion. This is related to another, important, consideration. As we saw, this is not a divine cult, it is a cult of Praxithea's husband Erechtheus, killed by Poseidon. The Erechtheion that was being built would be housing several cults, not least the poliadic cult of Athena, the deity who is giving the orders and who is very clearly not associating her sanctuary with that which is to be built for Erechtheus. This, in the Athenian audience's perceptions, would have helped to block the possibility that Athena's words would have been perceived to be referring to the Erechtheion.

It could be argued that no specific sanctuary was evoked for the audience by Athena's words because the sanctuary ordered by Athena was a sanctuary of the persona here referred to as the 'post-split' Erechtheus, while that mentioned by Herodotos had belonged to the 'complex' Erechtheus and this would have blocked the evocation of the latter, even as a focus for visualizing the former. However, this, I submit, is very unlikely; for in the eyes of the Athenian audience there was only one hero Erechtheus, though his persona may have been perceived to have more complexities and ambiguities and un-knowabilities than most. In earlier versions of Athenian mythology this Erechtheus was a primordial king, earthborn and the nursling of Athena; after Erichthonios was constructed and had taken over the mythemes that had made up the unambiguously primordial facet of Erechtheus, the latter shed those mythemes and eventually morphed into the persona focused on the war against the Eleusinians and the sacrifice of his daughters. But this transformation did not happen suddenly, with neat transitions or cut-and-dried transfers. Herodotos attests to the fact that the sanctuary on the Acropolis was perceived to be that of the earthborn Erechtheus after Erichthonios had been constructed, and Xenophon suggests that aspects of the persona of the 'complex' Erechtheus had not disappeared from the Athenian perceptions of Erechtheus, even after Erichthonios' myth had became the privileged representation of autochthony in the second part of the fifth century.[193] It is possible that one vehicle for

---

[193] Hdt. 8.55; Xen. *Mem.* 3.5.10 (p. 55 above).

the crystallization of the persona of the 'post-split' Erechtheus was Euripides' *Erechtheus.*

Because only fragments of the tragedy have survived, we do not know to what extent the persona of Erechtheus in Euripides' *Erechtheus* was explicitly and consistently defined as different from the persona of the earthborn nursling of Athena. It is likely that the king's parentage would have been mentioned and that this parentage would have been human—which would have distanced him from the earthborn nursling of Athena. For there are reasons for thinking that the core persona of this Erechtheus was not that of the earthborn nursling of Athena. Most importantly, the words through which Praxithea refers to the poliadic cult and the elements associated with it, 'ancient ordinances of our ancestors',[194] show that in the world of the tragedy the establishment of the poliadic cult had taken place a considerable time ago—certainly not in the reign of the previous king. The fact that by the 420s Erichthonios, who took over the primordial segment of Erechtheus, had been constructed may suggest that Erechtheus would have by then come to be perceived as the king who is defined by his victory over the Eleusinians.

However, it is not impossible that, besides this dominant characterization, there may also have been, in some parts of the tragedy, a certain, partial, vagueness in the representation of Erechtheus; it is not impossible that in the eyes of the Athenian audience he may not have been explicitly and consistently differentiated, and divorced, from the persona of the earthborn Erechtheus throughout the tragedy. In other words, it is not impossible that the distance between the earthborn Erechtheus and the king who fought and defeated the Eleusinians, sacrificed his daughter, and was killed by Poseidon may have been unstable, that it may have varied in the course of the tragedy, with some representations allowing the distinction to be implicitly blurred.[195] This would not be very different from Xenophon's reference to the hero, except for having a dynamic rather than

---

[194] *TrGF* 5, 24 F 360.45.

[195] I have discussed elsewhere other comparable zoomings and distancings in tragedy, and the textual devices that construct them; see, for zooming to and distancing from the world of the audience, Sourvinou-Inwood (1989, 2003a); for zoomings to and distancings from the schema 'normal Greek woman' helping construct Medea in Euripides' play, see Sourvinou-Inwood (1997b).

static form. If it is right, it would be part of the process of the construction and crystallization of the figure I call 'post-split' Erechtheus, as we shall now see.

Let us look again at Athena's words. But before considering further the meanings that (on my readings) the Athenian audiences would have constructed when hearing the words of Athena, I will say something very briefly about the ways in which such representations of cult foundations in tragedy were perceived by the ancient audiences. I have argued at great length elsewhere[196] that fifth-century tragedy was an important locus for religious exploration. On my reconstructions, tragedy was perceived by the fifth-century audiences not as a discrete unit, a purely theatrical experience, simply framed by ritual, but as a ritual performance; and the deities and other religious elements in the tragedies were not insulated from the audience's religious realities, but were perceived to be, to a greater or lesser extent, somehow close to those realities, part of those realities. Greek tragedy was, among other things, but very importantly, also a discourse of religious exploration, it was one important context where the religious discourse of the Athenian polis was explored and elaborated in the fifth century; and this religious exploration was intimately connected with the ritual context in which tragedies were performed, and within which tragedy had been generated.

As for the specific representations of cult foundations, it is necessary to locate them in the context of Greek religion. In Greek perceptions the divine world was ultimately believed to be unknowable, and human knowledge about the divine world, and about the right way of behaving towards it, was limited and circumscribed. Correlatively, Greek religion had no divinely revealed knowledge, no scriptures, and no professional divinely anointed priesthood. Cults were validated through tradition, in two ways: they were believed to have been founded by heroic figures who had lived in the heroic past when mortals had a closer connection with the divine and were often themselves descended from gods, and they had been shown to be efficacious in the past. I argued that tragedy, which often dramatized the foundation of cults by heroes at the instigation of divinities,

---

[196] Sourvinou-Inwood 2003a.

represented as interacting with mortals, became an important locus for this anchoring which was an important aspect of Greek religious discourse.

In this passage, the cult of Erechtheus is symbolically grounded in the heroic age; indeed, it is presented as resulting from a divine instruction, and is thus strongly validated. Specifically Athena's words give symbolic validation to the cult of the hero Erechtheus on the Acropolis which involved sacrifices of oxen and (as it is presented here) was focused on the persona of Erechtheus who fought against the Eleusinians and sacrificed his daughter to save the city, and was killed by Poseidon, a mytheme reflected in the epithet 'Poseidon', here accompanying the name 'Erechtheus'—a combination to which I shall return.

If it is right that Athena's words would have evoked for the Athenian audience the sanctuary of Erechtheus mentioned by Herodotos, this evocation would also have activated their knowledge that it had involved the cult of a hero Erechtheus who was earthborn and primordial. This knowledge, in interaction with the context, Athena ordering the foundation of a sanctuary to Erechtheus whose persona is focused on the war against the Eleusinians, may well have had the effect of helping to destabilize any perceived differences (which in our own logical perceptions appear self-evident and significant) between the cult recipient of the earlier sanctuary and the hero Erechtheus represented in the tragedy; it may have helped present the ritual nexus 'Erechtheus' as correlative with the figure of Erechtheus represented in the tragedy.

I shall return to this representation of Erechtheus on pp. 88–9 below. Here I need to consider further the question of the name. If what is being described by Athena is indeed a whole polis cult of the hero Erechtheus housed in its own sanctuary, as is also suggested by the similarities to the cult's reflection in the Homeric poems, how can we make sense of the surname Poseidon in ways approximating the ways in which the Athenian audiences would have done? Had the Athenians practised a cult of Erechtheus Poseidon, as well as of Poseidon Erechtheus? I believe this is an unlikely cultic modality, but this is inevitably a culturally determined judgement, and it may well be that this is what Athena is describing, an existing cult. If this was not the case, since there can be no doubt that the cult of Poseidon

Erechtheus was a cult of Poseidon, two readings appear 'logically' possible, though they were not necessarily both open to the Athenian audience—to whose assumptions we have limited access. First, that this passage is suggesting that there had also been once a cult of Erechtheus Poseidon, as well as the established cult of Poseidon Erechtheus; and second, that it is suggesting that the cult of Poseidon Erechtheus had begun as a cult of Erechtheus Poseidon.[197] I suggest that, given their perceptions of both Poseidon's hierarchical superiority, and his importance for the polis, the audience are unlikely to have constructed the latter meaning, that this important cult had begun as a cult of the hero Erechtheus. On the other hand, it is possible, I submit, that the audience had constructed the reading on which my translation is based, that what Athena is saying is not that Poseidon Erechtheus is Erechtheus, but that besides the cult of the god Poseidon with the epithet Erechtheus there was also a cult of the hero Erechtheus with the [surname] Poseidon.

I doubt that this reflected cultic reality. If it did not, one way the audience may have made sense of this would be to understand that this surname had fallen into disuse. But if this is right, how can we make sense of this Euripidean theological speculation, that there had also been, once, a cult of Erechtheus Poseidon, as well as the established cult of Poseidon Erechtheus, if no such cult existed in the last quarter of the fifth century in Athens? What meanings would have been constructed by the audience? Clearly, one meaning that would have been created was the strong evocation of the cult of Poseidon Erechtheus, which was part of the audience's assumptions. The evocation of this cult would have had the effect of activating, in the aftermath of Poseidon's hostility towards Athens, the audience's knowledge that all would be well, eventually, between Poseidon and the polis, without Athena directly naming the cult to the widow of

---

[197] One possible implication of the latter may be that, for this to be a possible reading for the audience, the two cults would have to have been housed in the same space even before the building now being built. But this is a possible, not a necessary implication, since the hypothesis that the cult of Poseidon Erechtheus had begun as a cult of Erechtheus Poseidon could have worked even if the two had not shared space in the Athenians' present and immediate past; for any such transformation would have been perceived to have taken place in the heroic, distanced, past, and the two may have been perceived to have separated since.

Poseidon's victim—and whether or not that accommodation between Athens and Poseidon was explicitly stated in the missing end of the tragedy.

In addition, in this context of maximum hostility between Erechtheus and his killer Poseidon, this statement would have constructed a cultic association between the god and the hero, of a kind that elevated the hero. This association with Poseidon would have had the effect of stressing the persona of Erechtheus that was focused on the war against the Eleusinians and so it would have helped crystallize the persona of the 'post-split' Erechtheus. That is, in the same way that the cultically established Poseidon Erechtheus evoked Poseidon in the persona that involved the contest and the war with the Eleusinians, the name Erechtheus with the epithet Poseidon (which, on my reconstruction, was a Euripidean construct that did not reflect cultic reality) evoked, and stressed, the persona of Erechtheus that was focused on that war and its associated mythemes.

If my analyses are right, and it was with the building of the Erechtheion that the cult of Erechtheus first came to share space, and an altar, with the cult of Poseidon Erechtheus, perhaps this relationship, and the new arrangements at the Erechtheion, may have been a matter of debate at the time; and this passage may also have constructed the meaning (at least for a segment of the audience) that taking over the sanctuary of Erechtheus for the Erechtheion and housing the cult of Erechtheus together with that of Poseidon Erechtheus was not problematic, because in the past the sanctuary of Erechtheus had been the sanctuary of a cult in which Erechtheus had the surname Poseidon, and so the merging of the spaces was not disrespectful to Erechtheus.

In these circumstances, I submit that Athena's words are not inconsistent with the conclusions of the analyses set out above: Poseidon Erechtheus on the one hand and Erechtheus on the other were distinct cult recipients; Poseidon Erechtheus was the god Poseidon with the epithet Erechtheus; Erechtheus had received both a whole polis cult and a cult as a tribal hero, in his own sanctuary, before the Erechtheion was built when he moved to share the space of Poseidon Erechtheus.

iii. 'Complex' Erechtheus, 'post-split' Erechtheus, and Erichthonios

I have been using the terms the 'complex' Erechtheus and the 'post-split' Erechtheus as convenient shorthand for referring on the one hand to the persona of the hero that first becomes visible to us, and on the other to the persona that he eventually acquired after the construction of Erichthonios. But this use must not be allowed to create a misleading impression of schematic distinctions. As we saw, in Athenian eyes there was only one hero Erechtheus; in the earlier versions of Athenian mythology he was a primordial king, earthborn and the nursling of Athena; after Erichthonios was constructed and had taken over the mythemes that had made up the unambiguously primordial facet of Erechtheus, Erechtheus eventually morphed into the persona focused on the war against the Eleusinians and the sacrifice of his daughters. That is, after the deployment of the primordial aspects of the 'complex' Erechtheus persona in the construction of Erichthonios, the 'complex' Erechtheus eventually lost his primordial and founding facet and became a figure of more limited scope in the Athenian mythological representations. He was located away from the primordial segment and he became above all the warrior king who sacrificed his daughter[s] to save the polis.

These mythopoeic processes were very complex and non-linear. For example, we saw, Xenophon's synoptical reference to Erechtheus, his nurture and birth and the war, evokes an Erechtheus whose persona was nearer that of the figure I call the 'complex' Erechtheus—since in other configurations some of the elements that are here combined belonged to the 'post-split' Erechtheus and others to Erichthonios. This shows that, for some time, the mythemes 'earthborn' and 'nursling of Athena', which had been part of the 'complex' Erechtheus and had subsequently gone into the making of the figure of Erichthonios, were not perceived to have been 'shed', divorced, from the persona of Erechtheus that was morphing into the 'post-split' Erechtheus. Then, we saw, Aristides' testimony showed that at least some (transformations of) elements from the nexus of the 'complex' Erechtheus had become associated with both Erichthonios and the 'post-split' Erechtheus.

As for cult, after Erichthonios became the founder of the Panathenaia we would expect him to have received offerings in connection with that festival, and he probably did. However, we do not have any explicit evidence concerning Erichthonios as a cult recipient, only, we saw, the information that he was buried in the sanctuary of Athena, which suggests that he received cult at his grave shrine which was perceived to be within Athena's precinct. Erechtheus, by contrast, was a very significant cult recipient, who was cultically paired with both Athena and Poseidon. Thus, Erichthonios' inheritance of cultic elements from the nexus of the 'complex' Erechtheus seems to have been somewhat circumscribed. It would appear, then, that when Erichthonios 'inherited' mythological material from the nexus of the 'complex' Erechtheus he did not inherit very much of the associated ritual material, he did not really, or at least not substantially, replace Erechtheus as a cult recipient; this inheritance, it appears, remained part of the persona of Erechtheus, who was both a tribal and a whole polis cult recipient.

iv. Praxithea, the wife of Erechtheus

In Euripides' *Erechtheus* Praxithea was the wife of Erechtheus. In Apollodoros' version of Athenian history[198] Praxithea is the name both of the wife of Erichthonios and also of the wife of (the 'post-split') Erechtheus. Erichthonios (who, in Apollodoros' version, set up the wooden image of Athena on the Acropolis, founded the Panathenaia, and was buried in the sanctuary of Athena Polias[199]) married a Naiad Nymph called Praxithea and they had a son called Pandion.[200] Pandion married Zeuxippe and they had two sons, Erechtheus and Boutes.[201] After Pandion's death the two

---

[198] Apollod. 3.14.6–15.1.
[199] Apollod. 3.14.7.
[200] Apollod. 3.14.6–7.
[201] Apollod. 3.14.8. I should note, incidentally, that there was a mytheme that Erechtheus was the son of Nemesis (Sud., Phot. s.v. Rhamnousia Nemesis): Erechtheus set up her statue, as she was his mother; she reigned in Rhamnous.

brothers divided their inheritance and Erechtheus married (a different) Praxithea and inherited the kingship, while Boutes inherited the priesthoods of Athena and of Poseidon Erechtheus.[202] The genealogical sequence according to which Erechtheus was the son of Pandion, who was the son of Erichthonios, is also found in Pausanias,[203] which may suggest that it was the common Athenian myth that crystallized some time after the figures of Erichthonios and 'post-split' Erechtheus were generated with the help of material from the nexus of the 'complex' Erechtheus.

The fact that after the 'split' both the wife of Erichthonios and that of Erechtheus were called Praxithea may indicate that the name was somehow significant. For the wives of Kekrops II and Pandion II did not have the same name as those of Kekrops I and Pandion I; Kekrops I was married to (another) Aglauros, Kekrops II to Metiadousa.[204] Pandion I was married to Zeuxippe, Pandion II to Pylia.[205] There is also an important semantic connection between the two wives called Praxithea: the first Praxithea was a Naiad Nymph; the second, the wife of the 'post-split' Erechtheus, was in Apollodoros the granddaughter of the river Kephisos, for she was the daughter of Diogeneia who was the daughter of Kephisos,[206] and therefore also bears traces of an association with minor freshwater deities. But according to Lykourgos, the Praxithea who was married to the Erechtheus who was king during the war with the Eleusinians, and whose daugher was sacrificed to save the city, the Praxithea who was a character in Euripides' Erechtheus, was the daughter of Kephisos[207]—and thus would have been perceived to be a Naiad Nymph. Also, a convincing supplement to a verse in Euripides' *Erechtheus* has Athena addressing Praxithea as 'daughter of Kephisos'.[208]

Whoever this Erechtheus may have been perceived to have been, whenever that myth was created (on this myth, see Parker 2005a: 407 n. 82), it would not have been the 'complex' earthborn one.

[202] Apollod. 3.15.1; cf. Harpocr. s.v. Boutês.
[203] Paus. 1.5.3.
[204] Apollod 3.15.5.
[205] Ibid.
[206] Apollod. 3.15.1.
[207] Lycurg. *Leoc.* 98–100.
[208] *TrGF* 5 F 370.63. See also Eur. *Ion* 1261 (cf. the commentary of A. S. Owen ad loc.).

Clearly, the minimal conclusion that we may draw from these data is that Praxithea was the name of the wife of the earthborn 'complex' Erechtheus and that she was a Naiad Nymph, the daughter of Kephisos, and that this was one of the elements that became attached to both the figures that were generated from the material of the nexus of this 'complex' Erechtheus. It would appear, then, that comparably to the generation of Erichthonios and the 'post-split' Erechtheus out of the nexus of the 'complex' Erechtheus, there was also a generation of two figures called 'Praxithea' out of the nexus of Praxithea the wife of the 'complex' Erechtheus: Praxithea the wife of Erichthonios and Praxithea the wife of the 'post-split' Erechtheus.

In Euripides' *Erechtheus* Athena appointed Praxithea, the wife of the 'post-split' Erechtheus, to be her priestess—after she had given her instructions concerning the cults of her husband and daughters. We saw that the nexus 'post-split' Erechtheus had inherited the mythemes 'Praxithea was the wife of Erechtheus' and 'the war against the Eleusinians' from the nexus of the 'complex' Erechtheus; did it also inherit the mytheme 'Praxithea became a priestess of Athena Polias' from this nexus of the 'complex' Erechtheus?

Let us begin by considering the established fact that in Athenian mythology at least one Praxithea, the wife of 'post-split' Erechtheus, was the priestess of Athena Polias. The name of a priestess of Athena Polias called Praxithea evokes, and raises questions about, the relationship of this figure to the *genos* of the Praxiergidai, who, as we shall see in detail in Chapter 3, were involved in the cult of Athena Polias and more specifically had a very important role in the festival of the Plynteria. Is it a coincidence that a priestess called *Praxi-thea* would have been perceived to have been ritually involved with a *genos* called *Praxi-ergidai*?[209] There is also another important aspect of Praxithea's persona that 'fits' the Plynteria: she was a Naiad Nymph, and who better to supervise washings of sacred clothes, especially if they were washed in fresh water (as, I will be suggesting, the *peplos* of Athena probably was) than a Naiad Nymph? As for the

---

[209] [Sourvinou-Inwood went on to contrast Praxithea, 'she who does the seeing', with the Praxiergidai, 'they who do the work'. But the *-thea* element in Praxithea surely relates to 'goddess', not 'sight'. R.P.]

statue's bath in the sea at Phaleron, Kephisos, Praxithea's father, was associated with the general area of Phaleron, since the river Kephisos flows into the sea at Neon Phaleron, where Kephisos had a sanctuary.[210] In fact, the ritual washing and at least some of the associated rituals could not have taken place very far from the place where the Kephisos flowed into the sea, since the point at which the procession reached Phaleron, having presumably gone through the Halade gate,[211] would not be very far from the mouth of the Kephisos.

As we saw, in the cultic myths shaping Athenian perceptions the festival of the Plynteria was founded a year after the death of Aglauros. If in those Athenian perceptions Praxithea, as well as the Praxiergidai, were involved from its beginnings, Praxithea would have been perceived to have succeeded Aglauros as the priestess of Athena Polias after the latter's death. On the version of the myth in which Aglauros killed herself to save the city during the war with the Eleusinians in the reign of the 'complex' Erechtheus this would not have presented a problem, since the Naiad Nymph Praxithea was married to the 'complex' Erechtheus, who had suceeded Aglauros' father Kekrops. But when it is Praxithea the wife of the 'post-split Erechtheus' who is the priestess of Athena there would have been a chronological gap between the time of Aglauros' death in primordial times and the time of Praxithea the wife of the 'post-split' Erechtheus, in the early, but not primordial, segment of Athenian history. That is, the two figures would have been perceived to have belonged not just to different times, but to symbolically distinct times. Would that matter? Perhaps not; but within this narrowly focused mythicoritual nexus glaring conflicts may not have been necessarily perceived as unproblematic. However, these chronological problems may have been capable of being accommodated within that nexus through the (implicit or explicit) representation that it was the first Praxithea, the one who after the 'split' was married to Erichthonios, and who, on this reconstruction, would also have been a priestess of Athena, who had been involved with the first Plynteria; this representation would also have involved some chronological

---

[210] On the sanctuary of Kephisos in Echelidai, on or near the Kephisos, halfway between Peiraeus and Phaleron at Phaleron, see Guarducci 1974: 57–66; Parker 2005a: 430–2.
[211] And thus following more or less the course of the present Syngrou Street.

problems, a gap, but this particular, much smaller, gap might have been capable of being symbolically compressed, or perhaps elided, in the Athenian perceptions, since both Aglauros and the first Praxithea had belonged to the primordial segment of Athenian history.

It is the story told in Euripides' *Erechtheus* as a whole that would have been perceived as being in conflict with the nexus of Aglauros. Not necessarily because Athena made this Praxithea her priestess, since there was no reason for the audience to assume that this entailed that she was the first priestess called Praxithea,[212] but because in this story in Euripides' *Erechtheus*, as in other versions of this myth, it was Praxithea's daughters who died to save the city in the Eleusinian war, not Aglauros. I suggested that Aglauros' self-sacrifice was cultically embedded. This does not mean that there was any problem about the daughters of Erechtheus also receiving cult, as indeed they did,[213] and I shall return to this cult and the myth below. Here I will mention that traces of a perception of a 'conflict' are not entirely absent. Thus, Phanodemos, who was an Athenian deeply involved with cultic activities,[214] says that the daughters of Erechtheus sacrificed themselves to save the city when an army from Boiotia had invaded and they are called Parthenoi Hyakinthides.[215] Jacoby[216] thought that this shows that Phanodemos' account of the relations between Athens and Eleusis was different from the current tradition, that he rejected the war, or represented it differently, or even silently passed it over. In my view, he moved the daughters of Erechtheus to a different war in an attempt to reconcile the cultically

---

[212] In Sourvinou-Inwood (2003a: 29) I assumed that Praxithea was presented as the first priestess of Athena *tout court* in this tragedy, cutting out entirely the Aglauros nexus. I now realize that in fact she would have been perceived by the audience, who made sense of the tragedy through perceptual filters shaped by their mythicoritual assumptions, as the first priestess of Athena in the newly 'confirmed' poliadic cult of the crystallized new polis that followed after the war against the Eleusinians. This in fact also fits Athena's formulation (Eur. *Erechtheus* TrGF 5 F 370. 95–7: cf. p. 80 above) 'And to you, who raised up again the foundations of this city, I grant to make burnt offerings for the city on my altars, being called my priestess.'

[213] For example, see, besides Eur. *Erechtheus*, Philochoros (*FGrH* 328 F 12), who speaks of sacrifices to the daughters of Erechtheus.

[214] See p. 258.

[215] Phanodemos *FGrH* 325 F 4.

[216] Jacoby 1954: i. 179–80 ad loc.

embedded myth that Aglauros killed herself to save the city during the war against the Eleusinians, with the notion that the daughters of Erechtheus also died to save the city and received cult.

The mytheme that it was the daughters of the 'post-split' Erechtheus and Praxithea who died to save the city was constructed as a result of the transfer of the war to the 'post-split' Erechtheus. However, Aglauros, the daughter of Kekrops, belonged to primordial times, and so the transfer of this war to a later king generated chronological problems, which, in their turn, generated various responses. First, in the cultic contexts the chronological 'discrepancies' between this and other Athenian myths as they had developed in the course of time were ignored, narcotized; for in those contexts the focus was on a particular segment of Aglauros' and the polis's history, rather than on its place in a coherent chronological system of Athenian history. The second set of responses, in the context of the wider mythologies about early Athens, involved strategies of new mythopoeic constructions in which Aglauros' self-sacrifice in the Eleusinian war was replaced, in certain contexts, by the sacrifice and suicide of the daughters of Erechtheus, though the cultically embedded myth of Aglauros' self-sacrifice remained part of an important mythicoritual nexus, in which, I will be arguing later, she was also associated with Praxithea.

v. Aglauros and others before Kekrops and after

The sacrifice of the daughter of the king in time of war is a common Greek mythological schema. I will now argue that there had been an earlier form of the myth of Aglauros in which she too had been the daughter of the king whose kingdom was threatened by war, until she saved it by her self-sacrifice. I will set out a series of arguments that, I submit, lead to a reconstruction of a myth of early Athens in which Aglauros had been the daughter of the 'complex' Erechtheus and the Naiad Nymph Praxithea, a version of early Athenian history in which the 'complex' Erechtheus had been the first king of Athens. Kekrops, on this reconstruction, was the product of a subsequent, albeit early, mythopoeic development, a manifestation of the tendency to elaborate the beginnings of Athens. He was constructed also with the help of transformations of mythemes that had been part of the nexus of the 'complex' Erechtheus, the first king of Athens.

I will argue that in an earlier form of the myths of early Athens (the 'complex') Erechtheus had been the first king of Athens and the father of Aglauros and Pandrosos and the husband of Praxithea; and that it is possible to reconstruct the main lines of this earlier Erechtheus nexus, which had included (besides the elements that belonged to the 'complex' Erechtheus as reconstructed here) also several mythemes that in the extant versions of the myths of early Athens are part of the figure of Kekrops. One such set of mythemes contained the mythicoritual nexus 'Aglauros and Pandrosos the daughters of Erechtheus' which was transformed into the mythicoritual nexus 'Aglauros and Pandrosos the daughters of Kekrops'. This transformation had the effect of separating Aglauros' self-sacrifice from her father's reign, and so from her status as daughter of the king.

As we saw, semantically, the first two stages of Athenian history represented by Kekrops and Erechtheus can be considered an elaboration of one stage; for both kings were associated, first, with autochthony, and, second, with the establishment and crystallization of Athena's poliadic cult and of the polis, that is, with the establishment of the main, most important, lines of things as they are now as far as the polis and the poliadic cult are concerned. Kekrops, who is usually represented as snake-tailed,[217] is closely comparable to Erechtheus; more specifically, he is a more visibly and intensely autochthonous version of Erechtheus. His autochthony is, as it were, wild autochthony. Kekrops can therefore be seen as (he is, formally, whether or not I am right that he was also 'genetically') a transformation of Erechtheus, governed by an intensification (and de-acculturation) of the element 'autochthony'. As we have seen, the development of the myths of early Athens, especially of the earlier segment, was strongly defined by a tendency towards elaboration; also, the parameter 'strengthening autochthony' was an important trend in Athenian ideology and mythopoeia. In addition, the generation of Erichthonios and 'post-split' Erechtheus out of the figure 'complex' Erechtheus shows that this mythopoeic modality was also part of the mythopoeic constructions of the myths of early Athens.

---

[217] See *LIMC* s.v. Kekrops; cf. Dem. 60.30.

The most important argument in favour of the reconstruction proposed here is that in the Homeric poems Erechtheus the earth-born is presented as the defining early Athenian king,[218] the dominant figure of Athens' past (when seen from the viewpoint of the age of the Trojan War): for, we saw, Athens is characterized as the land of Erechtheus,[219] and the present (the *Odyssey*'s present) day king's palace is referred to as the palace of Erechtheus.[220] This position of Erechtheus is correlative with the fact that the name Erechtheidai could be used for all Athenians,[221] as an extension from the meaning '(genetic) descendants of Erechtheus'[222]—an extension that is unlikely to have occurred after the Erechtheid tribe was created. This element 'naming the Athenians' was also shared by (on the reading proposed here was also transferred to) the figure of Kekrops.[223] In other words, in the earliest surviving manifestation of the myths of early Athens the elements 'autochthony', in this version combined with 'a close association with the poliadic deity', 'being a cult recipient', and 'defining the land', are part of the nexus of Erechtheus. This suggests the possibility that in that mythology Erechtheus was represented as the first, autochthonous, defining, king of Athens.

Another argument is based on the spatial arrangements on the Acropolis. The fact that before the building of the Erechtheion both *martyria* of the contest between Athena and Poseidon over the sovereignty of Athens, both the olive tree of Athena and the 'sea' created by Poseidon, were situated in the sanctuary of Erechtheus, while afterwards each was located in a space that either belonged to the relevant deity or to a figure associated with that deity, is very difficult to make sense of. This is, inevitably, a culturally determined perception. However, this state of affairs does make perfect sense in terms of what we know of Greek mythicoritual mentality if in earlier versions of Athenian mythology the contest had been associated with the 'complex' Erechtheus, if he had been first Athenian king, in

---

[218] See also Kearns 1989: 133; Parker 1996: 19–20.

[219] Hom. *Il.* 2.546–51.

[220] Hom. *Od.* 7.80–1.

[221] See for example Pind. *Isthm.* 2.19; Soph. *Ajax* 202.

[222] For which see e.g. Eur. *Ion* 24.

[223] See Hdt. 8.44.

whose reign had taken place the contest that established the poliadic deity of Athens.

This conclusion is reinforced by another, independent, argument that also concerns the poliadic cult. In the extant myths, elements concerning the poliadic cult that (in terms of Greek religious mentality) belong together are divided between Kekrops and Erichthonios—who inherited those primordial elements from the nexus of the 'complex' Erechtheus. That is, in the extant versions of the myths of early Athens the element 'establishment of the poliadic cult' is located in the reign of Kekrops, while the element 'the setting up in the temple of the statue that had fallen from the sky' is located in the reign of Erichthonios. In Greek cult foundation myths the element 'the setting up of the statue' is, I submit, part of the schema 'establishment of the cult'; therefore, this mythological configuration is probably the result of a state of affairs in which an earlier nexus 'establishment of the poliadic cult' was divided into two. Of course, the results of this fragmentation did not violate Greek religious mentality, but, I submit, in a cult in which a sky-fallen cult statue had an important place, the element 'setting up of the statue' is unlikely to have begun life outside the nexus 'cult foundation'.

If this is right, the construction of the figure of Kekrops as the first king, with the help of material from the nexus 'complex Erechtheus the first king of Athens', was a context conducive to such a mythopoeic fragmentation which allowed both kings to be represented as having been involved in the establishment of the cult, an outcome that was mythologically and ideologically desirable. For, on the one hand, it was desirable, and the mythopoeic process would have been shaped so as to ensure, that the new 'first king' Kekrops should have been involved in the establishment of the poliadic cult, because in Athenian self-perceptions the existence of Athens depended on Athena being its poliadic deity. On the other hand, the fact that (if this interpretation is right) Erechtheus was deeply rooted in the Athenian representations as being involved with the establishment of the poliadic cult of Athena, whose nursling he was, would have been conducive to his continuing to have a role in that establishment after the construction of Kekrops. This role was eventually inherited by Erichthonios when the nexus of the complex Erechtheus generated the figures of Erichthonios and the 'post-split' Erechtheus.

In these circumstances, I submit that the division in the extant myths of the nexus 'establishment of the poliadic cult' into two stages, one associated with Kekrops and the other with Erichthonios, was very probably the result of the division of a nexus 'establishment of the poliadic cult' into two, in the context of the elaboration of the very early history of Athens proposed here, through the construction of the figure of Kekrops as the first king with the help of the deployment of material from the nexus 'complex Erechtheus the first king of Athens'.

This argument may gain a little support from a related consideration that I will now set out, which pertains to the relationships between on the one hand Aglauros and the cult statue and on the other Aglauros and the various early kings. It is conceivable, but, due to the nature of the evidence, not demonstrable, that the *aitia* of the Plynteria and of the Kallynteria may indicate that a statue was perceived to have been part of the cult of Athena Polias during the priesthood of Aglauros, the cult's first priestess. As we saw, the foundation myth of the Plynteria involves sacred garments not being washed after Aglauros' death. In theory, sacred garments do not necessarily presuppose a statue; however, I believe that in ancient perceptions, in the specific context of the festival in which the *peplos* of the statue was washed, it is very unlikely that it would not have been understood to imply that Aglauros' priesthood included the existence of Athena's statue. According to the *aition* of the Kallynteria Aglauros, having become priestess, 'adorned' the gods. As we shall see in Chapter 3, this expression suggests the cleaning of the sanctuary and may or may not include the notion of cleaning (and perhaps adorning?) the statue. Consequently, I submit, these *aitia* (or at least that of the Plynteria) belonged to the same nexus as narratives about the beginnings of the poliadic cult in which the setting up of the statue was placed during Aglauros' priesthood.

In the extant versions (such as that in Apollodoros) that include the set of mythemes 'Erichthonios' birth led to Aglauros' death', Aglauros would have been dead long before Erichthonios set up the statue. Thus, the myth of the birth of Erichthonios leading to the death of Aglauros is in conflict with the association (if correctly reconstructed) between Aglauros and the statue, which in the later versions of the myth was set up by Erichthonios—a mytheme he

inherited from the 'complex' Erechtheus. These *aitia*, then, are unlikely to have been constructed in the context of the myth in which
the birth of Erichthonios led to the death of Aglauros, which, I have
aready argued, was not a cultic myth. In the variants narrated before
the construction of Erichthonios had taken place, that is, the variants
in which the 'complex' Erechtheus succeeded Kekrops, Aglauros was
alive and active in the reign of Erechtheus when she killed herself to
save the city. Therefore, the *aitia* of the Plynteria and the Kallynteria
are compatible with this variant of the early history of Athens in
which Erechtheus (husband of Praxithea), in whose reign Aglauros
killed herself, succeeded her father. They would also be compatible
with the variant in which Erichthonios inherited from Erechtheus the
role of statue founder—provided that it was not part of a nexus in
which Aglauros died soon after his birth, which, if it is right that this
was not a cultic myth, it would not have been.

However, all these mythemes would have belonged together more
organically, in a less forced way, in another variant, a variant in which
all these events would have been condensed into one reign. I therefore suggest that these mythemes are more likely to have been
generated together in the context of such a variant, in which the
establishment of the poliadic cult, the setting up of the cult statue,
Aglauros' tenure as the first priestess of Athena, Aglauros' death, and
the establishment of the Plynteria had all taken place in the reign of
an Erechtheus who was the first king of Athens, before Kekrops had
been constructed as the first king. In this variant the poliadic cult was
established by Erechtheus the nursling of Athena, who had also set up
the statue of Athena, while Erechtheus' daughter Aglauros became
the first priestess and killed herself to save the city; following her
death the sacred clothes were not washed, and this eventually led to
the establishment of the Plynteria.

The figure of Aglauros' mother provides another argument. For in
the extant myths, in which Aglauros is the daughter of Kekrops,
Kekrops' wife is either unnamed or she is called Aglauros, like her
daughter. In one story Kekrops' unnamed wife was the daughter of
the first king of Athens who was called Aktaios.[224] In the version in

---

[224] Paus. 1.2.6.

Apollodoros Kekrops was the first king of Athens[225] and he married
Aglauros, the daughter of Aktaios, who had not, in this version, been
a king of Athens.[226] As we saw, the notion that Kekrops was not the
first king of Athens is a further subsequent elaboration of the beginnings, known to, and rejected by, Philochoros.[227]

The fact that Kekrops' wife is sometimes nameless indicates that at
one end of her spectrum she is a shadowy figure defined by the roles
'Kekrops' wife' and 'Aktaios' daughter' and so also 'connecting link
between the two'—for her 'transfer' from Aktaios to Kekrops created
a connection between the two men and explains why Kekrops, who in
this version was not the first king of Athens, succeeded Aktaios, who
was. At the other end of the spectrum Kekrops' wife has a name, but
this name duplicates the name of one of Kekrops' daughters. Elsewhere, we saw, the duplication of names is the index of fill-in
mythopoeia, such as that involving the duplication of figures in
mythopoeic constructions aiming at creating systematic histories,
involving a coherent chronological framework based on lists of
kings, in which the duplications were a device for coping with
incongruities and apparent contradictions that emerged as a result
of the attempt to systematize the various versions of early Athenian
history.

Thus, Kekrops' wife was either a wholly shadowy figure defined by
her role, and without a name, or a figure with a name resulting from
the duplication of the name of one of Kekrops' (and her) daughters,
which makes it likely that she was constructed in a process of fill-in
mythopoeic elaboration and expansion. This contrasts strongly with
the figure of Praxithea the Naiad Nymph wife of (the 'complex')
Erechtheus who would have been Aglauros' mother in the condensed
variant of the myths of early Athens reconstructed here; in that
variant Erechtheus had been the first king and was married to
Praxithea the Naiad Nymph, an appropriate wife for a first king,

---

[225] Apollod. 3.14.1.

[226] Apollod. 3.14.2.

[227] See Philochoros (*FGrH* 328 F 92) and Jacoby (1954: i. 386–9 ad F 92–8). The
conception that Aglauros (and also Herse and Pandrosos) were daughters of Aktaios
emerges also, via a confusion between this Aktaios/Aktaion and another, in Suda s.v.
Phoinikeia grammata, part of which, but probably not the relevant part, comes from
Skamon of Mytilene, *FGrH* 476 F3.

since in Greek mythology Nymphs are very strongly associated with city foundations, correlatively with their close connection with landscape and locality.[228] In this particular case Praxithea's close connection with locality expresses another modality of autochthony: her husband was born from the earth, she was born of the most important river of the Attic plain.[229] This primordial couple, then, root Athens in the most comprehensive way into the soil of Attica.

The Naiads were connected with springs, wells, fountains, and also caves.[230] Aglauros and Pandrosos, and eventually, when she appeared, Herse, were clearly appropriate names for the daughters of a Naiad Nymph; the fact that Aglauros' sanctuary was associated with a cave[231] would also suit a daughter of the Naiad Praxithea.[232] Consequently, I submit, Praxithea the Naiad Nymph is a most appropriate wife for the first king of Athens and also a most appropriate mother for Aglauros, Pandrosos, and Herse.[233]

In these circumstances, I suggest, there are strong reasons for concluding that the sequence 'Kekrops the earthborn', usually perceived to have been half snake, then the earthborn Erechtheus, was constructed as an autochthony-strengthening elaboration of an earlier nexus in which a 'complex' Erechtheus was the first king of Athens. If this is right, this nexus of the 'complex' Erechtheus would have included the following elements: Erechtheus was the

---

[228] Sourvinou-Inwood 2005: 112–16, 265–7.

[229] If, as is most probable, given that Praxithea the wife of the 'post-split' Erechtheus was the daughter of Kephisos, the 'complex' Praxithea the Naiad Nymph was perceived to have been the daughter of Kephisos.

[230] Hom. *Od.* 13.103–8; cf. the commentary of A. Hoekstra on 104–12 and 217–18.

[231] On Aglauros' sanctuary see n. 10 above.

[232] Larson (2001: 6, cf. 126–7) classifies the daughters of Kekrops as "nymphlike in their association with Pan's sanctuary on the north slope of the Acropolis". However, the alleged association with Pan's sanctuary disappears now that the sanctuary of Aglauros has been identified as being on the east slope (Dontas 1983: 48–63), while the cave of Pan is in the NW slope (see e.g. Hurwit 1999: 4–6, 224). What they, and Aglauros especially, have is Nymph connections, which, I suggest, resulted from their being, in the earlier Athenian mythologies, the daughters of the Naiad Nymph Praxithea.

[233] The association is self-evident with regard to Pandrosos and Herse. As for Aglauros, 'the shining one, the bright one', this could perhaps be a reference to the water of a spring and therefore appropriate for the daughter of a Naiad Nymph.

first king of Athens; he was earthborn and the nursling of Athena; he was married to the Naiad Nymph Praxithea and they had two daughters, Aglauros and Pandrosos; the cult of Athena Polias was established in Erechtheus' reign, and his daughter Aglauros became its first priestess; after Athena's victory, the Eleusinians attacked Athens to reverse the result and establish Poseidon as the poliadic deity[234] and Aglauros sacrificed herself to save the city—the daughter of the king, but not sacrificed by her father, she was herself the active agent and perhaps not a virgin, if it was part of that earlier myth that she had at least one offspring by a god. After Aglauros' death Athena appointed Aglauros' mother Praxithea as her priestess. A year after that death the Plynteria festival was founded.

On this reconstruction, in the earliest Athenian mythology, the girl who died to save the city in the war with the Eleusinians was Aglauros, the daughter of the 'complex' Erechtheus in his pre-Kekrops phase and Praxithea, the Naiad Nymph. In Euripides' *Erechtheus*, and in other myths, the girl who died was also the daughter of Erechtheus and Praxithea, but this Erechtheus was not the first king, he was the figure shaped after the construction of Erichthonios, the 'post-split' Erechtheus.

In the myth of Aglauros only one person is mentioned as dying to save the city. In the myth of the daughters of Erechtheus in Euripides' *Erechtheus* one daughter was sacrificed[235] and her two sisters killed themselves because of an oath they had taken with their sister.[236] This myth in *Erechtheus*, then, is structured by the schema 'the daughter of the king is sacrificed to save the city' (which, on my reconstruction, had also structured the earlier myth of Aglauros) in combination with the schema 'a group of sisters die to save their country'.

If it is right that the figure of Kekrops was constructed with the help of material from the 'complex' Erechtheus in his pre-Kekrops phase, when did this construction take place? One certain *terminus ante quem* is provided by the date of the Kleisthenic reforms, when

---

[234] On Poseidon Pater at Eleusis, see n. 122 above.

[235] The oldest in Demaratos' summary, which, however, does not mention the death of the other sisters (Demaratos *FGrH* 42 F 4). In Apollod. (3.15.4) it is the youngest daughter who is sacrificed.

[236] Apollod. 3.15.4. See on this, Collard, Cropp, and Lee 1995: 151.

Kekrops was selected to be one of the ten tribal heroes.[237] The Kekropeion, the grave and hero-shrine of Kekrops at the south-western corner of the Erechtheion,[238] may conceivably have Peisistratos' rule as a *terminus ante quem*, if a large column was indeed erected to mark Kekrops' grave and if it was indeed of Peisistratean date.[239] A vase by Sophilos shows Aglauros and Pandrosos with their father, but the identity of the father cannot be established. I have argued that this image represented the contest between Athena and Poseidon over the sovereignty of Attica.[240] If my reconstruction is right, and Aglauros and Pandrosos were indeed the daughters of Erechtheus in earlier mythologies, and if Kekrops had not yet been constructed in Sophilos' time, their father at that time would have been Erechtheus, and it would have been Erechtheus who had the role in the contest that in the extant myths is performed by Kekrops.

Obviously, since Kekrops is Aglauros' father in the extant myths, his construction did not leave the myth of Aglauros unaffected. Given that her cultically embedded self-sacrifice was located in the reign of the 'complex' Erechtheus, there were, in theory, two possible outcomes of the mythopoeic shake-up resulting from the construction of the figure of Kekrops. The first, which is reflected in an extant myth, would involve Aglauros becoming the daughter of Kekrops, with her cultically embedded self-sacrifice to save the city still remaining located in the reign of the 'complex' Erechtheus—when the war with the Eleusinians took place. The second outcome would involve Aglauros remaining the daughter of the 'complex' Erechtheus. It is not impossible that this second outcome may also have been reflected in a myth which has not survived. It is even not wholly inconceivable that a story in a scholion (on Aristides'

---

[237] There is no assured pre-Kleisthenic representation: *LIMC* VI.i s.v. Kekrops, 1090.

[238] See e.g. Antiochos-Pherekydes *FGrH* 333 F 1; *IG* I³ 474.56–63.

[239] Hurwit (1999: 117 and 342 n. 76), noting that the precise date of the archaic monument is open to question; Korres 1994b: 41. But how certain can we be that there had not been any change in the use of space in that area where, we saw, such changes of space had certainly taken place when the Erechtheion was built? On the Kekropeion, see also Hurwit 1999: 145, 204; Gourmelen 2005: 293–5.

[240] Sourvinou-Inwood 2008.

Panathenaikos)[241] that is normally assumed to be based on a confusion between the daughters of the 'post-split' Erechtheus and Aglauros and her sisters may in reality have been reflecting a myth of this kind—or rather, more specifically, the confusion may have been the result of knowledge of a myth in which Aglauros was the daughter of Erechtheus. For according to that story, during the war between Athens and Eleusis Erechtheus received an oracle that he should sacrifice his daughter Aglauros and this he did, and then her sisters 'Ersa' and 'Pandrose' killed themselves because of an oath.

Whether or not there was a myth leading to the second outcome, the important question is, which myth became the cultic myth; for the two would not have coexisted as cultic myths, since such conflict in this narrowly focused mythicoritual nexus would have been beyond the parameters of tolerance of inconsistencies. Two arguments indicate that the variant that became the cultic myth was that in which Aglauros was the daughter of Kekrops, but her cultically embedded self-sacrifice took place in the reign of the 'complex' Erechtheus. First, in the extant myths the persona of Aglauros as the daughter of Kekrops is well established, and there is no trace of a filial link with Erechtheus. Second, the variant in which Aglauros was the daughter of Kekrops, but killed herself to save the city in the reign of Erechtheus, during the war with the Eleusinians, is actually attested in an important source, Philochoros.[242] On this reconstruction, after this reshaping of her myth, Aglauros' mythological nexus continued to contain the defining mytheme that she killed herself to save the city; this had to be located in the reign of the 'complex' Erechtheus, since it was during that reign that the war with the Eleusinians took place, and so it was. There would not have been serious problems with the notion that the daughter of Kekrops was also a priestess in the reign of her father's successor and killed herself to save the city. So this, I submit, was the cultic myth constructed after the creation of Kekrops.

After the 'split' that generated on the one hand Erichthonios and on the other (eventually) the 'post-split' Erechtheus, when the war

---

[241] Schol. on Aristid. *Or.* 1 Behr (*Panathenaikos*) 87; Dindorf III p. 112.10–15.
[242] Philochoros *FGrH* 328 F 105.

with the Eleusinians became attached to the 'post-split' Erechtheus, and was thus located a long time after Kekrops and his daughter Aglauros, the mytheme 'sacrifice of a girl to save the city', which was connected with the myth of the war with Eleusis, was reshaped and transformed. Through the deployment of the Greek mythological schema 'a king sacrifices his daughter' the mytheme of female sacrifice attached to the war took the form '(the "post-split") Erechtheus sacrificed his daughter' to save the city—as it appears in Euripides' *Erechtheus*. To put it differently, the earlier myth 'in the reign of the first, defining, earthborn king of Athens Erechtheus, his daughter Aglauros died to save the city', which was reshaped to 'in the reign of the earthborn king Erechtheus, Aglauros, the daughter of the first king, Kekrops, died to save the city', eventually generated the myth 'in the reign of the non-earthborn, "post-split" Erechtheus, the daughter[s] of Erechtheus died to save the city'.

Since Aglauros was cultically embedded, and her self-sacrifice was (inevitably) a cultic myth, this new myth would not have eliminated the myth of Aglauros' self-sacrifice, it would have become juxtaposed to it. Hence, we saw, mythopoeic activities such as that of Phanodemos, who says that the daughters of Erechtheus sacrificed themselves to save the city when an army from Boiotia had invaded;[243] such attempts are correlative with the attempt to reconcile the cultically embedded myth of Aglauros' self-sacrifice during the war against the Eleusinians with the notion that the daughters of Erechtheus died to save the city and received cult.[244]

In Euripides' *Erechtheus* the daughters of Erechtheus become the goddesses Hyakinthides whose cult was instituted by Athena.[245] The Hyakinthides are sometimes, as in *Erechtheus*, identified with the daughters of Erechtheus,[246] while sometimes they are presented as

---

[243] Phanodemos *FGrH* 325 F 4.
[244] Philochoros speaks of a sacrifice to 'the daughters of Erechtheus': *FGrH* 328 F 12.
[245] *TrGF* 5 24 F 370.65–89. On the Hyakinthides, see Parker 1987a: 212 n. 66; Kearns 1989: 59–63; 201–2; Larson 1995: 20, 101–6 passim; Parker 1996: 252; Kron 1999: 78–9 and n. 59 with bib.; Redfield 2003: 94; Parker 2005a: 399, 446. In *IG* II² 1035.52 a sanctuary Hyakinthion is mentioned, but no context survives.
[246] See e.g. Dem. 60.27; Phanodemos *FGrH* 325 F 4.

the daughters of the Spartan Hyakinthos.[247] Thus, in Apollodoros they are the daughters of the Lakedaimonian Hyakinthos who were sacrificed in the unsuccessful attempt to rid Athens of a famine and pestilence that had been inflicted upon them as a result of Minos' prayer for vengeance.[248] The myth in which the Hyakinthides are the daughters of Hyakinthos appears, because of their name, to be a more organic nexus than that in which they are identified with the daughters of Erechtheus. Indeed, it is not impossible that it was a perceived disjunction between the name Hyakinthides and the persona of the daughters of Erechtheus that encouraged the attempt by Phanodemos to explain the name Hyakinthides as resulting from something other than their parentage: according to Phanodemos the daughters of Erechtheus were called 'Hyakinthid maidens' because they were sacrificed on the hill called Hyakinthos.[249] As we saw, Phanodemos also said that these girls sacrificed themselves to save the city when an army from Boiotia had invaded;[250] I argued that this was the product of an attempt to reconcile the cultically rooted myth of Aglauros with the myth that it was the daughters of the 'post-split' Erechtheus who died and saved the city.

[247] See Apollod. 3.15.8; Harpocr. s.v. Hyakinthides, quoting the statement of Lykourgos in the speech *Against Lykophron* that they were the daughters of Hyakinthos the Lakedaimonian (whence Sud., Phot. s.v. Hyakinthides; Suda and Photios discuss the daughters of Erechtheus s.v. Parthenoi). Steph. Byz. s.v. Lousia says that Lousia was one of Hyakinthos' daughters, from whom was named the deme of the Oineis. On this version in which the two groups are separate, see also Frazer 1921: 118–19 n. 1 ad loc; Kearns 1989: 202. Mikalson argued that Erechtheus and Hyakinthos were originally local manifestations of the same divine figure and that the Panathenaia and the Hyakinthia were originally "the same annual festival", and that it follows that the Panathenaia was originally the annual festival of Erechtheus (Mikalson 1976: esp. 152–3). However, even leaving aside the question as to whether the similarities between the two figures and the two festivals are as close and significant as Mikalson suggests they are, in the same way that no figure can be 'the same' as another figure which belongs to a different religious system, neither can a festival be the same; mythicoritual material may be deployed to construct another, or both may be constructed from material that originated in (more precisely that at some point had belonged to) one nexus, but these are entirely different, very complex processes involving very complex bricolage, and the resulting crystallizations cannot be 'the same'.

[248] Apollod. 3.15.8.

[249] Phanodemos *FGrH* 325 F 4; see also Jacoby 1954: i. 178–80 ad loc. Phot. s.v. Parthenoi seems to ascribe this version to Phrynichos, *Monotropos*.

[250] Phanodemos *FGrH* 325 F4.

Parker remarked, with reference to the Hyakinthides and the daughters of Erechtheus, that the floating motif of the maiden sacrifice could attach itself to a particular king, and so to his hitherto non-existent daughters, and that since such daughters would not have had cult, there was a pressure to assimilate them to a cult group.[251] The pattern of appearance of the Hyakinthides and of their identification with the daughters of Erechtheus, and the disjunction between the name Hyakinthides and the persona of the daughters of Erechtheus, suggests that this is indeed what took place; that a pre-existing Hyakinthides cult came to be identified with the cult of the daughters of Erechtheus when Athenian mythopoeia constructed the mytheme that it was these daughters of the 'post-split' Erechtheus, rather than Aglauros, who died to save the city during the war against the Eleusinians.

To judge from their extant myths, as well as the very fact of their identification with the daughters of Erechtheus, we may conclude that, if it is right that the Hyakinthides had a pre-existing cult, their myth (of which the extant myths would be transformations) would have told a story of the Hyakinthides dying to save Athens. Of the two extant variants, in the first the Hyakinthides were the daughters of Erechtheus, in the second they were the daughters of the Spartan Hyakinthos, but their sacrifice was ineffective, they did not save the city. If the mytheme that Hyakinthos, the father of the Hyakinthides, was a Lakedaimonian was attached to their myth before their identification with the daughters of Erechtheus, the last quarter of the fifth century was a most suitable time for the tranformation of a myth of a Spartan's daughters saving (or not saving, whatever the variant may have been at the time) Athens to one in which the saviours were the daughters of an Athenian king.

It is indeed not impossible that both extant variants of the myth of the Hyakinthides were constructed at least partly in response to unease about a cultically rooted myth in which the city's salvation was brought about by the actions of persons whose nationality was the same as the present enemy's; and that this helped to generate two transformations of the myth: in the first the Hyakinthides became the

---

[251] Parker 1987a: 212 n. 66.

daughters of Erechtheus, in the second they were the daughters of the Spartan Hyakinthos, but their sacrifice was ineffective, they did not save the city.

As we saw above, the correlation between the fate of the Hyakinthides as described by Athena in Euripides' *Erechtheus* and the fate of the Athenian war dead as evoked by that formulation would have made the Hyakinthides be perceived as—among other things— mythological models for the Athenian war dead and their achievement of higher status in the afterlife, which usually took the form of heroization. Aglauros, we saw, had a cultically embedded connection with the ephebes, for whom she functioned as a paradigm. Euripides' *Erechtheus* constructed a representation of the Hyakinthides as paradigms for a new immortalization of the war dead. A new construction (whether or not crystallized by Euripides) of the daughter[s] of Erechtheus (instead of Aglauros) as the sacrificial victim[s] who saved the city in the war against the Eleusinians is deployed as a paradigm for (albeit not an exact representation, rather, a higher version, of) the immortality, especially the new form of celestial immortality, of the Athenian war dead.[252]

4. RECONSTRUCTING CULTIC MYTHS: A SUMMARY OF THE CONCLUSIONS

I will now summarize very briefly some of the most important conclusions set out in the previous sections.

Aglauros, the daughter of the first king of Athens (who in the extant versions was Kekrops), is one of the most important figures of Athenian mythology. She was the first priestess of Athena, and this is one of the two facets of her mythological persona that were cultically embedded from an early period—in the festivals of the Plynteria and Kallynteria. Aglauros' persona as the female who gave her life to save the city in the war against the Eleusinians during the reign of

---

[252] On the heroization and immortality of the Athenian war dead and on celestial immortality and the epitaph for the men who died in the battle of Poteidaia, see Sourvinou-Inwood 1995: 191–5, esp. 194, 202.

Erechtheus was embedded in her role in the maturation process of the Athenian youths that eventually crystallized into the *ephebeia* (and into her role as patroness of the ephebes)—and in her sanctuary, its position, and its function with regard to those youths. She and her sister Pandrosos, and eventually also Herse, when she was added to the pair to make it a triad,[253] were the mythological prototype of the *arrephoroi*, whose main patroness was Pandrosos.

In other words, before the pair Aglauros and Pandrosos became a triad, each of the two sisters was the main patroness of maturation rites of one or the other gender, male in the case of Aglauros, female in the case of Pandrosos. Both Aglauros and Pandrosos have a significant kourotrophic function, which is also correlative with their parentage, their descent not only from Ge, through their earthborn father, but also (on my reconstruction) from Kephisos through their mother Praxithea. This makes them par excellence appropriate kourotrophic figures.

The myth of Aglauros' and her sisters' involvement in the myth of Erichthonios was not cultically embedded from an early period—if at all; it was a later, fifth-century construction, and it does not refract the rite of the *arrhephoria*, though an element from that rite, 'forbidden to open, or look in, the basket', was deployed to help construct that myth. The myth of Aglauros' self-sacrifice was somewhat pushed into the background when the mythopoeic constructions generated by the construction of the figure of Erichthonios led to the creation of the myth that it was a daughter of (the 'post-split') Erechtheus who was sacrificed in the war against the Eleusinians and now receives cult together with her sisters who followed her in death, under the name Hyakinthides.

Erechtheus, in his earlier manifestations that are visible to us, was an *autochthon*, the nursling of Athena. This is the figure I call the 'complex' Erechtheus. He had a sanctuary on the Acropolis and he received a whole polis cult, to which was eventually added a tribal cult when Erechtheus became a tribal hero in the course of the Kleisthenic reforms. On my reconstruction, Erechtheus established the cult of Athena Polias and set up the goddess' statue, and founded

---

[253] Herse is not as deeply rooted in cult as the other two are.

the Panathenaia and invented the chariot. In the extant myths these
latter elements are part of the nexus of Erichthonios. For, at some
point, in the mythopoeic process of elaboration of the very early
history of Athens, elements from the nexus of the 'complex'
Erechtheus generated two figures, Erichthonios, who inherited the
primordial segment, and the figure I call the 'post-split' Erechtheus
who is focused on the mythological nexus of the war against the
Eleusinians.

The persona, including the cult, of Erechtheus was, and remained,
distinct from that of Poseidon Erechtheus. The latter cult was a
divine cult and Poseidon Erechtheus was the god Poseidon Gaieochos with the added epithet Erechtheus. When the Erechtheion was
built, but not before, the hero Erechtheus came to share an altar with
Poseidon Gaieochos Erechtheus.

The construction of the figures of Erichthonios and the 'post-split'
Erechtheus led to other mythopoeic constructions, including adjust-
ments, which affected the nexus of Aglauros, such as the creation of
the myth of the sacrifice of the daughters of Erechtheus, who were
worshipped as the Hyakinthides. However, Aglauros' self-sacrifice
was cultically embedded, and it did not disappear from the Athenian
representations; it was, I suggest, the cultic myth associated with the
location of the ephebic oath in her sanctuary and her primacy as a
witness.

Finally, I argued that in the earlier Athenian mythologies the
'complex' Erechtheus had been the first, defining, Athenian king.
His wife was Praxithea, a Naiad Nymph who was the daughter of
Kephisos, so that they constructed complex meanings of autochthony and rootedness in the land. Their daughters were Aglauros
and Pandrosos. Erechtheus founded the statue (and through this
the cult) of Athena Polias, of which his daughter Aglauros became
the first priestess. He also founded the Panathenaia including the
apobates competition, which was connected with his invention
of the chariot, first displayed at that festival. In his reign Athens
was threatened by the Eleusinians and after an oracle his daughter
Aglauros killed herself and saved the city. She was succeeded as
priestess of Athena by her mother Praxithea, in the early part of
whose tenure were first celebrated the Plynteria, which was, among

other things, a kind of commemoration of Aglauros' death, and probably also the Kallynteria, which commemorated Aglauros' actions as priestess of Athena in life.

Appendix: Eumolpos, the Hyades, and others in Euripides, *Erechtheus*[254]

a. Eumolpos and the Mysteries

Athena's speech continues from where we left it on p. 80 as follows.

ἃ μὲν κατ' αἶαν τήνδε <δεῖ> 'κπονεῖν κλύεις,
ἃ δ' αὖ δικάζει Ζεὺς πατὴρ ἐν οὐρανῶι
100   λέγοιμ' ἄν. Εὔμολπος γὰρ Εὐμόλπου γεγώ[ς
τοῦ κατθ]ανόντος

You have heard the tasks you must undertake in this land. Now I will tell you the judgment passed by Zeus in heaven.(100) For Eumolpos son of Eumolpos, who died.

There follow just line beginnings: 102 *Demeter*, 103 *who is to be born*, 104 *marrying*, 105 *and one* (fem.), 106 *and the* (fem.), 107 *and to/for the Hyades*, 108 *stars*, 109 *of/from Deo*, 110 (*things*) *not to be uttered*, 111 *toil*, 112 *of/from holy*, 114 *Kerykes*, 115 *But restrain*, 116 *piteous*, 117 *and the*. Praxithea's reply began at 118, but is lost.

So Athena went on to reveal the decisions taken by Zeus about the future; more specifically, about a major cultic issue that involved Eleusis and its relationship with Athens in this mythological universe in which Eleusis had been independent of Athens before it became part of it, after this war was won.[255]

---

[254] [These sections were added by Sourvinou-Inwood at a late stage to the main text of this chapter, between sections 3.iv and 3.v; I have re-located them as an Appendix. R.P.]

[255] I hope to have shown (Sourvinou-Inwood 1997a) that this myth does not reflect historical reality in the sense that Eleusis had been part of the Athenian polis from the time when that polis emerged and crystallized.

The extant part of the text leaves us in no doubt: the context of these verses was that of the Eleusinian Mysteries; also, as has been recognized, lines 100–1 undoubtedly refer to the foundation of the Mysteries by the later Eumolpos, the descendant of the one who has just died.[256] Thus, in this Euripidean version, the Mysteries were founded while Eleusis was already part of the Athenian polis. In other versions the Mysteries had been celebrated before the war, and were then incorporated in the Athenian polis that was constituting itself and its central cults.[257] According to one such version[258] Demeter was received by Keleos, king of Eleusis, when Pandion was king in Athens, which means in the generation before Erechtheus.[259] In one version the Mysteries were celebrated 'for the peace' (ἐπὶ τῇ εἰρήνῃ) after the war.[260]

The different myths about the foundation of the Eleusinian Mysteries[261] can be divided into two basic variants. In the first, in the *Homeric Hymn to Demeter*, the Mysteries were revealed by Demeter to Eleusinian heroes of the heroic past, including an Eleusinian Eumolpos.[262] The princes to whom Demeter revealed the Mysteries in this hymn[263] were Triptolemos, Diokles, Eumolpos, and Keleos. Earlier in the *Hymn*,[264] a longer list of Eleusinian princes consisted of Triptolemos, Dioklos,[265] Polyxeinos, Eumolpos, Dolichos, Keleos. This version stresses the divine authority of the rite, its revealed nature. In the strand of myths that make up the second variant, the Mysteries were founded by someone connected with Thrace, or Orphic poetry, or both; most commonly this founder is Eumolpos, either a figure of Thracian origin or a homonymous descendant of this Eumolpos, the son of Mousaios, to whom was ascribed eschatological poetry; in a somewhat later tradition the founder was Orpheus

---

[256] See on this, Collard, Cropp, and Lee 1995: 194 ad 100–1.
[257] See below and e.g. Paus. 1.38.2–3.
[258] Apollod. 3.14.7.
[259] On Pandion, see Kron 1976: 104–19; Kearns 1989: 81, 191–2. On Keleos: Kearns 1989: 176; Richardson 1974: 177–8; Clinton 1992: 100; Foley 1994: 41, 142.
[260] Schol. Eur. *Phoen.* 854.
[261] Some aspects of which I discussed in Sourvinou-Inwood 1997a.
[262] *Hymn. Hom. Dem.* 475–82.
[263] Ibid. 474–5.
[264] Ibid. 153–5.
[265] On the variation between Dioklos and Diokles, see Richardson 1974: 196.

himself.[266] The connection with Thrace, and correspondingly with Orphic poetry, expressed in these myths, undoubtedly refracted certain perceptions concerning eschatologies. I will say something briefly below about the circumstances of this mythopoeic construction.

In between these two variants of myths about the foundation of the Mysteries another variant can be reconstructed, which shares elements with both. It has been rightly thought[267] that the version in which the founder Eumolpos came from Thrace was a transformation of a myth in which the Mysteries were founded by an Eleusinian Eumolpos, the son of Poseidon, which was very suitable for an Eleusinian, since at Eleusis Poseidon was worshipped under the title 'father'.[268] Eumolpos, the eponymous ancestor of the Eumolpids,[269] is, of course, the mythological prototype of the hierophant,[270] and in some stories he is explicitly said to have been the first hierophant.[271] His name alludes to the beautiful voice that was desirable for hierophants.[272]

The mytheme that Eumolpos was the first hierophant was inextricably connected with the mytheme that he was the ancestor of the Eumolpids; he was the first hierophant because he was the ancestor of the Eumolpids, who provided the hierophants of the present; and the Eumolpids were hierophants in the cult now because they were descended from Eumolpos who was the first hierophant. The semantic gap between the persona of Eumolpos as the first hierophant and that of Eumolpos as the founder of the Mysteries, and the perception of such a gap, are, clearly, elastic. For the two personae were very closely connected. As the first hierophant, he was the first person to

---

[266] See Parker 1987a: 203–4; West 1983: 23–4. Orpheus is first attested as the founder of the Eleusinian Mysteries in [Eur.] *Rhes.* (943–4; on this cf. Graf 1974: 23–39; West 1983: 23–4). See also the differentiation between the activities of Orpheus on the one hand and Eumolpos (founder of the Mysteries) on the other in Lucian, *Fugitivi* 8. Eumolpos is sometimes said to have been the pupil of Orpheus (see Suda s.v. Eumolpos). On Eumolpos as founder of the Mysteries, see below and Parker 1987a: 203–4; Kearns 1989: 163; Richardson 1974: 198.

[267] See Parker 1987a: 203–4; Kearns 1989: 114–15.

[268] As Parker 1987a: 203 pointed out.

[269] On Eumolpos as ancestor of the Eumolpids, see e.g. Photius s.v. Eumolpidai; Schol. Aeschin. 3.18; Clem. Al. *Protr.* 2.20.2; Diog. Laert. 1.3.

[270] See Kearns 1989: 114; Clinton 1992: 75.

[271] In Hesych. s.v. Eumolpidai and Schol. Aeschin. (3.18) Eumolpos is said to have been the first hierophant.

[272] See on this desirability, Clinton 1974: 45: cf. *IG* II²3639, with Clinton 1974: 38.

Figure 1. Eumolpos on a red-figure skyphos, *c.*480 BC. BM E 140. © The Trustees of the British Museum.

have revealed the *hiera*, and this slides into the notion that he was the first to have revealed, and so founded, the Mysteries.

The earliest attested version of the myth of the foundation of the Mysteries, in the *Homeric Hymn to Demeter*, belongs to the first variant. In this myth Eumolpos was an Eleusinian prince—albeit, of course, not the founder of the Mysteries. It is this persona of Eumolpos as an Eleusinian prince that is also found in the other early attestations of his myth. A Hesiodic fragment which consists of three names, Eumolpos' and two others, associates Eumolpos with two

Eleusinian princes, Dolichos and Hippothoon, and therefore almost certainly represents him as an Eleusinian prince.[273] Eumolpos' persona as founder of the Mysteries is attested in a Pindaric fragment,[274] in which he also appears to have been represented as an Eleusinian ruler. For Eumolpos is characterized as a 'wise leader' who ruled 'with lawfulness that pleases the people' and is said to have 'established a rite for his citizens'. Thus this is an unambiguous instance of a Eumolpos who is both an Eleusinian king and the founder of the Mysteries.

A king who rules 'with lawfulness that pleases the people' or indeed a 'wise leader' are not the most appropriate descriptions of a ruler who led his people in a war that was lost. It is therefore unlikely that this Eleusinian Eumolpos led his people in a war with Athens. It could be argued that the figure so described here may have been the younger Eumolpos.[275] However, since after the war (in which, in the myths involving more than one Eumolpos, the Thracian Eumolpos was the leader) Eleusis no longer had its own king or ruler, these formulations stressing Eumolpos' role as a leader would not have been selected if the younger Eumolpos was being referred to.

This, then, is an Eleusinian Eumolpos, a ruler of Eleusis who did not lead his people in a war against Athens and who founded the Mysteries. Another representation of a persona of Eumolpos that combines the elements 'Eleusinian ruler' and 'hierophant' is seen in an Athenian image of about 480 BC.[276] In a scene showing the launch of the mission of Triptolemos Eumolpos, identified through an inscription, is represented seated and holding a sceptre, and therefore as a Eleusinian ruler; though he is not wearing the costume of the hierophant,[277] his persona as the first hierophant is evoked by his association with a swan, which signifies a beautiful voice. Eumolpos

---

[273] Hes. fr. 227M-W, cf. Euphorion fr. 35c Powell.

[274] Pindar fr. 346b 5–6. See on this fragment, Lloyd-Jones 1967: 206–29. See also Richardson 1974: 197 ad 154.

[275] See Lloyd-Jones 1967: 213.

[276] On the skyphos, London BM E 140: *ARV* 459.3; *Add* 243; Clinton 1992: 64 and figs. 51–4. It is true that Grecian dress does not necessarily indicate Grecian nationality at this date (cf. Orpheus). But the image shows Eumolpos (a) as a ruler, not military leader (b) juxtaposed with Triptolemos; so he should be Eleusinian. On other scenes from the first half of the fifth century that are, or may be, representing Eumolpos, see esp. Clinton 1992: 76–8, 138–9.

[277] On which, see Clinton 1974: 32–3, 48; Clinton 1992: 70 n. 38.

is depicted under one of the handles. Poseidon is represented under the other handle, seated to the left but looking backwards towards the Triptolemos scene; then, Amphitrite is shown to Poseidon's left, moving left towards Dionysos, and looking back; Zeus is shown behind Dionysos, then the swan, which is associated with Eumolpos, then Eumolpos, seated towards the direction of the swan and Zeus and the others, but looking back towards the scene with Triptolemos. Triptolemos is seated in his winged chariot with Persephone on the left carrying a torch and ears of corn and Demeter on the right, carrying a torch and about to pour him a libation; on Demeter's right, between Eumolpos and the Triptolemos scene, stands the (inscribed) figure of the Nymph Eleusis.[278] Eumolpos and Poseidon are symmetrical, probably because Poseidon was Eumolpos' father.

Finally, Eumolpos and other Eleusinian heroes are listed in Nikomachos' calendar as recipients of sacrifices offered by the Eumolpidai in the course of a festival.[279] That festival has generally been considered to have been the Eleusinia, but as Parker pointed out, this need not necessarily be the case; it is possible that the list relates rather to the Mysteries.[280] Eumolpos receives a sacrifice of a sheep. The list of heroic recipients[281] consists of Eumolpos, Delichos, or, the now accepted text, Melichos,[282] Archegetes, Polyxenos, Threptos, Dioklos, and Keleos. Threptos, Nursling, is undoubtedly a title of Triptolemos.[283] Therefore, this list of recipients of sacrifices performed by the Eumolpidai, very possibly in connection with the Mysteries, overlaps very substantially with the names of the princes listed in the *Homeric Hymn*. More specifically, all four princes to whom Demeter revealed the Mysteries in the *Homeric Hymn*,[284] Triptolemos, Diokles, Eumolpos, Keleos, are recipients of sacrifices by the Eumolpidai. If we then compare the list of these recipients to the longer list of the princes named earlier on in the *Homeric*

---

[278] Clinton 1992: 77 considers her a goddess. Shapiro 1989: 76 calls her the local personification.

[279] *LSS* 10 A 65–74 = Lambert 2002: A fr. 3. 65–74 (p. 365; *SEG* LII 48).

[280] Parker 2005a: 329 and n. 7; on these sacrifices, see Parker 2005a: 328–9.

[281] The divine recipients in ll. 60–3, which immediately precede Eumolpos, are Themis, Zeus Herkeios, Demeter, and Persephone.

[282] See on this, Lambert 2002: 378 ad 66.

[283] See also Kearns 1989: 170.   [284] *Hymn. Hom. Dem.* 474–5.

Hymn,[285] which consisted of Triptolemos, Dioklos, Polyxeinos, Eumolpos, Dolichos, Keleos, we find that, besides the additional presence of Archegetes[286] and the problematic relationship, if any, between on the one hand Dolichos and on the other Melichos (if this is indeed the correct reading), the other five names are the same. Thus, Eumolpos in his persona as an Eleusinian prince is cultically embedded in a set of gentilicial sacrifices performed by the *genos* whose eponymous ancestor he is in a whole cult polis context.

I will now consider the myths in which the founder of the Mysteries was someone connected with Thrace, or Orphic poetry, or both. All these myths are related to the significant representation of the prestige of the Thracian Orpheus in Eleusis and more generally in the realm of eschatological poetry.[287] As Kearns suggested, this mythopoeia that connected Eumolpos with Thrace was part of early syncretistic attempts to place together rites and teachings of a 'mystical' nature as essentially teaching the same wisdom.[288] However, it is interesting that the tradition that the founder was Orpheus himself appears later. This, and the very fact that the element 'Thrace' was inserted into the earlier nexus of Eumolpos the Eleusinian prince, may suggest that the myth of Eumolpos as founder was a very strong, embedded, representation that could not be easily obliterated. This suggestion converges, at least partly, with two known facts. First, as we have seen, the figure of Eumolpos as an Eleusinian hero was cultically embedded, and so was (at least insofar as the role of the first hierophant can blur into that of first revealer of the Mysteries) the myth of Eumolpos as founder—which may well have been also explicitly and emphatically cultically embedded, without any evidence of it having survived. Then, the group most concerned with preserving and increasing the prestige of Eumolpos, the Eumolpids, were a dominant voice in the Eleusinian sanctuary. So, as far as the mythologies directly associated with the ritual and sanc-

---

[285] Ibid. 153–5.

[286] On Archegetes being either Hippothoon or Eleusis/Eleusinios, see Lambert 2002: 378 ad 67.

[287] See Parker 1987a: 203.

[288] Kearns 1989: 114.

tuary are concerned, the myth of Eumolpos the founder could not easily have been displaced or elided.

Of course, Eleusinian mythology was not generated only at Eleusis, or in Athenian polis discourse. Therefore it is possible that it was not Eleusinian mythopoeia that created the myth that Eumolpos the founder of the Mysteries had come from Thrace; and several factors argue for that possibility. First, the Eumolpids were the dominant voice at Eleusis, and, whatever the prestige of its association with eschatological poetry, Thrace was not a desirable place of origin for an Athenian *genos*.[289] This is itself makes it unlikely that the figure of a Thracian, or Thracian-connected, Eumolpos was generated in the context of mythopoeic activities promoted by the Eumolpids. In addition, if it is right that this myth, which connects the Mysteries with Thrace, was part of a syncretizing mythopoeia, it is more likely than not that this did not take place in the context of the Eleusinian cult.

I shall return to this. First it is important to remember that, as we saw in *Erechtheus*, the myth in which Eumolpos the founder of the Mysteries was associated with Thrace competed with another myth that involved a Thracian Eumolpos.[290] To put it differently, there was another variant of the myth associating a Thracian Eumolpos with Eleusis, in which he was not the founder of the Mysteries. In the version of this latter variant found in *Erechtheus*, Eumolpos was a son of Poseidon who came from Thrace,[291] but the founder of the Mysteries was one of his descendants. That is, in this myth, the elements 'founder of the Mysteries' and 'associated with Thrace' decomposed into two different figures called Eumolpos.

---

[289] Indeed the long Schol. Soph. *OC* presents various answers to what is seen as the problem of how the Eumolpids, 'being foreigners', could have 'led the rites'.

[290] The two were presented as competing by later lexicographers. See Phot., Sud., Etym. Magn. s.v. Eumolpidai. In all these versions it is said, with reference to the Eumolpidai, that they were named either after Eumolpos the Thracian who invented initiation, or after Eumolpos the son of Mousaios. Given that their ancestor was perceived to have been the first hierophant, the Eumolpos after whom the Eumolpids were named was perceived to have been also the founder of the Mysteries.

[291] On the representation of Eumolpos as a Thracian, see Parker 1987a: 203–4; Collard, Cropp, and Lee 1995: 152–3.

The myths in which the Mysteries were founded by the Thracian Eumolpos[292] appear to be relatively marginal. More central is the other variant, in which the Eumolpos figure who was associated with Thrace had fought against Athens, while the Mysteries were founded by a homonymous descendant.[293] In Euripides' version the association between the foundation of the Mysteries and Thrace is more distanced, and another representation concerning Thrace is foregrounded, the defeat of a barbarian.[294] Thus, the direct association with Thrace has attached to the Eumolpos figure who was the leader of the army attacking Athens—but not the founder of the Mysteries.

We do not know whether or not in the earlier mythologies the leader of the Eleusinians in the war against Athens had been the Eleusinian Eumolpos who founded the Mysteries, but we saw that the representations in the Pindaric fragment and Makron's image suggest that he had not. Eumolpos the founder of the Mysteries did not lead a war against Athens in the variant in *Erechtheus*, where he was a descendant of the Thracian Eumolpos, and so still had a connection with Thrace, albeit a more distant one.[295]

But if it is right that the myth 'Eumolpos the founder of the Mysteries came from Thrace' was not the product of mythopoeia generated by the Eleusinian priesthood, but of an external, as it were, agent, Athenian or not, how and why would it have taken hold in

---

[292] See Plut. *Mor.* 607B; Lucian, *Fugitivi* 8; as one option in Phot., Sud., Etym. Magn. s.v. Eumolpidai (n. 290 above).

[293] See especially the nest of citations in Schol. Soph. *OC* 1053 (Istros *FGrH* 334 F 22; Akestodoros FHG 2.464; Andron *FGrH* 10 F 13); also Hesych., Phot., s.v. Eumolpidai; Marmor Parium *FGrH* 239 F 15. In Andron the figure called Eumolpos who founded the Mysteries and was the first hierophant was the fifth descendant of the Thracian Eumolpos, the son of Mousaios and great-grandson of the Eumolpos who was the son of Keryx who was the son of the Thracian Eumolpos. In the several attested variants of the version which had the Mysteries founded by a second Eumolpos, the founder Eumolpos was the son of Mousaios. Sometimes Mousaios is said to be the son of Eumolpos (Philochoros *FGrH* 328 F 208; Diog. Laert. 1.3). That is, in the versions of the myths in which there was more than one Eumolpos, Mousaios is sometimes the son of a figure called Eumolpos, as well as the father of Eumolpos the founder of the Mysteries. See also Graf (1974: 17–18). Hesych. s.v. Eumolpidai notes that there were many figures who had the name Eumolpos.

[294] On the meanings of Thrace in the Athenian *imaginaire* and their role in these myths, see Parker 1987a: 203–4.

[295] On Mousaios' perceived ethicity, see below.

the Athenian imaginaire? The syncretic impetus that inspired the creation of a myth associating the Eleusinian Mysteries with Thrace may have struck a chord with some sections at least of Athenian 'myth-producers' and 'myth-consumers'. But it is possible that another factor may also have come into play: it is possible to envisage Athenian ideological mythopoeia appropriating the notion of a Eumolpos connected with both Eleusis and Thrace, and deploying it in the context of the extensive mythopoeia about victory over barbarians generated after the Persian Wars; deploying it to reshape the myth of the war between Athens and Eleusis and present it as one more metaphor for the victory over barbarism. For the double nature of Thrace[296] allowed it to be deployed both in connection with things 'Orphic' and as a metonymically based metaphor for barbarians.

Since we do not know the date of the creation of the myth that connected Eumolpos the founder of the Mysteries with Thrace we cannot know how soon after that creation the 'competing' version was constructed; but it is clear that at some point Thracian ethnicity and the mytheme 'leader of an attack on Athens' were separated from the persona of Eumolpos the founder of the Mysteries in a process that generated that competing variant. If it is right that the earlier persona of Eumolpos the founder of the Mysteries included the element 'Eleusinian prince' but not 'led the war against Athens', it looks as though the decomposition resulted in, first, a partial reversion to the earlier persona of Eumolpos the founder of the Mysteries; and second, the construction of a figure of a Thracian who led the war against Athens and was not directly involved in the foundation of the Mysteries.

The variant in which the Mysteries were founded by an Eleusinian descendant of the Thracian Eumolpos was, when compared with the Thracian founder variant, desirable from one or more of the viewpoints of Athenian ideology, the Eleusinian sanctuary and the Eumolpids. In that variant the founder of the Mysteries and defining ancestor of the Eumolpids was represented as Eleusinian, with the Thracian ancestry largely elided though its dissociation from the founder and first hierophant; the Thracian was not connected with

---

[296] See also Parker 1987a: 203.

the Mysteries; and the leader of the attack against Athens was not connected with the Mysteries, which entailed the desirable representation of a less complex barbarian enemy, in the sense of one not made ambivalent through an association with the foundation of a religious institution that was of great importance to the Athenian polis.

Another variant, told by Pausanias,[297] is somewhat different: the Thracian Eumolpos was not the founder of the Mysteries but he became associated with them. Eumolpos, the son of Poseidon, had come from Thrace, and fought against Athens, survived the war—it was his son Immarados who was killed—which was concluded with the agreement that the Eleusinians would be subject to the Athenians in everything else, but they would 'conduct the ritual on their own' (ἰδίᾳ); and Eumolpos and the daughters of Keleos 'performed the rites' of the Two Goddesses. The implication of the formulation is clearly that the Mysteries had been celebrated before the war, that it was not Eumolpos who founded them.[298]

This makes the Thracian Eumolpos the ancestor of the Eumolpids, and a Thracian a significant hierophant. This, I submit, is unlikely to reflect Eleusinian mythology,[299] and indeed in one particular Pausanias explicitly states that it did not. For in this version Eumolpos was survived by Keryx, his youngest son; but, Pausanias adds,[300] the

---

[297] Paus. 1.38.2–3.

[298] See also Kearns 1989: 114.

[299] A scholion that may or may accurately reflect an earlier myth (Schol. Eur. *Phoen.* 854) tells a story that is also (as it were) in between the variant 'Eumolpos the founder of the Mysteries was associated with Thrace and led a war against Athens' and the variant 'Eumolpos the founder of the Mysteries was a separate person from the Eumolpos who was associated with Thrace and led a war against Athens'. In this story, Thracian ethnicity and war against Athens are not connected with the founder of the Mysteries; but they are attached to a figure, Eumolpos, king of the Thracians, who is both directly connected with the Eumolpids, who are named after him, and associated with the Mysteries in a less symbolically powerful way: he was the first foreigner to be initiated. Subsequently he allied himself with the Eleusinians in the war against Athens. Since barbarians were excluded from initiation in the Mysteries, and since in Athenian mythology the first foreigner in the sense of non-Athenian to be initiated was Herakles, or Herakles and the Dioskouroi (Xen. *Hell.* 6.3.6; Apollod. 2.5.12; Plut. *Thes.* 33; see also the Pindaric fragment 346), this story was not an Athenian myth.

[300] Paus. 1.38.3.

Kerykes themselves claim that Keryx was the son of Aglauros by Hermes, not of Eumolpos.

I revert to the variant in which Eumolpos the Eleusinian prince founded the Mysteries. Eumolpos' persona as an Eleusinian prince was, we saw, deeply rooted and cultically embedded; we also saw that Eumolpos' persona as the first hierophant and his persona as the founder of the Mysteries would have been perceived as very closely connected, since the first hierophant was the first person to have revealed the *hiera*, which had at least the potential of sliding into the notion that he was the first to have revealed, and so founded, the Mysteries. Thus, it can be argued that, in terms of formal relationships, the myth 'Eumolpos the Eleusinian prince founded the Mysteries' can be seen as a transformation of the myth 'Demeter revealed the Mysteries to the four Eleusinian princes' in the *Homeric Hymn to Demeter*; a transformation that might have resulted from an interaction of the myth 'Demeter revealed the Mysteries to the four Eleusinian princes' with the set of mythemes and representations 'Eumolpos was the ancestor of the Eumolpids', and 'Eumolpos was the first hierophant', and therefore 'Eumolpos was the first person to have revealed the *hiera*.' In the *Homeric Hymn to Demeter* the goddess demonstrated the performance of her rites, and taught her mysteries, to all four princes.[301] But since in the Mysteries there was only one hierophant, this could be 'rebranded', as it were: it could be presented as leaving space for one of the heroes to take on the dominant role, and so (on this reconstruction) the myth would have been further developed to include the notion that Eumolpos became the hierophant, which was eventually reshaped into the notion that he 'showed' the Mysteries, he founded the Mysteries.

I suggest that the myth that Eumolpos the Eleusinian prince founded the Mysteries was indeed constructed out of the myth of Demeter's revelation to the four princes in the *Homeric Hymn to Demeter*. This extension of the role of Eumolpos is undoubtedly the result of the important position of the Eumolpids in the Eleusinian cult. For when this cult becomes visible to us the Eumolpids and the

---

[301] *Hymn. Hom. Dem.* 473–9.

Kerykes have a major role in all aspects of the cult and the Eumolpids are the senior *genos*.[302] Since the mytheme that Eumolpos was the first hierophant was inextricably connected with the mytheme that he was the ancestor of the Eumolpids, and since the Eumolpids were, at least to a very large extent, in control of Eleusinian mythopoeia, it is surely difficult to doubt that it was Eumolpid mythopoeic activity that promoted Eumolpos into the figure of the founder.

b. Hyades and the daughters of Erechtheus

In this section I continue with the rest of Athena's speech. Because a scholion to Aratos[303] states that Euripides in *Erechtheus* says that the daughters of Erechtheus became Hyades, it is generally thought that in this tragedy Euripides identified the daughters of Erechtheus who became the Hyakinthides with the Hyades.[304] But in my view this belief is mistaken.[305]

A few words first about the Hyades. In one variant of their myth the Hyades were Dionysos' nurses, while in another they were the sisters of Hyas, a youth killed by a snake while hunting. In both variants the Hyades ended up as stars. This is a stable element across variants, because they were stars in the world of 'today', already in Homer,[306] and also in Hesiod, who mentions the Hyades with the Pleiades and Orion and instructs that when the Hyades, the Pleiades and Orion begin to set this is the ploughing season.[307] He

---

[302] See Chapter 7.

[303] Schol. Aratus, *Phaen.* 172.

[304] See on this identification, Collard, Cropp, and Lee 1995: 194, commentary ad 107–8; see also ibid. 153; Kearns 1989: 61–2. I accepted the identification without examining it further in my discussion of the Hyades and their relationship to Hyas and Dionysos (Sourvinou-Inwood 2005: 108, 339, 377–9).

[305] Gantz 1993: 218 considers the papyrus fragments to show that the information in the scholion that the daughters of Erechtheus became the Hyades is mistaken, since they became the Hyakinthides.

[306] Hom. *Il.* 18.486.

[307] Hes. *Op.* 614–17. See the notes of M. L. West ad loc. and of M. W. Edwards ad Hom. *Il.* 18.486. In Eur. *Ion* 1156–7: the Hyades are considered as a 'most clear sign' to sailors. Both Phot. and Sud. s.v. Hyades define them as the stars on the horns of the Bull.

also names the Hyades elsewhere, and calls them Nymphs resembling the Charites.[308]

I turn now to the question of the reliability of the scholion. The possibility of confusion was first raised by other scholars,[309] who pointed out one instance of a confusion in the attribution of a story to a Euripidean tragedy in the scholia to Aratos: Schol. Aratus, *Phaen.* 205 claims, as do two other related sources,[310] that in *Melanippe Sophe* Euripides tells a certain story about Melanippe's mother Hippo and Hippo's metamorphosis to a horse, which is in fact in conflict with the story of that metamorphosis in the extant fragment from the tragedy's Prologue.[311]

Let us consider the specific scholion[312] that includes the statement that Euripides in *Erechtheus* says that the daughters of Erechtheus became Hyades. It begins with a list of the different numbers of Hyades given by various authors. Then it states that they have the surname Hyades because they brought up Dionysos, and Dionysos was called Hyes (in support of which statement the scholion quotes a fragment of Euphorion). Then follows a comment about the relationships between the stars and the different numbers of the Hyades given by the different authors (including the statement that Euripides in *Phaethon* numbered them as three); then the next statement about their mythological persona is that while Euripides in *Erechtheus* says that the daughters of Erechtheus became Hyades 'being three', Myrtilos says that it was the daughters of Kadmos who became the Hyades;[313] and they were called thus, the scholion continues, for the reason that we said before—referring back to the explanation that the Hyades were called Hyades because they brought up Dionysos, and Dionysos was called Hyes.

The scholion's own voice, then, says that these catasterized females were called Hyades because they were the nurses of Dionysos, and

---

[308] Hes. fr. 291 M-W. On the Hyades, see also Hübner 1998: 762–3; Gantz 1993: 218. I have briefly discussed the Hyades elsewhere (Sourvinou-Inwood 2005: 108, 339, 377–9).

[309] Collard, Cropp, and Lee 1995: 194.

[310] Eratosthenes, *Katasterismoi* 18; Hyginus, *Astronomica* 2.18.

[311] Collard, Cropp, and Lee 1995: 194, 267–8.

[312] Schol. Aratus, *Phaen.* 172.

[313] Myrsilos *FGrH* 477 F 15.

then goes on to give, first, an alternative explanation of the name, Myrsilos' myth, which is a variation of this main representation; and, second, a totally different story about the mortal personae of the Hyades which it attributes to Euripides in *Erechtheus*: Euripides in *Erechtheus* says that the daughters of Erechtheus 'became Hyades being three'. This, then, unlike the other versions, does not explain why they were called Hyades. Also, when the scholion mentioned that Euripides in *Phaethon* said that there were three Hyades,[314] it did not add "(. . . in *Phaethon*) and in *Erechtheus*".

These formulations taken together raise the possibility that the scholiast or its source did not base the statement about the daughters of Erechtheus becoming Hyades in *Erechtheus* on a reading of the actual text of this tragedy. In other words, this statement may have been based on an inference, constructed on the basis of pieces of knowledge about this tragedy, above all the element that in *Erechtheus* the three daughters of Erechtheus gained celestial immortality, combined with the element that the Hyades were mentioned in the tragedy. It is possible that the compiler of this text—most of which was focused on the question of the number of the Hyades—knowing that in Euripides' *Phaethon* the Hyades were three, also knew that there were three daughters of Erechtheus and they had gained celestial immortality—like the Hyades—and that this led him to conclude that the two were identified.

I will now set out a series of arguments that will, I hope, show that it is extremely unlikely that in *Erechtheus* the Hyades were identified with the daughters of Erechtheus. The most important arguments are those based on the text. However, for reasons that will become clear below, I will begin with another argument. One objection depends on a distinction between two forms of a new strand of afterlife beliefs, celestial immortality. In my view, there is a difference between, on the one hand, astral immortality, a concept based on mythological representations, already seen in Hesiod, in which certain stars were identified with mythological figures, and on the other the celestial

---

[314] A reference to the Hyades is appropriate in Euripides' *Phaethon*, since Phaethon's sisters were, like the Hyades in one version of their story, sisters unrelentingly lamenting the death of a young male. (On Phaethon's sisters, see e.g. Gantz 1993: 32.)

immortality given to the daughters of Erechtheus, whose *pneuma* Athena installed in the *aither*.

Perceptions of celestial immortality—a concept which originated in philosophical thought—appear to have been fluid at that time.[315] But, as we saw, the specific expression used in Euripides' *Erechtheus* with regard to the daughters of Erechtheus evokes a formulation used in the public epitaph for those who died in the battle of Poteidaia[316]—and is also similar to that in a private epitaph of the fourth century, when what was reserved for the heroized war dead was extended to ordinary people.[317] The complex evocation of those specific immortalities of the war dead would have helped shape the Athenian audience's perception of the immortality of the Hyakinthides in the *aither* and this indicates, I submit, that the immortality of the Hyakinthides in the *aither* was perceived by the Athenians as describing something different from astral deification.

It could be argued that the possibility of understanding that immortality as *katasterismos* may nevertheless have been open to those Athenians; but there is nothing in the formulation to guide them in that direction, while—besides the evocation of the Poteidaia epitaph—the absence of any reference to stars would also have guided them away from such an interpretation. Elsewhere in Euripides there are references to astral immortality that are significantly different from the formulation concerning the daughters of Erechtheus.[318] Furthermore, other Euripidean formulations distance this notion of immortality in the *aither* from the notion of *katasterismos*. Thus, in *Suppliants* 534–5, '*pneuma* to *aither*, body to earth', which also evokes the epitaph for those who died at Poteidaia,[319] is a formulation, in the mouth of Theseus, that refers to normality, to what happens in

---

[315] On the concept of celestial immortality, see Burkert 1972: 357–68; Sourvinou-Inwood 1995: 194 and n. 342, with further bib., 202.

[316] *CEG* 10.

[317] *CEG* 535; see the discussion in Sourvinou-Inwood 1995: 202.

[318] Note the explicit references to stars in Eur. *Tro.* 1001 and Eur. *El.* 991–2, both referring to Kastor and Polydeukes. Incidentally, a different concept is expressed in Eur. *Or.* 1684–5 where Apollo says that he will take Helen to Zeus' palace by a journey through the stars (1684–5).

[319] See p. 79 above.

the normal course of events. The relationship of the afterlife representation in this *Suppliants* passage with that in *Erechtheus* is made more complex by another passage later on in the former tragedy: while in *Erechtheus* the voice of the deity in epiphany states both that she installed the *pneuma* of the daughters of Erechtheus in the *aither* and that their 'souls have not gone to Hades', in *Suppliants* 1140–2 another voice, that of the chorus,[320] says of the dead Argive heroes, 'the *aither* possesses them now, dissolved into the ashes of the fire, and they have flown and reached Hades'.[321] Collard is wrong in thinking that this is "a confused repetition of the conception of death in 533–4".[322] In my view, this other voice, this other possible articulation of a complex eschatological belief as it applied to these Argive dead, is a partial deconstruction that helped express a perceived uncertainty about (at least aspects of) celestial immortality, a set of beliefs that was in the process of being created and crystallized. In addition, and very importantly, it also helped construct a relationship of both closeness and distancing between these dead Argives of the heroic age and the Athenian war dead of the present, who did not go to Hades—like the figures who were eventually constructed as their paradigm, the daughters of Erechtheus.

The expectation that the earth will receive one's body and the *aither* something else, another component of the self which is not named in this instance,[323] is also expressed in Euripides' *Orestes* 1086–7. A comparable representation is also found in a fragment from Euripides' *Chrysippos*.[324]

In these circumstances, I suggest, the representation of celestial immortality in the *aither* in the last third of the fifth century may be reconstructed as involving a spectrum of possibilities; at the most positive end were located the daughters of Erechtheus, who did not go to Hades and are represented as deified mortals, an important

---

[320] See on this Collard 1975: 392–5.
[321] αἰθὴρ ἔχει νιν ἤδη, πυρὸς τετακότας σποδῶι, ποτανοὶ δ' ἤνυσαν τὸν Ἄιδαν.
[322] Collard 1975: 401 ad 1140b–2.
[323] See also M. L. West's note on Eur. *Or.* 1086–8.
[324] *TrGF* vol. 5 F 839.8–11, 'things born from the earth go back to earth, things sprung from heavenly stock go back to the pole of heaven'. Eur. *Hel.* 1014–16 is a transformation of such formulations that does not concern us here (see on this R. Kannicht's note ad loc.)

category of cult recipient that was expanding at that time;[325] then came the Athenian war dead, whose *psychai* went to the *aither*, and who did not go to Hades—though this is not explicitly formulated; while at the other end, which can be represented as normality in the heroic age, some component of the self goes up in the *aither*, but the shade of the person goes to Hades.

This state of affairs suggests, I submit, that in the assumptions shaping Euripides' selections there was a distance between on the one hand this immortality in the *aither* and on the other the concept of astral immortality. I am not convinced that there was a belief, at this time, that ordinary people became stars. For the passage in Aristophanes' *Peace* 832–9,[326] in which is expressed the belief that everyone becomes a star when they die, cannot be assumed to be an accurate reflection of contemporary doctrines of astral immortality, for comic modalities depend on polarization, exaggeration, and distortion; while the eschatological inflation that led to the construction of comparable beliefs about the common dead only appears later in the epitaphs.[327] If this is right, this is another way in which astral immortality would differ from the celestial immortality in the *aither* given to the Hyakinthides.

But surely, it could be argued, even if this is right, and the Athenian audience had not understood the celestial immortality of the Hyakinthides to have been a *katasterismos* at that point, on the hypothesis that Athena identified the Hyakinthides with the Hyades, she would have made it clear later on in her speech that the Hyakinthides became the Hyades. So, then, what is the problem? The answer to this question brings us to the consideration of the text, which, I will now suggest, provides more than one argument against the view that in Euripides' *Erechtheus* the Hyakinthides became the Hyades.

Let us first consider the structure of Athena's speech. The Hyades are mentioned in l. 107 of Athena's speech (cf. p. 111); in l. 108 there is a reference to stars (ἄστρων). In the earlier passage Athena spoke about the afterlife and cult of the daughters of Erechtheus, and their

---

[325] See Sourvinou-Inwood 2005: 329–45.

[326] Probably produced between 410 and 405 (see A. Sommerstein's edition, xix).

[327] See on such inflation and its expression, among the diversity of beliefs reflected in fourth-century epitaphs, Sourvinou-Inwood 1995: 201–7.

acquisition of the cult name Hyakinthides. She did not, I must stress, only give instructions about the cult that should be offered to them, she also gave information about the girls' postmortem fate: besides their deification which was expressed in terms of the cult, she mentioned the installation of their *pneuma* in the *aither*. The notion that Athena subsequently returned to this postmortem fate, to add that, incidentally, I forgot to mention, they will also become the stars Hyades, would be eccentric in itself. More significantly, if this had indeed been the case, if such a *katasterismos* had been presented separately, as part of the section that sets out the judgement of Zeus, there would be serious problems, as I will now try to show.

The segment preceding the announcement of what Zeus judges dealt with things that had just happened, including the afterlife fate of Erechtheus' daughters set in place by Athena, while the segment that sets out what Zeus judges deals with things that will happen in the future, especially the foundation of the Mysteries; the notion that Athena had just given Erechtheus' daughters this particular immortality in the *aither* and then went on to announce that subsequently Zeus would change it into another form of celestial immortality and turn the girls into stars is, I submit, theologically absurd. To put it more precisely. Either their celestial immortality in the *aither* announced by Athena had been understood by the audience to be the same as a *katasterismos* (which, I argued, was not the case), or it had not. If it had been understood to be the same, the allegedly katasterized girls would have had no place in a segment about the future; for if the audience had understood them to have been turned into stars by Athena, it would be almost comically implausible to imagine that Athena then returned to this issue later to say that Zeus would in the future rename them, give them the name 'Hyades'. If (as I believe to have been the case) the Athenian audience had *not* understood the girls to have been turned into stars by Athena when she installed their *pneuma* in the *aither*, we would need to believe that she tells their mother that she had given her daughters one kind of celestial immortality and then a little later she announces that actually Zeus had decided to give them another type of celestial immortality; this would be theologically absurd—and would involve a clumsy textual structure.

More concretely, and more importantly, there is another aspect of this fragmentary text that makes it extremely unlikely that the daughters of Erechtheus were identified with the Hyades in Athena's speech. The extant line-beginnings (p. 111) make it clear that the context in which the mention of the Hyades and of stars occurs in this fragment of *Erechtheus* concerns the Eleusinian part of the arrangements, and specifically the Mysteries; it is not connected to the daughters of Erechtheus and there is no visible break, or indeed space, to return to the family of Erechtheus. The Hyades occur at the start of line 107, in the middle of a section (lines 101–14, of fr. 370 K.) which is manifestly all concerned with the Eleusinian cult.

There is one further objection to the view that Euripides' *Erechtheus* identified the daughters of Erechtheus with the Hyades: the fact that, as we saw, the mythological persona of the Hyades, in its different variants, is entirely different from that of the daughters of Erechtheus. For, clearly, the two main variants of the Hyades myth have important elements in common—besides the *katasterismos*— neither of which is part of the myth of the daughters of Erechtheus: an association between a group of Nymphs/Nymph-like women and a young male, Dionysos in one case, Hyas in the other; and the fact that these two male mythological figures were connected, since Hyes was an epithet of Dionysos and Pherekydes called Dionysos' mother Semele Hyen.[328] I consider it implausible that the very different myth of the daughters of Erechtheus, who had already been manipulated into an identification with the Hyakinthides, would have further come to be structured through the schema of the Hyades with which their mythological persona had nothing in common,[329] and

---

[328] Kleidemos of Athens *FGrH* 323 F 27 (see Jacoby 1954: i. 84–5 ad loc.); Pherecydes *FGrH* 3 F 90a.

[329] Kearns (1989: 61–2) connects the daughters of Erechtheus with both child-rearing and Dionysos. The former she attempts to do via Hyakinthos and Artemis Iakynthotrophos and the Laconian festivals Hyakinthia and Tithenidia (which involved children); I suggest that, given the complex bricolage modalities through which mythicoritual material is deployed in the construction of mythicoritual nexuses (I have illustrated this with reference to Dionysos and others in Sourvinou-Inwood 2005), such convoluted indirect connections cannot be taken as evidence for the mythicoritual persona of the daughters of Erechtheus in Athens. As for the connection with Dionysos, even if it is right that there was a joint sacrifice of Dionysos and the daughters of Erechtheus, the mythological persona of the latter does not allow a

which would have distracted from the semantic constructs deployed in the earlier part of Athena's speech. On the other hand, if there was an intention to deconstruct and problematize these deified figures, would this problematizing element have been massively condensed and placed in the middle of the segment about Demeter and the Mysteries? I do not think that this is likely.

I will now return to the text of the fragment from Euripides' *Erechtheus* that involves the Hyades. Clearly, we cannot reconstruct the content of lines 105–9. But I would like to suggest some possible parameters for such a reconstruction.

With regard to the lines preceding these, after the reference in ll. 100–1 to Eumolpos the descendant of Eumolpos who has just been killed in the tragedy, ὃν χρῆ γεν[έσθαι, which I understand to mean 'who is to be born', in l. 103, undoubtedly refers to Eumolpos who is to be the founder of the Mysteries, whose lineage is then given, as is shown by 'having married', in l. 104, which surely referred to Eumolpos' father Mousaios, and probably also involved the naming of his mother Deiope.

Moving on to the Hyades, lines 107, where they are named, and 'stars' in 108 indicate that they referred to either the life and *katasterismos* of the Hyades, or to the night sky, or to both. The night sky, I suggest, was certainly involved, since 'stars' was followed by the letter λ, almost certainly from a form of λαμπρός, bright, which would indicate the night sky. The Hyades are among the specific stars mentioned in Euripidean tragedies when stars come into play in other contexts.[330] The fact that the context before and after these problematic lines was that of the Eleusinian Mysteries suggests that the night sky was indeed one focus of the lines under discussion.

connection with Dionysos in the girls' lifetime, and certainly not a kourotrophic relationship—which would have given them a common element with one version of the myth of the Hyades. (I say even if it is right that there was a joint sacrifice, because I am not totally certain that Jacoby's reading of a fragment of Philochoros (*FGrH* 328 F 12 and Jacoby 1954: i. 279 ad loc.) on which this depends is right, as I believe it is based on a rather oversubtle reading of the language of the scholion that gives us the fragment. On my reading, the scholion is simply adding to the recipients of 'sober' sacrifices listed by Polemon two more mentioned by Philochoros, namely on the one hand Dionysos and on the other the daughters of Erechtheus.)

[330] See Eur. *El.* 467–8, *Ion* 1150–8.

For the stars and the night sky are associated with the Eleusinian Mysteries also in other dramatic passages,[331] especially in connection with Dionysos—a deity importantly associated with those Mysteries.[332]

Since one of the important personae of the Hyades was that they had been the nurses of Dionysos before they became stars, if (in Athenian assumptions) Dionysos had been part of a nexus involving the night sky in connection with the Mysteries, the simple mention of the Hyades stars in this context would have evoked their *katasterismos* and its reason; it would therefore also have evoked Dionysos even if he was not explicitly named here. Insofar as, we saw, the Hyades were associated with the ploughing season, they also evoked agriculture, and thus were connected with Demeter and her cult, which is the focus of this segment. This would be a further, specific link between the Mysteries, and more generally the Eleusinian cult, and the Hyades—besides the association of the night sky with the Mysteries and also the association of both the Mysteries and the Hyades with Dionysos.

Some might argue that, if the parameters of this reconstruction are right, if it is right that these lines involved the night sky in an Eleusinian context, and perhaps also Dionysos, they would be a digression from a straight narrative line leading from Eumolpos' lineage to the foundation of the Mysteries—and perhaps also that this constitutes an argument against this reconstruction. But there are links between the 'digression' and both the 'Eumolpos' lineage' segment and the 'Mysteries and Demeter's cult' segment. Indeed it could be argued that the 'night sky' segment may have helped link these segments further together. I have already mentioned the links connecting the night sky segment with that of the Mysteries: besides the actual association of the night sky with the Mysteries mentioned above, there was also the association between the Hyades and ploughing, and thus agriculture and Demeter and her cult. Another link connects Eumolpos' lineage and the night sky, though it may or

---

[331] Soph. *Ant.* 1146–7, Eur. *Ion* 1074–86, Ar. *Ran.* 342–3, 'Eumolpos' ap. Diod. Sic. 1.11.

[332] See e.g. Tiverios 2004; Parker 2005a: 341. Indeed Aristides at least could represent Dionysos as being the *paredros* of the Eleusinian goddesses (Aristid. *Or.* 41 Keil [*Dionysos*] 10).

may not have been explicitly mentioned: Selene, who, as the mother of Mousaios, was Eumolpos' grandmother. The myth in which Selene was the mother of Mousaios appears in Plato and Philochoros, and therefore was probably an Athenian myth.[333] Selene may have been mentioned, but if not she would have been evoked, in this context in which the lines that deal with Eumolpos' lineage are followed by a reference to the night sky.

There are also various possibilities that further counter the notion of digression. For example, Athena may have presented these lines about the night sky as a fragment of Mousaios' work that she connected with the Mysteries, or that she may have said his son Eumolpos would somehow bring into play in his foundation of the Mysteries. For we are told in some sources that Eumolpos made known his father's work, and in one source this is mentioned together with his foundation of the Mysteries.[334] In later perceptions Dionysos was one of Mousaios' main subjects.[335] We are also told that he wrote about the Hyades.[336] Furthermore, Plato[337] attests to the notion that Mousaios and his son, who is undoubtedly Eumolpos,[338] told stories of how in the afterlife the righteous are rewarded and the impious and unjust punished. Thus, Mousaios and Eumolpos are mentioned together in connection with teachings which were popularly associated with the Eleusinian Mysteries (presumably teachings ascribed to them through the attribution to them of eschatological poetry).[339] Alternatively, Athena may have said that it would be Eumolpos himself who would write something that she cites or brings into play in connection with his foundation of the Mysteries. According to Diodoros, Eumolpos

---

[333] Pl. *Resp.* 364e; Philochoros *FGrH* 328 F 208.

[334] *FGrH* 239 A 15 (the Marmor Parium): '(Eumolpos) revealed the Mysteries at Eleusis and published (ἐξέθηκεν) the poems of his [father] Musaeus when Erechtheus son of Pandion was king of Athens.' The chronology here is different from that in *Erechtheus*. See also Sud. s.v. Mousaios: Mousaios' father was Antiphemos, his mother Selene . . . He wrote *Instructions for his son Eumolpos* in 4000 verses and other things.

[335] See e.g. Aristid. *Or.* 41 Keil (*Dionysos*) 2 (Kern *OF* 319 F 307).

[336] See Mousaios 2 B 18 D/K.

[337] Pl. *Resp.* 363c–d.

[338] See Graf 1974: 19; Parker 2005a: 362.

[339] See Parker 2005a: 361.

wrote Bacchic verses in which he spoke of Dionysos as ἀστροφαῆς, 'shining like a star'.[340]

If these lines in Euripides' *Erechtheus* were shaped by such representations, if Athena said that Eumolpos the founder of the Mysteries, the son of Mousaios, would somehow deploy material involving the night sky and perhaps Dionysos, either from his own, or from his father's, poetry in connection with the Mysteries, those verses would have effected a transition from Eumolpos' lineage to his foundation of the Mysteries.

---

[340] Diod. 1.11. 3.

3

Reading a Festival Nexus

Plynteria and Kallynteria

1. 25 THARGELION: DAY ONE OF THE PLYNTERIA

i. The analyses

I will now try to reconstruct the festival of the Plynteria[1] through the strategy set out in Chapter 1, which begins with setting in place what 'stable points' can be recovered from the available evidence.[2]

---

[1] On the Plynteria, see Deubner 1969: 17–22; Parke 1977: 152–5; Parker 1983: 26–8; Brulé 1987: 105–13; Parker 1996: 307–8; N. Robertson 1996a: 48–52; Bettinetti 2001: 147–54; Dillon 2002: 133–4; Parker 2005a: 478; see also Scheer 2000: 58–60, 69, 124. On the controversy concerning the procession at the Plynteria see below, and see esp. Christopoulos 1992: 27–39; Parker 1996: 307–8; cf. also Dillon 2002: 134; Humphreys 2004: 117 n. 22; Parker 2005a: 478.

[2] I cannot discuss here the Problematik of the iconography of the Parthenon's south metopes, but I need to say that the notion that south metopes 15–21 show myths and rituals pertaining to Athena's statues, the story of the arrival of the Palladion to Athens (which I will be discussing in Chapter 4, section 3 below), and the disrobing of the statue of Athena Polias, that is, the notion that these metopes allude to the Plynteria and the Panathenaia (see Hurwit 1999: 173–4, 349 n. 63), is mistaken on many grounds, not least (and most concretely) because of the many dissonances in the relationships between alleged action and representation. This is most striking in the case of the alleged representation of the ritual of disrobing the statue in metope 21: the semi-nudity of the woman on the right is a serious problem for an allegedly ritual scene—a fact mentioned by Hurwit (1999: 349 n. 63); but I will add that the nakedness and the figure's actual stance in relation to the statue taken together correspond to, are elements of a version of, the iconographical schema 'a woman takes refuge at a statue/shrine', which is also consistent with the representation of the second woman, on the left of the statue, and this is indeed how the metope

First, according to Xenophon,[3] Alcibiades arrived in the Piraeus on the day when the city was celebrating the Plynteria and the statue of Athena was covered up; and (Xenophon comments) some believed that this was ill-omened, since on that day no Athenian would venture to engage in any serious business. Plutarch[4] tells a similar story: he says that Alcibiades arrived on the day in which the festival Plynteria was being celebrated in honour of Athena, a day which the Athenians consider most inauspicious, *apophras*, for business of any kind, and that on that day, which he specified was 25 Thargelion,[5] the Praxiergidai performed secret rites (ἀπόρρητα ὄργια), having removed the adornment (*kosmos*) from, and having covered up, the goddess's statue. In this context, the *kosmos* of the statue clearly refers to its jewellery.[6] He adds that therefore the goddess was not thought to have received Alcibiades kindly or favourably, having covered her face and kept him at a distance. According to Pollux,[7] on *apophrades* days the sanctuaries were roped off, as for example, he adds, at the Plynteria, and on other similar days. Thus, on that day some (at least) temples were closed.[8]

These sources allow us to reconstruct the following elements of the Plynteria festival. First, it was celebrated in honour of Athena Polias and it involved her statue, which was covered up on 25 Thargelion. Second, this was an *apophras* day on which at least some other

is usually interpreted (see e.g. Simon 1975: 113; Castriota 1992: 152. On this group of metopes see also M. Robertson 1984: 206–8).

[3] Xen. *Hell.* 1.4.12.

[4] Plut. *Alc.* 34.1–2.

[5] On the date of the Plynteria, see Mikalson 1975: 160–4; Brulé 1987: 112–13; N. Robertson 1996a: 49; Lambert 2002: 374 ad 5–15; Humphreys 2004: 141; Parker 2005a: 478. For a recent discussion on the dates of the Plynteria and Kallynteria, see N. Robertson 2004: 127–36, who believes that the Kallynteria was a festival of adornment and that (N. Robertson 2004: 131–2) every second year the Kallynteria lasted two days, continuing on the 29th, because he takes the robe, φᾶρος, offered to Arthena on that day (see below) to be part of the Kallynteria. I discuss the dates of the two festivals below.

[6] N. Robertson (1996a: 49) thinks *kosmos* can refer to the *peplos*, but *kosmos* means ornaments, and we know that the statue indeed wore jewellery (see e.g. Ridgway 1992: 120; Mansfield 1985: 138–9, 144–5, 185–6 also discusses the jewellery worn by the statue).

[7] Poll. *Onom.* 8.141.

[8] See also Parker 2005a: 478.

temples were also closed. Of course, the strong emphasis on the inauspicious aspect of the festival must be set in context. That is, in the rhetorically charged context of both texts, in which the emphasis was on showing that the day was inauspicious for begining an enterprise such as Alcibiades', the focus is on the gloomy and the secret; any more neutral facet of the festival would have been ignored. However, even when these texts are set in context, the inauspiciousness and gloom of the day is still unambiguous, and the specific ritual acts mentioned are consistent with this inauspiciousness and gloom—the removal of the statue's jewellery, the covering up of the statue, the performance of secret rites. This last is the third element that we can reconstruct from the texts cited here, that the festival involved secret rites on 25 Thargelion. The fourth is that the *genos* of the Praxiergidai manipulated the statue and performed secret rites.

I should mention here that the olivewood statue of Athena Polias was believed to have fallen from the sky.[9] I assume that the statue showed the goddess standing. In my view the arguments for a seated statue are not compelling, those in favour of a standing one rather

---

[9] See Paus. (1.26.6). It is not totally clear whether this was perceived to be in conflict with the story reflected in Apollod. (3.14.6), according to which Erichthonios set up the statue of Athena on the Acropolis—and founded the Panathenaia (on the foundation of the Panathenaia see below, Chapter 5, section 2; and see e.g. Androtion *FGrH* 324 F 2). There can be little doubt that the mytheme that Erichthonios founded the Panathenaia was an Athenian cultic myth (see below, Chapter 5, section 2). But the mytheme that Erichthonios set up the statue of Athena on the Acropolis may or may not have been a cultic myth. If this mytheme was perceived to imply that this was the first statue of Athena, which it may not have been, it would have had implications concerning the cult served by Aglauros, the first priestess of Athena, whose mythicoritual nexus will be discussed later, and which was indeed an Athenian cultic myth. If that mytheme was a cultic myth and it implied that Erichthonios set up the first statue—a combination that I consider unlikely—it is still possible that the relationship between this myth and the nexus of Aglauros as the first priestess of Athena may have been ambiguous—in terms of modern logic, which would, however, be inappropriate for perceptions of relationships between myths, and of inconsistencies—'unresolved'. (I have discussed elsewhere the notion, and parameters, of inconsistencies in Greek mythology: [reference lacking].) One possibility is that in this context, in which (as will become clear in these discussions) the movements out of primordiality and to things as they 'now' are were multiple and complex, it remained ambiguous when the statue of Athena had fallen from the sky and been installed on the Acropolis, and that this ambiguity was part of the ancient perceptions of this nexus of representations.

more so.[10] In addition, as will become clear in Chapter 4 below, the
other well-known statue of Athena that had fallen from heaven, the
Trojan Palladion, was perceived by (among others) the Athenians as a
standing statue.[11]

Before continuing with the attempt to reconstruct stable points
that will allow the reconstruction of a ritual skeleton for the Plynteria, or at least the beginnings of one, I will open a parenthesis to
place the festival in the Athenian ritual universe by briefly considering the fact that the Plynteria was not only celebrated as a whole polis
festival. It was celebrated in at least some demes. The Thorikos
calendar informs us that at Thorikos this festival was celebrated in
Skirophorion (not in Thargelion like the central polis festival), when
the calendar prescribes that a choice sheep should be sacrificed to
Athena, a sheep to Aglauros, and to Athena a choice lamb.[12] It is
assumed that the two sacrifices to heroic figures that are listed next,
to Kephalos and to P[rokris], were also part of the same festival.[13]
This, then, appears to be complementary to the whole polis festival,
an additional deme celebration.

It is likely that the deme of Erchia also celebrated the Plynteria, for
it is likely that the sacrifices listed in the calendar of Erchia[14] as being
offered at the acropolis in Erchia on Skirophorion 3 were part of a
Plynteria celebrated in the deme.[15] The following sacrifices were
prescribed: a sheep to Aglauros (β 55–9); a young pig to Kourotrophos and a sheep $ἀν[τ]ίβους$, 'instead of an ox',[16] to Athena Polias
(a 57–65); a sheep with the restriction $οὐ\ φορά$, not to be carried

[10] For a discussion, see e.g. Hurwit (1999: 21); Ridgway (1992: 122) decides that
the statue was seated.

[11] On the different versions of the myth of the origin of the Trojan Palladion, see
below, Chapter 4.

[12] *SEG* XXXIII 147, Lupu (2005: no. 1, ll. 52–4): 'at the Plynteria to Athena a
selected sheep, to Aglauros a sheep'. On Aglauros outside the *asty*: Kearns 1989: 26–7;
Larson 1995: 26–7; Humphreys 2004: 141–2, 162–3, 188.

[13] Humphreys 2004: 162; Lupu 2005: 122, cf. 146–7. But Parker 1987a: 145
separates.

[14] *LSCG* 18.

[15] See N. Robertson 1983: 281–2, Humphreys 2004: 141–2, 188. The restoration
$Ἀγλαύ]ρωι$ in the Nikomachos calendar should be rejected (see on this Lambert 2002:
375–6).

[16] See on this: Daux 1963: 630; Jameson 1965: 157–8.

away, to Zeus Polieus (γ 59–64); and a sheep to Poseidon (δ 56–60).[17] Athena Polias was the main deity honoured at the Plynteria. Aglauros, it will become clearer below, was the secondary honorand. It is Ge who is the goddess Kourotrophos in Athens at this time and, we shall see below, Ge is associated both with Aglauros and with the Plynteria.[18] Zeus Polieus formed the ancient poliadic pair with Athena Polias, while she formed a complementary poliadic pair with Poseidon.[19] Consequently all these recipients are either connected with the Plynteria elsewhere in the extant evidence, or form a poliadic pair with Athena.

These deme cults must not be assumed to be straightforward reflections of the whole polis festival. But they do suggest some parameters concerning what was perceived as relevant to the Plynteria. At Thorikos, in which the name of the festival is mentioned, only Athena and Aglauros, and probably also a local hero and heroine, receive sacrifices.[20] This confirms the status of Aglauros as the secondary honorand which is indicated—albeit not in a straightforward way—by the *aition* connected with the festival, which will be considered below. As for the Plynteria celebrated at Erchia, if it is right that those sacrifices belonged to the Plynteria, they involved as cult recipients on the one hand the main and secondary honorand of the whole polis Plynteria festival and also Kourotrophos who as Ge received, we shall see, a sacrifice at the whole polis Plynteria, and on the other the two gods who formed a poliadic pair with Athena. If this set of sacrifices was indeed part of the Plynteria, this would suggest a strong poliadic element in that festival—at least as perceived at Erchia.

---

[17] Jameson suggested that in the missing lines of the fifth column of the calendar may have been listed an offering to Pandrosos (1965: 157). He associated these sacrifices with the Arrhephoria (1965: 157), but this was before the discovery of the Thorikos calendar which showed that there were at least some deme celebrations of the Plynteria, and that they took place in Skirophorion, not Thargelion. On the sacrifices on Skirophorion 3 in the calendar of Erchia, see also Jameson 1965: 156–8; Humphreys 2004: 177–88.

[18] On Kourotrophos in Attica, see now Parker 2005a: 426–8, cf. 222; see also Lupu 2005: 134 ad 20–1 with bib.

[19] Cf. Chapter 2, section 3.ii.

[20] It has been suggested (Humphreys 2004: 162 and n. 80) that oath taking and audit (*euthyne*) may have taken place in connection with the Plynteria.

In a fragmentary calendar of the first half of the fifth century, of a tribe or a phratry or a *genos*, the sacrifice of a sheep to Athena at the Plynteria is prescribed;[21] this festival was celebrated in the same month as the whole polis festival, in Thargelion. This therefore would appear to be a subdivision celebration that took place at the same time as the polis festival.

These epigraphical data, then, allow us to conclude, first, that the Plynteria was also celebrated by some polis subdivisions at the same time as the whole polis festival and by demes at least sometimes at a different date, in Skirophorion; second, they confirm that the main honorand of the festival was Athena and show that Aglauros was also an important cult recipient; and third, that sheep are appropriate sacrifices for both Athena and Aglauros at the Plynteria—with Athena the privileged recipient. Finally, if the Erchia sacrifices were indeed part of the Plynteria, it suggests that at Erchia at least this festival was perceived to have a significant poliadic element.

I will now continue the attempt to reconstruct stable points that will allow the reconstruction of a ritual skeleton for the Plynteria. We know that there was a procession at the Plynteria, for the lexicographers tell us that *hegeteria* was a cake of figs, more specifically dried figs, carried in the procession of the Plynteria.[22] I will be discussing the problems associated with the destination of this Plynteria procession in section 3. Here I will focus on the *hegeteria*. Athenaeus says that the Athenians call the fruit of the fig tree *hegeteria* because it was the first cultivated food to be discovered,[23] and Hesychios and Photios associate the *hegeteria* carried in the procession of the Plynteria with the notion that the fig was the first cultivated fruit eaten by the autochthons.[24] Can this tell us anything about the Plynteria?

Dried figs were associated with purification, for in the scapegoat ritual at the Thargelia in Athens, early in Thargelion, one scapegoat, *pharmakos*, wore a string of black dried figs, the other of white

---

[21] *IG* I³246 A 9–10; *LSCG* 2 A 9–10: a sheep to Athena at the Plynteria. This is generally considered not to be a whole polis calendar but one of a tribe or a phratry or a *genos* (see e.g. Jameson, Jordan, and Kotansky 1993: 108).

[22] See Phot., Hesych. s.v. *hegeteria*. See also Parker 2005a: 162–3.

[23] Ath. 3.74d. See also Phot. s.v. *hegeteria*. Ath.'s explanation obviously assumes an etymological connection with the *hēg-* root meaning 'lead'.

[24] See n. 22.

ones.[25] But here they are also specifically connected with primordial times and autochthony.[26] That this association is significant is shown by the fact that Aglauros, who, we shall see below, was significantly connected with the Plynteria, was also associated with primordial times and autochthony; for she was the daughter of the half-snake Kekrops, one figure of autochthony, and was also implicated in the other important myth of Athenian autochthony, that of Erichthonios.[27]

I shall discuss primordiality and autochthony further in section 2, where I shall also discuss Aglauros' relationship with the Plynteria and Kallynteria in more detail. Now I will consider some other evidence that will provide further stable points for setting up an interactive skeleton for the reconstruction of the Plynteria. But first I need to discuss what on the surface may appear to be a problem. How do we reconcile the fact that there was a procession during the Plynteria with the fact that on 25 Thargelion the temple was, like other temples, roped off? For roping off stresses enclosure and a procession consists of, and is defined as, movement from one place to another, which makes it very unlikely that a procession left the temple of Athena Polias on 25 Thargelion. I suggest that the procession left the temple on the second day of the Plynteria festival, on 26 Thargelion.[28] As we shall see, there are also other reasons for concluding that 25 Thargelion was part of a longer festival nexus which I will be trying to reconstruct here.

Of course, it could be objected that the procession may have begun outside the temple. However, if it can be shown that the statue was inside the temple at any point on 25 Thargelion, and that it was part of the procession, this objection would be shown to be invalid. That it was inside the temple on 25 Thargelion is shown by the texts of

---

[25] On the scapegoat ritual at the Thargelia in Athens and on the festival, which is a festival of purification and renewal, see Parker 1983: 25–6; Bremmer 2000: esp. 291–2; Parker 2005a: 185, 203–4, 211, 378, 382, 417, 481–3.

[26] Bettinetti (2001: 153) also notes the association, but does not see that, as we shall see in section 2, it fits excellently with the procession to Phaleron and bath.

[27] Cf. pp. 36–8 above.

[28] On that day, if the *IG* I[3] 7 restorations are right, the temple was symbolically sealed and the key held by the Praxiergidai. But symbolic sealing, we shall see, is a different matter, and did not prevent the movement of at least the Praxiergidai in and out of the temple. This is the whole point of them being given the key.

Xenophon and Plutarch cited above, for it is difficult to doubt that the secret rites, the removal of the jewellery, and covering up of the statue (by the Praxiergidai) would have taken place inside the temple of Athena Polias (which at the time was under the control of the Praxiergidai). More concretely, the notion in Plutarch that Athena did not receive Alcibiades kindly or favourably, having covered her face and kept him at a distance, corresponds to the statue being covered up inside the temple which was roped off. All this set the goddess apart during that day; and the covering up of the statue also involved a covering up of the goddess' gaze; the consequent diminution (or the potentiality of such diminution) of her protection may have been an element in the *apophras* nature of the day. As for showing that the statue was taken out in the Plynteria procession, it will become clear below that this was indeed the case and that therefore the notion that the procession took place on the 25th but began outside the temple is impossible; and that therefore the procession is very unlikely to have taken place on the 25th. I will now continue with the attempt to set in place further stable points for the reconstruction of the Plynteria.

The name of the festival, Plynteria, with its evident derivation from πλύνω, 'I wash', allows us to add an important element: that a ritual washing took place. In this context the washing was clearly that of Athena's *peplos*. The festival's *aition* confirms this. For according to this *aition*[29] (which will be discussed in section 2 below) after the death of Aglauros the sacred clothes were not washed (μὴ πλυθῆναι) for a year, and when subsequently they were washed the day 'acquired this name'.[30] The *aition*, then, confirms that the Plynteria involved the washing of sacred garments and indicates that Aglauros was associated with the Plynteria. I shall return to this in a moment. First it is necessary to set in place some further 'stable points' for the reconstruction of the ritual acts that make up the festival. The lexicographers give us the title of an office held by two girls in connection with Athena's statue that was clearly associated with the ritual washing and the Plynteria festival: Plyntrides. But these girls

---

[29] Phot. s.v. Kallynteria kai Plynteria; *Anecd. Bekk.* 1.270.3–5. See Parker 2005a: 381.
[30] Phot. s.v. Kallynteria kai Plynteria.

were also connected with the office entitled 'Loutrides', for our sources tell us that the Loutrides were also called Plyntrides. The title 'Loutrides' indicates the washing of the statue.[31] Thus 'Loutrides' corresponds to the washing of the statue, 'Plyntrides' to the washing of the *peplos*. The fact that the name Plynteria indicates the washing of the *peplos*, and not—so it has been claimed—the statue, has been felt to be in need of explanation.[32] In my view this is less of a problem than has sometimes been thought, for πλύνω can also refer to, and so 'cover', the washing of a statue perceived as a physical object—while λούω would refer to the statue only, it would not cover the washing of the *peplos*. The two different washings would correspond to the two office names Loutrides and Plyntrides. The fact that our sources tell us that the Loutrides were also called Plyntrides may reflect cultic reality or it may be the result of a confusion resulting from the fact that πλύνω covered both activities as did the name of the festival. If these were two distinct offices, the Loutrides washed the statue and the Plyntrides the *peplos*. Be that as it may, the name Loutrides makes it clear that the statue of Athena Polias, as well as its *peplos*, was washed, that Athena had a *loutron*, (ritual) bath (λουτρόν).

I suggest that if it is right that the term 'Plynteria' also covers the washing of the statue, this is correlative with the ambiguity between washing the statue and bathing the deity inherent in such rituals; for the washing of Athena's statue was both an act of πλύνειν and a *loutron* of Athena with the emphases shifting between the two. The perceptions pertaining to the Plynteria may have involved differential distances from the physical object that was the statue in the different parts of the festival. It is possible, indeed, I suggest, likely, that in the secret rites in which the Praxiergidai manipulated, covered up, washed, dressed the image of Athena Polias, the perceptual focus

---

[31] Hesych., Phot. s.v. *loutrides*. See also Deubner 1969: 18; Brulé 1987: 113; Parker 1996: 307; N. Robertson 1996a: 73 n. 74; Dillon 2002: 133; N. Robertson 2004: 137; Parker 2005a: 226. The κατανίπτης was probably a permanent office, not a function connected with the Plynteria rite (Parker 1996: 307).

[32] On the name Plynteria, see also Brulé (1987: 106), who points out that many names of festivals only partly cover the cultic activities occurring at those festivals. As Christopoulos (1992: 37) puts it, it is a case of the name of one part of a festival giving its name to the whole festival.

was on the physical object, so that the statue as a physical object may have been foregrounded;[33] while in the public part that was the procession[34] the perceptual emphasis was on the goddess herself—so that from that perspective the procession would have been taking the goddess for her *loutron*.

For reasons given above it must have been on 25 Thargelion that the procession took place and the statue was given a *loutron*. But, it may be argued, if 25 Thargelion was the first day of the Plynteria, would we not have expected some *plynein* to have taken place? It may well be that it did. For the woollen *peplos* may not have been washed in the sea. Perhaps it was washed in fresh water on the Acropolis on the first day of the Plynteria.

But before considering further evidence concerning the actions performed during the Plynteria, it is necessary to return to Aglauros and the *aition*. The association between Aglauros and the Plynteria will be discussed in section 2 below, but here I will stress that, first, that association is confirmed by the fact that in some deme calendars Aglauros receives an offering in connection with the Plynteria; and second, that the *aition* makes the Plynteria a commemoration of the first washing of the sacred garments that had been left unwashed for a year after the death of Aglauros, and so presents the festival as bringing about the end of a long period of pollution.

It is already clear, and will become even clearer below, that both the 'gloomy and inauspicious' and the 'ending of pollution' facet are important aspects of the Plynteria. The order in which these facets are enacted in purificatory rituals involves the 'gloom and pollution' facet being enacted first, followed by 'ending of pollution' rites. This is also the order of events in the *aition* narrative, first, the death of Aglauros and the pollution that follows it, then the cleansing of the sacred clothes and the institution of the festival. Both facets could in theory have been enacted on the same day. However, the extant texts indicate that the whole day of 25 Thargelion was extremely

---

[33] Though the perspective would change, when, as in Plutarch's text (*Alc.* 34.1–2), the focus shifts from the statue to the goddess in the attempt to relate the rite to Athena's intentions towards Alcibiades.

[34] See also Parker (2005a: 162–3) on the procession being the festival's unequivocally public part.

inauspicious, and we also found other reasons for considering 25 Thargelion different from the 26th, and locating the procession and *loutron* of the statue, which are 'ending of pollution' rites, on 26 Thargelion.

This, I submit, is what the available evidence, structured through the Greek ritual modalities insofar as we understand them, indicates: that 25 Thargelion was an extremely *apophras* day in which the temple of Athena Polias and at least some other sanctuaries were roped off; the statue of Athena Polias was denuded of jewellery, covered up, and kept in the temple, the goddess separate from the rest of the polis, in symbolic correlation to the mourning and pollution that followed the death of Aglauros; it is possible that one element of removal of pollution was already enacted on that day, as a ritual *prolepsis*, as it were, emphasizing the fact, expressed in the festival's name, that this day of pollution was part of a cleansing and renewal nexus.

I will now continue the attempt to reconstruct stable points for the reconstruction of the festival. Important information about the ritual nexus of which the Plynteria is part is reflected in a mid-fifth-century inscription, *IG* I³ 7.[35] In the 450s BC the polis allowed the Praxiergidai to record an oracle that set out their ancestral rites and prerogatives. There are in the surviving text two formulations introducing the setting out of the ancestral customs of the Praxiergidai, that is, those ancestral customs are structured into two unequal groups. The first only mentions dressing the goddess with the *peplos* and making the preliminary sacrifice to the Moirai, Zeus Moiragetes, Ge.[36] The second, the text of which is especially fragmentary, sets out a list of things which I will discuss in a moment. With regard to the first group, draping the *peplos* around the statue was the most important of the prerogatives of the Praxiergidai, indeed the Praxiergidai are defined as those who dress the statue of Athena in Hesychios.[37] This structuring of the prerogatives, then, is unlikely to be a non-significant choice; it is clearly a selection that mentions first, and thus highlights, the most important

---

[35] *IG* I³ 7 = *LSCG* 15.

[36] [ἀμ]φιεννύοσιν τὸν πέπλον τ[ἐν θεὸν καὶ προθύοσιν], *IG* I³7. 10–12. προθύω, if correctly restored (it fits the stoichedon line-length), can refer to sacrifices preliminary to other sacrifices or preliminary to other rituals.

[37] Hesych. s.v. Praxiergidai.

ritual duty of the *genos*. This most important ritual duty and privilege is coupled with one other: performing the preliminary sacrifice to the Moirai, Zeus Moiragetes, and Ge.

Given the importance of the dressing, and the overall structuring of the presentation of these prerogatives, we should not assume that the formulations, and the coupling of these two duties and privileges, are not significant. The question is, if they are significant what do they signify? One thing is clear: the order in which the two acts are listed is unlikely to be the order in which they were performed. For the placing of the laundered *peplos* around the statue was the ultimate goal, the culminating act, of the nexus of rites involving the manipulation of the statue and its apparel, while the preliminary sacrifice clearly took place before something significant.

One hypothesis is that the sacrifice was preliminary to the washing of the statue and *peplos*. For Ziehen[38] suggested that these sacrifices are comparable to a sacrifice at Olympia performed by the descendants of Pheidias, who received from the Eleans the privilege of 'making bright' ($\lambda\alpha\mu\pi\rho\dot{\upsilon}\nu\epsilon\iota\nu$) the statue of Zeus, and sacrificed to Athena Ergane before doing so.[39] However, in my view, the differences are too significant to allow us to use this either as evidence for the Greek ritual mentality or as evidence for the Athenian practice on the assumption that it influenced this rite. First, the nature of the recipients is very different; at Olympia it is the patron goddess of the activity that produced (and indeed maintained) the statue; in the case of the Praxiergidai sacrifice it is divinities with very specific functions, meanings, and connotations that correspond with the nature of the festival, as will become clear in a moment. In addition, 'making bright' is ritually significantly different from purifying by immersion in the sea.

I suggest that it is possible that the Praxiergidai offered the preliminary sacrifice as preliminary to the whole nexus of rites that included the removal of the *kosmos*, the washing of the *peplos*, the *loutron* of the statue, and so on. If this is right, the formulation in *IG* I[3] 7 would have involved first the mention of the ultimate goal, and ultimate privilege of the Praxiergidai, placing the laundered *peplos* around the statue, and then moved backwards to evoke the whole

---

[38] von Prott and Ziehen 1906: 61.
[39] Paus. 5.14.5.

nexus of rites that pertained to the statue and culminated in that act of dressing, through the mention of the first (and very important) rite of the preliminary sacrifice which evoked, because it also ritually encompassed, 'covered', the whole nexus, functioning as a *pars pro toto*.

The nature of the recipients of the sacrifice offers some support to this reconstruction. The Plynteria is connected with primordiality and the movement out of primordiality; in this festival the movement from pollution to purification is also (it will become clear) symbolically correlative with the movement from primordiality to heroic-age (and in this context so also present-day) normality. The Moirai[40] and Ge were symbolically associated with primordiality, and Ge more specifically with autochthony, while Zeus Moiragetes reflects the fact that these primordial powers are now integrated in the new order led by Zeus.[41] Thus the recipients of this sacrifice are connected with primordiality and autochthony, but also with the establishment of the new order and the orderly transition from one to the other. As will become progressively clearer in the course of this investigation, these are significant concepts in this ritual nexus, and especially in the particular segment involving the Praxiergidai dressing the statue with the laundered *peplos*.

In Euripides, *Melanippe Desmotis*, someone points out the importance of the religious roles performed by women, mentioning the role of women at Delphi and Dodona and adding that only women may perform holy rites for the Moirai and the anonymous goddesses.[42] Since the mention of Delphi and Dodona makes it clear that the context is one of reflection of cultic reality, not distortion, this gender differentiation clearly reflects Athenian cultic reality,[43] which

---

[40] On the parentage of the Moirai, see Hes. *Th.* 217 (where they are daughters of Nyx) and 904 (where they are daughters of Zeus and Themis: cf. the commentary of M. L. West on both lines); Gantz 1993: 7–8, 52–3. On the cult of Moirai in Athens, see Parker 2005a: 442 n. 96.

[41] See on the integration of Gaia into the new order at Delphi, Sourvinou-Inwood (1991: 227–9). This is symbolically correlative with another articulation of the same representation at Delphi, involving two of the three recipients of the Praxiergidai sacrifice: according to Paus. (10.24.4), statues of two Moirai, of Zeus Moiragetes and of Apollo Moiragetes, stood inside the temple of Apollo; Zeus Moiragetes and Apollo Moiragetes replaced the third Moira, according to Paus. See also Plut. *Mor.* 385C.

[42] *TrGF* 5 (45) F 495.18–20.

[43] See also on this, and on the 'anonymous' goddesses, Henrichs 1991: 175; Henrichs 1994: 37–9.

suggests that the preliminary sacrifice was performed by female Praxiergidai.[44]

With regard to the second group of prerogatives and duties, the first few lines following the rubric 'These are the ancestral customs of the Praxiergidai' (l. 14) are mostly impossible to read. Then, the word κόιδιον, fleece, occurs in a badly damaged part of the inscription (l. 17). The fleece is an instrument of purification.[45] After that, if the restorations are right, the text says that the archon is to seal the temple during the month Thargelion until the 28th and give the key to the Praxiergidai according to ancestral custom.[46] The archon sealed the temple in the sense of putting a seal on it that declared it symbolically, and mostly effectively, closed; he did not seal it in the sense of making it inaccessible to those who were allowed, and had business to conduct, within it.

All these activities concern the duties of the Praxiergidai with reference to the ritual nexus surrounding the Plynteria.[47] The sealing of the temple by the archon and the handover of its keys to the Praxiergidai—while normally they were the responsibility of the priestess—enacts, and helps to characterize, this period as 'abnormal' time. Thargelion was a month associated with purification and abnormality, above all through the festival Thargelia early in the month, which included the polis-purifying ritual of the scapegoat.[48] This aspect of Thargelion, the penultimate month, is correlative with the fact that purification and abnormality drift to the end of the year, before the renewal of the New Year,[49] though, of course, a renewal is

---

[44] There is another mention of the Praxiergidai sacrifices, in an honorary decree praising a priestess of Athena Polias, *IG* II²776, ll. 18–20; she allocated to the Praxiergidai for their ancestral sacrifice 100 drachmas from her own resources.

[45] See Parker 1983: index s.v. fleece.

[46] See Lewis 1954: 17–21. As Lewis noted (1954: 20) the temple is to be closed for the whole month of Thargelion, and from the fact that the Praxiergidai take over the temple for the whole month we may infer for them a connection with the Kallynteria which is nowhere explicitly stated.

[47] N. Robertson (2004: 111–61) has recently set out new readings and new interpretations of this decree. In my view, the text and restorations in *IG* I³7 are right, and objections to this text are culturally determined, inspired by the feeling that the restored text does not fit modern expectations.

[48] On the Thargelia and the scapegoat ritual, see n. 25 supra.

[49] Parker (2005a: 194–5) expresses scepticism with regard to the significance of the concept of New Year in ancient Athens and prefers (2005a: 210–11) concepts such as

itself enacted within the individual ritual nexuses—within the Thargelia, and through the concluding part of the Plynteria, or at the Kallynteria, a festival closely associated with the Plynteria, which, I will be arguing, most probably followed immediately after the Plynteria. Thus, the month of Thargelion can be said to be characterized by an interplay between pollution and purification, abnormality and normality. Abnormality is not, of course, equivalent to pollution. One way of perceiving the relationship between the two concepts is to consider 'polluted' as one version of 'abnormal'. Abnormality could also function as a symbol for pollution. With regard to the duration of this 'sealed temple abnormality', we should eschew culturally determined judgements as to whether or not such duration is plausible, or at least try to colour them through the one remaining memory of a model in our own cultural assumptions: the abnormal/purificatory ritual time of Lent lasts forty days and was once generally and strictly observed.

An important argument in favour of the reconstruction based on the restorations in *IG* I³ 7 is the following. On this reconstruction the Plynteria would have been the culmination, and have effected the end of, a period of abnormality and pollution that began when the Praxiergidai took over the temple's keys. This would be the ritual correlative of the situation in the festival's *aition*, in which the first washing of the sacred garments which the Plynteria commemorated came at the end of a long period of pollution.

If once again the restorations in *IG* I³ 7 are right, the text says that the Praxiergidai are to dress the statue with a *chiton* costing two mnai or pay a fine of one mna. They therefore had to provide a *chiton* for the statue to wear; the question is when would the statue wear this *chiton*? I suggest that this *chiton* was the garment worn by the statue after its *peplos* had been removed and before it was dressed again with the laundered *peplos*. (I criticize in an appendix to this chapter Nagy's suggestion[50] that the *chiton* was worn by the statue together with, not

---

festivals of renewal for those festivals (among which he mentions the Plynteria, the Kallynteria, and the Thargelia) that suggest the idea of purification or fresh beginning more emphatically than others.

[50] Nagy 1978a: 140–1. [The critique was part of Sourvinou-Inwood's main text: the editor has made it into an Appendix.]

in place of, the *peplos*.[51]) This *chiton*, since it was not the *peplos* normally worn by the statue, would be abnormal, and therefore appropriate for marking the abnormality of that period, part of the rites performed by the Praxiergidai while the temple was in 'abnormal' time and state, sealed, with the keys held by the Praxiergidai; that was why the Praxiergidai paid for the garment.

The fact that the archon sealed the temple and gave the key to the Praxiergidai, taken together with the information concerning the *chiton* to be provided by the Praxiergidai, leads us to infer that the priestess probably removed the *peplos* from the statue and handed it over to the Praxiergidai at the same time, in effect handing over responsibility for the statue to them, as the archon had done with regard to the temple. For while it is a temple's priestess who normally holds the key, acting towards the deity on behalf of the polis, the archon as a representative of the whole polis effected and sanctioned the temporary passing of responsibility for the temple from one human actor acting on behalf of the polis, the priestess, to another, the Praxiergidai.

The Praxiergidai then dressed the statue with the *chiton* which they provided. With regard to the *peplos*, we are not told that the Praxiergidai removed the *peplos* from the statue at the Plynteria. What we are told is, first, that on 25 Thargelion they removed the jewellery from the statue,[52] second, that on that same day they covered up the statue;[53] and also that they dressed the statue with the (laundered) *peplos*.[54] Before that, at some point, they would have received the *peplos*[55] in order to wash it, if, as is most likely, the Plyntrides who

---

[51] As well as the *himation* mentioned in *IG* II[2]1060 + *IG* II[2]1036, on which, see below. Mansfield (1985: 138, 139–44) thinks that in addition to the *peplos* various other garments were placed on the statue, because he not only assumes that the *himation* in *IG* II[2]1060 + 1036a was worn by the statue over the *chiton* but also that various garments listed in inscriptions as dedications (for example the garments mentioned in *IG* II[2] 776. 16–18 as having being dedicated by a priestess of Athena Polias) were all worn by the statue.

[52] Plut. *Alc.* 34.1.

[53] Ibid.

[54] *IG* I[3] 7. 10–11.

[55] I will argue in section 5 below that this is what is referred to in *IG* II[2] 1060 + *IG* II[2] 1036 fr.b ll. 1–2.

washed the *peplos* were members of this *genos*—or have it washed and returned to them if they were not.

ii. 25 Thargelion: a summary

At the beginning of Thargelion the archon sealed the temple and gave the key to the Praxiergidai and the priestess removed the *peplos* from the statue and handed it over to the Praxiergidai. When the Praxiergidai took over the statue they dressed it with a *chiton* costing two mnai which they provided.

On 25 Thargelion the sanctuary was roped off—a stronger version of the sealing on the temple in the course of Thargelion. This was an ill-omened day. On that day (conceivably on the evening and night that came before the daytime of the 25th) the Praxiergidai first offered the preliminary sacrifice to the Moirai, Zeus Moiragetes, and Ge; they then removed from the statue the *kosmos*, its jewellery, and its temporary dress, the *chiton*, then covered the statue up in an appropriate piece of cloth. They also performed 'secret rites' (ἀπόρρητα ὄργια). It is likely that it was on that day that the *peplos* (and probably the temporary *chiton*) was washed, in fresh water on the Acropolis, by the Plyntrides, two girls who were undoubtedly members of the Praxiergidai. On the morning of the 26th, as I will argue in section 3 below, a procession took the statue, covered up, to be immersed in the sea at Phaleron.

2. AGLAUROS, *AITIA*, PLYNTERIA, AND KALLYNTERIA

As we saw, the Plynteria was a festival of Athena Polias with which Aglauros was also closely associated. Aglauros is also involved in the *aition* of the related and connected festival Kallynteria, which is mentioned together with the *aition* for the Plynteria and will be considered below. Aglauros has already been presented in some detail in Chapter 2. As we saw there, her myths presented her as an ambivalent figure. Like her sisters, who also received cult, she is both a positive figure and a disobedient and foolish girl. On the one hand, in one well-established myth, she had been disobedient to Athena and with her sisters (or, in some versions, only one of her sisters) opened Erichthonios' basket and killed herself as a result. On the other, in another well-established myth, intimately connected with cult, she gave her life to save the city. On the one hand she dies to save the city, a schema intimately connected with a maiden, the schema 'a maiden dies to save the city',[56] on the other she is said to have had a daughter by Ares, Alkippe,[57] and the genealogy of the Kerykes claimed that Aglauros was the mother of Keryx by Hermes.[58] As Parker noted, as the most prominent Athenian females of the earliest times the daughters of Kekrops were ascribed descendants, but in their main myth they died virgins.[59] This is also connected, it has also been noted, with the instability of the mythological personalities of the Kekropids, and of the representations of primordial Athens in general.[60] Her association with autochthony and primordiality is an important aspect of Aglauros' persona: she was the daughter of the half-snake Kekrops, one figure of autochthony, and was also implicated in the other myth of Athenian autochthony, that of Erichthonios.[61] I shall return to this. First I will say something about her priestess.

A decree of the mid-third century BC honouring the priestess of Aglauros Timokrite[62] mentions that she had offered entry sacrifices, *eisitēria*, she had taken care that there was good order at the 'all-night festival' (*pannychis*),[63] and also she 'decorated the table'. I shall discuss these rituals in section 4 below, but here it is necessary to discuss the priesthood of Aglauros itself. The priestess of Aglauros is provided by the *genos* of the Salaminioi, as is mentioned in the report of the arbitration between the two branches of the Salaminioi[64] which says

[56] See e.g. Kearns 1990.

[57] See Hellanikos of Lesbos *FGrH* 4 F 38; Apollod. 3.14.2.

[58] Paus. 1.38.3.

[59] Parker (1987a: 210 n. 43). Gourmelen (2005: 59–60) thinks that the fact that Aglauros was the name both of Kekrops' wife and of one of his daughters means that Aglauros was both his wife and daughter—and that therefore he was surrounded by feminine powers, the mother (Ge) and the wife-daughter.

[60] See Redfield 2003: 121.

[61] On Aglauros' association with autochthony, see also Redfield 2003: 121–4.

[62] Dontas 1983 (*SEG* XXXIII 115). From *IG* II² 3459 we learn the name of another priestess of Aglauros, Pheidostrate, and the name and deme of her father, but nothing else.

[63] On *pannychides*, see Parker 2005a: 166, 182–3.

[64] *LSS* 19. 8–16; cf. Ferguson 1938: 3–5; Parker 1996: 309.

that this (like the other priesthoods held by the Salaminioi which included that of Athena Skiras) was a life priesthood and that the priestess should be elected by lot from both branches of the Salaminioi. Doubts have been expressed as to whether this was the whole polis cult priesthood of Aglauros. The problem is that in the Salaminioi inscription the reference is to a joint priesthood of Aglauros and Pandrosos (and more problematically Kourotrophos), while in later documents, such as that in honour of Timokrite, the priesthoods were distinct.[65] The most likely explanation of this discrepancy is that what had been a joint priesthood in the fourth century subsequently became divided into two.[66] The alternative has been suggested that this was a public cult but not a central polis cult, that it was a deme cult, since we know that there were deme cults of Aglauros.[67] However, first, there is no evidence that a *genos* could have held the priesthood of a deme cult—let alone for life; second, since the Salaminioi were spread in different demes,[68] a deme priesthood could hardly have been one for which to make the provision that the priestess should be elected by lot from both branches of the Salaminioi; and finally, if it had been other than the central polis cult the formulation, I submit, would have been likely to have been different, more specific, such as it is for the first mention of the priesthood of Herakles at Porthmos.[69] The whole polis priestess of Aglauros, then, was clearly provided by the *genos* of the Salaminioi. She was (in some manner or other) involved with the whole polis cult and sanctuary of Athena Skiras at Phaleron, at the very least to the extent that she was one of the recipients of loaves in the sanctuary of Athena Skiras at the Oschophoria festival—together with the priestess of Athena Skiras and the priest of Herakles and other officiants but not the other priest provided by the Salaminioi, that of Eurysakes.[70] In fact, it is extremely likely that, as Parker has argued, the *deipnophoria*, dinner-bringing, for

---

[65] On the problem, see Parker 1996: 311; Lambert 1999b: 114–15.

[66] See esp. on this, Parker (1996: 311). Lambert (1999b: 114–15) suggests that what had been a joint gentilicial priesthood became two priesthoods appointed by some other mechanism by the mid-third century.

[67] Kearns 1989: 139; Humphreys 1990: 246 n. 5. We know that it was not a *genos* cult (see Parker 1996: 311).

[68] See e.g. Lambert 1997: 96.

[69] *LSS* 19. 10–11.

[70] Ibid.; cf. Ferguson 1938: 36–7.

Aglauros, Pandrosos, and Herse, was part of the Oschophoria[71] and took place at the sanctuary of Athena Skiras at Phaleron. This would have associated the priestess of Aglauros provided by the Salaminioi who was one of the recipients of loaves in the sanctuary of Athena Skiras at the Oschophoria with a whole polis ritual in a whole polis sanctuary at a whole polis festival, thus confirming that this was a whole polis priesthood. This would also show that Aglauros and her sisters received offerings at the sanctuary of Athena Skiras at Phaleron.

As we saw, according to the *aition* for the Plynteria,[72] the sacred clothes had not been washed for a year after Aglauros' death, and when subsequently they were washed the festival 'acquired this name';[73] and the fact that Aglauros was strongly associated with the Plynteria indicated by this *aition* is confirmed by the fact that in at least one deme calendar she receives an offering in connection with the Plynteria.[74] However, the statement in a lexicographical source that the Plynteria was celebrated in Aglauros' honour[75] is a distorted refraction of her actual association with the festival; for not only is Aglauros a less important cult recipient than Athena in the deme calendars, but also we know that the Plynteria was a festival of Athena Polias, since we know that it was focused on the statue of the poliadic cult. In addition, according to Proklos, Aristokles of Rhodes (a first-century BC grammarian) said that the festival Bendideia was celebrated on 19 Thargelion, and that 'the festivals relating to Athena' come after that.[76] I will return to this when I discuss the festivals' dates in more detail.

The other 'festival relating to Athena' was, of course, the Kallynteria, to which I now turn. The *aition* in Photios[77] reads: 'Kallynteria. Because Agraulos is thought to have been the first, having become priestess, to have "adorned" the gods. And so they assigned Kallynteria to her. For

---

[71] Parker 2005a: 215–17.

[72] Phot. s.v. Kallynteria kai Plynteria; Anecd. Bekk. 1.270.3–5. See Parker 2005a: 381.

[73] Phot. s.v. Kallynteria kai Plynteria.

[74] See p. 138.

[75] Hesych. s.v. Plynteria: 'a festival at Athens which they conduct in honour of Aglauros the daughter of Kekrops.'

[76] Procl. *In Ti.* I.85.28–9.

[77] Phot. s.v. Kallynteria kai Plynteria. τὰ δὲ καλλυντήρια, ὅτι πρώτη δοκεῖ ἡ Ἄγραυλος γενομένη ἱερεία τοὺς θεοὺς κοσμῆσαι· διὸ καὶ καλλυντήρια αὐτῇ ἀπέδειξαν· καὶ γὰρ τὸ κοσμεῖν καὶ λαμπρύνειν ἐστίν. See Parker 2005a: 381, 474.

"adorning" is a form of making bright.' I have put 'adorned' and 'adorning' within quotation marks because, though the standard translation for the verb in question κοσμεῖν, 'adorn' may as we shall see be misleading. The entry in *Anecd. Bekk.* 1.270.1–3 explains Kallynteria 'from making beautiful (καλλύνειν) and "adorning" (κοσμεῖν) and making bright (λαμπρύνειν)' and connects the festival with Aglauros, who 'having become priestess "adorned" the gods'.

The notion in Photios that the Kallynteria was celebrated in honour of Aglauros is comparable to the claim in Hesychios[78] that the Plynteria was held in honour of Aglauros and is, like that, a distorted refraction of Aglauros' association with the festival. The Kallynteria, like the Plynteria, was a festival in honour of Athena.[79] Aglauros was probably a secondary cult recipient in the Kallynteria, as she was in the Plynteria.

What does 'adorned' the gods mean, and what does the *aition* tell us about the festival? The analogy of the formulations in Delos, where 'adornment' of Hera' ((ἐπι)κόσμησις τῆς ῾Ήρας) means the κόσμησις of the sanctuary of Hera and may or may not include the notion of cleaning (and perhaps adorning?) the statue,[80] suggests that the expression τοὺς θεοὺς κοσμῆσαι in Photios had a core meaning relating to the cleaning of the gods' sanctuaries.

A strong meaning of καλλύνειν pertained to cleaning. Parker, who concluded that it is uncertain if the Kallynteria festival was devoted to the cleaning of the temple or the adornment of the statue,[81] noted that καλλύνειν and associated words typically refer to cleaning rather than decoration. The notion of adornment and beautification was also included in them.[82] In the transmitted text of Photios,[83] κοσμεῖν

---

[78] Hesych. s.v. Plynteria.
[79] See also Parker 2005a: 474.
[80] See Bettinetti (2001: 144–7) who takes (ἐπι)κόσμησις to refer to the annual cleaning of sanctuaries and statues in preparation for the celebration of festivals. She cites (2001: 144 n. 26) Bruneau for the conclusion that (ἐπι)κόσμησις τῆς ῾Ήρας means (ἐπι)κόσμησις of the sanctuary of Hera but says that there is no reason why this would not include the care of the cult statue.
[81] Parker 2005a: 474–5.
[82] For example, acccording to Hesych. s.v. καλλύνεσθαι, καλλύνεσθαι equals κοσμεῖσθαι, καλλωπίζεσθαι. And Hesych. defines κοσμός (s.v.) as καλλωπισμός, κατασκευή, τάξις, κατάστασις.
[83] Editors print καὶ γὰρ τὸ <καλλύνειν> κοσμεῖν καὶ λαμπρύνειν ἔστιν, but the transmitted text (also accepted by Parker 2005a: 474) makes better sense.

is defined as also including the notion of λαμπρύνειν, making bright. This may indicate that in the understanding of Photios' ultimate source, the Kallynteria included actions that could come under the general heading of 'making bright', λαμπρύνειν. Making the temple bright by cleaning it and making it shine would fall into that category. It is not impossible that the notion of cleaning and making bright and perhaps also adorning the statue may also have been included. This prima facie may appear impossible, since the statue was washed at the Plynteria. However, we shall see, there are good reasons for thinking that the statue returned to its sanctuary cleaned and made bright during the Kallynteria when it was also adorned with its jewellery. If κοσμεῖν indeed included the notion 'adornment of statues', perhaps the festival included the ritual of putting the κόσμος, adornment (which had been removed on the 25th), back on the statue, and also whatever else may have been implicated in statue adornment, while λαμπρύνειν would indicate the notion of making brilliant the statue and the temple. If this is right, the ritual reality reflected in the names and *aitia* was complex.

The actions of sweeping and cleaning the temple at the Kallynteria would have needed to have been performed before the cleaned statue in the laundered *peplos* was returned there. However, as will become clear below, contrary to what may appear prima facie to be the case, this does not need to entail that the Kallynteria took place before the Plynteria. As we shall see, the reconstructed ritual scenarios that will be set out below can account for the Kallynteria following the Plynteria and still the statue being returned to a clean temple cleaned at the Kallynteria.

I turn now to consider an aspect of Aglauros' mythological persona that emerges from these cultic *aitia*. Her father Kekrops, being a civilizing figure in Athenian history, was strongly associated with both primordiality and movement out of it.[84] In the *aitia* of the Plynteria and Kallynteria Aglauros too is associated with the movement out of primordiality, in the sense that she is associated with the establishment of some of the things that are part of normality in the present. First, 'adorning' the gods was initiated by her. Second, the washing of the sacred garments in the Plynteria festival was the consequence of her

---

[84] See an extensive discussion in Gourmelen 2005: 209–67, cf. also 267–89; Parker 1987a: 197–8.

death. The two *aitia* create a symbolic alignment between pollution and primordiality on the one hand and purification and movement out of primordiality on the other. Incidentally, the fact that the *hegeteria*, which was connected with primordiality and autochthony in the ancient sources, was part of the Plynteria procession, and so of the abnormal time when the statue had left the Acropolis, confirms that in the nexus of the Plynteria and Kallynteria there was a symbolic alignment between abnormal ritual time and primordiality.

A third mytheme, not directly connected with the Plynteria, and not associated with pollution or its removal, also makes Aglauros, this time together with her sisters, an agent of the movement out of primordiality. According to this mytheme, the daughters of Kekrops (specifically, the formulation is, Pandrosos and her sisters) were the first to weave woollen clothes for mortals.[85] As Kearns noted, this mythological fact can hardly be unrelated to the weaving of Athena's *peplos* by the *arrhephoroi*,[86] particularly given that the *arrhephoroi* were specifically associated with Pandrosos.[87] If there were no woollen clothes woven by mortals prior to the daughters of Kekrops, Athena's statue before that cannot have worn what is 'now' its normal dress; the *peplos* as the normal dress of the statue of Athena Polias must have been introduced by Aglauros who was Athena's priestess—when she and her sisters wove woollen clothes.

This would appear to have another implication. If it was Aglauros who first dressed the statue of Athena Polias in a woollen *peplos*, before that the statue wore something that was not what is now Athena's normal dress.[88] I suggest that this is parallel to the

---

[85] Phot. s.v. *protonion*; cf. Suda s.v. *protonion*, which gives the variant Pandora. See also Gourmelen 2005: 161.

[86] Kearns 1989: 24. On the *arrhephoroi* and the daughters of Kekrops, see Burkert 1990: 40–59.

[87] See e.g. Kearns 1989: 24, 192. On the association with Herse, see Istros *FGrH* 334 F27 and Jacoby 1954: i. 643–4; Burkert 1990: 42–3; Kearns 1989: 161.

[88] It could be argued that all these suggestions are invalidated by the fact that there was a myth according to which Erichthonios set up the image of Athena which is on the Acropolis (Apollod. 3.14.6), which Apollodoros mentions together with Erichthonios' foundation of the Panathenaia. However, first, this may or may not have been the cultic myth; and second, it may or may not have been perceived to imply that this was the first statue of Athena. Furthermore, it is possible that the relationship between this myth and the nexus of Aglauros as the first priestess of Athena was perceived as 'unresolved': cf. n. 9 above.

reconstruction in section 1 above, according to which $IG I^3$ 7 indicates that the statue wore a *chiton* during the period before the Plynteria, when the Praxiergidai were in charge of the temple and the statue, in ritually abnormal time. For the *chiton*, which signified abnormality, also evoked the time before what was now normality was established, the time before Aglauros. The reclothing of the statue with the clean *peplos* would also have been partially evocative of Aglauros first establishing the woollen *peplos* as the statue's normal dress.

However, this is only partially evocative, not symbolically equivalent; for when Aglauros dressed the statue with the first woollen *peplos*, that *peplos* was new, and therefore corresponded rather with the new *peplos* placed on the statue at the Panathenaia, not the laundered *peplos* of the Plynteria. The priestess of Aglauros[89] was not involved in the laundering done at the Plynteria, which was assigned to the Praxiergidai; nor was it first performed aetiologically by Aglauros, even though it was associated with her death. On the other hand, since Aglauros was a cult recipient at the Plynteria, her priestess would have been involved in the festival's rituals—just not the washings. Since Aglauros is an agent in the *aition* of the Kallynteria, her priestess may have played a role in the course of this festival too. I will discuss this possibility in section 4.

3. THE PROCESSION TO PHALERON

i. The Problematik: the procession of the Plynteria and the Palladion hypothesis

I argued above that the procession left the temple on the second day of the Plynteria festival, on 26 Thargelion. There is disagreement as to the destination of the procession and so also as to the locality where the statue was washed, whether it only went a short distance away, or whether it went to Phaleron. That there was a procession at

---

[89] Though Aglauros had been a priestess of Athena Polias, her main ritual avatar in the present was not the priestess of Athena Polias, but, since she had one, her own priestess.

the Plynteria is, we saw, certain, because the lexicographers mention the *hegeteria*, a cake of dried figs, carried in the procession of the Plynteria,[90] which was associated with two concepts that were important at the Plynteria, purification and also primordiality and autochthony. So the statue was removed from its proper place, taken away covered up in a cloth, and washed. I will now set out the case that leads me to conclude that the procession of the Plynteria went to Phaleron, where the statue of Athena Polias was washed in the sea.

There has been much discussion as to whether the Plynteria procession was the same as the procession which, we are told by Philochoros[91] and some inscriptions of the last quarter of the second century BC,[92] took a statue of Athena to Phaleron escorted by ephebes. Burkert argued that it was not the same, that the statue escorted by ephebes was the Palladion, and that the *gennetai* involved were not the Praxiergidai but the Bouzygai.[93] I will argue in sections

---

[90] See Hesych., Phot. s.v. ἡγητηρία.

[91] Philochoros *FGrH* 328 F64b.

[92] *IG* II². 1006.11–12, 1011.10–11, 1008.9–10.

[93] Burkert 1970a, which was accepted by Mansfield 1985: 424–33; Brulé 1987: 105–6; N. Robertson (1996a: 49; with 72 n. 77) thinks that the bathing of the statue took place on the Acropolis. Contra, see esp. Nagy 1991: 288–306; Christopoulos 1992; Parker 1996: 307–8, esp. n. 63; on the controversy, cf. Dillon 2002: 134; Humphreys 2004: 91 n. 36, 117 n. 22. Nagy (1991: 290–4) has shown that the argument concerning the timing of the procession is wrong, and also discusses the use of the name Pallas (1991: 294–9). However, he (1991: 301–2, see also 306) also thinks that the procession to Phaleron was not part of the Plynteria because the Plynteria was a secretive and ill-omened festival while the ephebes' participation in the procession involved public display. But, as Parker (1996: 308 n. 63) noted, Nagy's argument underestimates the extent to which mixture of mood often characterized Greek ritual. To set this out in more explicit detail, I suggest that Nagy's view is based on the assumption that, because part of the Plynteria was secretive, the whole festival was secretive; he also does not take account, first, of the fact that the context in our sources is conducive to strongly emphasizing the ill-omened, and, second, of the fact that all processions were public, and since the Plynteria included a procession it had a public part, the very part that corresponds to the public rite that Nagy thinks could not have been part of this festival. Nagy's (1991: 302–6) own interpretation that the procession was a re-enactment of the evacuation and return of the statue of Athena Polias when Athens was evacuated before the battle of Salamis is implausible. Not only is the alleged rite unattested, the very event that this rite supposedly commemorated, the removal of Athena's statue when the city was evacuated, is not explicitly mentioned; it is not mentioned at all in Herodotos' narrative of the relevant events, while Plutarch cites Kleitodemos (*FGrH* 323 F 21 in Plut. *Them.* 10.4) for the story that when the Athenians were going down to the Peiraeus, the *gorgoneion* was lost

ii and iii that this view is mistaken, that the procession in question was indeed that of the Plynteria.

ii. The argument for the Plynteria

Let us look at the evidence. Philochoros says that the procession was organized by the *nomophylakes*. In one version of a fragment[94] the text says that the board of magistrates called *nomophylakes* 'dispatched' (ἔπεμπον) the procession for Pallas, in the other that they 'ordered' (ἐκόσμουν) the procession for Pallas when the image (τὸ ξόανον) was brought to the sea'.[95] The inscriptions deploy the following formulations. In *IG* II² 1006.11–12 the formulation is that the

from Athena's statue. Kleitodemos' story suggests that the statue had indeed been removed from the temple, but the absence of explicit references to this removal cannot legitimately be assumed to be coincidental; it may well indicate that the perceptions of this event were not of a type likely to encourage its commemoration. This is indeed what we would expect, for the removal of Athena's statue from her temple for protection was a negative, not positive, representation of the Persian Wars. More importantly, because more concretely, if Kleitodemos' narrative is taken to indicate the evacuation of Athena's statue by sea, it makes clear that it was the port of Peiraeus that was involved, not that of Phaleron, which was Athens's old harbour (see also Parker 1996: 308 n. 63). Nagy (1991: 305) tried to circumvent this insurmountable objection by suggesting that since Demetrios of Phaleron established the office of *nomophylakes*, and since the *nomophylakes* prepared the processsion to Phaleron, Demetrios may have changed the destination of the procession, from the Peiraeus to Phaleron, in order to glorify his place of birth. It is not certain that Demetrios created the *nomophylakes* (on the *nomophylakes* Jacoby 1954: i. 337–9 ad F 64; Rhodes 1981: 315, 580); but whether he did or not, changing the destination of an established procession from the Peiraeus to Phaleron would be a much more radical change in ancient eyes than may be assumed if both places are subsumed under the category 'Athenian ports' that obscures their specific differences in the Athenian conceptual universe. Such a change would, I submit, constitute a much less likely modality of ritual manipulation than the common one of enhancing the visibility and prestige of cults, rituals, and/or sanctuaries associated with the place of birth, or genealogy, that it is desired to enhance. That in this case would entail enhancing the visibility and prestige of this particular procession the destination of which was Phaleron, the religiously important procession to Phaleron at the Plynteria, which was part of a very important religious nexus pertaining to the poliadic cult, with the creation of, or alterations in, the institution of the *nomophylakes* being part of this process.

[94] Philochoros *FGrH* 328 F64b, (a) and (b).
[95] On the role of the ephebes and the *nomophylakes* in this procession, see Humphreys 2004: 117. On the *nomophylakes*, see Jacoby 1954: i. 337–9 ad 64; Humphreys 2004: 123–5.

ephebes 'joined in taking out Pallas (συνεξήγαγον τὴν Παλλάδα) to Phaleron and joined in bringing her in (συνεισήγαγον) again by torchlight (μετὰ φωτός) in all good order, and they also brought in Dionysos'; in 1006.75–6 the *kosmetes* of the ephebes 'escorted Pallas to Phaleron and joined in bringing her in from there by torchlight'. In *IG* II² 1011.10–11 the ephebes 'joined in taking out Pallas (συνεξήγαγον τὴν Παλλάδα) with the *gennetai* and brought her in again by torchlight in all good order, and they also brought in Dionysos'; in 1008.9–10 they 'took out Pallas to Phaleron and joined in bringing her back in from there by torchlight in all good order'.

Other scholars have already set out various arguments against the view that this procession was not that of the Plynteria but belonged to the cult of Athena at Palladion.[96] I will now add some further considerations.[97] I begin by examining one argument in favour of the Palladion that perhaps needs to be explicitly discussed again, and which appears to be the argument that convinced Brulé that this procession was not part of the Plynteria: "comment croire qu'un décret athénien appelle Pallas le *xoanon* de l'Acropole?"[98]

---

[96] See n. 93.

[97] Recently Bettinetti (2001: 150–3, see also 74–5) has revived Burkert's arguments without attempting to refute the case against them. She simply states that in the description of the Plynteria in the ancient literary sources there is no mention of a bath or an exit of the statue, but the emphasis is on the goddess being veiled inside the temple (Bettinetti 2001: 151). However, first, the veiled statue of Athena is not described as being inside the temple; no doubt it was inside the temple for part of the time, but the sources do not actually locate the veiled statue in a particular place. Second, Bettinetti's statement about what the sources do and do not say gives the impression that we have descriptions of the festival in at least one continuous narrative, while in fact we have a few snippets determined by the context. Third, her claim that there is no mention of a bath or an exit of the statue is not strictly true. We know that a procession was part of the Plynteria, and the (implicit) notion that this procession would not have involved the statue would need to rely on special pleading, especially given the (fragmentary) reference to the Praxiergidai 'taking out in procession' something in *IG* II² 1060 + 1036, which will be discussed below. We also know that the statue of Athena Polias did have a ritual bath (Hesych., Phot. s.v. *loutrides*). Finally, her argument does not take account of the fact that in the two extant sources the accent is on veiling because the context demands it. I should add that in an inscription of the first half of the third century BC from Kos (*LSCG* 154 B 24–5) that Bettinetti (2001: 159) herself mentions the undoubtedly correct supplement gives a text that speaks of veiling the statue of Kourotrophos and bringing it out in procession to the sea.

[98] Brulé 1987: 106. On the use of the name Pallas, see also Nagy 1991: 294–9.

To state the obvious, 'Pallas' is not the same as Athena at Palladion, or the Palladion, and the answer to Brulé's question is that it is not 'the *xoanon*' but the goddess that the decrees call 'Pallas'. For the expression that follows, which refers to Dionysos, makes it unambiguously clear that the formulations speak of the deities, not their statues; 'Pallas' in the inscription is the goddess, not her statue. In the archaic and classical dedications on the Athenian Acropolis, where there was more than one cult of Athena, the goddess was often referred to as simply 'Athena', without cultic epithet, and sometimes as 'Pallas'.[99]

Even more importantly, one particular text, *IG* II² 3474, which was inscribed *c*.130 BC,[100] and discovered near the Erechtheion, demonstrates that 'Pallas' was used to refer to Athena even when the focus was specifically on the cult of Athena Polias. It is inscribed on the base of a statue of the priestess of Athena Polias, Philtera, and refers specifically to the goddess's city-protecting functions while still addressing her (in verse) as 'Pallas'.[101] Clearly, then, in Athens the name Pallas was used generically for Athena, even when the focus was specifically on the cult of Athena Polias.[102]

Let us now examine the problem from another perspective. We know that a procession was part of the Plynteria and the festival's name and nature suggest that this procession went to a place where something was washed and cleansed. Is there any reason for thinking that this place was Phaleron?

---

[99] See the formulations in Sourvinou-Inwood 1997d: 168 and n. 26. Pallas: *CEG* 1. 179, 194, 201, 203, 240; 2.762. In addition, if it is right that the olivewood statue of Athena Polias also had the function of a palladion protecting the city (see e.g. Vian 1952: 256), that is, it functioned in ways comparable to those in which the Trojan Palladion had functioned, this may have been one of the factors facilitating the use of the generic name 'Pallas' for the goddess when the statue was taken out in the procession.

[100] Aleshire 1994: 337.

[101] Παλλὰς Ἐρεχθειδᾶν ἀρχαγ[έτι, σὸ]ν κατὰ ναόν/ ἅδε τοι ἱδρύθη Φιλτέρα ἱρ[οπόλ]ος.

[102] The argument of Mansfield (1985: 432), concerning *IG* II²3177, fails for the same reason. [I have omitted a short development in which Sourvinou-Inwood points out that in *Hymn* 5 Callimachus speaks of 'Pallas Poliouchos' even though the ritual presupposed in the Hymn does not concern Athena Polias but a Palladion. R.P.]

Purification in the sea is an established Athenian ritual modality and a strong modality of purification.[103] As Buxton noted, with reference in fact to the purifying bath of Athena, which he correctly places at the Plynteria, contact with the sea can constitute a new beginning, appropriate for the time of the year in which the Plynteria was celebrated, and in the Mediterranean the sea-shore, where this and comparable rituals took place, is a line, a boundary and the site of the transition between polluted and pure.[104] As we shall see, Phaleron was also another type of symbolic boundary, part of the symbolic frontier of Athens.

Phaleron was the nearest sea-coast from the centre of Athens and we know that it functioned as a locus for purificatory baths in Athenian rituals because it did so in the Eleusinian Mysteries: on the second day of the festival, called 'initiates to the sea', the initiates were purified in the sea at Phaleron.[105] The ritual formula 'initiates to the sea' makes clear that Phaleron was perceived to be the nearest sea from the city centre. It is, then, difficult to doubt that, if the statue of Athena Polias was washed in the sea at the Plynteria, this would have been done at Phaleron. I will now argue that there are further, different, reasons for connecting the Plynteria with Phaleron.

As we saw, since Aglauros had a significant place in the Plynteria, including as a cult recipient, her priestess would have had a role in the festival. As we saw, the priestess of Aglauros belonged to the *genos* of the Salaminioi; one of the religious centres of the Salaminioi was the sanctuary of Athena Skiras at Phaleron, whose priesthood the Salaminioi held. As we also saw, the priestess of Aglauros was (in some manner or other) involved with the whole polis cult and sanctuary of Athena Skiras at Phaleron, at the very least to the extent

---

[103] See also the purification of the statue in the sea in the pretend ritual in Eur. *IT* 1029–233. For the relationship between the Athenian audience's religious assumptions, including the Plynteria, and this rite in *IT*, see Sourvinou-Inwood 2003a: 301–3; and A. Kavoulaki's forthcoming monograph on the representation of processions in tragedy. On purification in the sea as a strong Greek modality of purification, see also Christopoulos 1992: 38; on cult statues purified in the sea, see also Bettinetti 2001: 158–60; on purifying statues in water in general, Parker 1983: 27; Scheer 2000: 58–9; Bettinetti 2001: 154–60.

[104] Buxton 1994: 102–3.

[105] Cf. Parker (2005a: 347 n. 87) and Travlos (1971: 160) for the position of the *Halade* Gate through which the *mystai* went out to go to the sea.

that she was one of the recipients of loaves in the sanctuary of Athena Skiras at the Oschophoria; since not all priests provided by the Salaminioi were recipients on that occasion, for the priest of Eurysakes was not, this may reflect a connection that is more than (though it obviously also reflects) the gentilicial association. In addition, we saw, it is extremely likely that the *deipnophoria* for Aglauros, Pandrosos, and Herse took place during the Oschophoria at the sanctuary of Athena Skiras at Phaleron.[106]

Wherever the Plynteria procession went, the activities that were performed there would have involved both secret rites performed by the Praxiergidai and public ones, since there was a public facet represented by any procession. I suggest that the actual *loutron* of the statue would not have taken place in public; the possibility that men may have been excluded from it is suggested by Kallimachos' hymn *On the Bath of Pallas*—which, of course does not refer to this rite, but was nevertheless structured by a common Greek ritual mentality which will be discussed below. If this is right, on my reconstruction, its destination would have been the sanctuary of Athena Skiras, where the men, and the public part of the procession in general, would have stayed while the female Praxiergidai took the statue to the sea and bathed it.

Even leaving my reconstruction aside, a movement of a statue of Athena to Phaleron that involved both a bath secretly performed by females and the public part that was the procession is more likely than not to have involved as a locus for part of the ritual the sanctuary, and so also the priestess, of Athena Skiras. This would fit a procession in which Aglauros and her priestess were involved, and therefore the Plynteria, not the cult of Athena at Palladion. Indeed, such a state of affairs, in which the Salaminioi had some involvement with the Plynteria and collaborated with the Praxiergidai, would constitute a satisfactory explanatory context for the fact that the priesthood of Aglauros was held by the Salaminioi, which has puzzled some modern scholars (as well as for a possible connection between the Salaminioi and the Praxiergidai outside the Plynteria—if

---

[106] As Parker (2005a: 215–17) has argued.

this is not a mirage).[107] To put it differently, if this reconstruction is right, the fact that the priesthood of Aglauros was held by the Salaminioi would be correlative with the involvement in the Plynteria of the sanctuary of Athena Skiras at Phaleron.

Another argument in favour of the view that the statue of Athena Polias was taken to Phaleron in the course of the Plynteria is provided, I will now argue, by an office attested in a very late period. A third-century AD inscription refers to a 'charioteer of Pallas', ἡνίοχος τῆς Παλλάδος.[108] This has been taken to refer to the charioteer of a chariot that took the statue of Athena at Palladion to Phaleron.[109] But there are serious objections to this scenario. To begin with, once it is realized that 'Pallas' means 'Athena' and not 'Athena at Palladion', it becomes clear that the office could have belonged to any cult and ritual of Athena. As we shall see, there are good reasons for thinking that the cult to which the charioteer of Pallas was attached was certainly not that of Athena at Palladion, and that it was part of the festival nexus of the Plynteria and Kallynteria. I should note that the fact that this office was almost certainly a late creation does not affect the arguments set out here. For, as I hope will become clear in the course of the discussion, the representations that came into play were earlier representations, which the creation of this office stressed but did not invent. These representations, I will be arguing, were part of the poliadic cult of Athena.

Burkert noted that the context of the inscription which mentions the charioteer is that of ephebic organization. The charioteer of Pallas

---

[107] Lambert (1999b: 124) argued that there may be a connection between the Salaminioi and the Praxiergidai other than that in the Plynteria; he suggested that in *IG* II² 2345, a list of names divided into *thiasoi*, where there is an overlap between membership of the *thiasoi* and membership of the *genos* of the Salaminioi, there may also be an overlap between membership of the *thiasoi* and membership of the *genos* of the Praxiergidai; it depends on making connections through the inscription on an altar of Herakles Agora I 1052 (on which see Jameson 2000: 217–27). As a supporting argument he says that since the Praxiergidai were concerned with the Plynteria, which is linked with Aglauros, and since the Salaminioi had a priestess of Aglauros "who may have served the state cult on the Acropolis", there may have been a cultic association between the Praxiergidai and the Salaminioi and this may have been reflected in both *gene* being associated with the group of *thiasoi* in *IG* II² 2345.

[108] *IG* II² 2245. 299–300.

[109] See Burkert 1990: 78 and 83 n. 8; Billot 1997–8: 16.

is clearly the same person as the *kosmetes* in charge of the ephebes named in the preceding lines, Ga[ios?] Kalpournios Proklos.[110] In a much earlier inscription,[111] we saw, the *kosmetes* 'escorted Pallas to Phaleron and joined in bringing her in from there by torchlight'. It would therefore seem possible that Kalpournios Proklos was the charioteer of Athena in the sense that he drove the chariot that took the statue of Athena to Phaleron in the procession that I am arguing was part of the Plynteria, and brought it back, as a symbolic correlative of his sending out and bringing back the statue and the procession that escorted it. However, if that is right, if being char- ioteer of Pallas was a regular part of the duties and privileges of the *kosmetes*, why should Kalpournios Proklos have been specifically named in this inscription as being the charioteer of Pallas? Would it not have been self-evident that the man who was named as *kosmetes* would also have been Athena's charioteer?

It is possible that he was named despite the fact that this was part of the *kosmetes'* role in order to stress a religiously important part of his duties. But it is also possible that the two offices were not inextricably connected, that, at least sometimes, they were distinct. The office of *kosmetes* was, of course, a senior one; if it was the case that the *kosmetes* was sometimes also the charioteer of Pallas and sometimes not, why did this happen? Surely anyone could drive a chariot in a procession—if that is what being charioteer of Pallas entailed. But there is another possibility: that driving the chariot was correlative with providing that chariot—in which case it is possible that the expense may have been too onerous for some *kosmetai*. For in Athens the word 'charioteers' denoted a class of 'richest' citizens who had to furnish chariots for public service.[112] Therefore it is not impossible that the charioteer of Pallas was the man who both furnished and drove the chariot whose driving made him the char- ioteer of Pallas.

---

[110] The praenomen Gaios is omitted in the naming of the charioteer of Pallas, but then the demotic is not included either, presumably precisely because he had already been fully named twice.

[111] *IG* II² 1006.11–12.

[112] Ael. Dion. fr. η 11 Erbse, 196 Schwabe.

For this is all we know, that there was an office called 'charioteer of Pallas', we cannot be certain that the chariot he drove was considered to be the chariot of Pallas (however likely that may be), and it does not matter anyway. Our concern is to determine in what sense someone was a charioteer of Pallas in cult and above all, to which cult did this office belong. The obvious explanation is that the name of the office means that Athena's charioteer drove Athena, which, given Athenian religious assumptions, means, in cult, a statue of Athena; that the name of the office reflected the fact that he drove the chariot which was transporting a statue of Athena. Since the procession to Phaleron is the one procession in which we know that the ephebes were involved in escorting a statue of Athena, and since the office of Athena's charioteer has clear ephebic connections, it seems reasonable to conclude that Athena's charioteer drove the chariot in which Athena's statue was taken in procession to Phaleron and brought back again.

However, this conclusion may be the result of a culturally determined judgement, and, in addition, it cannot, of course, provide any independent evidence concerning the identity of the cult of which the procession to Phaleron was part. Since I am here constructing a case for the view that this procession was part of the Plynteria/Kallynteria nexus, and did not belong to the cult of Athena at Palladion, it is desirable to try to consider whether there are independent grounds for ascribing the office of Athena's charioteer to a particular cult, whether we can independently locate this office in a particular cultic environment.

Since there is no direct evidence, we need to construct a strategy that would help us locate a charioteer of Pallas more generally in the Athenian conceptual universe. I suggest that a first step should be to consider how, if at all, chariots are associated with Athena's cults in Athens and especially also with the representation 'Athena being driven in a chariot'. Then we should try to determine whether there are any elements that recur in the various manifestations of that representation and perhaps also more generally in the contexts in which Athena's cults are associated with chariots. This should allow us to determine the cultic environment or environments to which such common elements had belonged and as a result to place the office of Athena's charioteer within the Athenian conceptual universe. I shall consider below what may or may not be deduced from this placing.

The most obvious association between a cult of Athena and chariots is the fact that there were chariot competitions at the Panathenaia; among these the competition in which a 'dismounter', *apobates*, jumped from a moving chariot and ran beside it was a symbolically very important event in Athenian perceptions.[113] I will consider below the *aition* of this competition and Athena's involvement.

An important manifestation of the representation 'Athena being driven in a chariot', indeed an important association between Athena and chariots, was located at the beginning of Athena's involvement with Athens and expressed in a privileged context: the representation of chariots on the west pediment of the Parthenon postulates that Athena and Poseidon arrived in a chariot at the time of their contest over the sovereignty of Attica.[114] Athena's chariot is driven by Nike, since she will be the victor of the contest (Poseidon's chariot is driven by his wife Amphitrite). Since this arrival led to Athena becoming Athens' poliadic deity and her cult being installed on the Acropolis, the arrival of Athena in a chariot may have come to be perceived as correlative with the installation of her cult on the Acropolis. It was certainly part of the privileged version of the story of the contest that led to the establishment of Athena as the poliadic deity of Athens, the establishment of the cult of Athena Polias.

Another manifestation of the representation 'Athena being driven in a chariot' was staged by Peisistratos and narrated by Herodotos and others:[115] the arrival of Peisistratos in a chariot accompanied by Phye, who was presented as Athena taking Peisistratos to the Acropolis. Connor[116] connected this story with the "cultural drama" involving a ceremonial appearance in the guise of a god and argued that in that performance Peisistratos presented himself as Athena's

---

[113] On chariot races, see Kyle 1992: 91–3; on the *apobates* race, see [Dem.] 61.23–9, with Crowther 1991: 174–6; Kyle 1992: 89–91.

[114] Irrespective of what particular moment in the story (if any) is represented on the pediment. See Hurwit (1999: 174–6) for the notion that it is unclear what particular moment in the story is represented on the pediment.

[115] Hdt. 1.60; Kleidemos *FGrH* 323 F 15; Arist. *Ath. Pol.* 14.iv; see also the discussion in Rhodes 1981: 205–6 ad loc. with a list of sources.

[116] Connor 1987: 42–47 = Connor 2000: 60–68.

assistant. He pointed out that in Kleidemos and in *Athenaion Politeia* Phye was the παραιβάτης, the 'goer-beside' or armed passenger alongside the charioteer, and therefore Peisistratos represented himself as Athena's charioteer. I believe that Connor is right that this is an important distinction.[117]

There is an iconographical parallel to this representation 'Athena as a kind of passenger in a chariot driven by an Athenian male' which also takes us back to the *apobates* and the Panathenaia. An image of the last decade of the sixth century shows Erichthonios driving a chariot and Athena running next to it as *apobates*.[118] This may be a refraction of a myth that functioned as a mythological paradigm for Peisistratos' performance, or it may be an expression of the idea that Erichthonios drove the chariot in an *apobates* competition when he first introduced the chariot and the *apobates* competition at the Panathenaia in the presence and/or with the approval of Athena.[119] For the chariot was believed to have been invented by Erichthonios, who first drove his invention at the first Panathenaia, and this is connected with the *apobates* competition.[120] According to the Atthidographers, Erichthonios was the first to celebrate the Panathenaia.[121] In this image, then, Athena' involvement with a chariot driven by a charioteer is associated with the Panathenaia and especially the *apobates*, and with primordial times. So, like her arrival in a

---

[117] He suggested that Athena is sometimes represented as *apobates* perhaps in reflection of her original arrival in Athens at the time of the contest with Poseidon.

[118] On the oinochoe Copenhagen National Musem Chr. VIII 340, *LIMC* Erechtheus no. 50.

[119] Two other images also show Erichthonios in a chariot in the presence of Athena: *LIMC* Erechtheus nos. 49, 51.

[120] See e.g. Marmor Parium *FGrH* 239 A 10; see Neils 1992b: 21; Parker 2005a: 254. The notion that the chariot was invented by Erichthonios is not in conflict with the notion that Athena and Poseidon arrived in a chariot at the time of their contest. For Erichthonios' invention introduced the chariot to the human sphere—a distinction made explicit, for example, in the story that the daughters of Kekrops were the first to weave woollen clothes *for mortals* (Phot., Sud., s.v. *protonion*; cf. Gourmelen 2005: 161).

[121] Hellanikos *FGrH* 323a F 2; Androtion *FGrH* 324 F 2; Marmor Parium *FGrH* 239 A 10; Istros *FGrH* 334 F 4; see Jacoby 1954: i. 25, 629–32. On these and the other *aitia* of the Panathenaia, see Parker 2005a: 254–6, 381. I return to these *aitia* in Chapter 5, section 2 below. I am not, incidentally, concerned here with the question of the relationship between Erechtheus and Erichthonios.

chariot for the contest represented on the Parthenon, this association is also connected with Athena's poliadic cult and with primordiality. There is also a connection with an aspect of the installation of the cult in this instance as well; for according to a myth reflected in Apollodoros, Erichthonios set up the statue of Athena on the Acropolis.[122]

How does the Peisistratos episode relate to these concepts, if at all? Clearly, since the performance related to the governance of the polis, and the message was that Athena was taking Peisistratos to her own Acropolis, which was dominated by her poliadic cult, that episode also involved, above all, Athena's poliadic cult. Connor cites Burkert's view that a kingship ritual underlies the *apobates* competition,[123] and suggests that the performance involving Peisistratos and Phye was a reversal of the ancient kingship ritual, for it is not Peisistratos who is seeking power, but Phye impersonating Athena who is the armed passenger, and also a different kind of reversal of the Panathenaic procession in which the citizens processed, some by chariot, to Athena's sanctuary. In Peisistratos' performance Phye impersonating Athena is returning to the Acropolis. I do not know whether or not a kingship ritual underlies the *apobates* competition, but though it is possible to see the performance involving Peisistratos and Phye as a reversal of the Panathenaic procession, it is also possible to see it as a more straightforward reflection of a procession that carried Athena, in the form of her poliadic statue, back to the Acropolis after it had been taken to Phaleron and purified in the sea.

If it is right that the schema 'arrival of Athena in a chariot' represented the notion of Athena's arrival and installation as the poliadic deity of Athens, a schema 'arrival of Athena's statue in a chariot' would be likely to have been part of the same nexus of representations, would be likely to have been part of the poliadic cult, and to have involved an arrival of her statue at the Acropolis.

Is this a culturally determined judgement? Perhaps it is. However, I suggest that our brief investigation has uncovered a strong connection between the representation 'Athena being driven in a chariot' on the one hand and the poliadic cult and primordiality on the other. It has established that the notion of someone driving a chariot in which

---

[122] Apollod. 3.14.6. This is not necessarily in conflict with the belief that the statue had fallen from the sky. Setting it up was an important ritual act.

[123] Burkert 1966, 1990.

Athena is riding is located in Athena's poliadic cult and strongly associated with primordial times. We also found that the notion of Athena's statue being brought back to the Acropolis in a chariot, which is what took place on my reconstruction of the Phaleron procession, would have been very significant in the Athenian imaginaire, for it would have been perceived as re-enacting, and evoking, the installation of Athena as the poliadic deity of Athens.

In these circumstances, I submit, it is very difficult to doubt that the charioteer of Pallas drove (and perhaps financed) the chariot in which the statue of Athena Polias was driven from and back to the Acropolis in the procession to and from Phaleron during the festival nexus of the Plynteria and Kallynteria. If the reconstruction of the mythicoritual environment to which the charioteer of Pallas belonged conducted above is right, this office would not have been part of the cult of Athena at Palladion; for the cult of Athena at Palladion was not the poliadic cult, and it was not associated with primordiality and the early history of Athens, since, as we shall see in Chapter 4, the Athenians only acquired the Palladion after the Trojan War, that is in the later part of the heroic age.

It could be argued that an office involving a chariot would be most likely to be part of the Panathenaia festival, which was symbolically connected with the chariot and the *apobates*. However, the particular representation 'Athena being driven in a chariot' is connected more strongly with other aspects of the poliadic cult, especially with the installation of the poliadic cult. Of course, if it is right that the office charioteer of Pallas was connected with the movement of a statue, this would exclude the Panathenaia. So either the charioteer of Pallas had a role in the Panathenaia that did not involve the movement of the statue in a chariot, or he was the driver of the chariot in which the statue was taken to Phaleron and brought back in the context of another festival nexus of the poliadic cult, the Plynteria/Kallynteria. The possibility cannot be excluded that the charioteer of Pallas may have had a role in both the Plynteria/Kallynteria nexus and the Panathenaia. But I suggest that the argument set out here leads to the conclusion that, whatever else he may have done, he almost certainly drove the chariot that took Athena's statue back to the Acropolis from Phaleron, and this was—among other things—a re-enactment of Athena's arrival and installation as the poliadic deity of Athens.

Yet another argument in favour of the view that the statue of the poliadic cult was taken to Phaleron in the course of the Plynteria emerges, I will now suggest, from the relationship between Phaleron and the locality Skiron, on the road to Eleusis, which was the destination of another procession from the centre that took place about two weeks after the Plynteria; for this relationship, I will argue, may suggest that a movement of the statue to Phaleron at the Plynteria would have had a special significance.

The first link between Phaleron and Skiron is provided by the names, Skiron on the one hand, and Athena's cult epithet at Phaleron, Athena Skiras, on the other, and the associated mythology.[124] Whether or not Athena Skiras had a sanctuary at Skiron is unclear, and in any case does not concern us here. Certainly, Athena was involved in the festival Skira or Skirophoria, the procession of which went to Skiron in Skirophorion. Another connection between Phaleron and Skiron is that, as Calame first pointed out, on a conceptual map Phaleron was in some ways correlative with Skiron:[125] Phaleron was perceived to be at the edges of the *asty*, at the interface of an extended city centre and the sea. Skiron was perceived as the border between the 'urban' part of the polis and the in-between, the not-*asty* and not-border/periphery segment of the polis. In certain contexts the in-between space and the periphery could be subsumed into a category not-*asty*, and Skiron could symbolically drift into the role of border between centre and periphery—hence the notion that it had been at the border between Athens and Eleusis which does not correspond to historical reality.[126] Also, I hope to have shown elsewhere,[127] the relationships between the centre of the *asty*, Skiron, and Phaleron are also implicated in the Eleusinian nexus.

The Skir- names and epithets are associated with both Athens and Megara.[128] In Attica they are associated with frontier areas; first,

---

[124] See p. 35.

[125] Calame 1990: 359; cf. 344–64 passim.

[126] [Sourvinou-Inwood's footnote ran 'Paus. 1.36.4: check', but that text does not speak of a boundary; Paus. 1.38.1 puts the boundary elsewhere, at Rheitoi.]

[127] Sourvinou-Inwood (1997a), which bears on all the matters discussed in this paragraph.

[128] For Skiron or Skeiron the Megarian, see Plut. *Thes.* 10.3; Paus. 1.44.6; Kearns 1989: 198.

frontiers between the Athenian polis and Megara: Salamis (whose ancient name was said to be Skiras and where there was a sanctuary of Athena Skiras)[129] and Eleusis; second, frontiers between the *asty* and the non-*asty* sections of the polis, Skiron and Phaleron. The two categories become somewhat blurred when it is considered that Skiron was understood as a mythological border with Eleusis and that Phaleron, being on the sea (and Athens' old harbour), could also be considered as on the frontier (in these conceptual, fluid, perceptions of frontier), especially while the Megarians held Salamis. This is illustrated with reference to that segment of the coast in the Athenian myth that presents itself as history, the story that Solon lured the Megarians into a trap, by dressing up youths in the clothes of the women who were celebrating the preliminary part of the Thesmophoria on the shore at Kolias.[130]

Processions are polysemic ritual movements. Among other things, they articulate, confirm, and stress relationships, between different sanctuaries and/or between different parts of the territory (above all various relationships between the centre and other parts of the territory), as well as perceptions pertaining to territory, such as, among other things, the notion of symbolically 'covering', ensuring, and reinforcing through ritual movements, divine protection for different parts of the city's territory.[131] The festival Skira or Skirophoria took place just over two weeks after the Plynteria, on 12 Skirophorion. Its local dimension, the celebrations by women in the demes, does not concern us here. It is the central polis facet of the festival that concerns us, the facet that involves a procession from the centre to the conceptual frontier at Skiron. The festival almost certainly belonged primarily to Demeter, but Athena clearly also had a role in it.[132] At this festival a procession went from the Acropolis to Skiron; in this procession the priestess of Athena Polias and the priest of Poseidon Erechtheus—and also the priest of Helios—walked out

---

[129] According to Strabo 9.393 Skiras was the ancient name of Salamis; sanctuary of Athena Skiras on Salamis: Hdt. 8.94.

[130] Plut. *Sol.* 8.4; Brumfield 1981: 82.

[131] See especially Graf 1996: 55–65.

[132] See e.g. Schol. Ar. *Thesm.* 834; Schol. Ar. *Ekkles.* 18. See on the Skira Brumfield 1981: 156–81; cf. also Deubner 1969: 40–50; Parke 1977: 156–62; Burkert 1983: 143–9; Calame 1990: 341–4; Parker 2005a: 172–7, 480.

under a canopy called *skiron*, carried by Eteoboutadai.[133] Their destination was a temple, almost certainly of Demeter and Kore, though Athena and Poseidon were undoubtedly worshipped there as well. The fleece called 'Fleece of Zeus', which is connected with purifications, was used in that procession.[134] As we saw a fleece was also mentioned in the Praxiergidai decree in connection with the Plynteria which, of course, had a strong purificatory facet.

If the reconstruction according to which the procession of the Plynteria went to Phaleron is right, then the two processions would form a kind of pair:[135] there would have been two ritual movements—just over two weeks apart—the first of the statue of the poliadic deity, the second of her priestess, from the centre to two symbolically significant, and corresponding, frontiers of the *asty*, at the sea, and at the conceptual frontier on the road to Eleusis—and back. Not only do these two places correspond with each other in the conceptual map of Athens, they are also connected through the cult of Athena Skiras, and also, more generally, the Skir- element. Because they were both symbolic frontiers, indeed symbolically charged symbolic frontiers, the ritual movement to these two mythicoritually connected localities, from the centre to Phaleron and from the centre to Skiron, symbolically covered, first, the whole *asty*, and then, through metonymy, the whole Athenian territory, whose connection to the centre and to the poliadic cult was reinforced through these symbolically charged movements.

These two processions, to Skiron and to Phaleron, that is, to the frontiers of the *asty*, belong, I suggest, to a special variant of Graf's category 'centrifugal processions', specifically a variant of the type of 'centrifugal procession that leads from the city centre to an outlying sanctuary'.[136] The two sanctuaries which (on the reconstruction proposed here) were linked to the centre and the poliadic cult through these two processions were pseudo-outlying sanctuaries, as it were: they were outlying as far as the *asty* and the symbolic centre

---

[133] Lysimachides *FGrH* 366 F 3.

[134] Suda, s.v. *Dios kôidion.*

[135] That the festivals of Thargelion and Skirophorion relate to each other within a wider, end of the year, ritual nexus is widely accepted (Burkert 1983: 135–58; N. Robertson 2004: 121).

[136] Graf 1996.

that was the sanctuary of the poliadic cult are concerned. If the reconstructed representation of the two processions as 'paired' is right, these two 'paired' processions, in the last two months of the Athenian year, which preceded the month in which was celebrated the whole polis festival of the poliadic deity, the Panathenaia, would have renewed the symbolic bonds between on the one hand the centre, and especially the poliadic cult, and on the other the *asty* and its interface, and through that the whole territory.

But if the conclusion drawn from all these converging arguments is right, how do we explain what appears to be the one remaining factor in favour of the view that what was washed in the sea was the Palladion, not the image of Athena Polias, namely the mytheme that appears to be an *aition* for the purification of the Palladion in the sea, the story in a Patmos scholion that it was brought down to the sea and washed by Demophon?[137] There are two possibilities, first, that two different statues of Athena were bathed at Phaleron, the statue of Athena Polias at the Plynteria, and the Palladion; and second, that the mytheme does not reflect an *aition* for a ritual involving the Palladion but is a later construct that does not reflect that cult. In Chapter 4 below I shall present a detailed case in favour of the second possibility.[138]

iii. 26 Thargelion: procession to Phaleron and *loutron*

I hope to have shown that there is a very strong case for concluding that the procession of the Plynteria took the statue of Athena Polias to Phaleron where it was bathed in the sea, and that this is the procession that is referred to by Philochoros and the inscriptions. I will now consider further what we can reconstruct of this procession,

---

[137] Schol. Patm. Dem 23.71. See also Parker's (1996: 308 n. 63) comment that the case for a procession associated with the Palladion rests merely on the story that the image was washed by Demophon.

[138] Of course the fact that the procession to Phaleron and the *loutron* are not mentioned in the *aition* of the Plynteria is not an argument against the notion that they were part of this festival. Even a superficial comparison between the *aitia* of Athenian festivals (conveniently set out in Parker 2005a: 380–3) and the rituals in those festivals shows that the match between myths and ritual actions can be far from close.

and the associated ritual, what ritual skeleton can be reconstructed for 26 Thargelion. I will not take into account here the comparative material that will be discussed in section iv, for reasons that will become apparent in that discussion, with one exception which will be appropriately signalled and concerns an individual ritual.

First, the date. I suggested in section 1 that the procession left the temple on what I argued was the second day of the Plynteria festival, on 26 Thargelion. Since the procession did not go out 'by torchlight', it went in the daytime after the night of the 26th, perhaps, as was the case with, for example, the Panathenaia procession, at daybreak. But the fact that the procession returned in torchlight means that that procession did not return on 26 Thargelion, but on the 27th.

Second, who is responsible for the procession? In Philochoros it is the *nomophylakes*,[139] in the inscriptions it is the ephebes, but not on their own. The ephebic inscription *IG* II² 1011[140] states explicitly that the procession to Phaleron was sent out, the statue taken out and brought back, by the *gennetai* and a unit representing the whole polis, in this case the ephebes. Of course, given the nature of the document, it is the ephebes' contribution that is at the centre—as was the case with the *nomophylakes* in the surviving reflections of Philochoros' text. In other ephebic inscriptions the *gennetai* are not mentioned explicitly, but their participation is indicated by the expressions 'joined in taking out Pallas' (συνεξήγαγον τὴν Παλλάδα) and 'joined in bringing her in (συνεισήγαγον) again'.[141] If my reconstruction is right, and this procession is indeed part of the Plynteria, the *gennetai* who were partly responsible were, of course, the Praxiergidai.

It is unclear whether the *nomophylakes* replaced the ephebes when the ephebate was discontinued under the oligarchic government of 322–318 or the ephebes replaced the *nomophylakes* when democracy was restored in 307/6, but the *nomophylakes* and the ephebes were functionally equivalent in representing the whole polis.[142] Thus, the procession that took the statue to Phaleron was the responsibility of a joint agency, on the one hand the members of the *genos* responsible

---

[139] Philochoros *FGrH* 328 F64b, (a) and (b).
[140] Quoted above, p. 161.
[141] See p. 161 above.
[142] See Humphreys 2004: 117.

for these rituals which included secret rites, and on the other one or other representative of the whole polis.

I argued that the procession's destination was the sanctuary of Athena Skiras at Phaleron, and that from that sanctuary the statue was taken to the beach by the Praxiergidai, I suggest only the female Praxiergidai, and bathed in the sea by the two Loutrides. I also argued that it is likely that the woollen *peplos* was not washed in the sea, but in fresh water on the Acropolis, on the first day of the Plynteria, 25 Thargelion. If that is right, it may have been taken to Phaleron in the procession, if the dressing of the statue with the laundered *peplos* took place at Phaleron; or it may have been left behind on the Acropolis and reunited with the statue when the latter was brought back to the Acropolis. I shall return to this question in section 5 below.

I suggested above that *IG* I^3 7, if correctly restored, indicates an intermediary period between the removal of the *peplos* and the washing of the statue, during which the latter was dressed in the *chiton* provided by the Praxiergidai. Whether or not this reconstruction is right, since the procession was part of abnormal time, the statue would not have been dressed in its normal dress, the *peplos*. Since we know that in the early part of the festival it was covered up in a cloth, I suggest that Athena's statue was taken to Phaleron covered up in a cloth—whether or not under that cloth the statue was wearing the *chiton* that, on my reconstruction, was provided by the Praxiergidai and was worn during the intermediary period of abnormality.[143]

The dressing of the statue with the laundered *peplos* by the Praxiergidai was a ceremonial act, and clearly would not have taken place as the statue was being brought out of the sea. But since this statue was perceived to be correlative with the goddess, it would not have been exposed naked as it was brought out of the water. So what had covered its nakedness at that moment? Certainly not the same cloth that had covered it before, in which it had been wrapped when it was

---

[143] If I am wrong and there was no period of abnormality, then what I suggested took place before the statue was dressed in a *chiton* would have happened on the day of the Plynteria; that is, on the day of the Plynteria the priestess removed the *peplos* and gave it to the Praxiergidai, who then removed the *kosmos* and covered up the statue.

'dirty' before the bath. It would have been wrapped up in a clean cloth, in a way comparable to that in which Aphrodite is shown being wrapped up in a cloth (albeit in these cases the goddess is not shown naked, but already dressed) as she emerges from the sea in representations of her birth.[144]

If the statue was dressed with the laundered *peplos* (by the Praxiergidai) at Phaleron, did this happen on the beach where, on my reconstruction, only the female Praxiergidai had performed the statue's purification, or in a more formal environment, that is, the sanctuary of Athena Skiras, a sanctuary of Athena at Phaleron with which both Aglauros as a cult recipient and the priestess of Aglauros were associated? Again, I shall return to this question in section 5.

Before the Praxiergidai dressed it in the laundered *peplos*, the statue would have worn the cloth in which it was wrapped when brought out of the sea, probably as a *himation*, and there would have been a change of garments from this *himation* to the *peplos* when the Praxiergidai dressed the statue. This cloth in which the statue was wrapped when it was brought out of the sea was perhaps a robe, *pharos*, such as the *pharos* made from pure wool that was offered to Athena on 29 Thargelion,[145] perhaps for next year's Plynteria, in a modality that helped convey the notion of continuity and endless repetition in the celebration of this festival and so also in the relationship between the polis and its poliadic deity. I suggest that it is likely that, as part of the same ritual stressing of the cyclical nature of the rite, one year's clean cloth that covered the statue as it came out of the sea eventually became next year's 'dirty' cloth that covered up the statue before it was purified.

In any case, this state of affairs, in which the clean statue was wrapped in a *himation* as it emerged from the sea, may well be echoed in a formulation in an inscription which will be discussed below:[146] if the formulation]ἱμάτιον ἐξάγωσιν in *IG* II² 1060+1036 fr. b.3, which, I argue, refers to the procession of the Plynteria, is to be

---

[144] See e.g. on the Ludovisi throne and on a Locrian pinax, Simon 1998: 217 fig. 235, 218 fig. 240.

[145] Lambert 2002: 3 A ll.7–8 on p. 374 (=*LSS* 10 A.7–8). For this calendar, see now the text and commentary in Lambert 2002: 353–99 (*SEG* LII 48).

[146] In section 5.

reconstructed ἕδος καὶ] ἱμάτιον ἐξάγωσιν, which is one of the two most likely reconstructions, it would appear to put some emphasis on the *himation*. I will discuss the formulation and those most likely reconstructions in the reading of the inscription. Here I will mention, both as a culturally specific eye-opener and as an illustration of Greek ritual mentality, that in one comparable festival that almost certainly involved the *loutron* of a statue emphasis was put on the carrying of the cloth: one of four -*phoros* offices in the procession for Artemis Daitis at Ephesos, which will be considered below,[147] was the σπειροφόρος, the carrier of a wrapping cloth, which would have enveloped the statue when it was taken out of the sea. This suggests that the possibility of an emphasis on the cloth used to wrap the statue as it came out of the water is not a culturally determined construct, but something that was consistent with Greek ritual mentality since it was attested in Greek ritual practice.

As we saw, a cake of dried figs called *hegeteria* was carried in the procession of the Plynteria and our sources connect this *hegeteria* with primordiality and autochthony. This, then, was a 'special food' that, since it was carried in the procession, would have been consumed at the procession's destination at Phaleron. As we shall see below,[148] 'special food' was also involved in at least two other rituals in which the deity's statue was taken out and washed in the sea. In those cases the statue is given some special food as offering by the sea—salt in one case, cakes of ground barley called *psaista* in the other. On that analogy, I suggest that it is possible that the *hegeteria* may also have been offered as a meal to Athena, possibly by the shore by the Praxiergidai—if not it would have been set in front of the goddess at the sanctuary of Athena Skiras.

Since the procession returned 'by torchlight', that is after the sunset that followed the day of 26 Thargelion, and since the Athenian day was reckoned from sunset to sunset,[149] the procession returned on the 27th, and at the end of the 26th it was still at Phaleron. I shall

---

[147] In section 3 iv.

[148] In section 3 iv.

[149] I am not convinced by the attempt to revise the established view and argue that days were counted from sunrise to sunrise (Pritchett 1979: 217–18, 1982); see the comment by Richardson (1981: 186), to which Pritchett's (1987: 179–88) response is equally unconvincing.

return to some of the rites of 26 Thargelion below, after I have briefly considered some comparative material.

iv. Other rites, other festivals: comparisons and reconstructions

I discussed the general methodological question of the deployment of comparative material in Chapter 1. One particular aspect of ritual logic that material from other cults can allow us to reconstruct is some of the parameters that shaped a festival nexus, and which therefore should help shape our attempted reconstruction. A procession that takes the cult statue to the sea where it is immersed in water and purified, and then returns it to its proper place (because, as we shall see, it also structures other festivals), constitutes a ritual schema, a composite ritual schema, shaped by the combination of more than one schema: procession is obviously one ritual schema, which here interacts with the schema 'removal of the cult statue from its proper place and return', which often occurs without a *loutron* in the sea, as, for example, in the case of the City Dionysia; 'purification in water' in the variant 'immersion in the sea' is another such schema and of course other schemata such as 'sacrifice', 'offering a meal to the deity', and ritual acts such as 'dressing the statue' also came into play. This composite ritual schema also has a variation in which the statue was taken to be washed and purified in a river.

I will now begin the consideration of comparative material that may help our attempted reconstruction of the Plynteria and Kallynteria with a more narrowly focused culturally specific eye-opener. If we simply assume that we can reconstruct what acts were involved in the cleaning of a temple, we will implicitly deploy culturally determined assumptions about what is likely to have been involved; such deployment is inevitable, but it can be somewhat restricted through considering what were the main lines of the acts involved in other rituals for which more information is available. Thus, we may infer that the physical sweeping and other obvious cleaning activities would be part of the process of cleaning a temple. But it is by considering another Athenian cult that we may get a less culturally determined idea of the things that were part of such notions in Athenian mentality.

A decree of the 280s BC concerning the cult of Aphrodite Pandemos in Athens mentions a procession and purification of the shrine and statues and other 'physical renewal' activities: it decrees that when the procession for Aphrodite Pandemos takes place the *astynomoi* are required to prepare a dove for purification of the shrine and wipe the altars and pitch the doors and wash the statues (λοῦσαι τὰ ἔδη).[150] This gives us an idea of what may be involved in the cleaning of a sanctuary; it should not be used as a parallel for filling in blanks, since, for example, the dove was goddess- and cult-specific. It provides some knowledge concerning the parameters that shaped the operation of ritual cleanings, that includes, for example, the fundamental connection between 'physical renewal' activities, washing the statues and purification, and the goddess- and cult-specific modality of purification.

Another variation of this type of use of comparative material is the reconstruction of knowledge about specific compatibilities between ritual elements. For example, comparative material can tell us that a purification ritual involving a statue being washed in the sea is compatible with sacrifice by the sea. This does *not* tell us whether or not a sacrifice by the sea took place at the Plynteria. But it does tell us that sacrifice by the sea in a purification ritual involving a statue being washed in the sea was compatible with Greek ritual mentality—at least in certain circumstances. For there is an example of a purification of a statue and sacrifice by the sea, if it is right that in a heavily restored prescription in a Koan decree from the first part of the third century BC [151] the priestess of Kourotrophos is to sacrifice a pig or a sheep by the sea as part of the purification of the statue of Kourotrophos. This is the prescription for an ad hoc purification, not part of a festival, that is, of a complex, articulated nexus, though the fact that it is stated that the priestess is to take out the statue according to established customs may conceivably suggest that a regular taking out of the statue and purification by the sea may also have been practised. Be that as it may, if the restorations are right, it indicates that sacrificing by the sea in the context of a purification of a statue by the sea was a Greek modality, not a culturally determined construct.

---

[150] *IG* II²659 (*LSCG* 39) 20–7; see Pirenne-Delforge 1994: 29–32; Dillon 2002: 134–5; Parker 2005a: 461. On cleaning and bathing statues, see esp. Bettinetti 2001: 143–60 (though see n. 97).

[151] *LSCG* 154 B 24–5; see Bettinetti 2001: 159; Lupu 2005: 42.

In an inscription from Kyzikos of the first century BC [152] a group of women holders of certain cult offices belonging to the cult of the Mother want to dedicate a bronze image of the priestess of the Mother, Kleidike, who had given them a gift towards the rites which they performed; they are the women who perform the 'adornments' (οἱ κόσμοι) for the Mother, the *hieropoioi* who are called 'of the sea' (θαλάσσιαι), and the priestesses who are joined with them. Bettinetti takes the role of the women who perform the 'adornments' to refer to the dressing of the statue, and suggests that the *hieropoioi* 'of the sea' may refer to women who purified the statue in the sea.[153] If this is right, the two groups would be performing the tasks which were performed by the Loutrides and other women of the *genos* of the Praxiergidai at the Athenian Plynteria. The priestesses who are joined with these two sets of cult personnel may be equivalent to the priestess of Aglauros being associated with these rites. The gift by the priestess of the cult whose statue is involved towards the rites performed by these women is reminiscent of the fact that the priestess of Athena Polias praised in the honorary decree *IG* II² 776, ll. 18–20, and had allocated to the Praxiergidai for their ancestral sacrifice 100 drachmas from her own resources. There are, then, some comparabilities and some differences between the ritual nexus at Kyzikos—on the interpretation followed here—and the nexus of the Plynteria in Athens.

A further level of complexity in the comparability of this ritual of the cult of the Mother with other Greek rituals is the fact that the Mother is an extremely complex and fluid deity, worshipped in Anatolia, in Greece, and in Rome. There were different cults and personalities of the Anatolian Mother, in different places, and they interacted with each other. Like all divine personalities, but, because of her particular circumstances, much more than most, she is constantly shape-shifting, developing and changing in the course of time, and through space, through—among others things—continuous interactions, assimilations, associations, influences, with a variety of other divine personalities, Anatolian and Greek.[154] However, this cult, and the cult of Artemis at Ephesos, another goddess whose

---

[152] Michel no. 537.
[153] See the discussion in Bettinetti 2001: 159–60.
[154] I have discussed this in Sourvinou-Inwood 2005: 135–40 with bib.

divine personality included Anatolian elements,[155] were Greek cults, whatever the origins of their constituent elements,[156] and therefore they were structured by Greek ritual logic, and Greek religious mentality in general.

The cult of Artemis at Ephesos included a festival, celebrated in honour of Artemis under the epithet Daitis, that was probably shaped by the ritual schemata 'removal of a cult statue from its proper place and return' and '*loutron* in the sea', in the version involving a procession taking the statue some distance from the sanctuary and its purification in the sea.[157] We know that the procession went to a place outside the city, which was probably near the sea,[158] and that a meal of salt was offered to the goddess there. According to the *aition*,[159] Klymene, the daughter of the king, had gone to this place with youths and maidens and the statue and had decided to entertain the goddess; so the maidens laid down the statue on a bed of celery and other unnamed plants and the youths entertained it with a meal of salt. When the next year this entertainment was not repeated the goddess was angry and sent a plague in which youths and maidens died; in response to an oracle they propitiated the goddess and gave her meals in the manner of the youths and maidens—and, it is understood, instituted this as an annual event.

The reason for thinking that a purificatory bath may have been part of this festival is as follows. As was pointed out by Heberdey,[160]

---

[155] See most recently, Morris 2001.

[156] I have discussed interactions between Greek and Anatolian elements in the construction of Greek divine personalities in colonial areas in Sourvinou-Inwood 2005: passim; see esp. 363–95.

[157] *Etym. Magn.* s.v. Daitis (p. 252.11 ff.). On this procession and festival, see Heberdey 1904; Nilsson 1906: 244–6; Calame 1977: 179–83; Bettinetti 2001: 229–31; Steiner 2001: 110. This procession cannot be the same as that in the local festival of Artemis at which Xenophon of Ephesos, *Ephesiaca* 1, 2–3 sets part of his story; for the latter involves a procession from the city to the sanctuary and there is nothing else that fits what little we know about the Daitis procession—other than the participation of maidens and youths, which is unlikely to have been limited to one procession. On processions in the cult of Artemis at Ephesos, see Knibbe 1995: 153–4. Dillon 2002: 216 wrongly ascribes this festival to Hera.

[158] Given the salt works mentioned in *Etym. Magn.* s.v. Daitis (p. 252.11 ff.). See Heberdey 1904: 211.

[159] *Etym. Magn.* s.v. Daitis.

[160] Heberdey 1904: 211–13.

an inscription of the first century BC[161] that lists certain fees includes a group of names of cult offices: a cult office involving the carrying of salt, ἁλοφόρος, another involving the carrying of celery, σελεινοφόρος, which clearly belonged to this procession in which salt was offered to the goddess; then follows μολπός, a musician; then σπειροφόρος, carrier of a wrapping cloth, and then κοσμοφόρος, carrier of jewellery.[162] It is likely that all four had a place in the same ritual, which, given the first two offices, would have been the procession for Artemis under the epithet Daitis.[163] I submit that the fact that there was a σπειροφόρος, carrier of a wrapping cloth, which indicates the need for a wrap, such as would be required if the statue was washed in the sea (for it would be enveloped in a wrapping cloth when taken out of the sea), adds support to the reading that in this festival the statue was washed in the sea. The office of κοσμοφόρος also provides support for this reading, for it indicates that the statue's jewellery was carried at some stage during the procession, and that therefore the statue and its apparel were manipulated, which in this context would suggest that the statue was bathed in the sea.[164]

If it is right that this procession involved the *loutron* of the goddess in the sea, what does the evidence tell us about this particular instance of the schema 'procession that takes the cult statue to the

---

[161] Wankel, Merkelbach, et al. 1979–81: no. 14. ll. 19–23.

[162] See Heberdey 1904: 212. See also Nilsson 1906: 244. An elaborate necklace has been discovered in the sanctuary of Artemis at Ephesos that appears to have belonged to the cult statue (Bammer 1991: 129 and pl. XXXVa–b; Bammer 1998: 440). There was also an office of *kosmeteira* in this cult (Knibbe 1995: 153 with refs.), but they could have done the 'adorning' anywhere and at any time, not necessarily (or not only) at this procession.

[163] The festival could conceivably, but need not, also have involved a δειπνοφοριακὴ πομπή, as mentioned in Wankel, Merkelbach, et al. 1979–81: no. 1577; see Heberdey 1904: 214; Nilsson 1906: 245–6.

[164] Bettinetti (2001: 231) acknowledges that these offices make us think of dressing and undressing the statue, but she does not believe this ritual included a *loutron*. The only (implicit) arguments set out in support of this belief are (Bettinetti 2001: 231 n. 720) first, that Heberdey's comparison with the Athenian Plynteria is invalid because she takes the view that there was no procession to Phaleron at the Plynteria and no *loutron* of the statue; and, secondly, Nilsson's (1906: 246) argument that if there had been a bath it would be odd that the *aition* does not mention it. However, the *aition* is focused on the name, and the correlation between ritual meal, the mythological meal, and the name; it cannot be assumed to have included a summary of the facts concerning the festival.

sea where the statue is immersed in water and purified'? First, maidens and youths had a significant ritual part and the *aition* is structured by a schema which also characterized other mythicoritual nexuses involving adolescents.[165] Second, the statue was offered a special, in this case abnormal, meal, and this was coupled with the abnormality of the statue reclining on celery. In other rituals, we shall see, it is the worshippers who sometimes recline on beds of a particular, religiously significant, plant in the course of ritual dining. Third, the carrying of the 'adornment' in the procession suggests that the statue was dressed and adorned before it was returned to the sanctuary. Fourth, the existence of the office σπειροφόρος suggests that the wrapping cloth, presumably for wrapping the statue when it was taken out of the sea, was perceived as a not insignificant element.

The Tonaia[166] was a festival celebrated in honour of Hera at Samos. It commemorated the miraculously foiled attempt to steal the goddess' statue and involved a procession from the city to the sanctuary, which was by the sea. The statue was removed from the temple and taken to the shore and hidden, searched for,[167] purified in the sea, and given a meal of *psaista*, cakes of ground barley, by the sea before it was eventually returned to the temple. Thus, in this festival, the schemata 'removal of statue from its proper place and return to it' and '*loutron* of the statue in the sea' are combined with another schema, the schema 'ritual search' which, like the schema 'removal and return of the statue', is sometimes part of a festival of advent. The Tonaia was indeed an advent festival celebrating (also) the deity's arrival.[168]

---

[165] See Calame 1977: 180–1, 187, 190, 192–3. The particular forms of the adolescents' involvement and the extent to which this festival includes transformations of initiatory rites do not concern me here.

[166] See Menodotos of Samos *FGrH* 541 F 1. See Burkert 1979: 129–30; Burkert 1985: 134–5; Graf 1985: 93–6. On the Tonaia, see also O'Brien 1993: 54–62.

[167] Every year the statue was carried to the shore, Menodotos of Samos (*FGrH* 541 F 1) tells us; given the *aition* he has just set out, the implication is that it was then searched for and found (see on this, Graf 1985: 95 n. 133, who classifies the Samian rite as a search ritual and compares it with other search rituals).

[168] Cf. e.g. Burkert 1997: 24. Some advent festivals included a ritual search. One type of ritual search is that in the Tonaia, involving a search for the deity's statue, which reflected and re-enacted a mythological search for a lost statue. A related type of ritual search, which also culminated in an event that gave material manifestation to the divine presence, did not involve the deity's statue, but something else related to the god. On search rituals in advent festivals, see also Sourvinou-Inwood 2005: 346–51.

The concept of primordiality was very significant in the Tonaia. First, the festival's *aition* involved both Karians and Leleges;[169] the Karians bound the statue with withies of willow (λύγος) when it was found and are associated with the ritual motif of wearing crowns of λύγος, the Leleges are connected with the foundation of the sanctuary. Second, the ritual included ritual dining on στιβάδες of λύγος, beds of willow leaves, crowned with wreaths of the same plant, Hera's sacred plant at that sanctuary.[170] In Greek religious mentality dining reclining on στιβάδες has connotations of dissolution of normality;[171] an established variant of this schema for ritual dining at a sanctuary during a festival involved, as here, reclining on beds of leaves of the relevant deity's sacred plant and wearing wreaths of the same plant.[172] At the Tonaia, as at the City Dionysia,[173] this schema goes together with a statue's removal and return, a re-enactment of a similar movement in the festival myth and also with dissolution of normality.

At the Tonaia the return of the statue to the temple was probably preceded by a stage in which it stood outside the temple on a base that has been discovered by the altar and has been connected with the goddess's 'epiphany' signalled by the statue's arrival.[174]

Clearly, in this festival also, the *loutron* of the cult statue is associated with abnormality and primordiality, purification, and special food offered to the statue by the sea. Here the removal and return of the statue is correlative with the nature of the festival as an advent festival. It is likely that for part of the festival the statue stood outside the temple by the altar. It is likely that this happened after the statue

[169] On Greek perceptions of the Karians and the Leleges, see Sourvinou-Inwood 2005: 268–75.

[170] στιβάδες of λύγος and λύγος the sacred plant of Hera at Samos: Menodotos of Samos *FGrH* 541 F 1; Nikainetos ap. Ath. 673a–c; Kron 1988: 138–41; cf. 138 n. 14 for references to discussions of στιβάδες; Graf 1985: 95. On στιβάδες see also e.g. Theocr. 7.67 ff.; and cf. Verpoorten 1945: 147–60; Versnel 1993: 242–3 and n. 48; further references and bib. in Burkert 1979: 164 n. 38; Henrichs 1982: 217 n. 44.

[171] Cf. Graf 1985: 95 with bibliography.

[172] I have discussed this type of ritual dining in Sourvinou-Inwood 2003a: 79–88.

[173] See Sourvinou-Inwood 2003a: 67–100.

[174] See Walter 1990: 53, also 52 fig. 42, 63. At least during part of the festival the statue stood outside the temple on a base by the altar: Graf 1985: 95–6. On the base, see also Walter 1976: 36, 98.

had been recovered, washed, and dressed, a display after its return, which expressed in concrete terms the arrival and presence of the goddess. In this festival there are two separate ritual movements before the statue was washed in the sea, first, the procession that went from the city to the sanctuary by the sea, and then the movement that involved the statue's removal from the temple and transport to the shore.

Whether or not an actual ritual is reflected in Kallimachos' hymn *On the Bath of Pallas* which speaks of a ritual at Argos, the *loutron* of a statue of Athena in the river Inachos,[175] the representation of the ritual in the poem was shaped and structured by Greek ritual knowledge and assumptions concerning either directly the *loutron* of a statue of Athena in the river Inachos, or the *loutra* of statues and the cult of Athena in general and Athena at Argos in particular. The fact that it was certainly the case that one statue of Athena at Argos was regularly undressed, since we know that there was a special term for the women who dressed it, Gerarades,[176] and therefore almost certainly washed it, makes it perhaps more likely that the poem indeed reflects or refracts an Argive ritual.

The hymn's first verse addresses the 'bath-pourers of Pallas', the maidens who undressed and bathed the statue. The statue is to be transported in a chariot drawn by horses, and this element, and Athena's association with chariots and horses, is stressed in this hymn.[177] The statue was dressed and beautified at the site of the *loutron*, for the girls are urged not to bring perfumes or alabasters or mirrors but olive oil for anointing Athena and a golden comb. It is possible that the statue was dressed again by the women called Gerarades who were the wives of Argive notables. The procession also involved youths who carried Diomedes' shield. The statue involved in this procession in Kallimachos' hymn is generally taken to be the Palladion,[178] and given the association with Diomedes' shield this is probably right. Since no male was allowed to see the statue

---

[175] On this rite in Kallimachos (*Hymn* 5): Calame 1977: 232–4; Dillon 2002: 132–3; Billot 1997–8: 12–17. On the cults of Athena at Argos, see Billot 1997–8: 7–52. On the question of the Trojan Palladion at Argos, see Billot 1997–8: 10–17.

[176] See *Anecd. Bekk.* 1.231.30–1; and see Billot 1997–8: 15, 46.

[177] Callim. *Hymn* 5. 2–12, 14, 43–4, 141–2.

[178] See esp. most recently, Billot 1997–8: 10–17, 52.

naked, the youths would not have taken part in the whole cere-mony.[179] For Kallimachos says that whoever sees 'city-holding Pallas' naked will be punished, and then he tells the story of the blinding of Teiresias, who saw Athena while she was bathing. He is saying that for a man to see the statue naked is equivalent to his seeing Athena herself naked.[180] According to Billot, this Argive procession inte-grated the education of both youths and maidens through specific pre-nuptial, pre-ephebic rites.[181] Be that as it may, it is certainly the case that, as in the festival at Ephesos, youths and maidens took part in this ritual.

The statue of Hera also received a ritual bath at Argos. Pausanias says that according to the Argives Hera bathed every year in the Kanathos spring and regained her virginity and this was told as part of the secrets during the rite they celebrate in honour of Hera.[182] As has been noted,[183] this suggests a rite involving only females in which the statue of Hera at Argos was washed. This *loutron* is clearly pre-nuptial, as was the bath of Hera's wooden image at the Daidala at Plataia.[184]

The composite schema 'removal of a statue from its temple to another place, immersion in the sea, and return' also probably structures another, possibly Athenian, ritual, this time of a male deity, that involves a very different type of immersion of a statue in the sea, which I have discussed elsewhere.[185] Plutarch and a fragment from Philochoros cited in a Homeric scholion, the text of which is uncertain, tell us that the Halaieis received an oracle that instructed them to dip Dionysos in the sea.[186] This seems to suggest a ritual

---

[179] Billot 1997–8: 13–14.

[180] Through this expression and also, in more complex ways, through the para-digm, which I cannot discuss, and which does not concern me here.

[181] Billot 1997–8: 15.

[182] Paus. 2.38.2–3. Cf. Hesych., *Etym. Magn.* s.v. Ἡρεσίδες: κόραι αἱ λουτρὰ κομίζουσαι τῇ Ἥρᾳ.

[183] See Dillon 2002: 132.

[184] On this pre-nuptial bath at the Daidala at Plataea, see Paus. 9.3.7 (with Schachter 1981: 246 n. 1); on the *aition* Plutarch fr. 157.6, see Schachter 1981: 245–6; Dillon 2002: 135; on the Daidala, see Burkert 1979: 132–4; Schachter 1981: 245–50; [Chaniotis 2002].

[185] Sourvinou-Inwood 2005: 190–206.

[186] Plut. *Mor.* 914D; Philochoros *FGrH* 328 F 191; cf. Jacoby 1954: i. 555–6 ad loc.; cf. Tümpel 1889: 681–96.

involving the immersion of a statue of Dionysos in the sea.[187] The location of this ritual is uncertain, it may have taken place at Halieis in the Argolid, but is more likely to have been Halai Aixonides in Attica.[188] I have argued that a ritual involving the immersion of a statue of Dionysos into the sea, and its retrieval, would be structured by two interacting schemata. One, the mythological schema 'Dionysos plunges into the sea', which helps structure the Homeric Lykourgos myth (in a scholion to which the fragment from Philochoros about this dipping rite is cited);[189] and two, a ritual schema associated with advent festivals, the schema structuring rituals in which the cult statue was removed from its usual place in the temple and then ceremonially brought back, after various rites had taken place— for example, at the Tonaia at Samos, we saw, after a search and other rites on the shore. I have argued that this 'dipping the statue' rite, the immersion of a statue of Dionysos into the sea and its retrieval, was part of an advent festival, in which the act involving the statue may have commemorated some mythological plunge of Dionysos, and in which the return of the statue was the focus of a ritual enactment of the god's arrival at his advent festival.

Whether or not this is right, there can be no doubt that the City Dionysia, which was structured by the schema 'removal of the cult statue from its proper place and return', was an advent festival. And we saw that of the festivals briefly considered here the Tonaia, which included the schema ritual search, also had a strong advent emphasis. What, then, of the removal and return of the statue of Athena Polias in the course of the Plynteria and Kallynteria nexus? Was that perceived to have involved, and brought about, the goddess's advent? I shall return to this question, and to a comparison between the applications of the schema 'removal and return of the statue' at the City Dionysia and at the Plynteria and Kallynteria nexus, after I have set out the attempted reconstruction of the ritual actions on 27 Thargelion.

---

[187] See Tümpel 1889: esp. 685–6; Burkert 1983: 208.

[188] See on this, Jacoby 1954: i. 555–6 ad Philochoros *FGrH* 328 F 191; Burkert 1983: 208 and n. 20; Tümpel 1889. On Halai Aixonides, see Parker 2005a: 63, 68–9.

[189] Schol. T Hom. *Il.* 6.136.

I will now consider to what extent, if at all, the comparative material briefly considered above can help our reconstruction of the Plynteria, either in terms of validation/invalidation or in any other way. First, the fact that the concepts of primordiality and abnormality were important in the Tonaia (in which purification was a major dimension in the *loutron* of the statue, as it was in the Plynteria) confirms that these concepts, which appear central to the Plynteria, were indeed central, that this is not a culturally determined reading; primordiality and abnormality were indeed significant to the festival, they were not incidental or marginal. There may be an element of primordiality and there is certainly one of abnormality also in another festival: the element of the statue reclining on celery at the festival of Artemis Daitis evokes the schema 'worshippers reclining on beds of a particular, religiously significant, plant in the course of ritual dining', which in the Tonaia and elsewhere is associated with dissolution of normality, at the Tonaia also specifically connected with primordiality.

Second, the fact that the statue was offered a special food both at the Tonaia and at the festival of Artemis Daitis suggests that the *hegeteria*, which was part of the evocation of primordiality at the Plynteria, was not a marginal element but an important one.

Third, the fact that at Argos (or at least in Kallimachos' hymn) the statue was transported for its ritual bath in a chariot, and that this element is stressed, appears correlative with the symbolic stress in Athens on the transportation of the statue in a chariot manifested, I argued, in the office of charioteer of Pallas who drove the chariot that took the statue of Athena to Phaleron and brought it back. In other words, this stress in the Argive ritual adds support to the view that the transportation of the statue in the chariot was not an incidental element of only utilitarian import, it was also ritually significant.

Fourth, the fact that at the Tonaia there were two separate ritual movements before the statue was washed in the sea, the procession that went from the city to the sanctuary by the sea, and the movement that involved the statue's removal from the temple and transport to the shore. This would provide a very partial comparability— with significant differences, of course—to my reconstruction, in which the Plynteria procession went to the sanctuary of Athena Skiras at Phaleron, where the main part of the procession would have stayed while the female Praxiergidai took the statue to the sea and bathed it and brought it back—though after that, differently from the different situation at Samos, the whole procession would have escorted it back to the Acropolis, while at Samos it was returned to its temple near the sea after a short display on a pedestal by the altar.

Fifth, as I already mentioned, the title σπειροφόρος in the procession for Artemis at Ephesos suggests that an emphasis on the cloth in which the statue was wrapped as it was brought out of the sea does indeed occur in Greek ritual practice.

Sixth, males were excluded from the washing and reclothing of the statue in at least some rituals. This exclusion is stated explicitly and emphatically with regard to Argos for the ritual bath of Athena and is inferred for that of Hera. The personnel mentioned in connection with the bath of the statue of Athena Polias in Athens, the Loutrides, like the Argive 'bath-pourers', were young girls. The women who performed the 'adornments' for the Mother, the *hieropoioi* who are called 'of the sea' and the priestesses who are joined with them in Kyzikos, were female. These comparanda cannot prove that men were excluded from the *loutron* part of the ritual during the Plynteria, that it was only female Praxiergidai (whether or not in the presence of other women, above all the priestess of Athena Polias and the priestess of Aglauros) who were involved, but they add support to this reconstruction that excludes males.

Seventh, in the reconstruction of 27 Thargelion which I will set out in section 4 below I will suggest that when the procession returned to the Acropolis the statue was not taken inside the temple, but placed outside by the altar where it stayed until the next day. I will suggest this for reasons that concern the festival nexus of the Plynteria and Kallynteria. The fact that, as we saw, at the Tonaia the statue probably stood outside the temple on a base that has been discovered by the altar gives some support to this reconstruction.

A final way in which the consideration of comparative material may legitimately help our reconstruction is by suggesting possibilities. I have already mentioned one such possibility in the course of the attempted reconstruction of 26 Thargelion: just as 'special food' was involved in the Tonaia, cakes of ground barley, and salt in the festival for Artemis Daitis, so too the *hegeteria*, also a special food, was carried in the procession of the Plynteria. Since in both the other festivals the deity's statue was offered this special food, by the sea in one case, it is possible that the *hegeteria* may also have been offered as a meal to Athena, possibly by the shore by the Praxiergidai—if not it would have been set in front of the goddess at the sanctuary of Athena Skiras.

The fact that the office of κοσμοφόρος appears to be associated with the procession at Ephesos suggests that in that procession a κοσμοφόρος had carried the goddess's 'adornment'. This in its turn would suggest that the statue was dressed and adorned before it returned to the sanctuary. In Kallimachos' hymn, we saw, the statue was dressed and beautified at the site of the *loutron*, for the girls are urged not to bring perfumes or alabasters or mirrors but olive oil for anointing Athena and a golden comb. But we hear nothing about jewellery being restored to the statue there.

On the basis of these analogies the possibility (no more) is suggested that at the Plynteria also the statue was dressed in the laundered *peplos* at Phaleron, by the sea; or, another possibility, that it was both dressed and adorned with its jewellery by the sea. What is certain is that the dressing of the statue with the *peplos* would have taken place away from the men's gaze; and though the *peplos* could have been fastened underneath the wrapping cloth, it is unlikely that a solemn ritual would have involved such undignified scrambling under clothes, it would have involved the statue standing and the *peplos* being solemnly fastened around it—and that is even without taking account of the strong possibility that the statue may have been anointed with oil as it was at Argos in Kallimachos' hymn. Therefore I suggest that the most likely reconstruction is that the female Praxiergidai dressed the statue in the *peplos*, which I suggested had been washed the previous day on the Acropolis, by the sea. They then carried the statue, now dressed in its *peplos*, back to the sanctuary of Athena Skiras nearby. They were still there at the end of 26 Thargelion, for the procession returned to the *asty* 'by torchlight', that is on 27 Thargelion.

Other rites may also have been performed at Phaleron on 26 Thargelion, such as sacrifices or the singing of hymns; but we have no evidence for them and so we cannot place them even tentatively.

In the next section I will try to reconstruct the skeleton of the ritual actions that took place on 27 Thargelion.

4. KALLYNTERIA: 27 AND 28 THARGELION. RETURN TO THE ACROPOLIS AND THE TEMPLE'S REOPENING

The inscriptions discussed in section 3.ii tell us that the procession returned to the Acropolis 'by torchlight' and that the ephebes brought back Athena from Phaleron 'in all good order'. If my reconstruction is right, the fact that the ephebes brought the statue back by torchlight means that the return to Athens of the procession and statue took place on 27 Thargelion, for the Athenian day was reckoned from sunset to sunset.[190] In our way of reckoning, the statue would have been absent for a full day, from the morning until well into the evening. On my reconstruction, 27 Thargelion was the first day of the Kallynteria. The washings had taken place during the Plynteria. At the beginning of 27 Thargelion the washings had been completed and the statue and those accompanying it in the procession were still at Phaleron, on my reconstruction at the sanctuary of Athena Skiras. On this new day the mood would have been different. As Parker noted, the day after the washings would have been joyous, "a period of especial liberation, with life beginning anew with purity".[191]

Let me consider the question of the dates further. When attempting to place the Kallynteria, Mikalson noted[192] that no meetings were attested for the period 24–8 Thargelion, and that the Kallynteria could be dated to any one of these days except the 25th, the day of Plynteria. On my reconstruction, the Plynteria lasted two days, 25 and 26 Thargelion. 27 Thargelion was also a festival day, since the procession returned from Phaleron. If we ask what festival it belonged to, the answer that imposes itself is, I suggest, the Kallynteria. For the Kallynteria was closely associated with the Plynteria in a variety of ways, besides, of course, the fact that they were both festivals of the cult of Athena Polias: first, they were both strongly associated with Aglauros, who was the second honorand after Athens in both; second, the ritual activities conducted in the two festivals,

---

[190] See above n. 149.
[191] Parker 1983: 28.
[192] Mikalson 1975: 164.

the washings of *peplos* and statue and the cleaning and making brilliant of the temple, were semantically connected, and were combined into one nexus in at least one other Athenian cult, the cult of Aphrodite Pandemos, where, we saw,[193] the washing of the statues and the cleaning of a sanctuary were part of the same cultic occasion; finally, and most importantly, the Plynteria and the Kallynteria are sometimes mentioned together by the lexicographers.[194]

Since we know that 25 Thargelion belonged to the Plynteria, there can be little doubt that Aristokles of Rhodes (a first-century BC grammarian) was referring to the Plynteria and the Kallynteria when, according to Proklos, he stated that the festival Bendideia was celebrated on 19 Thargelion, and that 'the festivals concerning Athena' come after that.[195] The reconstruction of the dates that I propose here is compatible with this statement.

I suggest that the Kallynteria followed on immediately after the Plynteria, beginning on 27 Thargelion, and including, and ending on, the 28th, when the temple was reopened. That is, I suggest that all the days from 25 to 28 Thargelion were festival days. We know that the 25th was the (on my reconstruction first) day of the Plynteria, and, we saw, *IG* I^3 7 tells us that the 28th marked the ending of the period of abnormality, which means that the 28th would fit the closure of this nexus of festivals in which abnormality (especially, but not exclusively, focused on pollution and primordiality) was a significant parameter, and the correlative restoration of normality.

But what, it may be objected, of the fact that Photios gives different dates, and places the Kallynteria before the Plynteria? Since Photios' date for the Plynteria, 29 Thargelion, is certainly wrong,[196] and so is his information that the Kallynteria were celebrated on 19 Thargelion,[197] there is no reason to consider trustworthy the order he ascribes to the two festivals which places the Kallynteria before the Plynteria.[198]

There are various possible reasons why a rationalizing compiler (perhaps the compiler who had structured the main lines of the entry

---

[193] See p. 181.
[194] See e.g. Phot. s.v. Kallynteria kai Plynteria; *Anecd. Bekk.* i. 270.
[195] Procl. *In Ti.* I.85.28–9.
[196] See Mikalson 1975: 163–4; Parker 2005a: 478 with bib.
[197] See Mikalson 1975: 163 cf. 158.
[198] See ibid.: 163–4.

in Photios) may have placed the Kallynteria before the Plynteria. First, the fact that logically the cleaning of the temple would have been expected to have preceded the washing of the statue. Second, a rationalizing compiler may well have assumed that the chronological order of the stories in the *aitia* would have reflected the order of the festivals; and that therefore the Kallynteria, the *aition* of which concerned Aglauros' acts as a priestess in her lifetime, would have been celebrated before the Plynteria, which was associated with events after her death. However, ritual logic operates in more complex ways, and it is not legitimate to assume that the mythological moments with which each festival was associated formed a linear temporal sequence that corresponded to the order of the festivals.

On this reconstruction, the Kallynteria corresponded to the 'return to normality' rites and joyful mood, culminating in, or at least encompassing, the reopening of the temple. If this is right, the Kallynteria would have included at one end the return of the statue to its sanctuary and at the other the reopening of the temple; in between—and leaving aside for the moment certain further rituals that will be considered below—this festival may also have included the replacement of the *kosmos*, the jewellery, of the statue on its return to the Acropolis, and it certainly (on my reconstruction) included the cleaning and brightening up of the temple, as part of the processes of the restoration of normality, and of renewal.

As we saw,[199] the *aition* of the Kallynteria shows that the cleaning of the temple was part of this festival; on my reconstruction that cleaning would have taken place on 27 Thargelion, before the temple reopened on the 28th. It is unlikely that in a festival nexus that involved the statue's removal from the temple that temple would have been cleaned after the cleaned statue had been brought back inside; therefore, I submit, when the statue was brought back to the Acropolis on the 27th it was not taken inside the temple of Athena Polias but was placed outside, probably near the altar.[200]

Before attempting to consider further the ritual acts surrounding the statue's return to the Acropolis we should first try to reconstruct

---

[199] See p. 154.

[200] Just as the statue of Hera probably stood outside the temple on a base by the altar in the Tonaia of Samos: p. 186 above.

how this return would have been perceived by the ancient Athenians. First, the return of the statue will have evoked Athena's arrival in primordial times that eventually led to the establishment of her poliadic cult. For, we saw, in Greek religious practices and perceptions the ritual schema 'removal of the cult statue from its proper place and return' evoked a deity's advent; it helped structure advent festivals and festivals that included an element of advent.[201] In such festivals the various ritual enactments of the arrival of the deity often presented themselves as commemorations of a mythological arrival of the deity or of the cult; the return of the statue was the focus of a ritual enactment of the deity's first arrival and it represented, gave concrete expression to, the deity's actual advent, in the present.

Of the festivals briefly considered above,[202] the Tonaia, we saw, had a strong advent emphasis and there may have been an advent festival in Athens that involved the immersion of a statue of Dionysos at Halai Aixonides, though the most important Athenian advent festival of Dionysos was the City Dionysia, which was structured by the schema 'removal of the cult statue from its proper place and return' and celebrated the introduction of Dionysos' cult in Athens: the removal and ceremonial return of the statue was a re-enactment, and celebration, of the introduction of the cult of Dionysos; the statue's return also gave concrete representation to the advent of Dionysos in the city in the present. Of course, the mythicoritual nexus 'advent' did not have as important a role in the cult of Athena as it did in that of Dionysos. Nevertheless, given that the statue's removal and return was, and would have been perceived as, a version of the advent schema, this schema and its associated perceptions would have been activated; and the return of the statue to the Acropolis would have been, I submit, inescapably perceived as evoking Athena's original arrival and conveying visually the notion of the goddess' advent and presence at the festival.

---

[201] See above section 3.iv. I have discussed advent festivals and divine arrivals in Sourvinou-Inwood 2005: 151–68, where I have set out the detailed arguments for some of the statements that follow. On advent festivals, see Burkert 1988: 81–7; see also Burkert 1985: 134–5; Burkert 1997: 24.
[202] In section 4.

The removal of any deity's statue brings about, and signifies, abnormality. But how was the removal of Athena's statue from the centre of the city to Phaleron perceived specifically? Clearly, this removal constructed some kind of a representation of absence; but it was a mock representation of an absence, because, of course, the statue was not removed outside the polis, it was moved to the frontier between *asty* and non-*asty*, and the goddess would not have been perceived as 'actually' absent in any case. It was a representation of a partly pretend absence. That is, the removal of Athena's statue constructed a representation of Athens without Athena Polias at the centre, but in the framework of the knowledge that she had not left the polis. Thus, this representation both was and was not a representation of a primordial age before Athena became the poliadic deity of Athens; insofar as Athena's metonymic sign that was her statue was absent from the centre, it could be perceived as such a representation of that primordial time; but insofar as the goddess and her statue were still in the city and Athena had not ceased to be the poliadic deity protecting Athens, the two representations were distanced, only to come together again at the return of the statue to the Acropolis, which also commemorated, and was also perceived as an image of, the cult's installation.

In these circumstances, it is clear that the return of the statue to the Acropolis was ritually important, for it brought about the end of the period of abnormality and was the representation of the goddess' advent; therefore, it is difficult to doubt that it would have involved, as other divine advents did, the performance of sacrifices. I will now argue that there is evidence that shows that sacrifices were indeed performed on the return of the statue, and that they were performed by the priestess of Aglauros. We know that the priestess of Aglauros performed sacrifices called εἰσαγωγεῖα, which by their name suggest a link with εἰσαγωγή, bringing in; and I will now argue that these εἰσαγωγεῖα were the sacrifices offered on the occasion of the return of the statue from Phaleron to the Acropolis on the evening of 27 Thargelion.

The argument is threefold. First, as we have just seen, the nature of the occasion suggests that it would have involved the performance of sacrifices. The second part of the argument concerns the honorary decree for the priestess of Aglauros Timokrite, which is dated to 247/6 or 246/5 BC: I will argue that there are good reasons for thinking that the εἰσαγωγεῖα performed by this priestess accompanied the εἰσαγωγή of the statue of Athena Polias from Phaleron. In the third part I will argue that if sacrifices were indeed performed when the statue returned to the Acropolis from Phaleron, the priestess of Aglauros was the most appropriate person to perform them.

I have already set out the first part of the argument. The second is based on the reading of the text of the inscription. The relevant section of the decree honouring Timokrite reads:

concerning the report that Aristophanes the son of the priestess of Aglauros made concerning the sacrifices which she sacrificed at the entry-rites (τὰ εἰσιτητήρια) to Aglauros and Ares and Helios and the Seasons and Apollo and the other gods to whom it was ancestral... the council and people should receive the blessings that occurred in the sacrifices for the health and security of the council and people of Athens and their children and wives and king Antigonos and queen Phila and their children. And since the priestess of Aglauros sacrificed the introduction sacrifices (τὰ εἰσαγωγεῖα) and the appropriate sacrifices and took care of good order in the all-night rite, and adorned the table, the priestess of Aglauros Timokrite daughter of Polynikos of Aphidna should be praised and crowned with a crown of olive...

It is not clear on what occasion she performed entry-rites (τὰ εἰσιτητήρια).[203] With regard to the introduction sacrifices (τὰ εἰσαγωγεῖα), it is normally assumed that they are the same sacrifices as the entry-rites.[204] For the immediately apparent logic of the text would suggest that the entry-rites would be mentioned again among the reasons why the priestess is praised, and since introduction sacrifices (εἰσαγωγεῖα) sound similar to entry-rites (εἰσιτητήρια) it is easy to identify them. However, I will now argue that a comparison with another decree of about the same time which has a somewhat similar structure suggests that another reading is perhaps more likely.

Let us consider the decree for Timokrite further. The first group of ritual activities mentioned is that of the sacrifices at the entry-rites concerning which the son of the priestess had reported. Immediately after this follows the resolution by the council to accept the blessings

---

[203] See Parker 2005a: 98 n. 31, 434 n. 64.
[204] See ibid.: 434 n. 64, though Dontas (1983: 56) thought that they were different.

that were produced through the sacrifices for the health and security of the council and the people and of the royal couple. Are these sacrifices that produced the blessings a separate group? Of course, all sacrifices in whole polis rituals were ultimately for the health and security of the council and the people and of the Athenians; but here something specific is referred to, since the resolution is taken to accept the blessings produced through these sacrifices in a context in which such blessings may have blurred into the notion of good omens produced in the sacrifices and reported upon. I suggest that the sacrifices for the health and security of the council and the people and of the royals were the ones that the priestess of Aglauros performed at the entry-rites, about which her son reported. These sacrifices at the entry-rites were clearly those on which the priestess of Aglauros was subjected to public audit (or, conceivably, the most important part of the activities for which she was submitted to such audit),[205] for which she was represented by her *kyrios* and which are mentioned as the subject of the report. I suggest that it was to these sacrifices in particular that the notion of the blessings (perhaps reported good omens interpreted as resulting in blessings) which it is resolved to accept referred.

There was a second part to the resolution—the structure being on the one hand to accept the blessings, on the other to praise and crown the priestess. The second part of the resolution, the resolution to praise and crown Timokrite, is introduced by 'and since' (ἐπειδὴ δέ), followed by a list of ritual activities that Timokrite had performed. So the resolution to praise and crown her is causally connected directly with a second group of ritual activities. This group unquestionably includes activities that had not been mentioned before (such as her role at the all-night rite). The question is whether the introduction sacrifices (τὰ εἰσαγωγεῖα) are identical with the entry-rites, or are, like the all-night rite, a new element (in which case her performance of the entry-rites, probably her most important ritual duty, will have been subsumed under 'the appropriate sacrifices' which follows).

I will now argue that this interpretation, which makes the εἰσαγωγεῖα a separate sacrifice, and not another term for the εἰσαγωγεῖα, gains some support from another honorary decree, a decree for the priestess

---

[205] *Euthyna* (on this, see Aeschin. 3. 18; see also Parker 1996: 125).

of Athena Polias, from the middle of the third century BC, *IG* II² 776,[206] which is therefore very close in time to the decree for the priestess of Aglauros. *IG* II² 776 is, moreover, close in structure to the decree for Timokrite. Unfortunately, the segment of the decree for the priestess of Athena that would be equivalent to the part which in the priestess of Aglauros decree refers to the entry-rites is missing. In addition, the 'praise and crowning' segment is much more elaborate in this decree than in that for the priestess of Aglauros. However, it is clear that in the section following 'and since' (ἐπειδὴ δέ) in this decree none of the major ritual duties performed by the priestess of Athena Polias is explicitly mentioned. The surviving part of this decree for the priestess of Athena contains the expression (*IG* II² 776. 6–11) 'should receive the blessings which the priestess says occurred in the rites which she sacrificed for the health and security of the council and people and their children and wives and king Antigonos and queen Phila and their offspring'. This is followed by 'and since the priestess', followed by an enumeration of a set of actions: she took good and zealous care of the adornment of the table according to ancestral custom, and of all the other things ordered by the laws and decrees, she always showed zeal towards the goddess, and she dedicated some garments, and she gave money to the Praxiergidai for the ancestral sacrifice from her own resources.[207] Clearly, then, the major sacrifices involved in the poliadic cult are not mentioned specifically and explicitly here—on my understanding they, or at least the most important among them, would have been in the missing part that would have referred to the 'report' (here presumably made by the husband of the priestess whom it is resolved to praise and crown in ll. 26–8). So, just as in the Timokrite decree the priestess's major duty (the entry-sacrifices) is not, on my reading, mentioned again explicitly but covered by the general reference to 'appropriate sacrifices', so in this one the major sacrifices performed by the priestess of Athena are not mentioned again explicitly but subsumed within 'the other things ordered by the laws and decrees'.[208]

---

[206] *IG* II² 776 of 260–56 BC. On the date, see Aleshire 1994: 336 and 337 note e.
[207] See on this, n. 44.
[208] An honorary decree for the priest of Asklepios Xypetaion, passed after 244/3 BC, has a similar structure: the 'and since' clause does in this case mention again the main sacrifice about which the priest reported, but also adds extra details (*IG* II²775; *SEG* XVIII 19).

If the foregoing argument is right, if the εἰσαγωγεῖα were indeed separate sacrifices, there is one ritual to which such sacrifices would have been appropriate in which we know that Aglauros was (and so her priestess would have been) involved, the 'introduction' of the statue of Athena Polias from Phaleron in the nexus of the Plynteria and Kallynteria, since Aglauros was the second most important cult recipient in that nexus and this entails a role for her priestess, and this nexus of the Plynteria and Kallynteria was the one cultic occasion besides the ephebic nexus with which Aglauros was strongly associated on her own, without her sisters.

I will now argue that (even if we leave aside the argument based on the decree for Timokrite), if sacrifices were performed when the statue returned to the Acropolis from Phaleron, as we would expect to have been the case, the priestess of Aglauros was the most appropriate person to perform them, for two important reasons. First, she was the most appropriate person to mediate between the two spaces involved in the movement of the statue. The bringing in, εἰσαγωγή, involved the movement of the statue of Athena Polias, and of the procession escorting it, from Phaleron to the Acropolis. On my reading, the starting point of the εἰσαγωγή was the sanctuary of Athena Skiras at Phaleron, one of the religious centres of the *genos* of the Salaminioi, of which the priestess of Aglauros was a member. Thus, the priestess of Aglauros was associated with both spaces and both sanctuaries.

Second, it would make ritual sense to have Aglauros' priestess perform these sacrifices. The fact that Aglauros was a ritual agent in the *aition* of the Kallynteria makes it more likely that her priestess was a ritual agent in the cultic activities of the present. More importantly, since Aglauros was the first priestess of Athena, she would have installed the statue and cult of Athena Polias. If it is right that one of the sets of perceptions through which the Athenians made sense of this ritual was that it was a re-enactment of the arrival of Athena and the establishment of her cult, this re-enactment of the establishment would have been conducted by Aglauros' closest symbolic equivalent, her priestess. A final argument is as follows. The time during which the cult statue is away from its temple is, we saw, a time of abnormality. The εἰσαγωγή was an important part of the process through which normality was restored. The priestess of Athena Polias was, above all, associated with normality in this ritual

nexus. For, if the reconstructions proposed here are right, she relin-
quished the key and control of the temple and statue to the Praxiergidai for this period of abnormality. Therefore, she would not have
been the most symbolically appropriate person to perform the
εἰσαγωγεῖα; there would have been a slight symbolic disjunction
between her symbolic correlation with normality and the nature of
the occasion. There was less of a symbolic disjunction and more of a
symbolic harmony between a rite that contributed to the restoration
of normality and a figure who was the avatar, as it were, of the first
priestess of Athena Polias, Aglauros, who had belonged (in a condensed symbolism) to the transition between primordiality and the
present normality, and, as the first priestess,[209] to the time when the
cult was established—a mythological priestess, whose cultic avatar
was her own priestess in the present. I submit that the priestess of
Aglauros was the figure symbolically more in harmony with
εἰσαγωγεῖα sacrifices connected with the εἰσαγωγεῖα of the statue
of Athena Polias.

As we saw in the decree honouring Timokrite, the priestess of
Aglauros also took care that there was good order at the *pannychis*,
'all-nighter', but we do not know which *pannychis* that was.[210] I will now
argue that it was an all-nighter that was part of the Kallynteria. To begin
with, the *pannychis* in which the priestess of Aglauros ensured good
order, which was, of course, part of a festival, would have to have been a
celebration in which Aglauros had a significant place.[211] A festival in
which we know Aglauros had an important place on her own (not with
her sisters) was the festival nexus Plynteria and Kallynteria, in which
Aglauros was the secondary cult recipient, which would be correlative
with her priestess having a secondary role in the *pannychis* (she was not
the one who actually conducted it)—the role of this priestess in this
nexus would have been secondary to the Praxiergidai in abnormal time,
to the priestess of Athena Polias in normal time.

Then there is a space for the *pannychis* in the Kallynteria as
reconstructed here. For the procession would have returned from

[209] See e.g. Jacoby 1954: i. 426 ad 328 F 105.
[210] On *pannychides*, see Parker 2005a: 166, 182–3; see also Parisinou 2000: 158–61;
Pritchett 1987. Cf. Dion. Hal. *Ant. Rom.* 2.19.
[211] Kearns (1989: 139) takes the *pannychis* to have been celebrated in honour of
Aglauros.

Phaleron some time well into the evening, so that a *pannychis* would naturally follow, especially if it is right that *eisagogeia* sacrifices were performed on the statue's return, since a ritual meal would then have followed, which would have taken the activities late and provided an occasion for an all-nighter. That is, since in this nexus the εἰσαγωγή occurred 'by torchlight', the sacrifices connected with that εἰσαγωγή would have happened relatively late in the evening, and this would be consistent with a *pannychis*.[212]

It is less likely that this *pannychis* occurred at a later stage of the Kallynteria, that it took place after the reopening of the temple and the restoration of the statue to its proper place inside the temple; for it is a *pannychis* before, rather than after, the culminating moment of the festival that would fit the pattern of the cult of Athena Polias as seen at the Panathenaia, since there can be little doubt that at the Panathenaia the *pannychis* took place before the procession and sacrifice.[213] This comparability should be seen in the context of the fact that the Panathenaia was not only a festival of the same cult as the Plynteria and Kallynteria, the cult of Athena Polias: it also involved a manipulation of the statue and its *peplos*, again like the Plynteria and Kallynteria, not in antithesis to the comparable action at the Plynteria and Kallynteria, but as an intensification: new *peplos* rather than newly cleaned *peplos*. As we shall see below, the Plynteria and Kallynteria on the one hand and the Panathenaia on the other were, among other things, also part of a nexus of renewal that began with a 'dirty' robe and concluded with a new robe at the Panathenaia.

---

[212] The reference by Athenagoras of Athens, *Legatio pro Christianis* 1.1, to τελεταί and μυστήρια held by the Athenians for Aglauros could conceivably refer to the *pannychis* of the Kallynteria.

[213] See esp. Parker 2005a: 256–7; cf. Burkert 1983: 155; Burkert 1985: 232. Pritchett (1987) argued against the established view that the *pannychis* of the Panathenaia took place the night before the procession and sacrifice. However I do not find the argument convincing and the sequence *pannychis* followed by the procession and sacrifices remains the most likely (see Parker 2005a: 256–7). I cannot discuss the argument in detail, but I will mention that it appears to rely on the assumption that there was a consistent relationship between *pannychis* and what he calls "the festival proper" (see e.g. p. 186), by which we may understand something like "the festival's central ritual core". But this is invalidated by the fact that his Eleusinian Mysteries case (Pritchett 1987: 186) does not work; for the procession to Eleusis, which is followed by the *pannychis*, is not the festival's central ritual core, which is the initiation, while at the Panathenaia procession and sacrifices are the central ritual core.

The comparability does not, of course, prove that a Kallynteria *pannychis* would have taken place on 27 (rather than 28) Thargelion, but it makes it much more likely, especially when the fact that there was a slot for an all-nighter on the 27th is also taken into account.

Furthermore, it is possible that both the Kallynteria and the Panathenaia may have been structured by a common schema '*pannychis*—new fire'; for it is possible that Athena's lamp was relit at the Kallynteria. According to Pausanias, the lamp that burned continuously day and night in the temple of Athena Polias, which was made by Kallimachos, was refilled once a year, on the same day every year, for the oil lasted for twelve months.[214] Whether or not it is true that Kallimachos' lamp contained enough oil to last for a year without being refilled, there was clearly only one ceremonial refilling, a once a year ritual, and that would have been the case also with the lamps that had preceded the one made by Kallimachos, when the oil would have run out more than once a year; any other refillings dictated by practical necessity would have been symbolically elided. Since lighting a new fire is a ritual of renewal, following dissolution,[215] and since the Kallynteria was the one festival in which renewal was focused on the temple, I suggest that it is very likely that Deubner's suggestion, that it was at the Kallynteria that the lamp of Athena was refilled and relit, is right.[216]

If this is correct, this extinguishing, refilling, and relighting, which would probably have been correlative with darkness and its removal, that is, sunrise, would most likely have taken place at the beginning of the daytime of the day on which the focus was on the temple, that is,

---

[214] On the lamp of Athena, see Paus. 1.26.6–7 (cf. Strabo 9.1.16); Deubner 1969: 20; Dillon 2002: 105. For a discussion of the lamp burning in the temple of Athena Polias, see Parisinou 2000: 20–31, cf. 32–5.

[215] Burkert 1970a/2000 and 1983: 190–6.

[216] Deubner 1969: 20, cf. Parke 1977: 152. Not everyone agrees: see Parisinou 2000: 31 and esp. Burkert 1970a: 11 = 2000: 241. Burkert suggests that extinction of the fire and its relighting will have taken place at the Panathenaia, when the new oil was available and used as a prize for the victors. However, at the Panathenaia the emphasis was on the sacrifices (and this is correlative with the new fire being brought for the altar), not on the temple as it is in the Kallynteria. Moreover, the relationship between the Plynteria and Kallynteria nexus on the one hand and the Panathenaia on the other, which includes comparabilities among the very many differences, appears to involve, we shall see, the more joyful versions of renewal drifting to the Panathenaia, with the darker tending to drift to the Plynteria and Kallynteria nexus. This would fit with the reconstruction followed here with regard to new fire: at the Panathenaia new fire for the altar, a more joyful, less 'dangerous' renewal; during the Plynteria and Kallynteria nexus extinguishing the fire before relighting it, corresponding to dissolution before return to normality and renewal.

at the sunrise of 27 Thargelion, after the end of the *pannychis*. If this is right the schema would be comparable to that at the Panathenaia, where there is a *pannychis* and at sunrise new fire is fetched from the Academy to the altar of Athena: the new fire is lit by the torch of the winner of the torch race which culminated in this act of lighting.[217]

Whether or not the lamp of Athena was refilled and relit on that day, on my reconstruction, in the course of the day of 27 Thargelion, which was still the first day of the Kallynteria, the temple was cleaned, adorned, and made brilliant. We are not told who the personnel who did the cleaning at the Kallynteria were, but given that the Praxiergidai still had control of the temple, and the *aition* tells us that Aglauros was the first to clean the sanctuaries of the gods, the cleaning was probably either done by, or under the responsibility of, the Praxiergidai, or some of them; the priestess of Aglauros, the avatar of the mythological figure who first performed this act, was probably also involved, perhaps in a supervisory role.

After the sunset of the 27th, on 28 Thargelion, normality was fully re-established: the temple was unsealed, the statue was returned to the cleaned temple, and the Praxiergidai returned the key to the archon, who returned it to the priestess of Athena.

I will sum up below the ritual acts that, on the reconstruction set out here, took place during the Plynteria and Kallynteria. First I must consider the inscription which contains (on my reading) two references relevant to the nexus of the Plynteria, *IG* II^2 1060 + *IG* II^2 1036.

5. WASHING THE NEW WOOL

IG II^2 1060 + *IG* II^2 1036 consists of two decrees,[218] of which the second (which is similar to *IG* II^2 1034 + 1943) honours the maidens who wove the Panathenaic *peplos* in 108/7 BC—not a year in which the Great Panathenaia was celebrated—and registers their fathers'

---

[217] Herm. in *Phdr.* 231e; cf. Burkert 1983: 155 and 1985: 232; Parker 2005a: 257.

[218] On this inscription see Nagy 1978a: 136–41 and 1978b: 307–13, esp. 311–13; Aleshire and Lambert 2003: 65–86 (= *SEG* LIII/I 143); Parker 2005a: 226–7.

request that they should be allowed to dedicate a silver phiale to Athena as a memorial of their piety towards the goddess. The list of maidens (like those in *IG* II^2 1034 + 1943 and 1942) is laid out by tribes. They are probably the group known from a lexicographer as the Ergastinai, 'workers' (of the *peplos*).[219] The much more fragmentary Decree I sets out general regulations concerning the *peplos* that were applicable every year, and prescribes that they should be honoured with a crown of twigs for having made the *peplos* well. Aleshire and Lambert think that, while it is likely that the date of this decree was the same as, or just before, that of II, it is not inconceivable that it may have been an old decree reinscribed.[220] For convenience I reproduce Aleshire and Lambert's text of decree I here:

fr. a

[- - - - - - - - - - - - - -]. νων κα. [- - - - - - - - - - - - - - - - - -]
[- - - - - - -] της καὶ οἱ ἀθλοθέτα[ι - - - - - - - - - - - - - - - - - -]
[- - - - - - - - -]καλῶς ποησαμένοις τὸν πέ[πλον - - - - - - - - - - - -]
[- - - - - - - - - -] τοῦ δήμου θαλλοῦ στεφά[νωι - - - - - - - - - - - -]
[- - - - - - - - - -πέ]πλου λευκὴν ἐσθῆτα H[- - - - - - - - - - - - - -]
[- - - - - - - - - - - ἀγων]οθέτης εἰς τὴν πομπ[ὴν - - - - - - - - - - - - -]
[- - - - - - - - - - - - - o [ ] καθ[- - - - - - - - - - - - - - - - -]

lacuna ?

---

[219] Hesych s.v. Ergastinai: 'those who weave the *peplos*'. For I agree that this is what these maidens were, though not everyone agrees that the girls who worked the wool who are honoured in these decrees were the same as those who wove the *peplos* (see the brief discussion of the issue in Parker 2005a: 227 n. 41). For a distinction could be made between the cleaning, combing, and spinning of the wool and the processes of making the warp, setting up the loom, and weaving. The question is discussed in Aleshire and Lambert 2003: 75–6, who set out a convincing argument (see especially 75–6) against Mansfield's view (see Mansfield 1985: 277–81) that the maidens in these decrees did not do the weaving but the cleaning, combing, and spinning. Aleshire and Lambert (2003: 76) conclude that it is doubtful whether they were responsible for the earlier pre-weaving stages of preparation of the wool, and that it is probably right that they are the Ergastinai and they wove the *peplos*. But I think that their argument simply shows that the weaving of the *peplos* was considered the most important stage and duty; it does not entail that the Ergastinai did not also prepare the wool or spin it. My position is that the maidens honoured in the decrees were the Ergastinai and they wove the *peplos*, but they also prepared the wool for a different year's *peplos*, a modality that stressed the cyclical nature of the polis's gift to Athena.

[220] Aleshire and Lambert 2003: 70.

fr. b.

[[c. 1.]] EX .... [. [c. 4-5.].]α ταῦτα πομπε.[.. [c. 3-4.].]. [- - - - - - - Πραξιεργί?]
- δαι παραλάβωσιν τὸν ἐφέτειον πέπλ[ο]ν [- - - - - - - - - - - - - - - - -]
ἱμάτιον ἐξάγωσιν, παραδιδότωσαν ταῖ[ς.] ... [- - - - - - - - - - - - - -]
συνεπιμελο<υ>μένου τῆς διαιρέσεως [- - - - - - - - - - - - - - - - - -]
ἡ βουλὴ καὶ ὁ δῆμος φαίνωνται διαι[ρούμενοι - - - - - - - - - - - -]
ας.   vacat

If the restoration 'Praxiergidai' in fr. b.1-2 is right, there is a
reference in decree I to the Praxiergidai receiving 'the current year's
peplos', then, after a gap, 'taking out (a/the) *himation*' (ἱμάτιον
ἐξάγωσιν), followed by 'let them hand over to the [feminine]', then
a gap and a reference to a division which was jointly supervised by an
official, presumably the *agonothetes*. The subject of 'hand over' was
undoubtedly the *athlothetai*, who oversaw the creation of the *peplos*.[221] The suggestion by Aleshire and Lambert[222] that what is being
divided may be the wool for next year's *peplos* is surely right. It is,
surely, because the issues concern the manufacture of the statue's
most significant dress that the prescriptions are given in this way, that
the dates for particular actions are specified with regard to ritual acts
concerning the statue's dress.

As I argue below,[223] the description of the *peplos* as 'the current
year's *peplos*'[224] suggests that the occasion referred to cannot be the
Panathenaia, and that the occasion was connected with the nexus of
the Plynteria. I suggested that at the beginning of the period of
abnormality in which the Praxiergidai were in charge, the priestess
removed the *peplos* from the statue and handed it to the Praxiergidai,
just as the archon gave them the temple keys.

Let us now consider the expression ending with ἱμάτιον ἐξάγωσιν.
Aleshire and Lambert note that ἱμάτιον "might be the object
of ἐξάγωσιν "lead out the cloak", but the usage would be odd with this
type of inanimate object and ἐξάγωσιν may rather be intransitive ... ,
"march out", or transitive governing a different object".[225] All these

---

[221] See e.g. Arist. *Ath. Pol.* 60.1; Nagy 1978b: 307–13; Rhodes 1981: 669–70 ad loc.
[222] Aleshire and Lambert 2003: 73.
[223] In the Appendix to this chapter.
[224] The various possible meanings of ἐφέτειος are discussed in Aleshire and
Lambert 2003: 72.
[225] Ibid.: 73.

difficulties disappear if ἐξάγωσιν refers primarily to a now missing ἕδος, statue. As we saw, formulations using the verb ἐξάγειν are used to refer to the procession that took the statue of Athena to Phaleron in the inscriptions considered above, which also date from the same last quarter of the second century BC as *IG* II² 1060 + *IG* II² 1036.[226] I suggest that in *IG* II² 1060 + *IG* II² 1036 the formulation was either something like [ἐπειδὰν ἕδος ὑφ'] ἱμάτιον ἐξάγωσιν, 'when they take out the statue under a *himation*,'[227] if *himation* refers to the cloth covering the statue when it is taken out; or, if *himation* refers to the cloth in which the statue will be covered up when taken out of the sea, [ἐπειδὰν ἕδος καὶ] ἱμάτιον ἐξάγωσιν, 'when they take out the statue and *himation*'. Either formulation would be an appropriate way of briefly referring to the procession of the Plynteria as reconstructed here. The reference to the *himation* together with the role of the Praxiergidai, who, unlike the ephebes, were concerned with the statue as above all a physical object which they manipulated at the Plynteria, would have foregrounded the aspect of the statue as a physical object and so might have shaped the choice of the word ἕδος.

Of the two likely reconstructions [ἐπειδὰν ἕδος ὑφ'] ἱμάτιον ἐξάγωσιν is self-explanatory. It may be asked why on the alternative reconstruction [ἐπειδὰν ἕδος καὶ] ἱμάτιον ἐξάγωσιν, in which *himation* would refer to the cloth in which the statue would be covered up when taken out of the sea, the *himation* needed to be specifically mentioned. Possibly because (besides the general concern with garments in this part of the inscription) it was closely associated with the Praxiergidai in the perceptions concerning this procession, as it would have been their responsibility to ensure that the *himation* was taken in the procession so that there would be an appropriate clean cloth to wrap around the statue as it was taken out of the sea. In any case, 'taking out the statue and *himation*' would be a very economical way of referring to the procession that took the statue to be washed in the sea at Phaleron.

The notion that the wool for next year's *peplos* was distributed in some kind of connection with the Plynteria nexus would be eminently consistent with the fact that this was about the time of year

---

[226] See p. 161.
[227] [R.P.'s translation: Sourvinou-Inwood left none.]

when shearing would have been conducted. Such distribution would allow the wool to be ceremonially washed in connection with the Plynteria, as part of the 'washing rites' (πλυντήρια ἱερά). Though the text of ll. b.1-3 is very fragmentary, the expressions 'when [the Praxiergi]dai receive the current year's *peplos*' and 'take out (a/the) *himation*' show that ritual actions are being set in a temporal sequence. There follows the instruction concerning the handover of what was doubtless the wool. There are, I suggest, two possibilities concerning this segment of the text. The first possibility is that the handover of the wool was to occur 'after the Praxiergi]dai receive the current year's *peplos*', but before (supplying something like καὶ πρὶν ἄν) 'they take out the statue and/under the *himation*'. The second possible reconstruction would be on the lines of: [ἔρια δὲ, ἐπειδὰν Πραξιεργί]δαι παραλάβωσι τὸν ἐφέτειον πέπλ[ο]ν, [συλλεγέτωσαν καὶ ἐπειδὰν ἕδος ὑφ'/καὶ] ἱμάτιον ἐξάγωσιν, παραδιδότωσαν, '[with regard to the wool, let them collect it after the Praxiergi]dai receive the current year's *peplos*, and [after] they take out [the statue and/under] the cloak let them hand it over ...'. The subject of 'let them collect', as of 'let them hand over', was undoubtedly the *athlothetai*, who oversaw the creation of the *peplos*.[228] The subject of 'take out' would have been understood to be the Praxiergidai, or the Praxiergidai and the ephebes.

If the first reconstruction is right the decree is saying that the wool would be distributed in the period in which the Praxiergidai were in control of the temple and before the procession to Phaleron—though not, obviously, on 25 Thargelion, since no Athenian would begin an enterprise on that ill-omened day. So why would the decree (on this reading) specify 'before the procession', and not, say, 'before 24 Thargelion'? I suggest that the reason why this particular selection was made was because it was this day and occasion that were the most important—which is why the elision of the 25th would have been implicit and unproblematic: in other words, I suggest that the day of the procession, the daytime of 26 Thargelion, was the day on which the new wool was washed, as part of the 'washing rites' (πλυντήρια ἱερά), probably in fresh water on the Acropolis. On this hypothesis, then, the inscription would be saying that the distribution has to be done in the period in which the

---

[228] See n. 221.

Praxiergidai were in control of the temple and *peplos* and before the day on which this new wool was to be washed, or, at the latest, on that day, before the Praxiergidai and the ephebes took out the statue—and, it is understood, obviously not on the 25th. The washing of the new wool in the same festival as that in which the current year's *peplos* was washed would have helped represent the offering of the *peplos* as a continuous, cyclical, enterprise that never ended—like, it was hoped, the relationship it symbolized.

On the second hypothesis the new wool was collected after the Praxiergidai had taken control of the temple and was distributed after they had taken out the statue, probably on that same day, (on my reading) the second day of the Plynteria, if the new wool was to be washed as part of the 'washing rites'—though the possibility cannot be excluded on this reconstruction that it may have been washed on the first day of the Kallynteria, while the temple was also being cleaned, and the statue had just been dressed in its (the current year's) laundered *peplos* the day before.

On either hypothesis, the washing of the new wool during this nexus would have helped represent the *peplos* offering, of the manufacture of which this distribution was the opening stage, as a continuous never-ending enterprise.

It was almost certainly the *athlothetai* who distributed the wool, joined by the *agonothetes*; the recipients were female. If the translation of the lines in fr. b.4-6 offered by Aleshire and Lambert,[229] "join in supervising the division so that the Council and the People may appear to di[vide justly *vel sim.*—?]" is right, it indicates strongly that the distribution is one in which more than one 'unit' was involved as recipients (since joint supervision was required to ensure justice). This is a major objection to the suggestion that the persons who received the wool are the Praxiergidai:[230] for the female Praxiergidai, and indeed the whole *genos* of the Praxiergidai, when considered vis-à-vis the polis, only constituted one unit. Another objection against that hypothesis is that 'Praxiergidai' is normally deployed in the masculine form that includes the whole *genos*.

---

[229] Aleshire and Lambert 2003: 70.
[230] Ibid.: 73.

We only know of one group of female recipients relevant to wool who were divided into different units: the group of maidens who wove the *peplos*, such as those honoured in decree II,[231] who were listed by tribes. I suggest that the wool was distributed to these tribally articulated maidens who wove the *peplos*; this would also make excellent sense of the fact that the distribution of the wool has a place in this decree which appears to be primarily focused on the relationship between the polis and the Ergastinai. Furthermore, the hypothesis that the recipients of the wool were the tribally articulated Ergastinai makes good sense of the notion that the participation of someone else, probably the *agonothetes*, was desirable in order to guarantee that the division would be perceived as fair, since the *athlothetai* were tribally articulated, in that they were appointed by lot one from each tribe.[232] Otherwise the accusation could have been formulated that some *athlothetai* favoured their own tribe while others did not.

Some girls appear as Ergastinai in more than one of the years for which inscriptions are attested.[233] In my view, the *peplos* was woven annually by a different group of girls of marriageable age,[234] whatever overlap there may have been between the groups of the different years. We do not know when the Ergastinai began their duties, or how long those duties lasted. Since the inscription under discussion and also *IG* II² 1034 + 1943 confirm that the maidens processed together with the *peplos* which they had completed, on the assumption that their service lasted for a year, there are two possibilities concerning the beginning of that year of office: first, that it took place after the Panathenaia and before, or at, the Chalkeia, when the new *peplos* was begun;[235] and second, that the Ergastinai finished their year of office not long before the decrees honouring them were

---

[231] As well as in *IG* II² 1034 + 1943 and *IG* II² 1942.

[232] Arist. *Ath. Pol.* 60.i. On the *athlothetai*, see also Rhodes 1981: 668–76; Nagy 1978b: 307–13.

[233] See e.g. Aleshire and Lambert 2003: 82–3 no. 50, 83 no. 52, 85.

[234] As Brulé noted (1987: 103), some of the maidens were *kanephoroi* at Delphi before being Ergastinai, and some others were *kanephoroi* at Delphi after they were Ergastinai.

[235] The weaving of the new *peplos* started at the Chalkeia, nine months before the Panathenaia, when the priestess of Athena Polias and the *arrhephoroi* set up the warp (*Etym. Magn.* 805.43 s.v. Chalkeia; Suda s.v. Chalkeia. On the weaving, see Barber 1992: 103–17.)

passed, which in the case of *IG* II^2 1034 + 1943 we know was in Gamelion.[236]

The Chalkeia took place at the end of Pyanopsion; the Plynteria and Kallynteria took place seven months later, late in Thargelion. Two months after that the Panathenaia were celebrated. On the first hypothesis, on which the change from one year group to the next took place after the Panathenaia and before, or at, the Chalkeia, the Ergastinai who were in office at the Plynteria and Kallynteria would not be the ones who would be weaving the *peplos* out of this wool next year after the Chalkeia; another group would have taken over. Though it may appear logical in our eyes that it should be those maidens who would use the wool who should receive it, in ritual logic a practice in which one year's group of Ergastinai received and washed the wool for next year's weaving would have been ritually significant: it would have helped convey the notion of continuity and the cyclical nature of the enterprise. Thus, the Ergastinai in office at the time of the Plynteria and Kallynteria would have received and washed the wool, though on this (the first) hypothesis, they would not be the ones who would weave it.

On the second hypothesis also the wool would be distributed to the Ergastinai who were in office at the Plynteria and Kallynteria; but on this hypothesis these Ergastinai would begin the weaving with this wool at the Chalkeia and then leave office (not long) before, or in, Gamelion, for the weaving to be continued by their successors.

To make the two hypotheses clearer I will illustrate them with the example of the concrete girls mentioned in decree II and I will consider 'now' to be the time of the decree, that is, some time in Gamelion (on the basis of *IG* II^2 1034 + 1943). I will call Group A the girls whose term of office had been completed when decree II was passed ('now'), the girls who had processed at the last Panathenaia and made the *peplos* now worn by the statue, whose honours are set out in decree II. I call Group B the immediate successors of group A, the girls who are in office 'now', at the time of the passing of the decree, and who are 'now' weaving the *peplos* that will be offered at the next Panathenaia. On either of the two hypotheses set out here,

---

[236] See also Aleshire and Lambert 2003: 77.

the wool from which they, group B, are now weaving the *peplos* would have been washed by group A. But on the first hypothesis group A had not done any weaving with the wool they had washed—while on the second hypothesis they would have begun the weaving of that wool, most of the weaving of which would have been done by group B. Group C are the girls who will succeed group B, on this first hypothesis after the Panathenaia and at, or before, the Chalkeia. On this first hypothesis, then, Group B, the Ergastinai now in office, will wash the wool from which Group C will weave the *peplos* next year.[237] On the second hypothesis group B will begin the weaving with this wool at the Chalkeia, leave office (not long) before, or in, Gamelion, for the weaving to be continued by group C. Also on this hypothesis, the weaving of the *peplos* now being woven had been begun (as well as the wool for it being washed) by group A, whose service on this hypothesis had finished not very long before the decree was passed. That is, on this hypothesis each year-crop would take over and continue the weaving begun by its predecessors, receive the new wool and wash it, complete the *peplos* and process at the Panathenaia, and then at some point spin the wool and then, after the Chalkeia, begin the weaving of next year's *peplos* that would be completed by their successors, after they themselves had finished their service and been honoured.

Both hypotheses involve continuities and overlaps that would have helped convey the notion of the cyclical nature of the polis's gift to Athena, but in the second the intertwining is clearer and more sustained: the group would wash the wool for the *peplos* that they themselves would begin for their successors to complete, expressing strongly the cyclical nature of the gift to Athena, in that each generation of Ergastinai were involved with two *peploi*, and both completed a *peplos* and left their work unfinished, thus reeling in the next

---

[237] In theory we cannot even totally exclude the possibility that the wool may have been distributed to Group A, the girls whose term of office had been completed, the girls who had processed at the last Panathenaia and made the *peplos* 'now' worn by the statue, whose honours are set out in decree II, and that this was part of a cyclical symbolism. A comparable interweaving between the different years and *peploi*, with the same symbolism, would have been involved if the wool was given to the girls who would take office in the following year and weave the *peplos* for the Panathenaia after-next.

generation who did the same thing, in a process that invites us to see it as never ending. A cyclical, never-ending, process is a common way of expressing everlasting continuity in the Greek collective representations.[238] The articulation of the duties of the Ergastinai proposed here would help to present the offering of the *peplos* as a continuous, cyclical, enterprise that never ends, and so help represent the relationship it symbolizes. between Athens and its poliadic goddess, as eternal and never ending.

This reconstruction would make the Ergastinai closely comparable to the *arrhephoroi*, who processed with the *peplos* for which their predecessors had begun (and probably performed some of) the weaving, and then they themselves started (and probably wove some of) the *peplos* which their successors would process with at the next Panathenaia.[239] This comparability leads me to conclude that this is the reconstruction most likely to reflect the ancient realities.

6. PLYNTERIA AND KALLYNTERIA: RECONSTRUCTIONS AND READINGS

i. Reconstructions: a summary

I will now sum up my conclusions, and set out what on my analyses are the most likely reconstructions of the basic skeleton of the nexus of the Plynteria and Kallynteria. First, at some point in the month of Thargelion the priestess of Athena Polias removed the *peplos* from the statue of Athena Polias and gave it to the Praxiergidai. The archon sealed the temple and gave the key to the Praxiergidai. The key is normally the responsibility of the priestess of a cult, hence the priestess is also often referred to as *kleidouchos* and is usually represented

---

[238] See the discussion of a comparable, albeit somewhat differently cyclical, never-ending, process in Sourvinou-Inwood 1986: 56–7.

[239] On the *arrhephoroi*, see most recently Dillon 2002: 57–60, with bib. on p. 311 n. 85; Parker 2005a: 219–23 with bib. On the date of the ritual in which one set of *arrhephoroi* were discharged and another began their service, see e.g. Burkert 1983: 150 and n. 61.

holding a key in Attic iconography.[240] Therefore the priestess of
Athena Polias would have given the key to the archon, thus relin-
quishing her authority over the temple for a limited abnormal time.
Authority over the temple rested with the polis and was normally
exercised by the priestess. On this occasion she symbolically 'returned' that authority, symbolized by the key, to the polis, in the
shape of the polis's more general representative that was the archon,
who sealed the temple and then handed over temporary authority
over it, for the period in which the temple would be symbolically
sealed, until 28 Thargelion, to the *genos* of the Praxiergidai. The
Praxiergidai were in charge of the statue; they had taken over the
peplos of Athena and dressed the statue in a *chiton* which they had
provided from their own funds.

25 Thargelion was an *apophras* day and the temple was roped off.
On my reconstruction, first the women members of the Praxiergidai
performed the preliminary sacrifice to the Moirai, Zeus Moiragetes,
and Ge, a sacrifice that was preliminary to the whole nexus of rites;
then they removed the statue's jewellery, and its temporary dress, the
chiton, and covered it up in an appropriate piece of cloth; they
performed rites that are referred to as secret. Two girls, the Plyntrides,
undoubtedly members of the *genos* of the Praxiergidai, washed the
peplos in fresh water on the Acropolis.

On the morning of 26 Thargelion a procession took the statue, still
covered up, to Phaleron in a chariot. It was probably also on that day
that the new wool, for the *peplos* that would be woven next year, was
washed by tribally articulated groups of Ergastinai. The procession's
destination was the sanctuary of Athena Skiras. From there the
female Praxiergidai carried the statue to the shore, where the Loutrides performed its ritual bath. When it was taken out of the sea the
statue was wrapped in a clean cloth which may have been placed
around it as a *himation*. At some point the female Praxiergidai
dressed the statue in the laundered *peplos* (which they had
brought with them) and offered it a meal involving the *hegeteria*, a
cake of dried figs—if not, this cake would have been set in front of
the goddess at the sanctuary of Athena Skiras, after the female

---

[240] See Connelly 2007: 92–104.

Praxiergidai and the statue had returned there and rejoined the rest of the procession. Whatever other rites may or may not have been performed at this sanctuary before the procession departed to return to Athens, this return of the procession and the statue took place by torchlight, and therefore on 27 Thargelion, which (on my reconstruction) was the first day of the Kallynteria. When the procession returned to the Acropolis the statue was not taken inside the temple, but placed outside by the altar where it stayed until the next day.

On the return of the statue and procession to the Acropolis the priestess of Aglauros performed 'bringing-in' sacrifices, εἰσαγώγεια. After this followed the *pannychis* (perhaps organized and conducted by the Praxiergidai, who were still in charge of the temple and the statue) in which the priestess of Aglauros was responsible for keeping good order. It may have been during this *pannychis* that this priestess 'adorned a table' for Aglauros.

Perhaps the statue was adorned with its jewellery some time after its return to the Acropolis, in public view. There was a priestess called Kosmo who, we shall see,[241] had a special responsibility concerning the adornment of the statue. But this was in normal time. In this still abnormal time it is possible that this task may have been performed by the priestess of Aglauros. It is possible that the extinguishing, refilling, and relighting of the lamp of Athena took place at sunrise on 27 Thargelion, after the end of the *pannychis*. In the daytime of 27 Thargelion the temple was cleaned, adorned, and made brilliant.

After the sunset of the 27th, on 28 Thargelion, normality was fully re-established: the temple was unsealed, the statue was returned to the cleaned temple, and the Praxiergidai returned the key to the archon, who returned it to the priestess of Athena.

ii. Readings and meanings

Greek festivals were complex, polysemic, multilayered, and multivocal. On my reconstruction, after a period of dissolution of normality, abnormality, and perhaps pollution, the first day of Plynteria marked, and brought about, on the one hand a polarization of

---

[241] In Chapter 5, section 2.

abnormality and pollution, accompanied by ill-omen and an association with death (with all its semantic satellites such as grief and pollution), and on the other the beginning of the removal of pollution, with the washing of the *peplos*, indicated also by the festival's very name, Plynteria.

In the nexus of the Plynteria and Kallynteria abnormality and pollution, we saw, were correlative with primordiality—in complex ways. The movement towards purification and transition to normality in this ritual nexus involved many stages, as did, in the Athenian perceptions, the transition from primordiality to things as they are now, the normality of the present. In ritual there was an abandonment of normality when the statue and the temple were given over to the Praxiergidai and the temple was symbolically sealed. This movement from normality to the abnormality of the period in which the Praxiergidai took over was a preliminary movement, comparable to the (literal) movement of the statue of Dionysos to the Academy before the beginning of the City Dionysia.[242]

In the festival nexus itself, the abnormality and the interplay between pollution and purification of Thargelion crystallized as pollution and ill-omen, an intensification of pollution and abnormality and ill-omen, on the first day of the Plynteria on 25 Thargelion; there was then a movement from the abnormal and polluted (in this nexus symbolically equivalent to the primordial) which were purged through the Plynteria, to the normal and purified, which was symbolically equivalent to, and re-established, the present normality, which began to be restored on 27 Thargelion, on my reconstruction the first day of the Kallynteria, and was fully completed on the 28th, when the temple was symbolically unsealed and its control passed out of the hands of the Praxiergidai. That is, the Plynteria effected a movement from the state of abnormality and pollution to purification and normality, but within this movement the interplay between the symbolic counters that structured this ritual nexus was extremely complex, and it shaped very complex relationships.

In the mythological nexus that is more directly correlative with this ritual nexus the primordial was replaced by a movement, which

---

[242] On which, see Sourvinou-Inwood 2003a: 69.

began in Aglauros' lifetime, towards things as they now are in the cult. Aglauros' assumption of the priesthood was correlative with the establishment of the poliadic cult, and Aglauros had set in place the normal arrangements for the temple and statue; correlatively, she was honoured in the Kallynteria, the festival when the cult's normal arrangements were restored. However, before that, the normality established in Aglauros' lifetime was replaced (in myth and ritual) by the polluted and abnormal state of affairs created by the unwashed sacred garments for the year after her death. This was then followed by a movement towards, once again, things as they are now: in myth (and ritual) this came about with the washing of the sacred clothes and the institution (in present-day ritual the conduct) of the Plynteria, which involved also the washing of the statue, and finally with the Kallynteria bringing about the restoration of full normality. Though, on my reconstruction, the movement out of abnormality took place in stages, and normality was not fully restored until the second day of the Kallynteria, the Plynteria could be seen as being symbolically correlative more with the polluted and the primordial and the Kallynteria more with the purified and the present day.

Clearly, the relationship between the ritual movements and their mythological correlatives are complex. There was a perceptual rewinding of time at the beginning of the Kallynteria, since the *aition* of the Plynteria derived from after Aglauros' death, but that of the Kallynteria from her actions while still alive. Several factors underlie this rewinding. First, Greek ritual logic demanded the sequence 'from pollution to purification': in this nexus there was a preliminary movement out of normality which was intensified into pollution and ill-omen at the beginning of the nexus, and then there is one movement, in stages: a movement (which can be seen as coinciding with the Plynteria) from the abnormal and polluted, which was correlative with the primordial, to the cleansed, a state that did not yet involve the full restoration of present-day normality, coinciding with the end of the Plynteria and the beginning of the Kallynteria; and then a movement from that state to present-day normality, which can be seen as coinciding with the Kallynteria, with normality being restored by the festival's end.

Second, correlatively with the movement from pollution to purification, from gloom and ill-omenedness to joy and propitious times, Greek ritual logic privileged the sequence 'first death, then life', and it is this sequence that is constructed through the celebration first of the Plynteria, which commemorated a time of grief and pollution after Aglauros' death, and then of the Kallynteria, which commemorated her deeds in her lifetime—as well as, like the Plynteria, activating her status as cult recipient in the present. A further factor is that the Kallynteria also celebrated the advent of Athena, which was given concrete form through the arrival, the return, of her statue to the Acropolis, which, among other things, evoked the installation of Athena as the poliadic deity.

It is possible to represent the nexus of the Plynteria and Kallynteria as being based upon two main, interwoven, semantic axes: first, that of dissolution of normality, abnormality, and pollution (correlative with primordiality) brought to an end by purification and return to normality; and second, the deity's advent, expressed through the statue's absence and return. The two axes are interwoven: 'advent' was also expressed with the help of the axis 'abnormality, dissolution of normality—return to normality', since the removal of the statue, which is a ritual element that helps convey advent ritually, has the effect of bringing about, and is a sign of, 'abnormality, dissolution of normality' before the return to normality was brought about by the advent.

The bringing about of renewal after the abnormality and dissolution, and correlatively with purification and the restoration of normality, was an important ritual outcome of the nexus of the Plynteria and Kallynteria. This nexus effects the renewal of the statue's garment,[243] of the statue,[244] of the temple, and of the very relationship between the goddess and the polis—through all these acts and especially through the re-enactment of the establishment of the cult. If it is right that the lamp was relit in the course of the Kallynteria, this would have been another strong element of renewal.[245] Through the renewal of the polis's relationship to Athena a general renewal was also brought about, a renewal of life, prosper-

---

[243] See e.g. Steiner 2001: 109: dressing statues in fresh finery brings about the renewal of the statue's power.

[244] See e.g. ibid.: 109–10: bathing the statue "represents an attempt to give renewed power to an image whose numinous quality has suffered depletion or impairment" (see also ibid. 111).

[245] See n. 216 above.

ity, blessings. I shall return to this question of renewal in the discussion of the comparisons between the nexus of the Plynteria and Kallynteria on the one hand and the Panathenaia on the other in Chapter 5. The involvement of the Praxiergidai and other *genē* in the Plynteria and Kallynteria will be discussed in Chapter 7.

[A very fragmentary new decree (Malouchou 2008), perhaps of the city, of the mid-second century BC is highly though tantalizingly relevant to this whole chapter. Only line beginnings survive, and these are, where the text begins, 1 [ἐν?]/δῦναι καὶ ἀμφιέσα[ι 2 τῶι Ἀγλαυρείωι 3 [τὸ γένος?]/ τὸ Εὐηνοριδῶν 4 [τοῦ ἱ]/ερέως θυσίας ἄφορο. Later line beginnings indicate allusions to offerings made for the council and people and the crops, give two dates, and mention Hestia. We have therefore references to what sounds like the putting of a garment on a statue ('to put on and fit round'), to the shrine of Aglauros, and to a hitherto unknown *genos* (on which see Lambert 2008). The first two of these elements suggest the possibility of a connection with 'the Plynteria/Kallynteria nexus', and perhaps therewith that some of the ritual action of that nexus took place in the Aglaureion. (A connection with the presentation of the new *peplos* at the Panathenaia cannot be excluded, but is less close to hand.) The role of the new *genos* would, if so, be a striking new datum. It had already been argued that the role of the Praxiergidai at these festivals was contested, because they felt the need to reassert their traditions, πάτρια, in *IG* I³ 7; the new decree might, Lambert 2008 suggests, give the name of their competitors, the Euenoridai. Sourvinou-Inwood would perhaps have preferred to envisage a collaboration between *genē*, with the Praxiergidai still the major partners.]

APPENDIX: NAGY ON *CHITON* AND *PEPLOS*

B. Nagy suggested (cf. p. 149) that the *chiton* mentioned in *IG* I³ 7 was worn by the statue of Athena Polias together with, not in place of, the normal *peplos*. I will now set out arguments against this hypothesis.

First, in *IG* I³ 7 the reference to the Praxiergidai dressing the statue with the *peplos* is separate from the requirement that they should provide a *chiton*. Second, and most importantly, in *IG* I³ 7 the reference to the Praxiergidai dressing the statue with a *chiton* follows immediately after the reference to the archon giving the Praxiergidai the keys to the temple after he had sealed it for the period until 28 Thargelion, which suggests that it was during that period that the Praxiergidai dressed the statue with the *chiton* they themselves had provided, which would be consistent with the fact that this is the period during which they were in charge of the statue. Clearly, this period in which the Praxiergidai were in charge, which is what the archon giving the Praxiergidai the keys to the temple involves, was considerably longer than the immediate preliminaries for the rites of 25 Thargelion; so an expensive garment was expected to be provided for the statue. On this reading, this was another part of the Praxiergidai being in charge: the priestess took off the statue's *peplos* and the Praxiergidai dressed the statue in a *chiton* they provided.

Since the Praxiergidai took control of the statue and the temple, we would expect the *peplos* removed from the statue by the priestess to have been handed over to the Praxiergidai. I will now suggest that there is some evidence that indicates that this is indeed what took place. In the inscription *IG* II² 1060 + *IG* II² 1036 (cf. p. 205), if the restoration 'Praxiergidai' in fr. b.1-2 is right, there is a reference to the Praxiergidai receiving 'the current year's *peplos*'.[246] This description suggests that the occasion referred to cannot be the Panathenaia, since at the Panathenaia 'the current year's *peplos*' slot was occupied consecutively by two different garments, first the *peplos* that the statue wore during the cultic year that ended at the Panathenaia, and then the new *peplos* at the centre of the ritual[247]—which entails that this expression would not have been a natural choice for referring to a *peplos* at the Panathenaia. It would, however, be an appropriate expression for an occasion situated between Panathenaia, in

---

[246] Cf. n. 224 above.

[247] To avoid accusations of circularity I must state explicitly the obvious: in the unlikely possibility that the new *peplos* was not wrapped around the statue at the Panathenaia, but at the Plynteria, there would still have been two *peploi* fitting 'the current year's *peplos*' at the Panathenaia: the one worn by the statue and the one whose offering is the centre of the ritual.

which 'the current year's *peplos*' came into play—in contrast to the one that was being woven for the next Panathenaia.[248] The one such occasion that we know about, in which, moreover, we know that the Praxiergidai had an important role, and the *peplos* was taken off the statue, is the Plynteria.

The Praxiergidai receiving the current year's *peplos* before, but in connection with, the Plynteria is consistent with what we know about their role, since, we saw, we are not told that the Praxiergidai removed the *peplos* from the statue at the Plynteria—only the 'adornment'. I suggested that it was probably the priestess who removed the *peplos* from the statue and handed it to the Praxiergidai, marking the beginning of the period of abnormality in which the Praxiergidai were in charge. On the first day of the Plynteria the *peplos* would be washed by the Plyntrides, who were undoubtedly Praxiergidai. The Praxiergidai would eventually wrap it around the statue again.

The third argument against the view that the *chiton* was worn together with the *peplos* is that if this *chiton* provided by the Praxiergidai was part of Athena's normal dress, worn all year round, it would have been too cheap at two mnai. Two mnai would be luxurious enough for a temporary abnormal dress, but, surely, too cheap for Athena's main dress, to judge from the general worth of two mnai.[249]

Another argument against the hypothesis that the *chiton* was worn by the statue together with the *peplos* is that the *peplos* and the *chiton* are presented as alternative garments in Athena's wardrobe in the Homeric scenes in which Athena removes her *peplos* and puts on a *chiton*, because the *chiton*, unlike the *peplos*, is appropriate for battle.[250] These scenes give us at least a glimpse of Greek perceptions and are not widely different from the situation in Attic iconography, where the two are also alternatives: the *peplos* seems to have been

---

[248] Robert Parker has pointed out to me that ἐπέτεια in inventories are the accessions of the past year. My answer to that is that the difference between the Panathenaia on the one hand and the inventories on the other is that in the Panathenaia both *peploi* play a *dynamic* role, the new *peplos* replaces the old and this replacement is at the centre of the festival, and therefore both are 'this year's *peplos*' at the Panathenaia.

[249] See e.g. Dem. 41.11.

[250] See *Il.* 5.734–7; 8.385–7. See also Loraux 1989: 264–7; Llewellyn-Jones 2001: 244–5.

more commonly worn by Athena in the earlier periods,[251] the *chiton* was especially, though far from exclusively, associated with the goddess's warrior persona, in certain times and contexts, and perhaps also with her Ergane persona.[252] A final argument in support of the notion that Athena was wearing a *chiton* during the 'abnormal' period before the Plynteria was discussed in section 1.i above.

An objection could be drawn from a notice in Pollux, which runs: '*Peplos.* This is an item of clothing with a double use, both for wear and for [*literally*] throwing over. That it can be an item for throwing over (ἐπίβλημα) can be inferred from the *peplos* of Athena. [*There then by contrast follows an example of a peplos used as a chiton, i.e. for wear.*]'[253] It could be argued that the fact that Pollux calls Athena's *peplos* an ἐπίβλημα suggests that it was worn over a *chiton*, since in itself ἐπίβλημα can denote an item of overwear. But the context in Pollux, with its distinction between 'wearing' and 'throwing over', shows that he cannot be thinking of the *peplos* as being worn by the olivewood statue over an actual *chiton*. One possibility is that Pollux may be referring to the colossal *peplos*, in which case there are two further possibilities: one, if this colossal *peplos* was draped around the statue of Athena Parthenos, as suggested by Lewis, it would have been referred to as an ἐπίβλημα, a garment thrown over; and two, if it was hung behind this cult statue in the Parthenon, it could have been referred to as an ἐπίβλημα in the sense of hangings.[254] The second possibility is that Pollux was referring to the *peplos* worn by the olivewood statue, which was perceived as being 'thrown over' it. If that is right, two different considerations suggest that it was not 'thrown over' a *chiton*. First, if the *peplos* was worn thrown over a

---

[251] Thus, for example, on Panathenaic prize amphoras it is only from the end of the sixth century that Athena wears a *chiton* instead of a *peplos* (Neils 1992c: 33); on the representation of Athena on the Panathenaic amphoras, see Ridgway 1992: 127. See also the two bronze statuettes illustrated in Ridgway (1992: 129); fig. 78 with *peplos*, fig. 77 with *chiton*, and the discussion pp. 129–30. See also Ridgway (1992: 140) for the changing fashions in Athena's dress.

[252] On the warrior type Athena, see Ridgway 1992: 127–31. On her Ergane persona, see ibid. 139.

[253] πέπλος· ἔσθημα δ᾽ ἐστὶ διπλοῦν τὴν χρείαν, ὡς ἐνδῦναί τε καὶ ἐπιβαλέσθαι. καὶ ὅτι μὲν ἐπίβλημα ἐστί, τεκμήραιτ᾽ ἄν τις καὶ τῷ τῆς Ἀθηνᾶς πέπλῳ, ὅτι δὲ καὶ χιτών . . . Pollux *Onom.* 7.50.

[254] For ἐπίβλημα can also mean tapestry, hangings (see L-S s.v. ἐπίβλημα I.2).

chiton, this *chiton*, and not the *peplos*, would have been the statue's dominant garment—or at least a garment as important as the *peplos*. This, in its turn, would entail that the polis did not renew Athena's garment either every year, or penteterically, but offered her a kind of luxurious accessory, while the Praxiergidai renewed her main garment; this, I believe is ritually less plausible than its alternative. Second, the argument concerning price mentioned above is relevant here as well: a two mnai *chiton* was too cheap for one of Athena's main, regular, garments.

Consequently, I submit, Pollux's text cannot support the view that the olivewood statue of Athena Polias wore a *chiton* and over it a *peplos*. If the *peplos* referred to by Pollux was indeed the one worn by the olivewood statue, it was not worn over a *chiton*; since it was considered an ἐπίβλημα it may have been draped over the statue—rather than fastened with pins and a belt.

4

Athena at the Palladion
and the Palladion myth

1. THE PALLADION IN ATHENS: INTRODUCTION
AND PROBLEMATIK

The reconstruction of the festival nexus of the Plynteria and Kallynteria in Chapter 3 partly intersected the cult of Athena at the Palladion, for it included the investigation of the hypothesis that the attested procession to Phaleron was not part of the Plynteria, but involved the Palladion. I hope to have shown that this hypothesis is incorrect. Nevertheless, it is desirable that one of its constituent elements, a mytheme in a Patmos scholion, should be further investigated in some detail in the overall context of a consideration of the myths that place the Trojan Palladion in Athens in connection with the figure of Demophon. The first, narrowly focused, reason why the investigation is desirable is because it will strengthen further the conclusion that the procession to Phaleron did not involve the Palladion. The more widely focused reason is because this investigation will entail a consideration of the cult of Athena at the Palladion, and, above all, of its associated mythology, which will allow us to consider another nexus of myths focused on an important statue of Athena, and determine whether it is possible to reconstruct which of them may have been cultic myths intimately associated with the cult. This is an interesting comparandum when set against the myths and representations focused on the olivewood statue of Athena Polias discussed throughout this book.

The myths that place the Palladion in Athens will be studied in the wider context of the myths about the Trojan Palladion, Athenian and non-Athenian. The mytheme at the centre of the narrowly focused enquiry, only attested in a Patmos scholion, says that Demophon brought the Palladion down to the sea and washed it, and it has been suggested[1] that this was an *aition* for a ritual bath in the Palladion cult—which, if right, would appear to sustain the hypothesis that the procession to Phaleron involved the Palladion and was not part of the Plynteria.

An *aition* is a myth created to explain a ritual. I will argue below that the consideration of the history of the myths associated with the Palladion cult and the placing of this particular mytheme within that history leads to the conclusion that the mytheme in the Patmos scholion was not an *aition* that corresponded to a ritual element in the cult. But there is also a separate argument that suggests that the story that Demophon brought the Palladion down to the sea and washed it is not an *aition*, independently from the discussion of the history of the mythological nexus associated with the Palladion, which is why I set it out here: the match between the myth and the presumed ritual ascribed to the Palladion cult by the hypothesis scrutinized here is significantly less close than may at first appear, since in one very important aspect there is not a match between the alleged *aition* and the presumed ritual action.

For in that mytheme, it was Demophon who brought the Palladion down to the sea and washed it. But if there had been a ritual involving a bath of the Palladion at Phaleron, the statue would have been washed either by the person holding a special priesthood, who would have been a member of the *genos* associated with the cult, the Bouzygai, or (as was the case with the Praxiergidai and the statue of Athena Polias) by an especially appointed member or group of members of that *genos*. In either case, the mythological correlative would have been Bouzyges, not Demophon. As we shall see in sections 2 and 3 below, Bouzyges did indeed play a role in one version of the myth 'the Trojan Palladion in Athens', and this corresponds to the role of the Bouzygai in the cult of the Palladion. This serious divergence between the mytheme and the rite for which it is supposed to be an *aition* constitutes on its own

---

[1] By Burkert 1970a.

a strong argument against the hypothesis that postulates this relationship.

In section 3 the story in the Patmos scholion will be considered in the context of the nexus of myths of which it is part, the myths that explain how the Trojan Palladion ended up in Athens. We do not know when the mythological nexus 'the Trojan Palladion in Athens' was first created, but as it was, obviously, part of the wider nexus that concerns the Trojan Palladion, and its acquisition by the Greeks through its theft by Diomedes and Odysseus,[2] I shall begin by discussing this wider nexus.

2. TROY, THE PALLADION, AND THE GREEKS

In the post-Homeric mythology about the fall of Troy, the Palladion protected Troy until Diomedes and Odysseus stole it,[3] after the Greeks discovered that the city could not be taken for as long as the Palladion was within its walls.[4] In most versions of the myth, the Trojan Palladion was god-given, which gave it special significance. In one version the statue had fallen from the sky.[5] In another, in a

---

[2] On the question of the Trojan Palladion at Argos, see Billot 1997–8: 10–17 with extensive bib. On the question of the Trojan Palladion at Sparta, see Billot 1997–8: 10, 12.

[3] I should mention that the extant versions of the myth of the theft of the Trojan Palladion which will be discussed in this section are incompatible with the myth which Plutarch ascribes to Derkyllos (*FHGr* IV 587; Plutarch, *Mor.* 309F [17A]) according to which, when the temple of Athena at Troy was burning, Ilos went in and seized the Palladion which had fallen from the sky and was immediately blinded because no man was supposed to see it—he later recovered his sight.

[4] See Konon *FGrH* 26 F 1.34.2 and Apollod. *Epit.* 5.10 where Helenos reveals this to the Greeks. In Schol. Lycoph. *Alex.* 658 an oracle was given to the Greeks to that effect. For sources for the theft of the Palladion (besides those discussed below), see Frazer 1921: ii. 226–9, commentary on Apollod. *Epit.* 5.13; J. Boardman and E. Vafiropoulou-Richardson, *LIMC* III.I s.v. Diomedes I, 397; for bib. Kron 1976: 149 n. 691; *LIMC* s.v. Diomedes I, 397–8; see also Gantz 1993: 642–6. On the Palladion see also Faraone 1992: 4, 7, 115; N. Robertson 1996b; Bettinetti 2001: 71–4. On the myth of the protective Palladion see also Scheer 2000: 91–6 esp. 91–4.

[5] In response to Ilos' prayer to Zeus: Apollod 3.12.3. The Palladion fell from heaven: Konon 26 *FGrH* F 34; Dion. Hal. *Ant. Rom.* 2. 66.5. On the provenance of the Palladion in general, see Bettinetti 2001: 71–3. On statues fallen from the sky, see Bettinetti 2001: 90.

fragment of Arktinos, *Ilioupersis*, considered dubious,[6] when Chryse married Dardanos she brought with her as her dowry the gifts of Athena, among them the Palladia (*sic*), and Dardanos took the statue to Troy, which he founded. Finally, in a different variant, the Palladion was manufactured by a *telestes* (initiator) and philosopher called Asios.[7] A statement ascribed, almost certainly incorrectly, to Pherekydes claims that Palladia was the name for the statues that fell from the sky.[8]

The Palladion and its theft are absent from the Homeric poems. Both are attested in the *Ilias Parva*[9] and, we shall see in section 3, probably also in Arktinos' *Ilioupersis*. I suggest that it is possible to reconstruct the context in which this myth was created.

The Homeric world was, for its historical Greek audiences, a distanced world that included direct contact with the gods, and in which the individual gods had different allegiances in the Trojan War, for different reasons. The Homeric poems were the end product of a long tradition of oral poetry which began probably in the Mycenaean, conceivably in the Early 'Dark Age' period; their world was made up of elements derived from many societies, each time perceived, handled, and made sense of through the perceptual filters of each generation of poets. This conflated picture, which resulted from the complex deployments and redeployments over the centuries of material that had originated in different societies, distanced the world of the poems from the world of the present, and this distancing helped construct the heroic age. Consequently, though the filters through which the world of the epics were viewed and manipulated by the poet were those shaped by the assumptions of eighth-century Ionia, the relationship between the assumptions and perceptions of eighth-century Ionia and the Homeric epics is extremely complex.

---

[6] *EGF* p. 65, where it is judged "fragmentum dubium". In my view this is not necessarily right; I will be discussing this fragment below.

[7] Suda s.v. Palladion. On this tradition that it did not fall from the sky, see Faraone 1992: 7, 117; Bettinetti 2001: 72–3 and n. 27. For sources on the Palladion, see Frazer 1921: ii. 38–41 ad Apollod. 3.12.3.

[8] *FGrH* 3 F 179, classified by Jacoby in the category 'uncertain, dubious or inauthentic' and not included at all in Fowler's equivalent category (Fowler 2000: 362–4). On the various terms used for the concept 'statue', see Bettinetti 2001: 25–63.

[9] In Proklos' summary: *EGF* p. 52.23–4; Arktinos: *EGF* p. 65.

I cannot, of course, try to discuss here the ways in which the world of the 'epic cycle' differed from the Homeric epics but it cannot be doubted that it did; for example, the large number of oracles and prophecies[10] entails that the guidance given by the gods in the world of the poems is comparable to that in the world of the audience.

I suggest that when the Trojan stories came to be reshaped and rewritten from the viewpoint of poets who shared the crystallizing ideologies of the early poleis, at the centre of which was the gods' guarantee of protection for these poleis, the destruction of a city was perceived to be a somewhat disturbing, symbolically threatening, concept. It is frightening to think that the gods might abandon a city despite the fact that the city had given them proper worship, and this was, again, explored centuries later in Euripides' *Troades*. One way of constructing a relatively reassuring conceptual framework for disaster (that did not entail a simple cruelty of indifferent gods who did not recognize the relationship of *charis*) is the perception of the victim's culpability, or, at the very least, 'contributory negligence'. Indeed in *Troades* this is the main explanation for the Trojans' sufferings: the Trojans are presented as responsible for their sufferings, which they (at least partly) brought upon themselves, by ignoring the warning of prophecy and letting Paris live. In addition, justice will be done, since the Greeks will be punished for their sacrilegious behaviour. This shows that the gods are not indifferent to human behaviour, and it also entails that there is order in the world.[11]

It is probably in that context, through the operation of these ideological parameters, that the myth of the protective Palladion and its theft by the Greeks was created, centuries earlier than the *Troades*, by one of the poets of the 'epic cycle'. For this myth gives a clear-cut answer to the problem of the loss of divine protection: it crystallizes divine protection into one sacred object, the loss of which 'explains' the loss of divine protection and the resulting Sack of Troy.

[10] See e.g. Griffin 1977: 48, who accepts the earlier view that this makes the world of the 'epic cycle' deterministic, a view which I believe is rather culturally determined (see text below).

[11] The statements made here are based on my discussions of this play and its Problematik in Sourvinou-Inwood 2003a: 350–61, 405–7.

However, as has been noted,[12] the belief that Troy fell because the Palladion had been stolen appears to be in some kind of 'conflict' with the story that Kassandra was raped at the Sack of Troy though she had taken refuge at the Palladion.[13] Like the belief that Troy fell because the Palladion had been stolen, the Locrian Ajax's rape of Kassandra at the Palladion gave, I will now argue, complex, but ultimately less threatening, answers to deeply significant questions. This rape at the Palladion was a sacrilege against Athena, and the fact that, for whatever reason, the Greeks did not punish the culprit gave an explanation as to why so many of the Greek heroes had problematic or disastrous *nostoi*: these disasters would have been seen as consequences of the sacrilege, which meant that it was not random bad luck in a frightening random world, but a punishment for an offence against a deity, and so ultimately all the gods. Indeed this point is made explicit in Euripides' *Troades*, for tragedy explored religious problems and gave, I have argued, ultimately reassuring (albeit complex) answers.[14] In the prologue of that tragedy Poseidon speaks of the sacrileges committed by the Greeks when Troy was sacked and Athena tells him of her purpose to bring a grim return home to the Greeks, because sacrilege was committed against her shrine when Ajax raped Kassandra and the Greeks did not punish him. This, then, is a clear-cut message of retribution for sacrilege, and at the same time an explanation for the unhappy fate of the Greeks returning from Troy. Insofar as it is an explanation, it is reassuring, since it establishes cause and effect and validates the notion of an ordered universe. For the most terrifying thing is a world that has no meaning, no order, and no plan.

Though the epic cycle is unlikely to have dealt with such a Problematik in ways comparable to the tragic explorations, its mythopoeia was inevitably shaped by cultural assumptions in which certain perceptions (for example that the world is an ordered universe, as well as the cultural anxiety that just conceivably it may not be)

---

[12] See Sourvinou-Inwood 2003a: 350–61.

[13] On Kassandra's rape, see (with bib.) Anderson 1997: 49–52, 199–202, 208–14, 217–29, 231–40 passim. On Kassandra as a suppliant at the Palladion, see also Bettinetti 2001: 178–9.

[14] See n. [not given].

shaped the construction of stories. In *Ilioupersis*[15] the rape of Kassandra at the Palladion is represented at the especially sacrilegious end of the spectrum of perceptions of that rape: Ajax, in dragging Kassandra away from Athena's statue, had dragged the statue with her.[16] This sacrilege would have been seen, I submit, as a cause of the Greeks' problematic *nostoi*.

But if the Palladion had been stolen, how could Kassandra's rape have taken place at the statue? And if Kassandra's rape took place at the statue, how was it possible for the Palladion to have been stolen?

I suggest that the perceived dissonance[17] between the two (obviously, independently created) important myths shaped the mythopoeic process in which the myth of the two Palladia was created. For it must not be assumed that this mytheme was a simple 'politically motivated' creation—though a privileging of the political and competitive over the dynamics of the mythopoeic process itself has shaped modern discussions of the multiple Palladia. Of course, the multiplication of Palladia, and various stories involving multiple Palladia, can be seen as correlative with the various claims, by various cities, to possess the Trojan Palladion, and eventually Rome's claim that Aeneas had taken it with him.[18] However, it does not follow that the mytheme of the second Palladion was invented solely, or even primarily, or at all, for that reason. Despite the apparent fit between multiple claims and multiple Palladia, we must not take it for granted that 'politics' and competition were necessarily the only, or indeed main, driving forces shaping this mythographical construction. Indeed it is possible that it was the existence of the myth that there was more than one Trojan Palladion that facilitated the emergence of the multiple claims.

The mytheme that there was more than one Palladion at Troy relates to mythemes that became important parts of the myth of the fall of Troy, that the Palladion had been stolen, and that Kassandra's

---

[15] Proklos' summary of *Ilioupersis, EGF* p. 62.23–4.

[16] See also e.g. Soph. *Ajax Lokros* (*TrGF* 4, pp. 102–23 FF 10a–18) fragment 10c, where Athena has just discovered the upsetting of her statue by Ajax when he violated Kassandra.

[17] I have argued that though we must not expect consistency in Greek mythology, nevertheless, its tolerance of plurality has certain limits: Sourvinou-Inwood 1997c.

[18] On the Roman versions of the Palladion myth, see R. G. Austin's edn. of Virg. *Aen.* 2, pp. 83–5 ad 2.163; Horsfall 1979: 374–5, 388–9; see also Bettinetti 2001: 77–80.

rape had taken place at the Palladion. The genuine god-given Palladion was necessary for Troy's protection. But a newly constructed 'imitation' Palladion, and indeed any statue of Athena, was sufficient to give protection to Kassandra, and to make it a sacrilege when that protection was ignored and the very statue dragged from its proper place; whichever statue was involved, the Lesser Ajax's actions were sacrilegious and offended the goddess. These semantic 'requirements' would correspond to a mythological construction in which there were two Palladia and the Greeks stole the genuine Palladion. Let us consider the surviving myths.

One version (for example the story in Konon[19]) claims that the Greeks stole one statue, the genuine Palladion. In another version they stole two Palladia. This latter version is reflected in images that will be discussed below. The earliest textual reference to the Greeks stealing two Palladia is in Ptolemy Chennos,[20] a story which may well be dependent on the third-century BC historian Apollas or Apellas of Pontos, whose surviving fragment says that there were two Palladia, both man-made, but not that the Greeks stole both.[21] The earliest known reference to two Palladia is in a story attributed to Arktinos' *Ilioupersis*,[22] according to which there were two Palladia at Troy, the one given to Dardanos by Zeus, which was hidden and remained in the city until it was captured, and an imitation one made to deceive those who had designs to steal it; the Greeks stole the fake one. The validity of this attribution has been doubted on grounds that are not necessarily as compelling as they may at first appear. I shall return to the question of which Palladion the Greeks stole below. But it is wrong to think that the authenticity of the reference to the story of the two Palladia does not "square easily" with the fact that Proklos' summary of *Ilioupersis* mentions the rape of Kassandra at the Palladion, and there is no suggestion that this Palladion was not authentic.[23] On the

---

[19] Konon *FGrH* 26 F1.34.

[20] Phot. *Bibl.* 190 p. 148 a29; cf. Tomberg 1968: 175–8.

[21] *FGrH* 266 F1 (see Jacoby 1954: i. 200–1).

[22] Cited in Dion. Hal. *Ant. Rom.* 1.68.2–69 (see also Satyros *FGrH* 20 F1; Domitios Kallistratos *FGrH* 433 F 10); classified by Davies *EGF* 65–6 as a "fragmentum dubium" of Arktinos, *Ilioupersis*. Horsfall 1979: 374–5 argues against its authenticity, but, we shall see, the basis of this rejection is mistaken.

[23] Horsfall 1979: 374.

contrary, we saw that this very potential dissonance was crucial in the mythopoeic process. As for the notion[24] that it only becomes necessary to invent pseudo-Palladia when the Romans claim the authentic one, it cannot be disproved beyond reasonable doubt (if we leave aside the question of the authenticity of Arktinos' fragment, to avoid circularity), since it cannot be shown that this Roman claim did not predate the 470s BC, when, we shall see, images showing two Palladia were painted, but I would suggest it is not very likely that it did.

The two Palladia also appear in one of the versions of the myth of the Trojan Palladion in Athens which will be discussed in section 3. For reasons of clarity of exposition I need to set out that story briefly here. According to an account in Polyaenus,[25] Diomedes gave the Palladion to the care of Demophon, Agamemnon demanded it, Demophon had an imitation one constructed and kept it in his tent; he gave the real one to an Athenian called Bouzyges to bring to Athens. When Agamemnon tried to take by force what was in fact the imitation statue Demophon and his men put up some resistance, to convince Agamemnon that they were protecting the true Palladion.

To return to the version according to which the Greeks stole two Palladia, which, we shall see, is represented in the images just mentioned: if the Greeks had stolen both Palladia, what about the dissonance with the rape of Kassandra? I suggest that no such dissonance would have been felt. One imitation Palladion was not symbolically different from another; so if the Greeks had stolen one imitation Palladion the Trojans would have been perceived (if such a question arose at all) to have simply constructed another. Once the genuine Palladion was stolen, any number of imitation Palladia could have been made and they were all statues of Athena that deserved respect. Certainly, by the early fifth century both myths were deeply rooted, and therefore (whether or not the mythological existence of more than one Palladion had been established) Athena's statue against which the Lokrian Ajax offended would have been conceptually cut loose from any perceived need to define its relationship to the protective Palladion. That this was indeed the case is indicated by the differentiation, in roughly contemporary Athenian scenes,

---

[24] For this Horsfall 1979: 375 cites R. G. Austin's note ad Virg. *Aen.* 2.163.
[25] Polyaen. *Strat.* 1.5.

Figure 2. Red-figure kylix by Macron (detail), showing the quarrel of Odysseus and Diomedes, each holding a Palladion. H. 12 cm. Inv. no. B-1543. The State Hermitage Museum, St. Petersburg, photograph © The State Hermitage Museum/Photograph by Vladimir Terebenin, Leonard Kheifets, Yuri Molodkovets.

between Athena's statue at the rape of Kassandra and the representations of the stolen Palladia. Until the late sixth century the Athena figure represented at the rape of Kassandra on Athenian vases was more an image of the goddess herself than of her statue, and was perceived to represent both goddess and statue, but subsequently Athena's statue was unambiguously represented,[26] and, at least on some images, it is shown as considerably larger than the Palladia represented in the two scenes from the 470s that will now be discussed, which were painted at about the same time as some of

---

[26] See Connelly 1993: 100–3, 114–16; Anderson 1997: 201.

the rape of Kassandra scenes with Athena's statue. This shows that the statue could at that time be thought of as very different from the Palladion stolen by Diomedes and Odysseus.[27]

The first of these images also offers the earliest evidence for some kind of association between Demophon and the Palladion. It is in an Athenian image painted a little after 480 BC, that includes a representation of Demophon, Diomedes, and two Palladia. This image, on side A of the cup St Petersburg, State Hermitage Museum, ST830 by Makron,[28] shows a quarrel between Odysseus and Diomedes (whose names are inscribed), each of whom is holding a Palladion in his left hand and a sword in his right. Each is represented next to the handle, facing in the direction of the other, and between them are four other heroes, whose names are also inscribed, one next to, and turned towards, each of the quarrelling heroes; the one next to Diomedes is named Demophon, the one next to Odysseus is named Akamas.[29] In the middle there are two more men, each facing in the direction of the hero nearest to him, on the left Agamemnon holding a sceptre and gesticulating towards Diomedes (and Demophon), on the right Phoinix, moving to the left but looking back towards Odysseus and Akamas. I shall return to Makron's image.

[27] Because the statue with Kassandra is differentiated from the Palladion represented in the theft scenes, and because the Palladion that was stolen was perceived to be the smallest (see Konon *FGrH* 26 F 1.34.2; see also Suda s.v. Palladion; Bettinetti 2001: 72 and n. 24) Moret (1975: 87–90) insisted that different statues were involved in the Rape of Kassandra and the theft of the Palladion, and that this understanding never changed.

[28] = St Petersburg, State Hermitage Museum, B1543 and St Petersburg, State Hermitage Museum, 649; *ARV* 460.13, 481, 1654; *Add* 244; *LIMC* Diomedes I no. 2; Sourvinou-Inwood 1990b: 405 pl. 5; Kunisch 1997: 135; 196 no. 338; pl. 113.338 (Kunisch considers this to be side B). It has been suggested that the image reflects the Ὀδυσσεὺς αὐτόμολος of Epicharmos in which, the hypothesis goes, Odysseus may have manufactured or otherwise procured a fake Palladion to present to the Greeks while Diomedes had stolen the real one from Troy (see e.g. Sechan 1926: 158 n. 2). But, as Kron (1976: 150) notes, besides the fact that the vase does not work as an illustration of a comedy, Demophon and Akamas would have had no place in Epicharmos' comedy; the content postulated for that play is pure speculation insecurely based on fr. 99 K/A.

[29] Kunisch (1997: 135 n. 642) says that the inscription normally considered to read 'Akamas' is destroyed to the point of illegibility.

Figure 3. Red-figure amphora showing Diomedes and Odysseus each holding a Palladion, with Athena between them. © Museum of Mediterranean and Near Eastern Antiquities, Stockholm, photographer Ove Kaneberg. Inv. no. MM1963.1.

Diomedes and Odysseus are also represented holding a Palladion each in another image of about the same time, which is therefore also structured by the schema 'two Palladia in Greek hands', on an amphora which shows Diomedes and Odysseus, fully armed, each holding a Palladion and facing each other with Athena between them.[30] Athena is standing between the two heroes, her lower body

---

[30] Amphora Stockholm Medelhausmus. 1963.1 (*ARV* 1643.33 bis; *Add* 210. (292.33 bis); *LIMC* Diomedes I no. 24).

facing one hero, while she turns to relate to the other; she is therefore shown interacting with both. The scene does not show fighting, but it is possible that, given the common schema 'deity represented between two fighting heroes', if the story of the fighting of the two heroes in connection with the two Palladia was already established, this image also would have been read as relating to the hostility, perhaps fighting, between Diomedes and Odysseus which is represented as being in abeyance in the image, in consequence, it would have been understood, of the presence of Athena, the goddess whose statues were the cause of the hostility. But it is probable that in the eyes of the ancient viewers it was ambiguous whether or not the image showed Diomedes and Odysseus after a fight, stopped by Athena; it is likely that both readings (that there had been a fight, and that there had not) were open to them. But what, I suggest, is clear, is that the schema would have evoked the knowledge that at some point they did quarrel. The fact that there is more than one image representing Diomedes, Odysseus, and two Palladia indicates a story known at Athens at that time.[31]

A third, very fragmentary, classical representation of the theft of the Palladion involving two statues dates from the end of the fifth or beginning of the fourth century: on a fragment from an Attic krater two Palladia are shown inside a temple.[32] According to Tiverios who published this fragment, Diomedes and Odysseus would have been represented outside the temple and possibly other figures, such as Athena, Helen, and Theano.[33]

---

[31] The story of the theft of the Palladion had been explored in tragedy (see Soph. *Lakainai TrGF* 4 pp. 328–30 FF 367–369a). See Arist. *Poet.* 23.1459 b 6. On this tragedy see also below.

[32] Tiverios 1988.

[33] Ibid.: 328. He (1988: 329) connects the appearance of Demophon and Akamas on Makron's cup with the acquisition of the Palladion, and this to the threat to Athens during the Persian Wars and the strengthening of morale resulting from the notion that Athens possessed the true Palladion, for he takes that cup as showing that this tradition of the Palladion in Athens was known in Athens at least as early as the beginning of the fifth century. He supposes the representation of the two Palladia on this krater fragment to be similarly connected with the Peloponnesian war.

The two Palladia also appear in a fourth classical image,[34] on a fourth-century South Italian vase of 360–50 BC.[35] In that image Diomedes and Odysseus, each holding a drawn sword and a Palladion, are moving away from, but looking towards, Athena who is on the left. Athena is pointing towards the Palladion held by Diomedes or also to a woman on the right whose identity is problematic. She is wearing a diadem on which is fixed a long veil which hangs down her and she is holding an object that is difficult to identify. It could be a key, in which case the woman would be a priestess, or, as Moret has argued, it may be a torch, in which case it is held in an unusual way.[36] If the object is indeed a torch, it does not follow that the woman is Hekate or Persephone.[37] I shall return to this. A shield is shown above the two heroes, and this shows that the scene is located in the sanctuary.[38] The stances of Odysseus and Diomedes and the ways in which they are holding the drawn swords do not support the notion that they are fighting with each other and Athena puts an end to it; they are naturally alert in hostile territory.[39]

The element of the two Palladia connects this image to the scene on Makron's cup and to that on the amphora; Athena interacting with the two heroes connects it more closely to that on the amphora. The quarrelling Diomedes and Odysseus on Makron's cup are represented together with other Greek heroes who are intervening in the quarrel. The non-quarrelling Diomedes and Odysseus on the South Italian scene appear to be located in the Trojan sanctuary. Athena is present and interacting in both the image on the amphora and the South Italian scene located in her sanctuary. The representation of Athena in friendly interaction with Diomedes and Odysseus who are stealing (in the South Italian vase) or have just stolen (on the Attic amphora) the Palladia conveys the idea that Athena looked benignly on the theft of her statues from Troy. This idea may or may not have been expressed in a tragedy in which Athena

[34] They also appear on a clay mould for a plaque of the Roman period (*LIMC* Diomedes I no. 41 and ill. on p. 402).
[35] The Apulian oinochoe Paris Louvre K36 (*LIMC* Diomedes I p. 401 no. 25).
[36] Moret 1975: 79–80.
[37] As ibid.: 80 suggested.
[38] See ibid.: 80–1.
[39] See also ibid.: 79.

appeared to the two heroes and gave them her support. The woman is combined with the scene's location in the Trojan sanctuary, but she is not interacting with the others and may well have been understood to be, not part of this moment of the narrative, but an emblematic element that belongs with, and complements, the story. The way she is holding the object in her hand, especially if it is a torch, suggests that it is at rest, not in use at this particular moment.

The identification of the woman primarily depends on the object she is holding, which characterizes her. If it is a key, the woman would be a priestess. There was one priestess involved in the myth of the theft of the Palladion from Troy: according to one version of this myth Theano, the priestess of Athena at Troy, gave the Greeks the Palladion. This mytheme is only attested in late sources,[40] but it has been suggested that a fragment of Sophokles' *Lakainai* (*Spartan Women*), which deals with the theft of the Palladion, the fragment *TrGF* 4 F 368, which justifies the Greek position in the war, would more naturally be addressed to a Trojan, and later sources make Theano hand over the image.[41] The title of Sophokles' tragedy indicates that the chorus were Helen's attendants, and so they were discovered by, or contacted, Helen[42]—after they had entered Troy through a sewer.[43] But Helen would make excellent sense as an intermediary who would put them in contact with Theano, and a

---

[40] In Schol. Lycoph. *Alex.* 658 Theano, the priestess of Athena at Troy, gave the Palladion to Diomedes and Odysseus. In Suda s.v. Palladion Diomedes and Odysseus looted (ἐσύλησαν) the Palladion from the sanctuary after Theano, who was a priestess and guardian of the statue, had betrayed it.

[41] On Sophokles' *Lakainai*, see also Sechan 1926: 156–9, 599 with earlier bibliography. On the suggestion concerning F 368, see ibid. 156, though Sechan himself takes the view that nothing proves that Theano was convinced by the argument; but, in my view, his argument that the fact that the priestess is running in fear as Odysseus and Diomedes steal the Palladion on the South Italian vase Naples 3231 shows that she did not give it to them willingly is mistaken; for there were clearly different treatments of the story, and, we shall see, whichever version was reflected in *Lakainai*, there is some reason for thinking that Theano went together with the version of the two Palladia, and the Naples vase only involves one. On the suggestion that F 368 would more naturally be addressed to a Trojan, see more recently Gantz 1993: 643. See also Lloyd-Jones 1996: 197; see also ibid. 361 ad fr. 799.

[42] Gantz 1993: 643.

[43] *TrGF* 4 F 367.

chorus of Laconian women would be complicit with the Greek heroes. An Attic vase of about 420 BC,[44] which has been thought to reflect Sophokles' play,[45] shows Helen, whose name is inscribed, between Diomedes, who is holding the Palladion, and Odysseus. Helen, then, in this depiction of the theft, is associated with the one Palladion version, but this does not mean that she may not also have been associated with the two Palladia version in some stories.

To return to the South Italian scene with the two Palladia. If the object held by the woman is a torch, held in an unusual way,[46] as though it is resting in the woman's hands, rather than being shown in use, I suggest that Theano is again the most likely candidate: she is shown holding, but probably not using, a torch that represents the fact that she guided the Greek heroes and helped them in their quest. Helen may or may not have also helped them in the story shown on this vase, which may or may not be a version of the story that is also reflected in Sophokles' *Lakainai*, but whether or not she did, the torch would have been more appropriate for characterizing Theano, for it would have been Theano who would have physically guided them to the Palladion, undoubtedly lighting the way with a torch.

In theory Makron's image would be compatible with a story in which only one Palladion was stolen and the other was discovered after the Sack. However, first, there is no reason to think that the quarrel between Diomedes and Odysseus, which is shown in Makron's image, was located at any other time than immediately after the theft of the Palladion: in the extant narratives, in the *Ilias Parva* and probably also in Sophokles' *Lakainai*, the strife between Diomedes and Odysseus is located at the time of the stealing of the Palladion.[47]

---

[44] Panathenaic amphora Naples 81401 (H 3235); *ARV* 1316.1; *Add* 362; see esp. *LIMC* Diomedes I no 27.

[45] See Sechan 1926: 158–9 with bib.

[46] Moret 1975: 79–80.

[47] *Ilias Parva* fr. 9 *EGF*; see also on this Gantz 1993: 643. Lloyd-Jones 1996: 361 ad fr. 799 agrees with the view that fr. 799 was part of Sophokles' *Lakainai* and belonged to the quarrel between Odysseus and Diomedes while they were returning to the Greek camp with the Palladion (Radt *TrGF* 4 p. 542 had included fr. 799 in the Incertarum Fabularum category).

Second, the decision to represent on the amphora the two heroes alone with Athena and not fighting (for if they were fighting the image would have been perceived as an extract from which the other Greeks were omitted) suggests a context involving only these three figures, and such a context involving Diomedes, Odysseus, and the Palladia belonged to the story of the theft of the Palladion. Third, the South Italian scene which shows the two heroes with two Palladia is located in a sanctuary, and so shows them stealing two Palladia. So the story that the Greeks stole two Palladia can be securely dated to at least as early as the 350s BC. In fact, given the combination of the two Palladia and the presence of Athena that connects the South Italian scene to that on the Athenian amphora, it is difficult to doubt that it reflects the same story as the one reflected on that amphora. We may therefore conclude that the myth that the Greeks had stolen two Palladia, which means that they had certainly stolen the genuine one, was current in Athens at, or before, the 470s BC.

According to the logic of the myth, for Troy to have fallen, the Greeks had to have stolen the true Palladion; either the one and only Palladion which was the true one, or, if there was also an imitation statue, they must either have taken the genuine Palladion or both the fake and the genuine statue. However, Dionysios of Halikarnassos claimed that in Arktinos' *Ilioupersis* the Greeks stole the fake Palladion—a claim the validity of which, we saw, has been doubted. Not all the reasons for doubting the attribution of this story to Arktinos' *Ilioupersis* are valid, but the notion that the Greeks had stolen the false Palladion and nevertheless Troy was taken does create problems, not least in invalidating the oracles revealed to the Greeks by Helenos which led to the theft of the Palladion.[48] We cannot exclude the possibility that the notion that even a god-given Palladion could not protect Troy may have been explored in the epic cycle, but as this would have destabilized the complex web of myths and perceptions of which the theft of the Palladion is part, it is perhaps less likely than its alternative, that the mytheme 'the Greeks

---

[48] See also Gantz (1993: 644 and 876 n. 78), who suggests that it is possible that the story that the Greeks stole the fake Palladion was wrongly attributed to Arktinos, that it is possible Dion. Hal. was working from an interpolated text.

stole the fake Palladion' was a creation either of Dionysios of Halikarnassos or of a source Dionysios used which shared his ideological
perspective. Since the notion that the Greeks stole the fake is a
necessary correlative to Dionysios of Halikarnassos' story (and concern) that Aeneas brought the Palladion, the genuine Palladion, to
Rome, for which it was necessary that the genuine Palladion should
still be in Troy during the Sack, I suggest that this mytheme, that the
Greeks stole the fake, is the result of an alteration of Arktinos' text
either by Dionysios of Halikarnassos himself, or, perhaps more
probably, by a source which, like Dionysios of Halikarnassos, privileged the idea that the Palladion was in Troy when the city fell and
was taken to Rome by Aeneas.[49]

Consequently, Arktinos' *Ilioupersis* may well have told the story
that there were two Palladia, one genuine and one fake, and the
Greeks took away the genuine one, or both, which was then modified
by Dionysios of Halikarnassos or his source who viewed the myth
from a very different ideological perspective from that of the archaic
and classical Greek world, in which the destruction of Troy was
dependent on the loss of the genuine Palladion. A possibility that
cannot be excluded is that there may have been versions of the myth
in which it had been unclear whether Diomedes and Odysseus had
stolen the genuine Palladion, until Troy fell, thus demonstrating that
they had.

To continue the consideration of the two Palladia version of the
myth, it is possible that the mytheme of Theano's help to the Greeks,
the story that she handed over the Palladion to them, belongs in the
framework of this variant of the myth. I will now present the case for
suggesting that Theano's help was part of a myth in which there were
two Palladia and the genuine Palladion was hidden, as in the version
attributed to Arktinos.

The notion that the Palladion was handed over to Diomedes and
Odysseus by Athena's Trojan priestess would have added authority to
the Greek acquisition of the statue; but this is likely to have been the

---

[49] Elsewhere Dion. Hal. says that others say that Aeneas who knew the Palladion
well took it and brought it to Italy, while the Achaeans stole the copy (*Ant. Rom.* 2.
66.5).

result of this action, not its narrative motivation. This semantic space 'narrative motivation for Theano to give the Palladion to Diomedes and Odysseus' roughly corresponds to the interaction between two mythemes 'the Trojans had hidden the genuine Palladion and put the imitation one on display' and 'the Greeks stole the true Palladion'. In other words, in a version in which two Palladia were involved and Diomedes and Odysseus stole the true Palladion—or both the true and the imitation one—and in which the true Palladion was hidden, the heroes' inability to find the true Palladion corresponds to the mytheme 'Theano gave the Palladion to Diomedes and Odysseus' for which we are trying to reconstruct the narrative motivation.

Since the Palladion was a cult statue, in Greek eyes there would be no question as to where it would have been in normal circumstances: it would have stood in Athena's temple (as it did, for example, in [Eur.] *Rhesos* 499–502, where Hector says that Odysseus stole the statue from Athena's precinct). Therefore the notion that the Greek heroes needed Theano's help to get hold of the statue would seem to belong together with the mytheme that the Trojans had hidden the genuine Palladion and replaced it with an imitation one. It is therefore possible that the mytheme that Theano gave the Palladion to the Greeks was part of the variant of the myth that there were two Palladia, one genuine and one fake—and in one version the Greeks took away the genuine one and in another both. Such a combination of two Palladia and Theano would coincide with the reading of the South Italian vase suggested above, according to which the woman with the torch was Theano and her representation indicated that she had guided the Greek heroes to the true Palladion—probably the one now in the hands of Diomedes, next to Theano, in the direction of which Athena is shown pointing.

Let us return to Makron's image. This image is certainly not a representation of the parts of the myth involving Demophon bringing the Palladion to Athens that we know about, but it has been suggested, we shall now see, that it depicts an earlier moment of the myth of the Athenian acquisition of the Trojan Palladion at Troy.

The story represented in Makron's image may have had versions which continued with Diomedes giving the Palladion to Demophon followed by Demophon's hostile relationship to Agamemnon and the rest of the myth reflected in Polyaenus. That is, the antagonistic relationship between Diomedes and Odysseus in the image may have provided a possible context for the construction of the mytheme 'Diomedes (or Diomedes and Odysseus) entrust the Palladion to Demophon', which structures one version of the 'Palladion acquired by the Athenians at Troy' variant. This is indeed how Kron interpreted the scene: that Agamemnon orders the quarrelling heroes to leave the decision to the Greek leaders who are represented on the other side of the cup (six men with staffs, some seated, some standing) and to entrust the Palladia to Demophon and Akamas.[50] Kunisch goes further and reads the scene in more specific detail: Diomedes and Odysseus are quarrelling about who stole the genuine Palladion from Troy, while on the other side are shown the Greek leaders who will entrust the genuine Palladion to Demophon's custody.[51] If he is right, then this image refracts an early version of the myth 'Demophon acquired the Palladion at Troy'.

Whether or not there was such a specific story, if a story involving Demophon acquiring the Palladion was established before Makron's cup was painted, the representation of Demophon on that cup would for the Athenian viewers have evoked his role in that story. If the story involving Demophon acquiring the Palladion and Agamemnon trying to seize it (a version of the story told by Polyaenus) was established before Makron's cup the same would be true of the figure of Agamemnon. Unfortunately, the image cannot prove the existence of such a story; for we cannot be totally certain that the representation of Demophon and Akamas corresponded to a story concerning the Palladion; Makron might have given them a prominent position simply to strengthen the Athenian element in the scene. This is less likely, given Demophon's connection to the Palladion and to Diomedes in stories about the Palladion attested later, but it cannot be totally excluded.

In any case, the minimum that can be reconstructed on the basis of this image is that the elements 'two Palladia in Greek hands at Troy', 'fighting among Greeks over the Palladia' (in the version of the quarrel between Diomedes and Odysseus), 'Demophon's involve-

---

[50] Kron 1976: 150–1.   [51] Kunisch 1997: 135.

ment of some kind' appear in a representation of *c.*480 BC before they reappear in a different form in Polyaenus' version of the myth of the Athenian acquisition of the Palladion at Troy.

The mytheme 'two Palladia in the possession of the Greeks', one of the elements that were deployed in a modified form in Polyaenus' version of the myth, appears both in Makron's image and on the almost contemporary amphora mentioned earlier.[52] The element 'fighting between Diomedes and Odysseus' may have been evoked by, but is not actually represented in, the second image. It could be argued that these images may refract a tragedy that involved the theft of two Palladia; that the fact that two vases by different vase-painters painted at about the same time showed the two Palladia, and that the two Palladia were only represented again twice, once at the end of the fifth or beginning of the fourth century, the second time in the middle of the fourth century in Apulia, is a pattern of appearance that would fit iconographical depictions inspired by a tragedy.[53] If this is right, the different images would be different refractions of the tragedy, in the sense of different iconographical constructions representing a story inspired by, but not necessarily closely reflecting, a tragedy.

If the representation of Athena interacting directly with the two heroes on the amphora and, most vividly, on the South Italian vase is a reflection of a tragic scene—and it would fit the pattern of direct, non-distanced, human–divine interaction in early tragedies[54]—it is not impossible that in that tragedy Athena may have ordered the Palladion to be taken to Athens. The tragedy may have created the mytheme that identified the Palladion in Athens with the Trojan Palladion.

---

[52] See n. 28.
[53] We do not know when Sophokles produced *Lakainai*, but many scholars would consider Makron's vase especially to be too early to be reflecting a tragedy by Sophokles. I do not agree, and I have already suggested that the cup should be downdated to some time after 480—Makron appears to have been active until at least 470—and that the tondo may reflect, may have been in one way or another inspired, by another early tragedy of Sophokles: Sourvinou-Inwood 1979: 48–58.
[54] Sourvinou-Inwood 2003a: 462–9.

3. THE PALLADION IN ATHENS

I will begin my investigation of the Palladion in Athens with a few facts about the realities of the Palladion cult. To start with the basics, there is evidence for two cults 'at Palladion' (ἐπὶ Παλλαδίῳ), that of Zeus the priesthood of which belonged to the *genos* of Bouzygai,[55] and that of Athena, the priesthood of which almost certainly also belonged to the *genos* of Bouzygai.[56] In the 420s Athena's cult is referred to as Athena 'at Palladion', ἐπὶ Παλλαδίοι.[57] Athena at Palladion does not describe a cult whose statue was the Palladion. For this formulation is no different from Poseidon 'at Sunium' (ἐπὶ Σουνίῳ), and so it should be understood to be Athena at Palladion, comparable to Zeus 'in Palladion' (ἐν Παλλαδίῳ) and Zeus 'at Palladion' (ἐπὶ Παλλαδίου). Athena at Palladion would mean Athena at the court Palladion, or Athena at a place called Palladion, after which the court was also named, not necessarily Athena at the sanctuary Palladion. Of course, we know that eventually the name Palladion came to be associated with the Trojan Palladion and the statue of Athena at Palladion came to be identified with the Trojan Palladion.

The lawcourt at Palladion was south-east of the acropolis near Ardettos.[58] It was certainly not at Phaleron, as, we shall see, the Patmos scholion and some other late sources claim. Boegehold[59] takes these late sources at face value and suggests that there were two separate sanctuaries called Palladion, the one in the *asty* and the one "near Phaleron", which housed the Palladion and where the homicide trials were held. "Near Phaleron" is an evasion; if the

---

[55] *IG* II² 3177: ἱερ]εὺς τοῦ Διὸς τοῦ ἐπὶ Παλλαδίου καὶ Βουζύγης; cf. *SEG* XXX 85. 10, 17–18 ὑπὲρ τοῦ Βουζύγου καὶ ἱερέως Διὸς ἐμ Παλλαδίωι *IG* II² 5055 (on the seat of the priest in the theatre of Dionysos): Βουζύγου ἱερέως Διὸς ἐμ Παλλαδίῳ. On the *genos* Bouzygai see Toepffer 1889: 136–49; Parker 1996: 286–7; see also Storey 2003: 135–6, cf. 186.

[56] This is suggested by the myth according to which Demophon gave the Palladion to an Athenian called Bouzyges to bring to Athens (Polyaenus *Strat.* 1.5).

[57] *IG* I³ 369.73 [426/5–423/2] Ἀθ]εναίας ἐπὶ Παλλαδίοι Δεριονέοι; ibid. 90: Ἀθεναίας ἐπὶ Παλλαδίοι. We do not know what Δεριονέοι refers to.

[58] Kleitodeimos *FGrH* 323 F18; cf. Travlos 1971: 412–13.

[59] Boegehold 1995: 47–8.

sources are taken seriously this sanctuary and court must be located at Phaleron; indeed one of those sources, we shall see, specifies that it was set up by the sanctuary of Athena at Phaleron, which means Athena Skiras. However, in the absence of other evidence, it is not legitimate to take these late sources at face value—especially since, we shall see, they contain other elements of late mythography that do not accurately reflect cultic reality.[60]

This brings us to the investigation of the mythological nexus 'the Trojan Palladion in Athens'. The story that the image was washed by Demophon is only mentioned in the Patmos scholion to Dem. 23.71.[61] It is one variant of the myth of the acquisition of the Palladion by the Athenians and the foundation of the 'at Palladion' lawcourt. The Patmos scholion to Dem. 23.71 says that the lawcourt at Palladion was founded by Demophon, following an oracle; having found out about those who had been killed at Phaleron, he buried them and founded this lawcourt, which was called at Palladion because Demophon took the Palladion that had been brought by the Argives with Diomedes down to the sea and, after purifying it from the pollution of the murders, set up the statue and founded the lawcourt in that place. The deaths which this scholion refers to as murders (φόνοι) were the killings of the Argives in the battle at Phaleron which took place when Diomedes and the Argives on their return from Troy disembarked at Phaleron and mistook it for hostile land, as a result of which Athens acquired the Palladion.[62] I shall return to this. First let me open a parenthesis to give Pausanias' version of this story.

According to Pausanias,[63] cases of involuntary homicide were brought at the court at Palladion and everyone agrees that Demophon was the first to be tried there, but there is disagreement with regard to the charge. "They say" that after the Sack of Troy Dio-

---

[60] That these sources contain demonstrable confusions has also been acknowledged by others (see e.g. N. Robertson 1996b: 398).

[61] The scholion is cited by Burkert 1970a: 364 n. 31; see the text of this scholion and of the related one ad Dem. 23.27 in Jacoby 1954: i. 80.

[62] The Patmos scholion to Dem. 23.71 does not tell this story, which is narrated in the Patmos scholion to Dem. 23.27—as well as, we shall see, in other sources (see e.g. Paus. 1.28.9; Suda s.v. ἐπὶ Παλλαδίῳ).

[63] Paus. 1.28.8–9.

medes and his Argives, while returning home, disembarked at Phaleron and did not realize that it was Attica, but thought that it was enemy territory. There was a battle, since the Athenians did not recognize the Argives either, and Demophon marched out to help and killed some of them, seized the Palladion, and went off with it. But an Athenian man was knocked down by Demophon's horse and killed. Demophon was then brought to trial, some say by the relatives of the man killed by his horse, others say by the *koinon* of the Argives.

To return to the Patmos scholion. Though that scholion locates the battle at Phaleron, it does not specify Phaleron, or any particular locality, for the purification of the statue in the sea, or for the foundation of the lawcourt; the setting up of the Palladion and the foundation of the lawcourt happened "in that place" and therefore by the sea where the statue had been purified. Some other late sources, we saw, place the court at Phaleron; the localization in the Patmos scholion, then, is a vaguer version of the Phaleron localization. Given that, as we saw above, the lawcourt at Palladion was at the south-east of the acropolis near Ardettos, not at Phaleron, what does the confusion about its localization in these sources tell us? Clearly, since the text of the Patmos scholion contains an important confusion, and belongs to a tradition that is based on that confusion, it is not, as it stands, a reflection of cultic reality; but could it be a radical distortion of an *aition* connected with the cult of Athena at Palladion, does the mytheme 'Demophon took the Palladion down to the sea and washed it' refract an element of cultic reality of the cult of Athena at Palladion? This is our central question.

Let us consider some other late sources that also place the court at Phaleron. Pollux 8.118 says that some Argives who, on their return from Troy, had disembarked at Phaleron and mistaken it for hostile land, were killed by the locals and left unburied, until eventually Akamas made it known that they were Argives and had the Palladion with them, so they were buried and following an oracle they were called Ἀγνῶτες, 'persons unknown'; and in that place (αὐτόθι) the Palladion was set up and the lawcourt was founded in which are tried involuntary killings. Schol. Aeschin. 2.87 gives basically the same version, except that it does not mention the oracle or the appellation Ἀγνῶτες, and mentions instead that they found the Palladion and set it up 'beside Athena at Phaleron' (παρὰ τῇ Ἀθηνᾷ τῇ Φαληροῖ), and having buried the dead they founded a lawcourt there (ἐκεῖ).[64] These versions which say that the Palladion was founded 'in that place' resemble the version referred to in the Patmos scholion to Dem. 23.71 also in that they include the element of corpses left unburied, though, we saw, the Patmos scholion is somewhat more vague as to locality, not mentioning Phaleron; it also does not include the identification of the dead Argives with Ἀγνῶτες. Let me open a parenthesis to say something about Ἀγνῶτες in order to try to set the parameters of the relationships between these accounts and cultic reality.

At Phaleron, Pausanias says,[65] besides the temple of Athena Skiras, and of Zeus some distance away, there were also altars of the gods called unknown (ἄγνωστοι) and of heroes and of the children of Theseus and of Phaleros (who the Athenians say was an Argonaut), and also an altar of Androgeos, son of Minos, which is called altar of Heros but well informed locals know to be an altar of Androgeos. The cult recipients mentioned by Pausanias, then, are unknown gods, not heroes,[66] and Pausanias' formulation indicates that he saw the different categories of cult recipients he mentions as separate. He does not even associate Phaleros with Demophon and Akamas, since he mentions the version in which Phaleros was an Argonaut. Since Pausanias identifies an altar of Heros as that of Androgeos on the basis of what he was told by well-informed locals,[67] the fact that he does not identify the unknown gods with the dead Argives in this context, or even when he discusses the incident with the Argives,[68] shows that this was not an identification that had any reality for those well-informed locals. This identification, then, was either a later cultic development or, most likely, a mythographical construct, an

---

[64] The first part of the story and then the foundation of the court are also told in the Patmos scholion to Dem. 23.27. The scholion's reference to 'Athena at Phaleron' is a fragment of authentic cultic knowledge, wrongly applied.

[65] Paus. 1.3.4.

[66] See also Philostr. *VA* 6.3 where 'altar of unknown *daimones*' could refer to either gods or heroes, but the context makes it unambiguously clear that these were unknown gods.

[67] On this hero, see Kearns 1989: 40.

[68] At 1.28.9.

element of late mythography which gives a distorted version of the earlier cultic realities—conceivably as a result of someone interpreting a (real or relative) proximity of the altars of ἄγνωστοι to those of Akamas and Demophon as denoting a significant association, which in the context of Akamas, Demophon, and Phaleron evoked the myth of the battle with the Argives, and so interpreted them as dead Argives. Be that as it may, it is clear that the association between the dead Argives and the Ἀγνῶτες[69] does not reflect Athenian mythico-ritual realities of the classical or Hellenistic period and that an element from another nexus has been incorporated into the myth of the acquisition of the Palladion after a battle at Phaleron.

Pollux's book 8 was written, or at least completed, after he was appointed to a chair of rhetoric in Athens,[70] therefore when writing it he was aware of Athenian cultic realities. How do we explain the fact that he located the Palladion court at Phaleron? There are various possibilities. Given the corrupt state of the text that has reached us, the first possibility is that the incorrect information may be the result of textual corruption. However, there are two objections against this hypothesis: one, the fact that what we may call 'the "on the spot" (αὐτόθι) mytheme' that locates the Palladion at Phaleron appears in many late sources of the myth and is also contained in the summary of Phanodemos' narrative which will be discussed below; and two, the fact that the element of the Ἀγνῶτες belongs together with the localization of the Palladion at Phaleron. The second, most likely, possibility is that Pollux was following an earlier and apparently authoritative source, perhaps from a summary that was itself misleading, and placed the Palladion at Phaleron. I would like to suggest that if a major polis procession had taken the Palladion from the *asty* to Phaleron for a ritual bath and brought it back again, this knowledge would have been too much part of Pollux's assumptions to allow him to place the Palladion at Phaleron—which the Ἀγνῶτες element told us that he did. Be that as it may, Pollux's text as we have it deploys a transformation of an actual Athenian cultic element in a way that appears to anchor the localization of the Palladion to Phaleron.

---

[69] On 'unknown' cult recipients, see C. Harrauer, s.v. Agnostos Theos, *Neue Pauly* 1 (1996), 264–5 with bib.
[70] *OCD*³ s.v. Pollux, Iulius.

Consequently, and given the fact that the Patmos scholion is a version of the mytheme 'the Palladion court and sanctuary were founded at Phaleron', which is based on a confusion, it would appear to be extremely unlikely that this scholion alone should contain this one correct reflection of cultic reality which is not found in any other text, the *aition* of a ritual act that was part of the cult of the Palladion. On the contrary, I would suggest, the fact that transformations of cultic elements located at Phaleron and belonging to different cults were deployed in other versions of the mytheme 'Palladion court and sanctuary founded at Phaleron' opens up the possibility that the narrative reflected in the Patmos scholion may also have included a cultic element taken over from another nexus and incorporated into the myth by later mythography;[71] in other words that the story that Demophon took the statue down to the sea and washed it may have been a transformation of an element, also located at Phaleron, taken over from the Plynteria nexus, the bath of the statue of Athena Polias, and attached to the myth of the Palladion.

I will now consider the whole nexus of myths associated with the Palladion and its Athenian cult and try to locate the whole tradition to which the Patmos scholion belongs inside that nexus. There are, it will become clear, two main variants of the myth 'the Trojan Palladion in Athens'. In one variant the Athenians, normally Demophon, acquired the Palladion at Troy and then brought it or sent it to Athens. In the second variant the Palladion was acquired on Athenian soil. This second variant occurs in two main versions, one involving Agamemnon and another, to which the Patmos scholion belongs, involving a battle at Phaleron. I will argue below that the variant according to which the Athenians acquired the Palladion at Troy is the earlier variant of the myth of the Trojan Palladion in Athens; and that of the two versions of the second variant the story involving Agamemnon was created before that of the battle at Phaleron.

The earliest reference to the Trojan Palladion being in Athens is in a fragment of Lysias' speech *In defence of Socrates against Polycrates*, which, according to a scholion, said that Demophilos (*sic*) seized the Palladion from Diomedes (presumably while still at Troy) and took it

---

[71] For such taking over of cultic details, see n. 64 on Athena at Phaleron.

to Athens.[72] According to the account in Polyaenus,[73] mentioned above, which also places the Athenian acquisition of the Palladion at Troy, Diomedes entrusted the Palladion to the care of Demophon. Agamemnon demanded it, and Demophon had an imitation one constructed and kept it in his tent; he gave the real one to an Athenian called Bouzyges to bring to Athens. When Agamemnon tried to take by force what was in fact the imitation statue Demophon and his men put up a certain amount of resistance, to convince Agamemnon that they were protecting the true Palladion. Agamemnon was indeed deceived, and took away the false one. This myth certainly correctly reflects one cultic element of the cult of Athena at Palladion, its association with the *genos* Bouzygai.[74]

The fight between Demophon and Agamemnon in Polyaenus' version is one version of the more general element 'fighting among two Greek heroes in connection with two Palladia'; that element also appears in Makron's image, though there Demophon and Agamemnon, though visually prominent, are not the main combatants. Since in Polyaenus' version the central element is the acquisition of the Palladion by Demophon, Demophon is the central character. Agamemnon's role as Demophon's antagonist can be seen as reflecting his profile in Greek myth, established through the story of Achilles and Briseis, as the leader who removes their booty from other heroes' tents—of which his action in this story is a variation.

The narrative element of the Athenians' mock fighting to convince Agamemnon that Demophon and his men were protecting the true Palladion in Polyaenus' narrative presupposes Agamemnon's awareness of the existence of two Palladia, one of which was an imitation.

---

[72] According to Schol. Aristid., Dindorf III p. 320 (Lysias fr. 272a–b Carey).

[73] Polyaenus *Strat.* 1.5.

[74] It is however a culturally determined judgement to assume that because this myth establishes the connection of the Bouzygai with the Palladion cult it must have been a gentilicial myth, as assumed by Toepffer (1889: 146), followed by e.g. Kron (1976: 150). This is the product of a cultural habit of preferring a *cui bono* argument, perceived and presented in culturally determined terms, which include the assumption of antagonism and competition between polis and *genos* (since no other *genē* came into play in the cult), over the issue that was in fact the most religiously significant in ancient eyes, namely to anchor the cult in the heroic age—to put it differently, the privileging of the political and the utilitarian over the religious and the symbolic.

This sits less comfortably in Polyaenus' version, in which the imitation Palladion was made by Demophon (presumably, we are to understand, in secret), than in the story that two Palladia were taken from Troy, versions of which are represented in the images discussed in section 2. Polyaenus' narrative may therefore have been constructed out of a story in which Agamemnon tried to remove the Palladion from Demophon's tent after both Palladia had been entrusted to the Athenian hero. Be that as it may, Polyaenus' version was, it seems, created with the help of a partial transformation of at least parts of the story one version of which appears in Makron—of which Polyaenus' version may well echo a continuation.

Polyaenus presents a relationship of friendship between Demophon and Diomedes, and a relationship of hostility between Demophon and Agamemnon. The relationship of friendship between Demophon and Diomedes is consistent with the fact that in Makron's image it is Demophon who is more closely associated with Diomedes, since it is Diomedes whom Demophon is trying to restrain. The version of the myth in Dionysios the Rhodian or Samian, according to whom Odysseus and Diomedes entrusted the Palladion to Demophon,[75] perhaps echoes this relationship of friendship between Demophon and Diomedes found in Polyaenus' narrative, though it cannot be excluded that, if Kron and Kunisch are right,[76] and Makron's image assumes a version in which it was the Greek leaders who had decided to entrust the Palladia to Demophon, it was some reflection of this story that was echoed here. The story in Lysias involves a hostile action, the Palladion was snatched from Diomedes and taken to Athens, but the man who did this was not Demophon, but Demophilos, clearly a constructed variation on Demophon which allowed a hostile acquisition without affecting Demophon's friendly, or at least, not overtly hostile, relationship with Diomedes. In the story in Polyaenus the hostile interaction is displaced onto Agamemnon.

The stories in Lysias, Polyaenus, and Dionysios Rhodios are versions of the variant in which the Palladion was not acquired on Athenian soil but was brought to Athens by an Athenian. The most

[75] Dionysios *FGrH* 15 F3.
[76] See p. 244 above.

popular variant, to which the Patmos scholion also belongs, is that in which the Palladion was acquired by the Athenians on Athenian soil. The major difference between these two main variants is that the one in which the Palladion was acquired on Athenian soil also contains an aetiology for the foundation of the lawcourt at Palladion. I argue here that the variant in which the Palladion was acquired on Athenian soil is later than, and derivative from, that in which it was acquired by an Athenian at Troy.

There are two main versions of the myth 'the Palladion was acquired on Athenian soil and these events led to the foundation of the lawcourt at the Palladion'; one is that of which the Patmos scholion and most other late sources are versions, and another— which is the earliest surviving reference to the variant of the myth in which the Palladion was acquired on Athenian soil—appears in a fragment of Kleitodeimos. According to Kleitodemos,[77] Agamemnon arrived in Athens with the Palladion and Demophon seized the Palladion and killed many of his pursuers. Agamemnon was not happy about the situation, so they set up a trial, involving fifty Athenians and fifty Argives, who were called *ephetai*. Presumably Kleitodeimos concluded with the statement that this is why this court was set up there and is called Palladion.

This version includes 'the hostile relationship between Demophon and Agamemnon over the Palladion' narrative element encountered also in the variant 'the Palladion was acquired at Troy and brought to Athens by an Athenian'. Agamemnon's presence at Troy was natural, and his actions structured by a schema of behaviour characterizing Agamemnon at Troy,[78] while Agamemnon's presence in Athens is much less so, and in the extant summary of Kleitodemos's narrative appears unmotivated. This suggests that the theme 'hostility between Agamemnon and Demophon over the Palladion' probably first appeared in the 'acquisition of the Palladion at Troy' variant of the myth. If we compare the myth in Kleitodemos with the two versions of the variant 'the Palladion not acquired in Athenian soil' in Lysias and Polyaenus we see that Kleitodemos' version combines, first, the elements 'hostility between Demophon and Agamemnon' and

---

[77] Kleitodeimos *FGrH* 323 F 20.
[78] Cf. e.g. his appropriation of Briseis.

'minor fighting' of Polyaenus' version, second, a transformation of the element in Lysias 'Demophilos seized the Palladion' in which Demophilos is replaced by Demophon, and, finally, a construction of an aitiology for the lawcourt at Palladion.

If it is right that Makron's image refracts a story that included the entrusting of the true Palladion to Demophon, this would date the myth 'acquisition of the Palladion by Demophon at Troy' to the early fifth century. The earliest known reference to the myth of the Palladion in Athens, in Lysias, also belongs to the variant in which the Palladion was acquired at Troy. It is not necessarily chance that this variant is the one first attested. This pattern of attestation would fit with the hypothesis tentatively proposed in section 2, that the pattern of appearance of the images with the two Palladia may show them to be refractions of a tragedy, and that Athena's interaction with Diomedes and Odysseus may have included the issuing of instructions concerning the fate of the Palladion, which involved its being taken to Athens.

The assessment that it seems 'logical' that the simpler story of a Trojan Palladion acquired at its place of origin was earlier than the more complex story of an acquisition on Athenian soil and the subsequent foundation of a court is a commonsense argument and so inevitably based on a culturally determined judgement. However, the consideration of some of the relationships mentioned above leads to a less culturally determined argument that runs as follows. A main schema structuring Kleitodemos' story, 'fighting between Demophon and Agamemnon over the Palladion in Athens', is a transformation of the schema 'fighting between Demophon and Agamemnon over the Palladion at Troy' reflected in Polyaenus. Kleitodemos' story is a transformation of the variant located at Troy, rather than vice versa; for the schema 'fighting between Demophon and Agamemnon over the Palladion at Troy' is more organically integrated in its story than the schema 'fighting between Demophon and Agamemnon over the Palladion in Athens' is in its story. The construction by Kleitodemos of his version involved, first, the addition (to the Polyaenus type variant) of a transformation of an element that occurs in the other variant of the 'Palladion acquired at Troy', in Lysias: the element 'Demophilos seized the Palladion' in a transformation in which Demophilos is replaced by Demophon; and second, and above all, it involved the event being relocated to Athens and having bolted on to it an etymology for the Palladion court.

The fact that Kleitodeimos' story was, first, created by transformations of elements that structured two versions of the 'Palladion acquired at Troy' variant and, second, included an additional element, an aitiology that is consistent with Kleitodemos' own preoccupations, suggests that the story was invented by Kleitodemos, who was an *exegetes*, an expounder on ritual matters,[79] and who was interested in aitiologies of the Athenian landscape.[80] This will have been the earliest version of the variant that the Palladion was acquired on Athenian soil.

Kleitodeimos' version of the story of the acquisition of the Palladion in Athens involved a hostile relationship between Demophon and Agamemnon; other variants of this version occur in the extant sources.[81] But it is the second version of the myth 'the Palladion was acquired in Athens and these events led to the foundation of the lawcourt at Palladion' that is more commonly found in the later texts, the version that involved the battle at Phaleron. The earliest attestation of this second version is in Phanodemos, who is another early Atthidographer. According to Phanodemos, we are told,[82] when the Argives were sailing back from Troy, they arrived at Phaleron, and since they were unknown to the Athenians they were killed. Later on, Akamas discovered this, and, as the sought-for Palladion had been found, in accordance with an oracle they established a lawcourt on the spot (αὐτόθι).

This is clearly a summary of a longer narrative. In the summary the emphasis is on the foundation of the lawcourt, not on the Palladion, which is mentioned almost *en passant*. This and other similar summaries of Phanodemos' narrative are probably the sources that underlie, at least partially, the late accounts that include the confusion that the lawcourt was located at Phaleron or at least by the sea—located through αὐτόθι and similar expressions. If the word αὐτόθι

---

[79] See *FGrH* 323 F 14; F 28; Jacoby 1954: i. 57, 70 and ii. 70 n. 2 (noting that it is unclear what type of *exegetes* he was, possibly *pythochrestos*).

[80] See Kleitodemos *FGrH* 323 F 7 (the Pnyx).

[81] See e.g. Harp. s.v. ἐπὶ Παλλαδίῳ; see Jacoby 1954: i. 80.

[82] Pausanias Atticista e 53 Erbse (Phanodemos *FGrH* 325 F 16).

was part of Phanodemos' text it clearly was not used to locate the lawcourt at Palladion at Phaleron, since we know (and the well-informed Athenian Phanodemos knew) that this court was not by the sea but in the main part of the *asty*. In this respect, then, this is a misleading summary of Phanodemos' text. We cannot reconstruct with any certainty what the word αὐτόθι referred to in his text. Nevertheless, I suggest that the following reconstruction of the outline of Phanodemos' narrative would account for the extant summary. "They consulted the oracle and the god said that the Palladion should remain in Athens; so Demophon set up the Palladion and there (αὐτόθι) they founded the lawcourt", that is they founded the lawcourt in the same place where the Palladion was set up (the locality of which we Athenians all know).

The summary as it stands gives the impression that it was the foundation of the court that the oracle had ordered. This is correlative with the fact that the court at Palladion was the focus of this lexicographical narrative, which was therefore structured accordingly. In my reconstruction it was the setting up of the Palladion, the foundation of the cult of the Palladion, that was primary, and the foundation of the court was its adjunct. The fact that in this reconstruction the oracle would, as so often, be ordering the foundation of a cult gives, I submit, some support to that reconstruction—especially when the lexicographical focus of the summary is taken into account.

This myth told by Phanodemos, then, presents another version of the acquisition of the Palladion on Attic soil from that told by Kleitodemos, and (to judge by the incomplete summary) a somewhat different version also of the aitiology of the foundation of the court at Palladion, though here also the victims involved were Argives. In both versions there was some fighting, but while in Kleitodemos' version the fighting was the result of Demophon's seizing of the Palladion which had been in the possession of Agamemnon, in Phanodemos' version the Athenians were not really culpable, and the acquisition of the Palladion was a by-product of a disastrous misunderstanding.

Phanodemos' myth deploys the Greek mythological schema 'people disembark in a place and are mistaken for enemies while in fact they are friends and/or allies', which embodies the concept 'battle with friends and/or allies (in this case the Argives) for which one (in this case the Athenians) is not culpable'.[83] In Phanodemos' version of the 'Palladion in Athens' myth this schema is expressed through narrative elements that also appear in other versions of that myth: first, 'fighting', which was also part of the story in Kleitodemos' version and also in Polyaenus'; and second, a modification, a destructive manifestation, of 'Demophon's friendly relationship to Diomedes', in the form in which friends fight each other by mistake, except that here this fighting between friends is placed at some distance from Diomedes and Demophon themselves: Diomedes is not mentioned and Akamas has replaced Demophon, but even Akamas was not involved in the fighting. Phanodemos' myth allows a combination of fighting and friendly relations with the Argives but at the same time, when compared to Kleitodemos' version, presents the Athenians in a more positive light. They had not done anything wrong to acquire the Palladion. In addition, if I am right about the oracle's role in Phanodemos' story, this acquisition had been sanctioned by the god. Both elements, the significant change and the more positive presentation of the Athenians, fit Phanodemos' profile as a historian: he was Athenocentric and he, at least sometimes, changed established myths radically. For example, while in most versions of her myth the animal which replaced Iphigeneia and was sacrificed in her place was a hind, in Phanodemos' version it was a bear,[84] and, moreover, the sacrifice probably took place at Brauron, not Aulis.[85] He also located the rape of Persephone in Attica.[86] Since the parameters of difference between the version in Kleitodemos and that in Phanodemos coincide with two important characteristics of Phanodemos' mythography, the myth of the acquisition of the Palladion in Athens after the Argives had disembarked at Phaleron may well have been Phanodemos' creation.

---

[83] See e.g. Apollonios Rhodios' version of the myth of Kyzikos (*Arg.* 1.947–1077; cf. also Apollod. 1.9.18; Hyginus, *Fab.* 16) or the involuntary parricides of Althaimenes (Apollod 3.2.1; Diod. Sic. 5.59.1–4) and Telegonos (Proklos' summary of *Telegony, EGF* p. 73); Soph. *Odysseus Akanthoplex TrGF* 4 pp. 374–8; see Arist. *Poet.* 1453 b31–6.

[84] Phanodemos *FGrH* 325 F 14.

[85] See Jacoby 1954: i. 186–7 ad 325 F 14. See on this localization, Euphorion fr. 91 Powell (Schol. Ar. *Lys.* 645.)

[86] Phanodemos *FGrH* 325 F 27.

I suggest therefore that the mythological nexus 'the Palladion was acquired on Athenian soil and these events led to the foundation of the lawcourt at Palladion' was the creation of fourth-century Atthidography, first Kleitodemos and then Phanodemos. If this reconstruction is even approximately right, the story of the purification of the Palladion is certainly not an ancient cult myth of the sanctuary of Athena at Palladion, reflecting and explaining an ancient ritual practice; I will now argue that it is also extremely unlikely to have been a later myth created by a Atthidographer like Phanodemos to explain a procession to Phaleron and a ritual bath of the statue.

To begin with, the superficial impression of plausibility that may be implicitly created by the coincidence in locality needs to be deconstructed. For the identity of Phaleron as the nearest sea-coast to the *asty* and part of the symbolic frontier of Athens is sufficient reason for its role in both the Palladion myth and the purification of the statue, whichever statue that was. To put it differently, once the schema 'people disembark in a place and are mistaken for enemies while in fact they are friends and/or allies' was deployed to construct the myth, the selection 'Phaleron' for the location of the event was determined by the fact that Phaleron was the ancient harbour and also a symbolic frontier of Athens. So the 'coincidence' of Phaleron as the place of the battle and of the bath of Athena's statue cannot be used as an argument to suggest that the two are part of the same mythicoritual nexus.

Then, if this story of a purificatory bath of the Palladion indeed reflected a ritual element, this would have helped anchor the myth to the cult's realities. Therefore, I submit, it would have been prominent in the narratives telling the myth—especially in new mythopoeic constructions. Thus, if it is right that, as I suggested, both early Atthidographers were constructing drastic transformations of the 'Palladion in Athens' myth, if these radically innovative myths had included a narrative element that anchored these myths in the cult's ritual realities, that element would have been prominent not marginal—especially in Phanodemos' myth. If Phanodemos had created an *aition* that explained a procession to Phaleron and a bath of the Palladion, this *aition* would have connected the newly created myth, specifically the newly invented locus of the Palladion acquisition, to a cultic reality, thus anchoring the new myth to a ritual. If that had been

the case, this *aition* would have had a prominent place in Phanodemos' narrative of this newly created myth. Consequently, even given
the lexicographical bias, it would have been unlikely not to have been
included in any of the extant sources except the Patmos scholion.
Of course, it could be argued that the perceptual filters through
which these summaries were composed were different from Phanodemos' and this explains the omission. However, first, if the element
did have a very prominent place however different those perceptual
filters may have been, the omission still appears problematic, especially since its inclusion would only have involved the addition of two
words, 'and' and one other: in the summary of Phanodemos' story[87]
instead of simply 'after the Palladion had been found ... in accord
with an oracle' something like 'after the Palladion had been found
[and purified] ... in accord with an oracle'; in Schol. Aeschin. 2.87
something like 'once they had found [and cleansed] the Palladion,
they established ...'

Second, the Patmos scholion (which is vague with regard to the
localization of the purification and the court) belongs to a tradition
that contains a significant confusion and includes elements belonging to different cultic nexuses and is, therefore, not a reliable
source—as well as being certainly shaped by filters much more
remote from those of Phanodemos than most of the other sources.
Third, unless Pollux's text is extremely corrupt, his omission of the
aition would not be explicable in terms of different perceptual filters,
since, if there had been a procession and bath of the Palladion in
Athens (especially if it was of the importance suggested by the
inscriptions), a resident in Athens could not have been unaware of
it, and that would have led to the decision to include a narrative
element that tied up the myth to the cult, to Athenian realities.
Perhaps more significantly, if the mytheme had been an *aition* and
therefore had a prominent place in Phanodemos' and other narratives, and inevitably also in the Athenian perceptions of the ritual and
associated myth, it would have been unlikely to have been omitted
from Pausanias' narrative about Demophon's acquisition of the
Palladion at Phaleron. I would also suggest that if the myth had

---

[87] Pausanias Atticista e 53 Erbse (Phanodemos *FGrH* 325 F 16).

involved the explanation of a procession to Phaleron, the bath of the statue there, and a procession back to Athens, it is unlikely that any source that read such a narrative would have mistaken αὐτόθι to be referring to the foundation of the sanctuary and court at Phaleron.

We do not know if Phanodemos' narrative included the mytheme that at first the Argives had not been buried. It is not included in the summary of his narrative, so, even if it was part of that narrative, it is probably unlikely to have been a prominent part. In the versions in which the Argives were at first left unburied, if the Palladion was eventually discovered among the corpses there would have been a space in which an ancient reader could have filled in the notion that the Palladion was purified. If this was the context of the construction of the mytheme that Demophon purified the Palladion, if it was created to fill in the gaps of a particular version of the narrative, not as an *aition* explaining an important ritual, its uniqueness in the extant sources becomes more easily intelligible: there would have been no space for it in any but the versions that included the unburied dead motif. But even among those versions that included that motif it is only found in the Patmos scholion, not in Pollux, nor in any of the other accounts, and this, I suggest, makes it likely that this mytheme was created by a late mythographer who filled in the gaps by spelling out what was not spelt out because the focus of the myth was elsewhere; it was not an *aition* for a ritual, it was not part of the cult.

Indeed, since we saw that two other instances of the version that includes the localization of the Palladion at Phaleron incorporated in the myth an element that pertains to a different ritual nexus (the Ἀγνῶτες), and an element that refers to another cult (the alleged proximity to the sanctuary of Athena (Skiras)), the possibility cannot be excluded that the Patmos scholion may reflect the appropriation of another element located at Phaleron which was part of a different cultic nexus, the purification of the statue of Athena Polias during the Plynteria. That is, the story that Demophon purified the Palladion in the sea might have been created under the double impetus of a mythographical trend to elaborate and fill in perceived gaps on the one hand, and on the other the knowledge that a ritual bath of a statue of Athena took place at Phaleron, the purification of the statue of Athena Polias at the Plynteria.

In these circumstances, I submit, the discussion of the mythological nexus associated with the cult of Athena at Palladion has shown, at the very minimum, that the reliability of the Patmos scholion as a source for Athenian ritual is highly dubious and that it is extremely unlikely that this mytheme is a refraction of the *aition* for an (important) Athenian ritual.

I add a final observation about the Palladion at Athens. The possession of the Trojan Palladion was a religiously and culturally prestigious thing. Presumably it also offered the possibility that it would give extra protection to the polis. The olivewood statue of Athena Polias which had fallen from the sky undoubtedly also had a city-protecting function comparable to, though not explicitly stated to operate in the same strong terms as, the Trojan Palladion.[88] I suggest that there was one particular ideological context which would be especially conducive to the construction of a mytheme that would reinforce the idea of divine protection for the city through the 'acquisition' of the Trojan Palladion by the Athenians: the years immediately after the Persian Sack of Athens, after the very survival of the polis had been in doubt. Athens did survive while Troy had not, and it may have been in this context in which Athens might have suffered the same fate as Troy, but did not, that the notion emerged that the Palladion, whose theft from Troy allowed its destruction, ended up in Athens and added its protection to that of the cult statue of Athena Polias.

---

[88] Vian (1952: 256): the miraculous statue that fell from the sky, whatever its appearance, warlike or peaceful, had the function of a palladion and its power extended to all domains of national activity.

5

Athena Polias, Panathenaia, and the *Peplos*

1. THE CULT, THE FESTIVAL, AND THE *PEPLOS*

Chapter 5 consists of a set of discussions concerning certain aspects of the Panathenaia,[1] including its *aitia*, and some aspects of the cult of Athena Polias. A central focus of the investigations is the offering of the *peplos* to Athena and the ways in which the Panathenaia related to the Plynteria. I also engage with the much discussed topic of the Parthenon frieze, for I believe that certain readings of this representational nexus, and of the *peplos* itself, have taken insufficient account of the system of religious representations of which this offering was part. This is especially true, it will become clear, of a few relatively recent suggestions concerning the *peplos*, which I discuss in the Appendix to this chapter, since they have implications for an important part of the Panathenaia and also for the relationship between the Panathenaia and the Plynteria.

I will begin with a brief look at the priestly personnel involved in the cult—at least those offices of which we know—and the *genē* which provided them. The most important priesthood, that of Athena Polias, was provided by, was the privilege of, the Eteoboutadai,[2] who also held the priesthood of the god who disputed with her

---

[1] On the Panathenaia, see now Parker 2005a: 252–69 with earlier bib. See also the notes below.

[2] Drakon of Athens, in *Peri genon*, *FGrH* 344 F1. On the priestess of Athena Polias, see Dillon 2002: 84–9.

for the role of poliadic deity, Poseidon Erechtheus.[3] It is not known if, but it is not unlikely that, the Eteoboutadai also provided the priestesses Kosmo and Trapezo, also called Trapezophoros, who were assistants to the priestess of Athena Polias.[4] Some sources say that these priestesses, Trapezo[phoros] and Kosmo, managed all things together with the priestess of Athena, doubtless as her assistants rather than equals;[5] others say that the priestess Trapezo[phoros] set the *trapeza*, table, before Athena, and the priestess Kosmo adorned the statue of Athena.[6] The two claims are not necessarily contradictory; they were probably assistant priestesses and these were the special areas of responsibility of each.

The one ritual act that we know was performed by 'Eteoboutadai' was that, in the procession from the Acropolis to Skiron at the Skira/Skirophoria, the priestess of Athena Polias, the priest of Poseidon Erechtheus, and the priest of Helios walked out under a canopy called *skiron*, which was carried by "Eteoboutadai"[7]—obviously a small number of their members.

The *genos* of the Eteoboutadai can be considered as the elite *genos* within the gentilicial elite that provided gentilicial priesthoods. This prestige was derived partly from the fact that they held the priesthood of the poliadic deity, and partly from a special claim to nobility of birth which is detectable in the extant sources from at least as early as the fourth century.[8] They claimed descent from Boutes,[9] brother

---

[3] On the Eteoboutadai, see Toepffer 1889: 113–32; Parker 1996: 290–3, esp. 290; see also Humphreys 2004: 105–6; [Lambert forthcoming b].

[4] See Parker 1996: 290. Dillon 2002: 84 says that they "might well have been drawn" from the women or girls of the *genos* of the Eteoboutadai.

[5] According to Harpocr. s.v. *trapezophoros*, both Lykourgos in the 'On the Priestess' and Istros (*FGrH* 334 F 9) say that *trapezophoros* is the name of a priesthood and she and Kosmo 'manage everything together with the priestess of Athena'; for their subordinate status: Jacoby 1954: i. 634–5 (ad Istros *FGrH* 334 F 9).

[6] Trapezophoros: *Anecd. Bekk.* I. 307; Kommo [*sic*] = Kosmo: ib. I. 273.6.

[7] Lysimachides *FGrH* 366 F 3.

[8] See Parker 1996: 290 and e.g. Apostolios 8.62.

[9] On Boutes, see Kearns 1989: 152–3; see also Toepffer 1889: 115–17. Boutes had an altar in the Erechtheion (Paus. 1.26.5) and a priest, presumably an Eteoboutad, a fragment of whose seat, dating from the second half of the fourth century BC, inscribed 'of the priest of Boutes', was discovered in that area (*IG* II² 5166: see on this Parker 1996: 290, who also discusses the alternative interpretation in which Boutes is a sacral title).

of Erechtheus and son of king Pandion. In Apollodoros' version of Boutes' genealogy, Erichthonios (as we saw in Chapter 2) married the Naiad Nymph Praxithea and their son was Pandion.[10] Pandion, according to Apollodoros, married Zeuxippe and they had two sons, Erechtheus and Boutes.[11] After Pandion's death the two brothers divided their inheritance and Erechtheus married Praxithea and inherited the kingship, while Boutes inherited the priesthoods of Athena and of Poseidon Erechtheus.[12]

It is possible to see this version as correlative with, and perhaps resulting from the interactions of, three representations: first, the representation in cultically embedded myths that the earliest priestesses of Athena had been members of the royal family (Aglauros, Praxithea); second, the knowledge that the Eteoboutadai were not descendants of the last, or even the last pre-Neleid, Athenian royal family; and third, the perceived importance of genealogical continuity in the relationship between a cult and the associated gentilicial priesthood.[13]

There may also have been specialized minor priestly offices serving the Acropolis cults, conceivably as a result of a proliferation of offices in later periods. This is suggested by the office of the *kataniptes*, 'washer'; we are told that this was the name of a priesthood, and that its holder washed away 'dirt collecting under the *peplos* of Athena (τὰ κάτω τοῦ πέπλου τῆς Ἀθηνᾶς ῥυπαινόμενα)'.[14] If, as is very likely, the *kataniptes* was a permanent office, not a function connected with

---

[10] Apollod. 3.14.6–7.

[11] Apollod. 3.14.8.

[12] Apollod. 3.15.1. Considered logically, the myth in Apollodoros is in conflict with the myth in Euripides' *Erechtheus* in which Athena made Praxithea, wife of the 'post-split' Erechtheus, her priestess. But it would not have been in conflict with a myth in which Praxithea, the Naiad Nymph and priestess, was the wife of the 'complex' Erechtheus. If a myth that Boutes inherited the priesthoods while his brother inherited the kingship was part of the early versions of the myths of Athens, before the figures of Erichthonios and the 'post-split' Erechtheus were generated out of material from the nexus of the 'complex' Erechtheus, that brother would not have been Erechtheus and there would have been no conflict with the notion of Erechtheus' wife Praxithea as priestess.

[13] [Only fragments remain of a planned treatment of the Eteoboutads in the historical period.]

[14] *Etym. Magn.* 494.25; see Deubner 1969: 19 n. 14. I will not discuss here the problem of what exactly he washed.

the Plynteria rite,[15] it might conceivably have belonged to the Prax-iergidai in that it involved washing and the *peplos*. However, as Parker noted,[16] if it was a permanent office there is less reason to connect it with the Praxiergidai. In addition, I would add, it may be that the Praxiergidai, who handled the temple, the statue, and the *peplos* in a ritually abnormal period, operated only in abnormal time; if this is right, then the function of a permanent priest involved with minor cleanings in normal time would have contrasted with the major washings by the Praxiergidai in abnormal time, and therefore the *kataniptes* would not have been a member of the Praxiergidai. I have already mentioned the offices held by members of the Praxiergidai during the nexus of the Plynteria and Kallynteria, of which we know of the Plyntrides and Loutrides.

Priesthoods of other deities were involved in the cult of Athena Polias, not least the priesthood of Poseidon Erechtheus, and also, I shall be arguing below, that of Zeus Polieus; but the priesthoods that directly concern us are those serving cult recipients directly concerned with the *peplos* and the nexus of the Plynteria and Kallyn-teria, that is, Aglauros and Pandrosos. As we saw in Chapter 3, the priestess of Aglauros, who was provided by the Salaminioi, was involved in the Plynteria and Kallynteria, in which Aglauros was the second honorand, after Athena. The Salaminioi also provided the priesthood of Pandrosos. We saw in Chapter 3, section 2 that in the Salaminioi inscription the reference is to a joint priesthood of Aglauros and Pandrosos (and more problematically Kourotrophos), while in later documents, such as the mid-third-century decree in honour of the priestess of Aglauros Timokrite, the priesthoods were distinct; and that the most likely explanation of this discrepancy is that what had been a joint priesthood in the fourth century subse-quently became divided into two.

I turn now to the Panathenaia itself. It was, of course, the par excellence 'panathenaic' festival in the sense defined in Chapter 1. The Great Panathenaia, established in 566/5 BC,[17] was a more spec-tacular and grand version of the festival of the Lesser Panathenaia.

---

[15] On this see esp. Parker 1996: 307 and n. 2.
[16] Ibid.: 307 and n. 2.
[17] See ibid.: 89–92.

On the reconstruction followed here (which, we shall see, includes acceptance of the hypothesis that a *peplos* was offered to the goddess every year) both Lesser and Great Panathenaia consisted of a *pannychis*, the procession and sacrifices, the offering of the *peplos* as well as a crown as an excellence award,[18] and competitions, including the torch race.[19] Though the Lesser Panathenaia included some competitions[20] it was, of course, the Great Panathenaia that had a very large agonistic part, with many competitions in a variety of fields; some were confined to Athenians, and were often tribally organized, some open.[21] An act that appears to have been performed at the Lesser, and undoubtedly also at the Great, Panathenaia that echoes aspects of the Kallynteria is a *kosmesis*, adorning, of the great altar.[22]

I accept Mansfield's view that two different *peploi* are reflected in the sources.[23] On my reading of the thesis of the two *peploi* (in which both would be decorated with a Gigantomachy), a *peplos* woven by the *arrhephoroi* and the Ergastinai, '(wool)-workers', appropriate in size, was offered at the Panathenaia every year, including the years of the Great Panathenaia, as a new dress for the olivewood statue;[24]

---

[18] See Parker 2005a: 265.

[19] On the torch race being held at the Lesser Panathenaia, see Kyle 1992: 96 and 207 n. 113 with bib.

[20] See e.g. Lys. 21.2, 21.4.

[21] See on these competitions Parker 2005a: 256–7 with bib.

[22] *LSCG* 33 (RO 81) B 29; the word κόσμησις is restored.

[23] In his unpublished dissertation (Mansfield 1985) Mansfield argued that there were two *peploi*, one offered annually, woven for the statue of Athena Polias by the Ergastinai—*arrhephoroi* (which in his view, but not mine, were one and the same [see n. 27 below and chapter 3 n. 219]) and a tapestry with a representation of the Gigantomachy woven by professional weavers, displayed on the Panathenaic ship and dedicated to Athena at the Great Panathenaia, commemorating the Athenian victories in the Persian Wars and presumably displayed as a wall hanging inside the Parthenon or the temple of Athena Polias (Mansfield 1985: passim, esp. 5–7, 16–17, 51, 55). He suggested that the practice of dedicating the *peplos*-tapestry to Athena every four years probably began at one of the Great Panathenaia following the Persian invasion (Mansfield 1985: 52–3; on the large *peplos* and the Panathenaic ship see 51–78; on the ship: 68–78). Mansfield's unpublished dissertation is cited by, among others, Barber (1992: 113) and Hurwit (1999: 45, 333 n. 63).

[24] Parker 2005a: 268–9 takes the view that a *peplos* was only offered at the Great Panathenaia. If I am wrong, and there was only one *peplos*, offered at the Great Panathenaia, most of my analyses would change, but not radically, in that instead of an annual renewal it would be a penteteric one, and the cyclical nature of the enterprise would simply involve a much longer cycle.

a second, large, *peplos* was woven by professional weavers and displayed at the procession of the Great Panathenaia as a sail on the Panathenaic ship, and then either draped around the colossal statue of Athena Parthenos,[25] or, as is more likely, hung behind this cult statue in the Parthenon—or simply deposited in one or the other temple, of Athena Polias or Athena Parthenos. I am only concerned with the *peplos* that I believe was offered annually and worn by the olivewood statue.

The weaving of the new *peplos* started at the Chalkeia, nine months before the Panathenaia, when the priestess of Athena Polias and the *arrhephoroi* set up the warp.[26] The fact that the *arrhephoroi*, who were female children, the marriageable maidens referred to as Ergastinai,[27] and at least one married woman, the priestess of Athena, were involved in the weaving entails that representatives of the three stages of women's lives as perceived by the Greeks took part in this endeavour, which in its turn entails that, symbolically, all Athenian females would have been deemed to have participated in the *peplos*'

[25] As Lewis (1979/80: 28–9) suggested.

[26] *Etym. Magn.* 805.43 s.v. Chalkeia; Suda s.v. Chalkeia: see the texts in Parker 2005a: 465. On the weaving, see Barber (1992: 103–17). On the Chalkeia, see Parker (2005a: 464–5). The lexicographical sources speak of "the priestesses with the *arrhephoroi*". If this plural is reliable, the priestesses involved besides the priestess of Athena Polias may have been the priestess of Aglauros (Aglauros was Athena's first priestess and, with Pandrosos, associated with weaving wool: cf. p. 157), the priestess of Pandrosos when the joint priesthood was split (cf. p. 153), and perhaps also Kosmo and Trapezo, if it is right that they were involved in 'all things' with the priestess of Athena Polias (cf. n. 5), and not just in adorning the statue and setting a table before the goddess. Mansfield (1985: 280) thinks that the priestesses referred to were the priestess of Athena Polias, Kosmo, Trapezo, and possibly the priestess of Pandrosos.

[27] On the Ergastinai, see Hesych. s.v. Ergastinai; Brulé 1987: 99–105; Dillon 2002: 58. N. Robertson (2004: 149) thinks that the office of the Ergastinai was invented at the end of the second century BC. But at whatever date this function may have become formalized into the office reflected in the inscriptions, there is no reason to doubt that marriageable maidens had always participated in the weaving of the *peplos* (see also Brulé 1987: 105). The various females involved in the weaving of the *peplos* have also been discussed by Mansfield (1985: 277–81), who argued (on the basis of a particular reading and interpretation of the inscription *IG* II² 1060 + 1036) that the *peplos* was woven by the *arrhephoroi* and that the most probable interpretation is that Ergastinai were the *arrhephoroi* (1985: 279–80)—he also suggested that four *arrhephoroi* may have been involved in the creation of the *peplos* after two of them had begun the weaving.

creation.[28] Since in the Greek symbolic system weaving characterized women, through the symbolic participation of all Athenian females, the whole of the Athenian polis would have been deemed to have participated in the manufacture of the new *peplos* which they were offering to the goddess.

[28] On the number of priestesses involved see n. 26 above. Apollodoros of Athens *FGrH* 244 F 105 (cf. Schol. Eur. *Hec.* 467) shows that there was disagreement as to whether only maidens wove the *peplos* or married women as well. For our purposes this is not important since the 'married women' category is symbolically present in the priestess's participation. Nevertheless, the fact that the question was a live issue confirms, I suggest, that these female categories were significant in connection with the *peplos*. There are two refractions involving the weaving of the *peplos* in Euripides, and I hope to have shown that they are less straightforward than has sometimes been assumed (Sourvinou-Inwood 2003a: 306–7, 340). In *Hekabe* 444–83 the captive Trojan women agonize about their future and wonder where they will end up. First they envisage the possibility that they will be taken to Delos, and mention the sacred palm and laurel and the singing of the Deliades, with whom they imagine they might sing. The Athenian audience would have perceived them to be mistaken, for foreign slaves would not have been perceived to have taken part in such hymn singing together with citizens, even in the heroic age. The references to Delos, the palm, and the laurel would have zoomed the world of the play to that of the audience's realities, while the erroneous nature of their imaginings would have distanced them from those realities. This distancing would be even stronger when the chorus speculate that they may be taken to Athens, where they imagine they may be involved in the weaving of Athena's *peplos*. This would have zoomed the world of the play to that of the audience's realities, but since in those realities the *peplos* was not woven by foreign slave women they would have perceived this as another distorted ritual image, which would have led them to see the chorus as even more pathetic, for things would be even worse than they think: they would be excluded from the cultic roles which they imagine they would perform. In *Hekabe*, then, the relationship between text and cultic reality is one of serious distortion. So we cannot know if this passage refracts the participation of Athenian married women (other than the priestess[es]' initial involvement) in the weaving of the *peplos*. The situation is different in *IT* 221–8, where the pathos is created when Iphigeneia contrasts her present life with the life she would have had as a normal girl, the bloodthirsty rite she is performing with the ritual duties she would have performed as a normal maiden, celebrating Hera with song and dance, and weaving the image of Athena in the Titanomachy. The worship of Hera is the obvious cultic service for the daughter of the king of Argos. The reference to weaving the image of Athena in the Titanomachy inevitably evoked for the Athenian audience their own weaving of the *peplos* of Athena. The fact that it is the Titanomachy rather than the Gigantomachy she would be weaving is part of the distancing of Iphigeneia, a heroic-age non-Athenian, from Athenian realities. But the shaping parameter here is distancing, not distortion. The pathos of her situation was, I submit, conveyed effectively precisely because Athenian virgins of Iphigeneia's age group, marriageable maidens, in fact wove the *peplos*.

The offering of the new *peplos* was the most important gift made to the poliadic goddess by the polis, a gift that took a long time to manufacture and symbolically involved the labour of the whole city. Because it was the most important gift offered to the poliadic deity, it inevitably expressed and symbolized, among other things, the relationship of reciprocity between the polis and its poliadic deity. Because the relationship between a polis and its poliadic deity was also a metonymic symbol, as well as an intense version, of its relationship with all the gods, the offering also expressed the relationship of reciprocity between the polis and all the gods, the gods who alone guaranteed the city's continued existence and prosperity.[29]

The dressing of the statue in a new *peplos*, the renewal of the goddess's dress, was, of course, ritually polysemic. Insofar as it involved renewal, it also suggested the renewal of the relationship between the polis and its poliadic deity at the poliadic festival. In addition, if the creation of the *peplos* was symbolically perceived to begin at the Chalkeia and end with its presentation to the goddess at the Panathenaia, the biologically based, and therefore universal, association of nine months with human pregnancy could not but have imbued the enterprise of weaving the new *peplos* with the metaphorical colouring of the production of a child, which not only added to the gift's perceived importance, but also gave it the connotation of an important new beginning, appropriate for signifying the renewal of the relationship between the polis and its poliadic deity—and through her with all the gods—at the poliadic festival.

2. THE AITIOLOGICAL MYTHS

I will now discuss the three *aitia* associated with the Panathenaia.[30] The first of these *aitia*, the one that appears to be most deeply rooted in the Athenian representations, is the myth that the Panathenaia was founded by Erichthonios. In this myth Erichthonios invented the

---

[29] Sourvinou-Inwood 1990a: 306–7 = Sourvinou-Inwood 2000: 23–4.

[30] On the notion that the Panathenaia celebrated Athena's birthday, see now Parker 2005a: 256. On these *aitia*, see also Parker 2005a: 254–6, 381.

chariot and first drove his invention at the first Panathenaia and this is connected with the *apobates* competition.[31] The myth of the foundation by Erichthonios connects the festival with autochthony and primordial times and also with a specifically Athenian competition.[32]

The second myth associated with the Panathenaia says that the festival was founded by Theseus—just as Theseus synoecized Athens, that is founded the city as it now is. According to the Atthidographers, Erichthonios was the first to celebrate the Panathenaia,[33] and the myth that the founder was Theseus was combined with the myth of Erichthonios' foundation in the version according to which before Theseus the festival was called Athenaia, and then became Panathenaia.[34] This distinction between Athenaia and Panathenaia corresponds to the distinction between pre-synoecism and post-synoecism, post-Theseus Athens and it (or something like it) may always have underlain (whether or not in an articulated form) the myth that Theseus founded the Panathenaia. It is, among other things, a representation dependent on the semantic nexus 'Theseus synoecized Athens': a refounded festival expresses the 'new', 'refounded' synoecized polis.

Finally, the third myth associated with the Panathenaia claims that the festival was celebrated for the death of the giant Asterios or Aster.[35] This may have been a cultic *aition* current in Athens, or it may have been a learned construct.[36] The Gigantomachy, we shall

---

[31] See e.g. Marmor Parium *FGrH* 239 A 10; see Neils 1992a: 21; Parker 2005a: 254.

[32] As Parker (ibid.: 254–5) puts it, this *aition* "associates the festival with authentic, autochthonous Athenian-ness" and also highlights the *apobates* competition, which only the Athenians had practised since ancient times.

[33] Hellanikos *FGrH* 323a F 2; Andretion *FGrH* 324 F 2; Marmor Parium *FGrH* 239 A 10 (see Jacoby 1954: i. 25–6, 629–32; cf. Istros *FGrH* 334 F 4). Cf. Philochoros 328 F 8–9 (see Jacoby 1954: i. 631). On Istros see also n. 34 below.

[34] Paus. 8.2.1. Istros (*FGrH* 334 F 4) supposedly stated that it was before Erichthonios' foundation that the festival was called Athenaia. But as Parker (2005a: 255 and n. 9) observes, it is very likely that Istros too ascribed the change to Theseus, and has been misrepresented through abbreviation. Jacoby (1954: i. 629–32 ad loc.) does not exclude the possibility that Istros spoke of an Athenaia before Erichthonios.

[35] Schol. Aristid. *Panath.* 189 p. 323 Dindorf. See the discussion of the scholia below. See also, on the myth, Vian 1952: 262–5; Ferrari Pinney 1988: 471.

[36] See the discussion in Parker 2005a: 255. Ferrari (1994–5: 223) argues that a flood of pictures representing the Gigantomachy on Attic vases begins to appear in the 560s and that this is connected to the reorganization of the Panathenaia at 566,

see, was an important representation at the Panathenaia. The notion of a victory over any Giant has meanings dependent on those of the Gigantomachy, which will be discussed below. But the question is, why is it this particular Giant's death that is commemorated, are there any meanings created by the identity of this particular Giant, with this particular name? I shall begin the discussion of this with a consideration of his name.

In Greek mythology Aster- names, and specifically Asterios and Asteria, are associated with primordial times and autochthony, and also, more generally, with what we may call 'times before now'. Thus, Asteria was the former name of Delos, for Asteria was a Titanis, sister of Leto who was transformed into the island of Delos.[37] Asteria was also the former name of Miletos, and Asteri- names are involved, in connection with autochthony, in the foundation myths of Miletos,[38] above all through the figure of Asterios, son of the autochthonous king Anax. Another association between an Asteri- name and primordiality and autochthony is located in the Argolid: Asterion was the name of a river in the Argolid who was one of the judges adjudicating whether the Argolid belonged to Hera or Poseidon— they found in favour of Hera.[39] So this Asterion also has mythological connections with primordiality as well as, being a river, with autochthony.[40] Clearly, then, the name Asterios was associated with primordiality and autochthony; more specifically the Asterios of Milesian mythology was a primordial king associated with autochthony. I shall return to these associations below. First I shall consider the myth that the Panathenaic Games commemorated the death of the Giant Asterios.

which she suggests spurred the production of representations of its foundation legend, the victory at the Gigantomachy, and specifically Athena's victory over Asterios. As we shall see, there can be no doubt that the Gigantomachy had a great symbolic importance at the Panathenaia.

[37] On this myth, see Rutherford 2001: 250–2, 371. Vian (1952: 262–5) discusses Asterios and his name. He mentions also some other places which had earlier had Asteri- names (p. 264), but does not make the general link with primordiality.

[38] I have discussed the foundation myths of Miletos in great detail in Sourvinou-Inwood 2005: 268–309.

[39] The story is in Paus. 2.15.5, 2.17.1–2.

[40] In Hom. *Il.* 2.735, Asterion is a city. A non-primordial Asterion was an Argonaut (Ap. Rhod. 1.35; Paus. 5.17.9) and so was an Asterios (Ap. Rhod. 1.176).

This myth is only attested in two scholia to Aristeides, which contain two versions of an *aition* involving the death of a Giant. The first, which is ascribed to Aristotle, claims that the festival was celebrated for the death of the Giant Aster, who was killed by Athena.[41] The second scholion ascribes the foundation of the Lesser Panathenaia to Erichthonios for the death of the Giant Asterios and that of the Great Panathenaia to Peisistratos.[42] The latter is simply a distorted refraction of the reorganization of the festival in 566/5 that involved the establishment of the Great Panathenaia.[43] The notion of Erichthonios being the son of Amphictyon is clearly a corruption of the established mytheme that Erichthonios was the successor of Amphictyon.[44]

Of course in the Athenian conceptual universe the association of the killing of a Giant with the Panathenaia belongs in, and evokes very strongly, a particular mythological context, the Gigantomachy, and especially Athena's victorious role in the Gigantomachy,[45] in the gods' triumph over disorder and chaos, which was celebrated at the Panathenaia through its representation on Athena's *peplos*.[46] The Gigantomachy was also represented on the pediment of the 'old temple' of Athena, in which the olivewood statue which wore the *peplos* had stood[47]—as well as on the east metopes of the Parthenon,[48] and on the inside of the shield of the statue of Athena Parthenos.[49] It has been suggested that the Gigantomachy was represented in Athena's *peplos* because, as is shown by this myth of Asterios, the Gigantomachy was the foundation legend of the Panathenaia.[50] Be that as it may, the

---

[41] Schol. Aristid. *Or.* 1 Behr (*Panathenaikos*) 189, Dindorf III p. 323 (Dindorf prints killed by the Athenians); [Arist.] *Peplos* F 637 Rose.

[42] Schol. alt. Aristid. *Or.* 1 Behr (*Panathenaikos*) 189, Dindorf III p. 323, which Rose includes in [Arist.] *Peplos* F 637.

[43] See on this, Parker 1996: 89–92.

[44] Paus. 1.2.6, Apollod. 3.14.6.

[45] See also Parker 2005a: 255, 265. On the association between the Gigantomachy and the Panathenaia, see Vian 1952: 246–65. For the Panathenaia as a celebration of the victory at the Gigantomachy, see Ferrari Pinney 1988: 471–3; Ferrari 1994–5: 223.

[46] See e.g. Ridgway 1992: 123–4.

[47] See e.g. Hurwit 1999: 123–4.

[48] See e.g. ibid.: 170–1.

[49] See e.g. ibid.: 171, 187.

[50] See Ferrari Pinney 1988: 471–3; Ferrari 1994–5: 223.

fact that Asterios is not one of the Giants represented elsewhere as Athena's important adversaries is correlative with Asterios' connotations and meanings. The primordiality and autochthony signified by his name are correlative with the primordiality and autochthony signified by the myth that Erichthonios founded the Panathenaia— correlative, but not, we shall now see, the same.

Since the Asterios of Milesian mythology was a primordial king associated with autochthony he is semantically related to the Athenian autochthonous earthborn king Erichthonios. In addition, neither was the first bringer of autochthony in the line of their local kingship. Erichthonios was himself earthborn but he was also the successor of other autochthonous kings, most notably Kekrops.[51] Asterios was the son and successor of the autochthonous king Anax. As well as these correlations between Erichthonios and the primordial Milesian king, there are also symbolic correlations and differences between Erichthonios and the Giant Asterios who was killed by Athena. All Giants were sons of Gaia; Erichthonios was also a son of Gaia. But, as the son of Hephaistos and Athena's nursling, Erichthonios was a positive figure, a good primordial, autochthonous king, a culture hero, while Asterios, Athena's enemy, was a wild man who set himself up against the gods.[52]

If we leave all chronological considerations aside for the moment,[53] the sequence 'Athena kills a Giant—Erichthonios founds the Panathenaia in commemoration of this victory' connects the Panathenaia first with the defeat of savagery and chaos and then with a civilized primordiality and autochthony. When to this sequence is also added the third aitiological myth, that Theseus expanded and [re]founded the festival, the three myths taken together construct, and connect the Panathenaia with, a progression, from savage autochthony to the good autochthony of a civilizing

---

[51] Whether Erichthonios was Kekrops' direct or indirect successor is not relevant to our concerns. It is possible that in earlier genealogies Erichthonios had succeeded Kekrops (see Parker 1987a: 200; and Chapter 2 n. 109).

[52] Erichthonios was born as a result of Hephaistos' seed falling on the earth; according to Hes. *Theog.* 183–5 (cf. the note of M. L. West ad loc.) the Giants were conceived from the blood of Ouranos, when Kronos castrated him. So the latter conception can be seen as a wild savage version of the former.

[53] The complex chronological and related problems will be discussed below.

king to the civilized reign of Theseus in which things as they are 'today' were set in order. Consequently, I suggest, the three myths are likely to have been created in relation to each other—possibly at the same time, but it is perhaps more likely that the other two were constructed in connection with the most deeply rooted *aition*, that of Erichthonios' foundation. The fact that there are significant correlations between Erichthonios and Asterios points in the same direction, at least for this myth, in that it suggests that the myth that the Panathenaia commemorated the death of the Giant Asterios who had been killed by Athena was constructed in connection with, to become part of, the myth that Erichthonios was the founder of the Panathenaia.

In these circumstances it appears most probable that the version which combines the *aition* involving Asterios' death with that of Erichthonios as founder is primary, as it were, and the version in which Erichthonios is not mentioned and the Panathenaic Games are simply said to have been founded to commemorate the death of the Giant (if it was ever told as a story, as an alternative to the Erichthonios *aition*, which is not certain[54]) was secondary, parasitic as it were, on the combined version. Perhaps the extension back to Asterios and the times of chaos occurred when the myth that Theseus [re]founded the Panathenaia came to create, together with that of Erichthonios as founder, the sequence 'from civilized and civilizing autochthony and primordiality to the high heroic age and high civilization'. This sequence would have opened up a semantic space for extension at the other end, especially given that the sequence 'chaos—establishment of order' is often associated with foundations in Greek mythology. Another parameter shaping the new myth was primordiality and autochthony and the strengthening of autochthony: I suggest that in this mythopoeic process the semantic similarities between the Athenian autochthonous king Erichthonios, who founded the Panathenaia, and Asterios, the primordial king associated with autochthony in Milesian mythology, attracted the name Asterios into the sphere of the aitiological mythology of the Panathenaia, in which it was

---

[54] The failure to name Erichthonios in the version that omits him (n. 41 above) need not be significant, since the emphasis in that condensed list is on dead persons 'for whom' games were founded, not on founders.

deployed to construct another figure partially correlative with, but strongly antithetical to, Erichthonios, Asterios, the Giant killed by Athena.

Other parameters that shaped this mythological construction were, first, the symbolic importance at the Panathenaia of Athena's victorious role in the Gigantomachy, the gods' triumph over disorder and chaos, which was a reaffirmation of the cosmic order of the reign of Zeus, and, second, the schema 'Greek Games originated in funeral Games for a particular individual'.[55] The interaction of these two parameters would have helped construct the myth that the festival was established to commemorate the death of a particular Giant.

I will now consider a major problem. How did the foundation of the Panathenaia by Erichthonios relate chronologically to the Gigantomachy? The answer to the question when the Greeks would have perceived the Gigantomachy to have taken place is not unproblematic. Insofar as it was a cosmic event that determined the nature of the cosmos, we would 'logically' expect it to have been perceived to have taken place in the time before human history began. However, there is an element in it that places the Gigantomachy very much after human history began, the fact that Herakles fought in it, on the side of the gods; for he belonged to the central segment of the heroic age. Indeed the human presence is stressed by the fact that the help of a mortal is necessary for the gods to defeat the Giants.[56] Herakles, of course, was not an ordinary mortal; but it is in his capacity as mortal, which he was in his lifetime, albeit a mortal son of Zeus, that, we are told, he takes part in the Gigantomachy. Therefore, one of the meanings created by this mytheme was a mortal involvement in the Gigantomachy, a human stake in the outcome, in the gods' victory—though it was deconstructed by the activation of the perception that (when viewed through the eyes of archaic, classical, and post-classical Greeks) Herakles was ambiguously mortal.

---

[55] See also Parker 2005a: 255.
[56] See Apollod. 1.6.1; cf. e.g. Pind. *Nem.* 7.90. On Herakles in the Gigantomachy Vian 1952: 193–5, 211–14, 217–22, and passim (see Index). On the myth and its sources, textual and iconographical, see Gantz 1993: 445–54. On Herakles at the Gigantomachy, see also Ferrari (1994–5: 222–5), who argues that the vases that show Herakles with Athena in a chariot pertain to the Gigantomachy, the victory celebration after the defeat of the Giants.

Be that as it may, the mytheme of Herakles' participation would appear to de-anchor the Gigantomachy from cosmic time and locate it within human history.[57] Would that have been a possible Greek representation of the time of the Gigantomachy, that it took place in the generation that preceded the Trojan War? The victory of the Olympian Gods in the Titanomachy led to the establishment of the cosmic order as it now is, the establishment of the reign of Zeus. Thus the Titanomachy was inescapably perceived as being 'out there' in time, at the very beginning of the time of which 'now' is part, in 'cosmic' time before human history. But the Gigantomachy was different, insofar as it involved the reaffirmation of the cosmic order of the reign of Zeus rather than its first establishment. For the Gigantomachy reaffirmed the gods' victory over disorder and chaos and reaffirmed their reign.[58] It is thus a representation of reassurance, reassurance about the cosmic order, its stability and future. The fact that it was possible to perceive it as taking place in the world of human history and that a human contribution was of crucial importance may have strengthened that reassurance, may have constructed the more strongly reassuring meaning that whatever threat to the cosmic order may emerge, the gods will defeat it, with the collaboration of humanity.

This set of representations may be one of the reasons why an extremely small number of images of Titanomachies[59] contrasts with the vast number of Gigantomachies—and why the Gigantomachy became one of the metaphors through which the Greek victories

[57] According to Vian 1952: 217, when the Greeks began to systematize their mythology, they found situating the Gigantomachy in cosmogonic chronology awkward, because the nature of the conflict invited a placing at the beginning of the reign of Zeus, but Herakles belonged to the generation that preceded the Trojan War. He thinks that fourth-century writers tried to resolve the contradictions and he accepts the attribution to Hekataios of Abdera of the invention attested (unattributed) in Diod. Sic. 1.24.2 of a second, much earlier Herakles, and remarks that usually the preference was to insert the old cosmogonic theme into the life of Herakles. The rationalization of the two figures of Herakles was not part of the established perceptions of the classical period, as, for example, Pind. *Nem.* 7.90, or images of Herakles in the Gigantomachy, make unambiguously clear.

[58] The defeat of Typhon by Zeus is, of course, part of the same semantic nexus.

[59] On the sources for, and possible representations of, the Titanomachy, see e.g. Gantz 1993: 44–5.

over the Persians were represented as a victory of civilization over barbarism, which of course increased much further the popularity of Gigantomachy images. Another, probably stronger, reason, is that the Giants represented chaos and disorder in an unambiguous way, while the Titans represented the older order,[60] which was ambivalent. For in the Greek collective representations the age of Kronos had ambivalent characteristics, including savagery and disorder,[61] and ambivalence is fundamental in the character of Kronos.[62] Nevertheless, it is central to the Greek perception of the cosmos—a perception expressed, above all, in Hesiod's succession myth in the *Theogony*— that the reign of Zeus established a superior order in the world, that Zeus' assumption of sovereignty was a decisive step in the movement from primordial darkness and chaos to an ordered cosmos.

To return to the question of when the Greeks perceived the Gigantomachy to have taken place. Though Herakles' participation seems to bring it down within human history, this could not entirely obliterate the nature of the Gigantomachy as a cosmic event: the perception that it happened alongside human events could not but be destabilized by, for example, the notion that some geographical features of the present, which also existed in the heroic past, were created in the course of this battle between gods and Giants.[63] Consequently, I suggest, in Greek eyes also, the time of the Gigant-omachy, and indeed the nature of the time of the Gigantomachy, was ambiguous and ambivalent. This complexity and ambiguity of the temporal location of the Gigantomachy may have been perceived by the Greeks as related to the unfathomable nature of divine time—and perhaps also the unfathomable notion of a human who became a god, but who functioned as a human in his lifetime.

In these circumstances, I suggest that the chronological relation-ship between the Gigantomachy and the reign of Erichthonios is virtually unfathomable. From the viewpoint of a perception that

---

[60] See also Vian 1952: 287.

[61] See esp. Versnel 1987: esp. 132–3; Versnel 1993: 95–7; cf. also Vidal-Naquet 1981: 82, 86.

[62] Versnel 1993.

[63] See for example, Apollod. 1.6.2; Strabo 10.5.16 [489].

placed the Gigantomachy before human history, the reign of Erichthonios would have taken place long after that battle. In that case Erichthonios would have been perceived to have founded the Panathenaic Games to celebrate Athena's victory long after the event.[64] From the viewpoint of a perception that placed the Gigantomachy in Herakles' lifetime, Erichthonios would have lived a considerable time before the Gigantomachy. However, there is yet another chronological indication, which may or may not reflect established myth, which places the Gigantomachy before the birth of Erichthonios: according to Euripides, *Ion* 987–1003, Athena gave to Erichthonios at his birth two drops of the blood of the Gorgon who was killed in the course of the Gigantomachy.

It is possible that Athenian cultic mythopoeia (if the *aition* according to which the Panathenaia was founded for the death of the Giant Asterios was ever an Athenian myth) or the mythographer (if not) may have treated any perceived 'conflict' in ways that disguised what appears to us to be a problem; or that strategies of conflict avoidance implicitly developed by the Athenians shaped their perceptions of the myth in ways that did not foreground such conflict. Thus, for example, to start with the latter possibility, the Gigantomachy may indeed have been perceived, as suggested above, as free-floating in the Greek imaginaire, and not, paradoxical though this may seem to us, anchored by, and in, Herakles' lifetime. That is, it is possible that, if both the Gigantomachy and the foundation of the Panathenaia by Erichthonios were cultic *aitia* of the festival, it was somehow feasible to perceive the Gigantomachy both as a cosmic event in the past of the cosmos (which is what the allusion in Euripides, *Ion* 987–1003, would suggest) and as a reaffirmation of the cosmic order in the course of the heroic age; or at least that it was somehow possible both to perceive the Gigantomachy as a cosmic event and to believe that Herakles had taken part in it.

Alternatively, it may have been the case that the mytheme that Athena killed the Giant Asterios did not place this killing in the course of the Gigantomachy, but presented it as a separate victory, which was semantically a mini-Gigantomachy and prefigured (if the

---

[64] See also Parker 2005a: 255.

battle with the Giants was indeed perceived to have taken place later), and certainly evoked the Gigantomachy. So, on this hypothesis, the killing of a Giant by Athena was an *aition* of the Panathenaia, while the Gigantomachy would have been a kind of metaphorical *aition*, as it were. This possibility would be consistent with the name Asterios, which evokes primordiality and autochthony; for a Gigantomachy that was perceived to have taken place in Herakles' lifetime would have belonged to the high heroic age, not to the primordial times evoked by Asterios' name.

Yet another possibility would be that in the narrative articulations, and in the Athenian perceptions of such articulations, the picture beyond the core mytheme 'Athena killed a Giant, the Panathenaia commemorates this' remained vague, opaque.

Be that as it may, the mytheme 'Athena killed the Giant Asterios', whether it was perceived as part of a Gigantomachy, or as a pre-figuration of a Gigantomachy that was to take place in Herakles' lifetime—or, more generally, and perhaps more probably, as a meta-phor for an ambiguously located Gigantomachy—would have evoked the nexus of meanings concerning the Olympians' reaffirma-tion of the present cosmic order and the reign of Zeus defeating chaos and disorder.

Whether or not the aitiological association of the Panathenaia with the Gigantomachy was an Athenian myth, the fact that the battle between the gods and the Giants was represented on Athena's *peplos* meant that one of the representations of the poliadic relationship between Athens and Athena expressed at the Panathenaia associated that relationship with the Gigantomachy. In that representation Athena's role in the Gigantomachy was emphasized by the context. (Of course, if the myth that connects the Panathenaia with the death of Asterios was indeed a cultic myth in Athens, this emphasis and the association between the poliadic relationship and the Gigantomachy would have been even stronger.) The Gigantomachy, especially in the versions which emphasized Athena's role, stressed Athena's persona as a cosmic victor over chaos. Thus, this representation of the poliadic relationship as associated with the Gigantomachy repre-sented the poliadic deity, and so also the protection she gave to the polis, as all-powerful.

3. PANATHENAIA AND PLYNTERIA

Though much more lavish and spectacular, and much more significant in the ideology of the polis, the Panathenaia was ritually a
simpler festival than those making up the nexus of the Plynteria
and Kallynteria, consisting, as it did, of a *pannychis*, a procession
escorting the multiple offerings (that is, the *peplos*, the sacrificial
victims, and the crown), sacrifices, the clothing of Athena in the
new *peplos*, and competitions.[65]

Both the Great Panathenaia and (perhaps especially) the 'unclut-
tered' Lesser Panathenaia are, in a way, a kind of continuation of the
nexus of the Plynteria and Kallynteria. Insofar as the Kallynteria
commemorated the installation of the poliadic cult, the Panathenaic
procession and offerings belong to a later moment, when the cult was
already established, and the polis brings offerings to honour and
please the goddess and renew that established relationship. Insofar
as at the Plynteria the *peplos* was washed and the statue was dressed in
this laundered *peplos*, the Panathenaia, in which the goddess was
offered, and the statue was dressed in, a new *peplos*, involved a kind
of intensification of the actions at the Plynteria.

The notion that the Panathenaia symbolically belonged with an
already established cult of Athena Polias is mythologically not inconsistent with the festival's *aitia*. The myth of the foundation by
Erichthonios fits well with this symbolic characterization of the
Panathenaia, since the poliadic cult of Athena had been installed in
the reign of Kekrops and its first priestess had been Aglauros.[66] The
myth that the Panathenaia was founded by Theseus would also,

---

[65] I have argued elsewhere (Sourvinou-Inwood 2003a: 72–81, 89, 99–100, 104)
that there was a comparable relationship between the other 'panathenaic' festival, the
City Dionysia, and the 'older Dionysia', the Anthesteria.

[66] As we saw (pp. 98–9), the myth in Apollod. 3.14.6 that Erichthonios set up
Athena's statue may or may not have been a cultic myth and it may or may not have
been perceived to imply that this was the first statue of Athena. As has become clear in
these discussions, the movements out of primordiality and to things as they 'now' are
were multiple and complex, and I suggested that in this context it may have remained
ambiguous when the statue of Athena had fallen from the sky and been installed on
the Acropolis, and that this ambiguity may have been part of the ancient perceptions
of this nexus of representations.

obviously, fit well with this notion, though I suggested that it is likely that Theseus' foundation was always perceived to have been a second foundation, reflecting the synoecized polis. But what of the third myth that the festival commemorated the death of the Giant Aster or Asterios? If my analysis in the previous section is right, this *aition* was part of the myth that the Panathenaia was founded by Erichthonios, therefore the same considerations apply as with the other versions of the 'Erichthonios as founder' myth that do not involve the death of a Giant. In addition, it is possible to argue that the Gigantomachy would also fit symbolically with the notion of the Panathenaia belonging to a moment when the cult was already established, and the polis was bringing offerings to honour and please the goddess and renew that established relationship; for since, as we saw in the previous section, the Gigantomachy represented the reaffirmation, not the first establishment, of the cosmic order under the rule of Zeus, the two can be seen as symbolically correlative, in that both involved not beginnings, but reaffirmation and renewal.

This semantic location of the Panathenaia at a moment when the poliadic cult is already established, and the polis brings offerings to honour and please the goddess and renew that established relationship, is ritually expressed through the fact that, unlike the procession of the Plynteria, which went outwards to Phaleron carrying the statue, and its return procession (on my reconstruction part of the Kallynteria) which brought the statue back to the Acropolis, the Panathenaic procession came from the polis to pay homage and bring gifts to the goddess in her sanctuary. This, on Graf's classification, is a centripetal procession.[67] Similarly, unlike the nexus of the Plynteria and Kallynteria, the Panathenaia was not preceded by, nor did it begin with, a period of abnormality and pollution; it celebrated an already established relationship between Athens and its poliadic deity.

The Panathenaia was an open and joyful festival which involved the whole polis, while the Plynteria included secret and exclusive rites, some of which were performed on a day that was inauspicious, ominous, at the culmination of a period of abnormality. On my

---

[67] Graf 1996: 57–9; on the Panathenaic procession, ibid. 58–9.

reconstruction, the restoration of order took place during the asso-ciated second festival of the nexus, the Kallynteria. As we saw in Chapter 3, section 6.ii, renewal was an important ritual outcome of the nexus of the Plynteria and Kallynteria, the renewal of the rela-tionship between the goddess and the polis and through it a renewal of life, prosperity, blessings. The Panathenaia also involved a renewal of the relationship between Athens and its poliadic deity and an attendant general renewal.[68] Thus the two nexuses together would have been perceived as achieving a two-act renewal, as it were, thus reinforcing the renewal brought about by each individual nexus on its own.

Greek renewal rituals have a gloomy, dark facet involving dissolu-tion, and then a new beginning and joy, a joyous facet associated with the establishment of the new order. At the Plynteria and Kallynteria the facet of the renewal nexus that pertains to pollution, ill-omened-ness, and purification is, we saw, strong. At the Panathenaia it is the joyful facet that is strong and that of gloom and dissolution invisi-ble.[69] But if the Panathenaia is considered together with the nexus of the Plynteria and Kallynteria, as a pair in a nexus of renewal, these apparent oddities structure themselves into a pattern that is consis-tent with Greek ritual logic: the joyous facet has drifted primarily to the Panathenaia and the gloomy facet to the Plynteria (even when taken together with the Kallynteria, and by comparison with the Panathenaia).[70] Clearly, then, these festivals were perceived to be, among many other things, also part of a nexus of renewal[71] focused on the statue, which began with a 'dirty' robe (and dirty wool), progressed to a cleaned robe (and cleaned wool for next year's new *peplos*) at the completion of the Plynteria, and concluded with a new robe at the Panathenaia. The new robe indicates, and brings about, a stronger renewal than a newly laundered one.

---

[68] On the 'new year renewal' aspects of the Panathenaia, see Burkert 1983: 154–5.

[69] See also Burkert 1985: 232. The sequence *pannychis*—lighting of the altar fire (Burkert 1985: 232) is the closest that on observable evidence the Panathenaia comes to a gloom–joy sequence.

[70] This does not mean that there was no joyous facet in the nexus of the Plynteria and Kallynteria (see also Parker 1996: 308 n. 63).

[71] Burkert 1983: 135–61 discusses the Panathenaia as part of a whole cycle of New Year festivals.

Both nexuses were associated with primordiality and auto-chthony, the Panathenaia, we saw, through its *aitia*, the Plynteria and Kallynteria in manifold ways. The *aitia* of the Plynteria and Kallynteria locate the festivals symbolically at the beginning of the movement out of primordiality and towards things as they now are; those of the Panathenaia stress the movement from chaos and negative primordiality to positive primordiality and beyond, to the 'high' civilization of the peak of the heroic age. All these moments, and all these movements, are focused on the poliadic cult of Athena Polias.

4. THE *PEPLOS* ON THE PARTHENON FRIEZE: A READING

My justification for engaging with the much discussed topic of the Parthenon frieze, and especially of the *peplos* scene, is my belief that certain discussions of these images have taken insufficient account of the system of religious representations of which the *peplos* was part.[72] I begin by mentioning here, for clarity's sake, that, as has been almost universally accepted, and will be further confirmed in the course of the discussion, the representation, on a temple of Athena, of a ritual

---

[72] I cannot engage with the vast bibliography on this topic, so my engagement (here and below, in the course of the discussion) will be selective. On the figures with the *peplos* on the frieze see most recently the discussions with bib. in: Neils 2001a: 67–70, 166–71 cf. 184–5; Dillon 2002: 45–7; Hurwit 2004: 146, 230, 236 (see also Hurwit 1999: 179–86; 222–8); Neils 2003: 159. Among recently expressed views, Dillon (2002: 45–7) identifies the woman as the priestess of Athena Polias, the man as the *archon basileus*, the smaller child as a girl, and the two girls with the objects on their head as the *arrhephoroi*. For Neils (2001a: 67–70, 166–71), the scene shows the *peplos* being folded after the presentation; the man is a priest because of his unbelted short-sleeved *chiton* (2006: 167, 168–9); the woman is a priestess (p. 167); the girls are most likely the *arrhephoroi* (p. 168); the younger child is male, and he is the priest's assistant (pp. 168–71). She expresses the same views in Neils (2003: 159). Hurwit (2004: 230, 236) accepts the reading that the central scene is the Panathenaic *peplos* scene and identifies the figures as a young temple boy helping the *archon basileus* with the robe; the woman is the priestess of Athena Polias or the Basilinna, the two girls are *diphrophoroi* or *arrhephoroi*.

manipulation of a large cloth refracts (in ways to be further discussed) the offering of the *peplos* to Athena at the Panathenaia.[73]

The *peplos* scene is at the very centre of the frieze, above the entrance, over the position of (though not, of course, directly over) the door that led from the *pronaos* to the cella; it is located in the most ritually important place. Its prominence is further increased by the fact that it is framed by two groups of deities: what the ancient viewers saw through the columns framing the frieze's central part above the entrance of the temple was a representation involving the *peplos* and framed by deities.[74] These deities are shown on a larger scale than the mortals; they are turned away from the *peplos* scene, and facing in the direction of the arriving procession. They are the Twelve Olympians—a version in which Dionysos is included instead of Hestia—who are represented seated, and two minor deities who are shown standing, Iris, associated with Hera, and Eros, associated with Aphrodite. The Twelve Gods received worship as one cultic entity in Athens.[75] The Altar of the Twelve Gods in the Agora, dedicated by Peisistratos, son of Hippias,[76] stood in the middle of a small shrine enclosed by a low precinct wall and came to be considered the centre of Athens, since it was the central point from which distances were measured.[77]

---

[73] Since, I believe, for various reasons, some of which have been set out by others and some of which will emerge in the discussion below, that the scene is not mythological in the sense of representing something believed to have happened only once in the heroic past. The most thoroughly argued, rich, and interesting mythological interpretation is that of Connelly (1996).

[74] See also Jenkins (1994: 35) on the relationship between the deities and the *peplos* scene and the ways in which this is affected by the position of this segment of the frieze and the way it was viewed through the fourth and fifth columns of the peristyle; and (ibid. 35–42) for the significance of the *peplos* on the frieze and its relationship with the other sculptures on and in the Parthenon. On the various relationships of the different parts of the sculptural decoration of the Parthenon to each other from the viewer's viewpoint, see also Osborne 1994.

[75] On the Twelve Gods, see also Phillips 2002: 860. On the inscribed seat of the priest of the Twelve Gods in the *prohedria* of the theatre of Dionysos (*IG* II² 5065), see Maass 1972: 132.

[76] Thuc. 6.54.6–7. He was probably archon in 522/1. The recent reconsideration of the altar by Gadbery has also concluded that 522/1 was the date of its construction (Gadbery 1992: 447–89 esp. 487). On the Altar of the Twelve Gods, see Travlos 1971: 458–61; Shapiro 1989: 133–41 with bib.

[77] Hdt. 2.7; cf. Dontas 1983: 60 and n. 37.

The divinities immediately next to, and framing, the *peplos* scene are Athena on one side and Zeus on the other. They are the city's two poliadic deities: while Athena is the main poliadic deity, Zeus, the sovereign of the gods, is also worshipped as Zeus Polieus, with a sanctuary on the Acropolis, to the north-east of the Parthenon.[78] As the main poliadic deity, and the recipient of the gift shown in the image, Athena stands next to the *peplos* that is being folded—though she is shown turned away from it; Zeus' status as the sovereign god is signalled in the frieze through the fact that he is the only deity shown sitting on a throne rather than a stool. Athena and Zeus have an especially close connection to each other here, both because they are the two poliadic deities shown in a context which, through the representation of the *peplos*, brings poliadic relationships to the fore, and also because the east pediment, above this part of the frieze, represented the birth of Athena and so Zeus' close relationship to her of both father and—almost—gestating mother.[79]

What are we to make of the·fact that Athena, Zeus and all the other gods are shown with their back to the *peplos* scene?[80] Let us begin by trying to reconstruct the effects created by the represented spatial relationships. First, the general effect is that the turned backs help create a visual separation of the *peplos* scene from the gods, and this, in combination with the change in scale, sets off, separates and also gives prominence to, the *peplos* scene, at the very centre of the frieze. The gods are represented as both connected to the *peplos* scene and separated from it.

More complex relationships are created, we shall now see, at the more detailed level. Before considering them I should make clear that I am not, of course, suggesting—especially given the position of the frieze—that the ancient viewers consciously noticed all the details I will be setting out, and systematically worked out their meanings.

---

[78] On the sanctuary of Zeus Polieus, see Hurwit 1999: 190–2, cf. 40; on the cult of Zeus Polieus and the Dipolieia: Deubner 1969: 158–74; Parke 1977: 162–7; Burkert 1983: 136–43; Sourvinou-Inwood 1990a: 307–8, 310, 313–14 = Sourvinou-Inwood 2000: 24–5, 27, 30–1; cf. N. Robertson 1992: 15; Parker 1996: 299.

[79] On the Parthenon pediments, see Palagia 1993; Palagia 2005: 225–59. On the relationship between Athena and Zeus in general, see also Neils 2001b: 219–32.

[80] For the notion that this representation depicts the deities sitting in a semicircle, and the argument against it, see below and n. 82.

However, those ancient viewers were familiar with the language of Greek iconography and so (at some point in the conscious–unconscious spectrum) minor variations (which we need to work out through systematic concentrated observation) registered, in the sense that they contributed to the complex process of meaning creation through which they made sense of the image.[81]

I will now consider in detail the ways in which the *peplos* scene related to the divine groups that framed it. Athena sits, next to the child manipulating the *peplos*, with her back almost, but not quite, fully turned, her torso in a marginally three-quarter (rather than fully profile) position, while the child turns its back on her fully; the almost but not quite vertical lines of Athena's back outline, her gently curving arm, and the leg of her stool, correspond to the child's straight vertical created by the vertical fall of its *peplos*. At this point, then, the separation of the two segments is sharp. Zeus, on the other side of the *peplos* scene, is not fully turned away, his torso is in a more fully three-quarter stance and his bent arm is resting on the back of the throne. This corresponds to the complex stance of the girl next to him, which associates her not only with the *peplos* scene in which she belongs, but also with the viewer and—to a more limited extent—the gods. Under Zeus' arm the vertical of the throne's back corresponds to the almost vertical of the lower part of the girl's body. Here, then, the separation is not as radical as on Athena's side. Thus, on Athena's side, where the semantic connection of the goddess with the *peplos* is close, the iconographical separation is strong; on Zeus' side, where the semantic association is weak, the iconographical separation is less radical. There would therefore appear to be a comparable balance between separation and connectedness on the two sides, constructed through different interactions between iconographical elements and the semantic assumptions with the help of which the iconographical elements were made sense of by the contemporary viewers. This suggests that a complex balance between separation and connectedness between the *peplos* scene and the gods (especially Athena and Zeus) was a significant factor in the shaping of the selections that generated this set of images.

[81] See Sourvinou-Inwood 1991: 12–13.

The care taken with the relationships of the figures at the interface between the gods and the *peplos* scene shows that this interface was significant; and therefore that these interface segments, in both groups, on both sides, should not be taken out of their context and their significance ultimately elided—as it is in readings that seek to translate the represented relationship between the *peplos* scene and the gods into a different, pseudo-realistic relationship, such as that the gods should be understood to be sitting in a continuous semi-circle.[82] This kind of reading is based on the assumption that the intermeshed juxtaposition of the gods and the *peplos* scene had a 'real-life' reference, that it would have been made sense of as representing a visible ritual act in the presence of invisible gods. However, given that the idiom of Greek iconography includes the emblematic

---

[82] Neils has revived and elaborated the notion that the gods were sitting in a continuous semicircle. On her argument they can be interpreted as taking part in a *theoxenia*, sitting in a semicircle in front of, and facing, the temple (1999: 5–20). However, first, as I just argued, the care taken at the interface between the gods and the *peplos* scene shows that this interface is significant. Second, as I hope to show, the ancient viewers constructed significant meanings from the image as it stands, in its own terms, and they would not have discarded those meanings in order to translate the representation into something else that seems realistic to the modern viewer. It may well have been a reading open to the Athenian viewers that the image represents the gods attending a *theoxenia* rite. But even if this is right, it would be a separate issue whether or not such reading would entail that the gods would be understood to be represented as sitting in a semicircle in front of the temple. Perhaps it cannot be excluded that it was open to Athenian viewers to interpret the representation of the gods on the frieze as implying a semicircular sitting arrangement. But even if that were the case—and I believe it is unlikely—this would be one elaboration of one possible reading; it would not entail that the image was not made sense of in its own terms, but was translated into a realistic correlative. The realist interpretation is inspired by, and implicitly based on, the combination of two types of culturally determined expectations. First, expectations about what is logical, perhaps above all the perception that the gods would not turn their back on the *peplos* scene and especially Athena would not turn her back on the gift offered her; second, the unconscious privileging of the descriptive narrative mode, in this case the assumption that ancient viewers would have translated what they saw into the narrative 'the gods are turning their back on the *peplos* offering'. Furthermore, if the main meaning, and a significant parameter, shaping selections, had indeed been that the gods were sitting in a continuous semicircle in front of, and facing, the temple with the *peplos* ceremony taking place in the centre, the *peplos* scene (which on that reading would have to be the depiction of an actual ritual act, not a more complex refraction) would be incongruously unspectacular and mundane when considered from the point of view of 'watching', especially given the prominence of its position and the privileging of its viewing by the gods.

modality, it is not legitimate to make such an assumption; for the grouping may have been understood to be conveying a conceptual relationship between the *peplos* scene and the gods, comparable, for example, to those represented on the document reliefs in which Athena is shown shaking hands with the poliadic deity of another city to indicate alliance, friendship, and commitment between the cities.[83]

Let us therefore consider what is actually depicted. What does this particular arrangement of the images of the gods and the *peplos* scene do? As we saw, it gives prominence to the *peplos* scene and this, and the representation of a special connection to the gods, reinforces the meaning created by the scene's central position, that it is religiously very important. The gift of the *peplos* was at the religious centre of the Panathenaia—as it is of the frieze. But what of the separateness from, and connectedness to, the gods, the intermeshing, the framing and complex separation at the interface, what, if any, other, more specific, meanings does this particular version of the intermeshing of the *peplos* scene with the divinities construct?

Meaning is created also with the help of relationships of similarities to, and differences from, the other elements in the system of which each element is part.[84] Let us, then, first consider how the gods relate to the segments on their other side, and so to the rest of the frieze. As we saw, they are turned towards the procession. They are not directly facing it, for immediately next to each group of seated deities, between them and the procession, is represented a group of standing figures—whose identities do not concern me here.[85] Standing figure E23 is turning his back on Hermes and on the other side three standing figures, E43, 44, 45, are shown turned away from

---

[83] See e.g. Lawton 1995: 30, 88 no. 12 pl. 7; on the iconographical schema, see pp. 36–8.

[84] Other elements in the image and in addition other elements that might have been chosen in the place of the one under consideration (see Sourvinou-Inwood 1991: 11).

[85] I will only mention that if they are the Eponymous Heroes (see e.g. Hurwit 1999: 186, 225) they would represent another category of polis-protecting being, and this would be consistent with the reading offered here, which puts the emphasis on poliadic relationships. But I believe they are more likely to be mortals. See Jenkins 1994: 77, 80–1.

Aphrodite who is gesticulating in the direction of the standing figures and the procession. Clearly, this relationship between the gods and the procession is very different from that between the gods and the *peplos* scene. In the case of the procession gods and ritual do not intermesh, but the gods are turned in the direction of the ritual, while the standing figures (possibly heroes, more probably mortals) are shown with their backs to the gods whom they separate from the arriving procession. Thus, one of the meanings created by this representation is that the gods relate to the procession but the members of the procession do not relate to them, in other words, that the gods are watching the procession, while the mortals are not aware of their presence.

The differences between this set of relationships and the complex ways in which the *peplos* scene relates to the two groups of gods that frame it further confirm that the gods are not represented watching the *peplos* scene, but as being in some way connected with it. The question is how; more generally, what meanings did this set of images, the *peplos* scene intermeshed with divinities, construct, in the context of the frieze as a whole? First, the *peplos*, the most important gift offered to Athena, expressed and symbolized the relationship of reciprocity between polis and poliadic deity. A polis's relationship with its poliadic deity was its most important relationship with the divine world; it was an intense version, a part, and at the same time also a metonymically based symbol, of its relationship to all the gods, both a close relationship with a particular deity and a focus and symbol of the relationship with the divine world, the 'contract' with the gods which ensured the polis's survival and prosperity. For a city's continued existence and prosperity depended on, and was guaranteed by, its relationship to the divine world, a kind of divine, finite, guarantee.[86] That relationship was based on reciprocity. Because the poliadic relationship was also a symbol for the polis' relationship with the divine world in general, the *peplos* offering also expressed the relationship of reciprocity between the polis and the whole of the divine world.

---

[86] Sourvinou-Inwood 1990a: 306–7 = Sourvinou-Inwood 2000: 23–4.

Second, in this context, in which this poliadic relationship was at the forefront, the representation of the Twelve Gods plus two minor deities would also have evoked the divine world as a whole, that is, the deities would have been perceived as the specific gods represented, the twelve most important gods, who were also worshipped as one cultic unit, and at the same time as a metonymically based metaphor for the divine world as a whole, the gods who guaranteed the city's survival and prosperity. The construction of the metaphor was facilitated by the representation of Iris and Eros, for they are minor deities, associated with, but not part of, the Twelve Olympians, and so in ancient eyes they inevitably evoked all the other gods. Finally, while in the *peplos* scene the focus is on the main poliadic deity, Athena, to whom the rite is addressed and whose temple the frieze adorns, in the representation of the gods both poliadic deities are prominent, at the centre, immediately framing the *peplos* scene and, we saw, relating to it in ways involving comparable measures of connectedness and separateness. Zeus, as the sovereign of the gods, was the ultimate guarantor of the cosmic order and so the city's fate. This double nature of Zeus, poliadic deity and sovereign of the gods, would also have brought to the fore the interplay between poliadic deities and the divine world as a whole, both of whom, together and separately, protected, and guaranteed the survival of, the polis.

Consequently, this segment of the frieze, above the entrance to the temple, is an iconographical articulation of the relationship, based on reciprocity, between the polis and its poliadic goddess, shown as part of the relationship between the polis and the whole divine world, which was represented by the Twelve Gods plus two minor deities, and also by the city's second poliadic deity, Zeus, the sovereign of the gods, who was the ultimate guarantor of all order and so also of the city's fate, a part of his persona signalled in this image through the throne. In other words, this segment of the frieze represented iconographically the 'contract' between the polis and the gods who guaranteed the city's survival.[87]

---

[87] That the east side of the Parthenon represents the collectivity of the Olympian gods, and not just the poliadic deity, as important for the polis, has been noted by others (see Palagia 2005: 233–4).

Of course, the representation is polysemic. Since the gods are shown watching the procession, the ancient viewers clearly opened up the frame outwards, taking in, together with the gods, also the part of the procession shown on the outer parts of the east frieze—as well as the parts they had already seen while walking around the temple towards the east side. So the gods were also perceived as being present at a festival, watching its procession. In this context, a reading that opened up the frame from the central segment expressing the 'contract', to the procession watched by the gods, which was part of the festival of which the offering of the robe is the centre, also constructed the meaning that the gods looked benevolently upon Athenian rites; and so the frieze represents all the gods involved in the relationship of reciprocity—though it was focused, above all, on the poliadic goddess.[88] To put it differently, the *peplos* scene is framed by the Olympian gods and the nexus '*peplos* scene and Olympian gods' is framed by a procession in the direction of which the gods are turned as it arrives on both sides. This iconography corresponds to significant, interrelated, ancient perceptions. At the centre the gift to the main poliadic deity that above all symbolizes the polis's intense relationship of reciprocity with the deity; this is framed by both poliadic deities, the secondary one of whom is the sovereign of the gods, and so also represents and reinforces the relationship with all the gods; and this is framed by the Twelve Gods (plus two), also representing all the gods, who are in a relationship of protection and reciprocity with the polis, and are themselves framed by a procession which also expresses reciprocity. Thus, the *peplos* scene taken together with the two groups of divinities with which it is intertwined is a condensed expression, at the ritual centre, above the entrance, of the central representation conveyed by the whole frieze: the reciprocity of the relationship between the polis and the gods, which is especially focused on, and represented most strongly by, the relationship between the polis and its poliadic deity which the Panathenaia celebrated.

It is difficult to doubt that the system of images that make up the frieze, located on a temple of Athena and centred on the representation

---

[88] On the Twelve Gods being present at certain rites and festivals, see Sourvinou-Inwood 2003a: 95–6, with bib.

of mortals manipulating a *peplos*, corresponds to realities and perceptions relating to the Panathenaia.[89] Does the frieze, then, reflect the Panathenaia procession and festival? This may well have been the dominant reading in the eyes of the ancient Athenians, that it depicted facets of the Panathenaia, neither specifically the Little Panathenaia, nor specifically the Great Panathenaia, but a set of refractions of selected realities and perceptions concerning the Panathenaia nexus that were ritually important and/or represented important aspects of the polis. But it is possible that another reading was also open to Athenian viewers. It has been suggested that the procession could be seen as also evoking other processions and festivals, in honour of other deities.[90] Such an interpretation can now be anchored more concretely, since, on my reading, it would also be religiously connected to the central part of the east frieze, it would be correlative with the opening up, on the east frieze, of the semantic frame of reference from the poliadic nexus to all the gods, and the iconographical expression of the 'contract' based on reciprocity; in other words, it is possible that the notion of all the gods being involved in this reciprocity was in fact represented more strongly through the depiction of ritual elements that evoked the cult of other deities. It is also possible that there was, in Athenian eyes, or at least some of them, a certain (unresolvable) ambivalence as to whether the images on the frieze evoked rituals and perceptions concerning the Panathenaia alone or also other rituals honouring other deities. The location of the frieze, on a temple of Athena, and the *peplos* scene with its emphasis on the poliadic relationship, would have anchored, I submit, the Panathenaia as the dominant theme, and perhaps also the dominant reading.

[89] My formulation is not very radically removed from that expressed by Jenkins (1994: 42): "The *peplos* scene provides an unequivocal Panathenaic context; for the rest the frieze does not aim to document the event itself. It serves, rather, as a visual metaphor of the spirit of the Panathenaic festival, as it was conceived in Perikles' day, embodying and reinforcing the communal values of the city, but at the same time transcending it." (See also Jenkins 1994: 24–6; cf. 26–34, 42.) There are differences between this reading and mine, which will become clear in the course of the discussion.

[90] See Hurwit (1999: 227–8); he accepts that the Panathenaia are "given pride of place on the east frieze", but thinks that this festival is one of many rituals distilled on the frieze which surveys "the rich panorama of Athenian sacred life".

I will now consider briefly the *peplos* scene and try to set out the parameters for the identification of the individual figures. A woman is receiving two young girls who are holding, and carrying on their heads, certain objects. On her other side a man in priestly dress[91] and a child are manipulating a cloth. Ancient Greek viewers (who shared Greek religious knowledge and the conventions of Greek iconography) with even minimal knowledge of Athenian rituals would have identified the cloth as the *peplos* offered to Athena and as a result they would also have identified the woman at the centre of this scene, and of the frieze, as the priestess of Athena Polias. For this most prestigious position in a situation connected with the *peplos* and Athena in her poliadic persona coincides with the profile of only one figure, the priestess of Athena Polias.[92] Those viewers would have identified the man as a priest assisted by a child, and the two girls as being somehow involved with the ritual. I suggest that these are the minimal parameters for our reconstruction of the scene's meanings in the eyes of the non-Athenian Greeks. What can we reconstruct about how the Athenians made sense of it?

Clearly, they would know the identity of the girls and of the man in priestly dress, and also the precise sex and status of the assisting child—which I will not discuss here, other than to say that if it is a girl she would be an *arrhephoros*, if a boy an assistant of some kind,[93] and that I will be arguing that it is extremely unlikely that the child is an *arrhephoros*. Since we do not share the ritual knowledge that

---

[91] Mantis (1990: 80, 84, 85) noted that the short-sleeved Ionic *chiton* worn by this figure was the typical dress of a priest in the classical period.

[92] She is not, as has been thought possible (Hurwit 1999: 225), the *basilinna*, even if the man is the *archon basileus*. For the *basilinna* only had a role in the specific ritual nexus, a specific part of the Anthesteria, a particular Dionysiac festival, which also included a part in which Dionysos, impersonated by the *basileus*, was married to the *basilinna*. (On this aspect of the Anthesteria see Hamilton (1992: 53–6) with testimonia—though I do not find the scepticism well grounded—and most recently Humphreys 2004: 252–3, 270–1, cf. 232–7; and esp. Parker 2005a: 303–5). The fact that no other ritual role for the *basilinna* is mentioned in the highly charged context of [Dem.] 59, where another such role performed by a woman who was not entitled to perform it would have added weight to the speaker's argument, entails that the *basilinna* did not have any other (at the very least) significant ritual role, and that in its turn entails she could not have been represented in the *peplos* group on the Parthenon frieze.

[93] See e.g. Neils 2003: 159.

allowed the Athenians to identify the man, we need to reconstruct his identity by narrowing down his profile as much as possible. First, he is almost certainly a priest, for he is so characterized by his dress. Second, the treatment of the image (his presence in the scene at all, and his position near, but not quite at, the centre, in a back-to-back juxtaposition to the priestess) presents him as an important figure in this nexus, but not quite equivalent to the priestess, who is at the very centre. Whatever his precise identity, then, his office clearly made him symbolically perhaps almost, but certainly not quite, equivalent in importance to the priestess at this ritual. I submit that we have sufficient access to Athenian ritual assumptions to know that there are three figures whose roles would very roughly fit this slot at this ritual: the two with whom the man has so far been identified by various scholars, the *archon basileus* and the priest of Poseidon Erechtheus, and also a third, the priest of Zeus Polieus.

The *archon basileus* elected the *arrhephoroi*,[94] and if the child is a girl she would be one of the *arrhephoroi* handing over the finished product of their ritual labour—more accurately of the ritual labour of which the *arrhephoroi* did part—to the man responsible for their selection. However, for this interpretation to be tenable it would have to be assumed that the *archon basileus* wore priestly dress when playing a ritually important role. Also, I will suggest that the child is extremely unlikely to be an *arrhephoros*.

The notion of an office almost, but not quite, symbolically equivalent to the priestess's at this ritual would fit the priesthood of Poseidon. Indeed, this is one of the two main proposed identifications of this figure, that he is the priest of Poseidon Erechtheus.[95] My initial reaction to that identification was rather negative, for it seemed to me difficult that the priest of the deity defeated in the contest for the position of Athens' poliadic deity should have a central cooperative role in the most important poliadic rite. But Robert Parker persuaded me that, since the contest story ultimately

---

[94] On the *basileus* and the *arrhephoroi*, see also Brelich 1969: 234; and esp. Parker 2005a: 220.

[95] Mantis, who, we saw, noted (Mantis 1990: 80, 84, 85) that the short-sleeved Ionic *chiton* worn by this male figure was the typical dress of a priest in the classical period, concluded (Mantis 1990: 78, 80, 85) that this figure is very probably the priest of Poseidon Erechtheus.

ends in conciliation, there need not be a problem with such a role.[96] If that is right, then perhaps the very participation of the priest of Poseidon would have been important in conveying the reconciliation, after the contest represented on the west pediment, especially the fact that Poseidon also protects Athens and Athens in turn honours Poseidon. However, I believe that there is an argument, albeit not a strong one, against this identification. In the frieze, just beyond the *peplos* group, Athena is represented sitting next to Hephaistos, not Poseidon; that is, she relates spatially on the one hand to Zeus, who, like her, frames the *peplos* scene, and on the other to Hephaistos. The second juxtaposition may relate to the fact that it was at the Chalkeia, probably a joint festival of Athena and Hephaistos,[97] that the loom for the weaving of the *peplos* was set up, and it may also reflect Hephaistos' role at Athena's birth which was represented on the pediment above, but that is not the point. The pairing of Athena and Hephaistos (and the different 'pairing' of Athena and Zeus) contrasts with the fact that she was not paired with Poseidon in this context, that the pair Athena–Poseidon was not prominent here; and this may suggest that the man involved with the *peplos* was not the priest of Poseidon. To look at this differently, if the pair Athena–Poseidon had been prominent in the assumptions shaping the selections that generated this part of the frieze, those selections, I submit, would have associated Athena with Poseidon.

I would like to suggest that another male would fit the semantic slot unproblematically: the priest of Zeus Polieus.[98] Though it is possible to consider Athena Polias and Poseidon as an alternative poliadic pair, both the names and the cults show that Athena Polias and Zeus Polieus were the older and more deeply embedded

---

[96] On the myth of the contest, see Parker 1987a: 198–200. On the reconciliation, see the end of Eur. *Erechtheus* after the defeat of Eumolpos' attempt to replace Athena with his father Poseidon; cf. Parker 1987a: 201–4.

[97] On the Chalkeia, see Parker 2005a: 464–5.

[98] On the priest of Zeus Polieus, see esp. Parker 1996: 299. The importance of this priesthood is illustrated by the fact that the seat of the priest of Zeus Polieus in the *prohedria* of the theatre of Dionysos (*IG* II² 5024) was in the central segment of the front row, like that of the priest of Dionysos Eleuthereus (*IG* II² 5022). This inscribed seat of the priest of Zeus Polieus is of Hellenistic date, probably second century BC (see Maass 1972: 104 and pl. VI, see also 43–4, 50–3).

poliadic pair.[99] In the myths of the contest through which Athena became the poliadic deity of Athens the dominant relationship is, of course, the antagonistic relationship between Athena and Poseidon. But Zeus also has a role; in one variant he is a kind of mediator;[100] in another he is a supporter of Athena, and it seems that fragments and refractions of a myth associated with the expressions 'Seats of Zeus' and 'Vote of Zeus' reflect a tradition in which Zeus' role in the judgement was especially important.[101] This role of Zeus in the process that led to Athena's establishment as Athens' poliadic deity can be seen as a refraction of the cooperative relationship between Athena Polias and Zeus Polieus.

The *peplos* scene is either a refraction of a poliadic rite, or an image combining elements pertaining to that rite, and it is framed by the city's two poliadic deities, the principal one, Athena, who is the rite's recipient, and Zeus, with whom she forms the main poliadic pair. There are two adult ritual actors, shown in a cooperative relationship; a woman in the most prominent position and a man in a slightly inferior position; the woman is the priestess of Athena Polias, the man is a priest; I suggest that the priesthood that corresponds most closely to this semantic and iconographical slot is the priest of Zeus Polieus—a reading that would also be consistent with the poliadic emphasis on the frieze in general: the priestess of Athena Polias and the priest of Zeus Polieus are represented in connection with the central poliadic rite and framed by the two poliadic deities. If the male is indeed the priest of Zeus Polieus then the two priests in

---

[99] See e.g. Sourvinou-Inwood 1990a: 307–8, 310, 313–14 = Sourvinou-Inwood 2000: 24–5, 27, 30–1.

[100] See e.g. Apollod. 3.14.1.

[101] Hesych. *s.v.* Διὸς θᾶκοι καὶ πεσσοί (after the headword in Hesych. follows "some write ψῆφοι") tells us of a myth according to which during the contest Athena begged Zeus to give her his vote and in return promised that Zeus, here referred to as Polieus, would have a particular sacrificial privilege. (Incidentally, θᾶκος ... Διός in Aesch. *PV* 831, a reference to Dodona, is probably a transformation of this established expression.) According to Phot., Suda s.v. Διὸς ψῆφος the place in which Athena and Poseidon were judged was called Διὸς ψῆφος; they quote in illustration Cratinus fr. 7 K/A, ἔνθα Διὸς μεγάλου θᾶκοι πεσσοί τε καλοῦνται. Also according to Suda Διὸς ψῆφος was a proverb that referred to things divine and inviolable. In Callim. fr. 260.24–6 (*Hekale* fr. 70.9–11 Hollis) Athena obtained the land by the vote of Zeus and the twelve other immortals (cf. Hollis 1990: 236 ad 70.10).

the *peplos* scene would be the priests of the two deities framing the image in a chiastic arrangement, the priest of Zeus Polieus nearer Athena, the priestess of Athena Polias nearer Zeus, and this would have made the *peplos* scene visually intermesh more closely with the group of gods in Athenian eyes—while still remaining significantly apart.

Before trying to reconstruct (as much as possible) the ways in which the ancient viewers would have made sense of the two girls I need to say something briefly about the relevant scholarly discourse—for reasons that will, I hope, become apparent—and in the process bring out some significant data.[102] The preferred identification has generally been that they are two *arrhephoroi*[103]—especially recently, after the case for this reading was set out in detail by Wesenberg.[104] However, Hurwit expressed the view that they seem a little too old to be *arrhephoroi*.[105] I have argued elsewhere (an argument cited by Wesenberg) that this age reading is incorrect, and that the girls are not too old for this office: I have argued that age representation in Greek iconography is conventionally constructed, and that the iconographical schema through which these two girls are depicted corresponds to the age of about 10 and 11 and is therefore consistent with that of the *arrhephoroi*.[106] Wesenberg produced a strong argument for the view that the girl V32, who is interacting with the priestess, is holding a lamp.[107] But he also argued that the two girls are not carrying cushioned stools, as the traditional interpretation has it, but trays on which they carry, wrapped up tightly, the mysterious cult objects given to them at the sanctuary of Aphrodite in the Gardens, which they are handing over to the priestess of Athena, and that the group of the *arrhephoroi* and the

---

[102] Some of the following readings may well need modifying in the light of a forthcoming important study of this part of the frieze by O. Palagia.

[103] See e.g. Deubner 1969: 12, 31; Simon 1983: 66–9.

[104] See e.g. Neils 2001a: 168; Dillon 2002: 45–7; Neils 2003: 159. The argument in Wesenberg 1995: 149–78, esp. 151–64.

[105] Hurwit 1999: 225 and 2004: 230.

[106] Sourvinou-Inwood 1988: 58–9, 100–1 n. 285 cited by Wesenberg 1995: 157 n. 51.

[107] Wesenberg 1995: 160–3.

priestess is separate from that of the priest and the child manipulating the *peplos* and represents the rite of the Arrhephoria.[108]

There are several independent arguments against this interpretation. First, the Arrhephoria was a secret rite and therefore it would not have been appropriate to represent it on the frieze of a temple, especially on the outside. Secondly, and more concretely, it is probably right that the girls are carrying on their heads trays or flat baskets rather than stools, but what are shown on these trays/baskets cannot be cult objects wrapped up tightly, for they are solid (squashed) oval masses with an upper contour consisting of an unbroken curve (and more generally, where the state of preservation allows us to see, a roughly smooth surface); so they cannot be cult objects, for they do not have the variously undulating contour that would indicate objects wrapped in a cloth, however tightly. If the assumption shaping the sculptor's selections had been that the girls were carrying cult objects tightly wrapped to cover them from view, the surface and upper contour of the squashed ovals would have been broken, more or less undulating. Third, the trays are too shallow; they are too shallow to be referred to as *kistai*, as the receptacles carried by the *arrhephoroi* are referred to in a late source,[109] and they are certainly far too shallow to relate to Erichthonios' basket as shown in the fifth century.[110] Finally, Wesenberg's reading entails the implausible state of affairs that a minor rite, and one associated with the dissolution of the end of the year, rather than the new beginning and re-establishment of order expressed in the Panathenaia,[111] would have been selected to be shown in the most central part of the frieze and given more prominence than the major rite of renewal of the major poliadic festival which expessed the relationship of reciprocity between Athens and its poliadic deity—with three

---

[108] Wesenberg 1995: see esp. 158–9; see also 164–8, cf. 176–8.

[109] In Schol. Ar. *Lys.* 642. On the basket of the *arrhephoroi* and the hypothesis that the name is derived from that of a particular type of basket, see N. Robertson 1983: 247–50.

[110] See e.g. the examples illustrated in Reeder 1995: 253 no. 66, 257 no. 69, 265 no. 73.

[111] The *arrhephoroi* rite associated with the dissolution of the end of the year: Burkert 1983: 150; re-establishment of order at the Panathenaia: Burkert 1983: 154.

figures as opposed to two, and most importantly, with the priestess of Athena Polias being part of a minor dissolution rite rather than the major renewal ritual of the major poliadic festival.

In these circumstances, I submit, while Wesenberg's identification of the girls as the *arrhephoroi* is right, his conclusion that they and the priestess form a separate group representing the Arrhephoria rite is not. The fact that the girl V32 is holding a lamp (if this reading is right, and I think it is) does not entail that she is represented during the night rite of the Arrhephoria. For if the arguments set out above against the Arrhephoria rite interpretation are right, this reading was not open to the Athenian viewers whose assumptions would have led them to see it as an element that simply belonged with, and emblematically characterized, an *arrhephoros*. It is not legitimate to assume that every element in the scene contributed to the construction of a snapshot picture of one particular moment. On the contrary, the fact that the *peplos* scene is framed by two groups of gods would have encouraged, for the ancient viewers, readings that did not privilege a descriptive narrative modality or a moment-specific representation.

I do not know what the girl V31 is holding in her left hand;[112] the objects they both carry on their heads are probably flat baskets or trays with squashed ovals on top. These ovals, which are solid, may well be cushions, even if they are (probably) not carried on stools. But the possibility cannot be excluded that they may be loaves of bread (probably wrapped in cloth); we know that there was a special bread associated with the arrhephoroi called *anastatos.*[113]

Clearly, the Athenian viewers would have unproblematically recognized the two girls as *arrhephoroi* if the *peplos* scene refracts a rite that was part of the Panathenaia, but what if it is simply an image conveying the relationship of the *arrhephoroi* with the *peplos* and the

---

[112] The usual interpretation for this object is a footstool (see Jenkins 1994: 79). Simon 1983: 67 suggested an incense box.

[113] Paus. Att. a 116 Erbse, Suda s.v. *anastatoi* (a kind of *plakous*); cf. Ath. 3.114a. Mansfield 1985: 272 remarks that it is not known in connection with what specific rite the *anastatoi* were made, or what made them distinctive. I suggest that the name, which indicates bread or cake made to rise up, combined with the classification as a *plakous*, may indicate the type of shape that would roughly correspond to these objects carried on the flat trays.

priestess of Athena?[114] I suggest that even in that case Athenian viewers would have unproblematically identified the girls as *arrhephoroi*, through the combination of their age and proximity to, and association with, the *peplos* and the priestess—unless that identification was blocked. I submit that it was not. Admittedly, given that we cannot identify the objects they are carrying with any degree of certainty, nor can we be certain that there was not a rite involving other girls and those objects, we cannot be totally certain that the identification '*arrhephoroi*' had not been blocked. But there are many reasons for concluding that this was not the case. First, while we know that the *arrhephoroi* are of the age that corresponds to these two figures, and had a symbolically important role connected with the *peplos*, we do not know of any other girls of this age being involved with the *peplos* in a way important enough to be shown in this condensation of the most important poliadic rite.

Second, if Wesenberg's persuasive argument that V32 is holding a lamp is right, that would be an important emblematic element in the construction of the figure. Third, whatever the objects carried on their heads are, it is unlikely that they could have blocked the *arrhephoroi* identification. Even if the 'flat trays' are in fact stools with cushions, the carrying of such objects is a non-specific cultic act which would have been performed by a variety of persons in different contexts, including the *arrhephoroi*.[115] Of course, if they are, as I think is not impossible, trays with bread, whoever else may have been associated with bread,[116] certainly the *arrhephoroi* were connected with a special type of bread which may well correspond to the oval object on each girl's head, and so (whether or not such bread was part of a rite connected to the *peplos*) it would be seen as helping to characterize the girls as *arrhephoroi*.

[114] Whether or not a rite is refracted, the image certainly presents these relationships.

[115] It certainly would not mean, given the context, that the girls were *diphrophoroi*, metics' daughters carrying stools behind the *kanephoroi* (see e.g. Ar. *Ekkl.* 730–7; Ar. *Av.* 1550–2; Hesych. s.v. *diphrophoroi*; see Dillon 2002: 38, 45, 206).

[116] Incidentally, I hope to have shown (Sourvinou-Inwood 1988: 142–6) that the *aletrides*, who, we are told (see e.g. Schol. Ar. *Lys.* 643), ground the grain for the sacrificial cakes, were not an office in the cult of Athena, but in that of Demeter, associated with the 'sacred ploughing' ritual.

The *arrhephoroi* probably had some role in the *peplos-*focused part of the Panathenaia, at least in the procession.[117] Whether or not they did, they are certainly at the Panathenaia in the reality of this image, in which they are interacting with the priestess of Athena Polias, whom the *peplos* places unambiguously at the Panathenaia. In the eyes of the Athenian viewers, *arrhephoroi* at the Panathenaia, whether or not they reflected an actual ritual involvement in the festival, were the new *arrhephoroi*, those who replaced the girls who had completed their office the previous month.[118] These new *arrhephoroi* were the ones who would be starting the weaving of the new *peplos,* with the priestess, in three months' time. Consequently, their presence, especially in the company of the priestess, would have also evoked the idea of the new *peplos* that these *arrhephoroi* and the priestess would begin at the Chalkeia for the next Panathenaia; and this would have indicated that the *peplos* offering was a cyclical enterprise, a never-ending activity, one year's presentation soon followed by the preparation of next year's one.

This representation, that the *peplos* offering was a cyclical enterprise, was further reinforced in Athenian eyes by the group of the man and child manipulating the *peplos*, which, I will now try to show, evoked past offerings. The child is unlikely to have been a third *arrhephoros*: from what we know of the *arrhephoroi* we might have expected either two or four to be represented together, not three, and we would also have expected all the *arrhephoroi* represented to be wearing the same garments—since wearing special garments did come into play in this office.[119] If the child is not an *arrhephoros* handing over the new *peplos* to the *archon basileus,*[120] it is an assistant helping the man to manipulate the *peplos*. If we eliminate all

---

[117] Since we know that white dress was associated with the *arrhephoroi* (Harpocr. s.v. *arrhephorein*), πέ]πλον λευκὴν ἐσθῆτα in fr.a l.5 of decree i in *IG* II² 1060 + 1036 may well refer to the *arrhephoroi* processing with the *peplos*, i.e. at the Panathenaia, wearing a white dress.

[118] See Burkert 1983: 150; Simon 1983: 41 n. 10.

[119] Harpocr. s.v. *arrhephorein*.

[120] If the child were a third *arrhephoros* handing over to the *archon basileus* the fruit of the labours of the *arrhephoroi* at the Panathenaia, she would not have been one of the *arrhephoroi* who had taken part (however small or great that part may have been) in the weaving of the *peplos* being offered, but one of their successors.

preconceptions in the reading, the manipulation of the cloth seems more indicative of a folding up than an unfolding; in other words, on this reading, the image shows the man and child folding up the old *peplos* before they put it away—after the statue was dressed with the new *peplos* that the polis has just offered to Athena. If this is right, the image would have evoked last year's presentation, and also the other old *peploi*, past offerings, that were stored in the sanctuary.[121] This segment of the scene, then, like the segment consisting of the two *arrhephoroi*, also opened up the image to a different time frame, in this case past Panathenaia and past offerings.[122]

On this reading, the frieze looks forward and back from its own 'now'. But where would the ancient Athenians have perceived the 'now' of the frieze to be located? If the frieze indeed evoked other festivals as well as the Panathenaia, it would not have been perceived as having a reference outside itself; there would have been no other 'now' to which the 'now' of the frieze would have corresponded, the image would not be reflecting any real-life referent. If it reflected only the Panathenaia, this reflection may have been perceived to be a wholly generic one, which each viewer located wherever they wished, along a spectrum of possibilities that probably included a conceptual expression of the Panathenaia and a contemporary generic one. Or it may have been perceived to be located in the heroic past. Perhaps all these possible readings were open to the fifth-century viewers; or perhaps the very divergences from the Panathenaia of their day which have worried modern scholars may have been perceived by the

---

[121] For the existence of a *peplotheke*, a place for the storage of old *peploi*, see Nagy 1978a: 138 n. 6; see also Mansfield 1985: 55–6.

[122] The notion that the representation of the old *peplos* evokes the timeless repetition of the ritual has already been expressed by M. Robertson 1975: 11. Because his reading is much closer to the descriptive narrative mode than mine, Robertson thinks that the casual air of the gods shows that they are waiting for the procession to pass, and so that the new *peplos* has not yet been offered, but he comments that the folded cloth is the old *peplos*, "its four year service finished, implying the timeless repetition of the ritual". On my reading, the (annually occurring) renewal of the garment has already taken place, and the representation of the old *peplos* together with the evocation of the future *peplos* through the *arrhephoroi* constructs the notion of the offering as a cyclical activity and so, it is hoped, everlasting. Of course, the frieze itself timelessly repeats the ritual, but I suggest that the *peplos* scene actually constructs the *peplos* offering as a cyclical activity.

Athenians to be distancing the festival of the frieze to the heroic age, so that a generic heroic age may have been the privileged reading of the 'now' of the Panathenaia in the frieze. If it was perceived as distanced to the heroic past, this was a generic heroic past, not the first Panathenaia, not an event that could function as a mythological paradigm, for the festival on the frieze is represented as part of a cycle.

Perhaps, however, the representation on the frieze was mostly perceived as a wholly generic (not a heroic age generic) refraction of the Panathenaia (and perhaps also of other festivals) generalized, and conceptually (as opposed to historically) paradigmatic; if so, this would have emphasized further the everlasting nature of the rituals and of the relationships they expressed and symbolized. I shall return to this.

First I will open a parenthesis to say something about the priestess. The context identifies the mortal woman in the *peplos* scene as the priestess of Athena Polias, for she is at the centre of a set of images expressing the reciprocity of the relationship between the polis and the gods, especially focused on the relationship with the poliadic deity. Whatever the exact relationship of the scene to cultic reality, it clearly expresses realities and perceptions concerning the offering of the *peplos* at the Panathenaia. This offering is therefore the focus of the image and the representation of the priestess at the centre of the image is consistent with the view that she dressed the statue with the new *peplos* that was the central symbol of the relationship between the polis and Athena.

Furthermore, if my argument concerning the cyclical nature of the *peplos* offering is right, it offers support for this view. For, if it is right, the meaning 'the *peplos* as a cyclical offering' was created through the visual depiction of the notion that this year's (new) *peplos* (the new *peplos* which in the 'now' of the frieze has just been wrapped around the statue) is one point in a cycle of endless repetition of weaving, offering, and dressing the statue with a new *peplos* every year[123] as an expression of the everlasting relationship between Athens and its poliadic deity; this entails that the centre of the construction, the

---

[123] Or, if I am wrong, penteterically.

pivot, in a backwards and forwards movement between different time frames[124] was 'this year's *peplos*', which therefore had to be anchored in the image, which means it had to be represented, signalled or evoked, through a separate iconographical element, an element other than the *arrhephoroi* (who evoked next year's *peplos*), and the priest and child (in which last year's *peplos* was represented and past dedications evoked); in other words, if the argument is right, this year's *peplos* was signified through the spatially central element of the priestess. In that case it would follow that the priestess had a strong connection with this year's *peplos*. Consequently, the frieze cannot support the hypothesis that the statue was dressed by the Praxiergidai at the Panathenaia, but it does offer some support for the reconstruction according to which the priestess wrapped the *peplos* around the statue.

The *peplos* scene on the frieze has seemed tame and domestic to some modern eyes. But in Athenian eyes the representation of the poliadic gods, and then, in the wider frame, all the gods, framing the *peplos* offering (and being themselves surrounded by the procession) was an iconographical expression of one facet of the 'contract' between the polis and the gods, especially focused on the poliadic deity, which ensured Athens survival and prosperity; within the poliadic festival, in the midst of the Olympians who symbolize all the gods, the offering of the *peplos*, which above all expressed and symbolized the reciprocity of the relationship between gods and mortals, of which that with the poliadic deity is the intense version, is represented as part of a continuous cycle.

A mythological representation of the establishment of the poliadic relationship between Athens and Athena is depicted on the image that a viewer coming into the Acropolis and walking towards the Parthenon would see first: the contest between Athena and Poseidon on the west pediment.[125] Of course that scene is polysemic,[126] but a dominant meaning was the poliadic relationship that was at the

---

[124] If the viewer read from right to left, time moved forwards, if from left to right it moved backwards, but it was only in interaction with the other elements in the scene that the right segment evoked past dedications and the left future ones.

[125] On the Parthenon pediments, see Palagia 1993.

[126] See e.g. Osborne 1994: 143–4, cf. 145–6.

centre of Athens's existence and prosperity. The frieze displays the same relationship, in another modality, one which allows the inclusion of the mortal side and the stressing of reciprocity; at its centre, just before the visitor will enter the temple, the poliadic relationship with Athena is represented through the city's gift which symbolizes that reciprocity and is here shown as part of the polis's relationship with all the gods.

This set of meanings, taken together with the particular circumstances of this temple and this time, may explain the choice of subject to represent on the frieze, the refraction of a polis ritual rather than a mythological representation. At some point after the Parthenon had been designed and began to be built with the traditional sculptural decoration of mythological scenes, it was decided, apparently as an afterthought, to add this frieze,[127] which, on the reading offered here, depicted in ritual terms the poliadic relationship between Athens and Athena, the goddess whose temple was being adorned, opening up to include, first, the second poliadic deity, who was also the sovereign god and so also represented the relationship with all the gods, and then the other Olympians with two minor deities, who also represented the entire divine world. This would have had a special resonance on the Parthenon, not only because of its place in Athenian religious and civic ideology, but also because of its history: its predecessor, the so-called 'Older Parthenon', had been burnt by the Persians while it was still under construction, in circumstances in which it had seemed that the polis would not survive, that the gods had abandoned Athens. For cities did perish if they were abandoned by the gods. Troy certainly did. But in the case of Athens, at a crucial moment Athena sent a miraculous sign (her burnt olive tree miraculously germinated a shoot) that signalled that her guarantee of Athens's existence was still valid and Athens would live.[128] So in this temple, that evoked the past danger, as well as its overcoming thanks to the gods' protection, a set of images suggested that that protection would never end.

---

[127] Korres 1994a: 92–114, 115, 118–19, 120.
[128] Hdt. 8.55. See Sourvinou-Inwood 1990a: 306–7 = Sourvinou-Inwood 2000: 23–4.

Modern readers may choose to interpret this set of images as a statement of imperial confidence. In ancient eyes this would have been partly deconstructed; that is, ancient viewers, I suggest, would have made sense of the images through filters that also included the perception of the precariousness of the human condition and the belief that the survival and prosperity of cities depended on the goodwill of the gods; therefore they would have also perceived strongly the element of what, for want of a better definition, we may call 'prayer and expression of hope'.

APPENDIX: THE *PEPLOS* AT THE PANATHENAIA.
A CRITIQUE OF OTHER READINGS

I will now consider the two hypotheses concerning the dressing of the statue with the new *peplos* that I mentioned earlier. The first of these hypotheses claims that the new *peplos* was not wrapped around Athena's statue at the Panathenaia, when it was presented to her, but at the Plynteria or the Kallynteria, many months later.[129] The second hypothesis claims[130] that it was not the priestess of Athena Polias who dressed the statue with the new *peplos*, as has always been assumed,[131] but the Praxiergidai, the *genos* who put the *peplos* around the statue at the Plynteria.

I will begin with the first hypothesis, according to which the statue was not dressed with the new *peplos* at the Panathenaia. Simon suggested that Athena was disrobed at the Plynteria. At the Panathenaia

---

[129] At the Plynteria: Simon 1983: 66; Shapiro 1989: 29–30 and n. 88; Neils 1996: 185; cf. also Hurwit 1999: 333 n. 63. At the Kallynteria: N. Robertson 2004: 111–61. [I have omitted Sourvinou-Inwood's detailed critique of Robertson's interpretation of the Kallynteria, an interpretation largely based on his argument that the duties of the Praxiergidai listed in *IG* I³7 are new, not, as the text itself claims, traditional; Sourvinou-Inwood rejects that argument. R.P.]

[130] Mansfield 1985: 378–9, see also 290–6; Barber 1992: 113; Neils 1992b: 17; Neils 1996: 185; Steinhart 1997: 475–8. Neils (1992b: 17) says it was "presented to the goddess" by the Praxiergidai, though elsewhere (Neils 2001a: 167–9 and 2003: 159) in discussing the *peplos* group on the frieze she identifies the female figure as the priestess and the man as a priest.

[131] See e.g. Rhodes 1981: 568–9 ad 49.iii.

"the image need not have been clothed with the new *peplos*, which was instead added to Athena's treasures."[132] Shapiro agreed with this view, that the old *peplos* was removed and the new one placed around the statue at the Plynteria and not the Panathenaia.[133] Hurwit formulates this hypothesis as follows: "If a *peplos*-dress was presented to Athena Polias each year, it may seem strange that it was thought necessary to disrobe the statue and presumably wash the cloth at the Plynteria festival just two months before the presentation of a new one at the annual Panathenaia." He then mentions Simon's and Shapiro's suggestions and continues, "If so the brand new *peplos* (and not simply a laundered one) could have been draped over the statue of Athena Polias at the Plynteria."[134]

It is true that, when considered logically, it appears strange that the statue should have been undressed and dressed again twice within a relatively short period. This would make it logically economical to assume that only one disrobing and rerobing had taken place. Since we know that the statue was undressed and dressed again at the Plynteria, and there is no evidence that tells us explicitly that this also happened again at the Panathenaia, such an assumption would lead to the conclusion that it was only at the Plynteria that the statue was undressed and dressed again. However, the situation looks very different when we try to block the intrusion of utilitarian logic and reconstruct as much as possible the perspective of Greek ritual logic. I will now set out two different arguments based on such reconstructions, the conclusions of which converge to indicate that the statue was dressed with the new *peplos* at the Panathenaia, not at the Plynteria.

The first argument is that since it can be shown that the disrobing and rerobing of the statue at the Plynteria was different, and had very different meanings from, any disrobing and rerobing that could have taken place at the Panathenaia, the second 'disrobing and dressing' at the Panathenaia was far from redundant. Whether the *peplos* was removed, as I suggested, before the Plynteria, or at the beginning

---

[132] Simon 1983: 66.
[133] Shapiro 1989: 29–30 and n. 88.
[134] Hurwit 1999: 333 n. 63.

of the Plynteria, it was certainly done in a period of abnormality, touched, or dominated, by pollution and ill-omen. This was not the case at the Panathenaia. At the Plynteria the rerobing followed the statue's ritual bath in the sea and would have taken place on the beach at Phaleron. This was not the case at the Panathenaia.

A second argument is based on another aspect of the nature of the Panathenaia. The Panathenaia was the symbolically strongest locus of the renewal of the poliadic relationship. The offering of a new *peplos* helped bring about, and at the same time symbolized, that renewal. The notion that the statue was not dressed with the new *peplos* at the Panathenaia would entail that this fundamentally important religious act would have been split into two, the offering of a new *peplos* at the Panathenaia and then the robing of the statue with that new *peplos* ten months later at the Plynteria in Thargelion; it would also entail that the completion of the renewal of the relationship between Athens and its poliadic deity would have taken place not at the major poliadic festival, but many months later in the course of a festival in which ill-omen and pollution were very strong.

I will now discuss the second hypothesis under consideration here, which claims that it was the Praxiergidai and not the priestess of Athena Polias who, at the Panathenaia, dressed the statue with the new *peplos*.

There is no direct evidence to indicate who dressed the statue with the new *peplos*. Nevertheless, there is, I suggest, one, not insignificant, argument in favour of the hypothesis that it was the priestess of Athena Polias who performed that ritual act. The offering of the new *peplos* was, we saw, symbolically the most important gift made to the poliadic goddess by the polis. Since the priestess was the most important representative of the Athenian polis in its relationship with the poliadic deity, there is a symbolic match between the gift and the priestess, which is expressed in, among other ways, the fact that the priestess was involved in the setting up of the warp at the Chalkeia.

What, then, are the arguments in favour of the Praxiergidai? The underlying assumption is that since the Praxiergidai were involved with Athena's clothes at the Plynteria, at which festival they dressed the statue, we would expect them to be the ones who also dressed the statue at the Panathenaia.[135] However, this assumption, like the hypothesis that the statue was only undressed and rerobed at the Plynteria, is based on the blurring of important distinctions and differences between the two ritual sequences, and between the Plynteria and the Panathenaia.

Steinhart claims that the fact that Hesychios (s.v. Praxiergidai) says that the Praxiergidai clothed the ancient statue of Athena without mentioning a specific occasion entails that they clothed the statue on every occasion, they always had that duty, and not simply at the Plynteria.[136] Clearly, the validity of this argument depends on three separate assumptions. First, that the lexicographer had access to both accurate and precise information; second, that Hesychios was not overgeneralizing when he wrote his lemma; finally, that the lemma had not been shortened, a very bold assumption, given that Hesychius' lemmata were indeed abridged during transmission. In these circumstances, I submit that little weight can be placed on Hesychios' specific formulation.[137]

The rest of Steinhart's case concerns the *peplos* scene on the east frieze of the Parthenon: he identifies the two figures who are manipulating the *peplos*, the man and the child, as Praxiergidai.[138] I have set out my reading of the *peplos* scene in the context of the Parthenon frieze in section 4 above. But whether or not the reading of the *peplos* scene

---

[135] Barber 1992: 113; Neils 1992b: 17. Neils (1992b: 17, 194 n. 18) cites in support of this statement Mansfield 1985 (as does Barber loc. cit.) and Romano 1988: 127–33 (who however does not say this).

[136] Steinhart 1997: 477.

[137] Mansfield is one of the scholars who believe that the Praxiergidai, and not the priestess of Athena, draped the new *peplos* on the statue at the Panathenaia (1985: 378–9, see also 290–6). This belief is based on his own readings and interpretations of *IG* I[3] 7 and *IG* II[2] 1060 + 1036. With regard to *IG* I[3] 7 he cites Hesychius in apparent support of his interpretation of ll. 10–11 as entailing that the Praxiergidai draped the statue with the new *peplos* at the Panathenaia (1985: 378), the argument which I have just discussed. He also set out objections to the text of *IG* I[3] 7 (1985: 398–404) which, in my view, are culturally determined, in that the text is rejected when it does not fit modern expectations of what seems logical and reasonable, as for example in the argument that if the temple had been sealed, with an affixed official seal, the Praxiergidai would not have been able to enter the temple even with the keys. This argument takes no account of the likelihood that the seal would not have physically barred entrance to the temple, which would have been symbolically sealed as part of the abnormal time.

[138] Steinhart 1997: 475–8.

I offered is compelling, the identification of the man and the child as members of the *genos* of the Praxiergidai is, I will now argue, mistaken. Steinhart's argument is that the man is not a priest, because Athena was served by a priestess, nor is he the *archon basileus*, because the *archon basileus* is not attested in connection with the handover of the *peplos*; therefore the most likely identification is that both he and the child are members of the Praxiergidai, the *genos* closely connected with the *peplos*.[139] However, first, as became clear in section 4, the fact that Athena was served by a priestess does not entail that the priest of another deity could not have a place in the image; and second, since we know so little about the handover, Steinhart's argument that the *archon basileus* is not attested in that connection has no substance. As for the Praxiergidai being the *genos* connected with the *peplos*, I have, I hope, set out the significant differences between the Plynteria, in which the Praxiergidai officiated, and the Panathenaia, that make it illegitimate to assume that what was valid for one festival would also be valid for the other. If anything, the presumption should be the opposite. Steinhart's argument that the proximity of the two figures to the priestess of Athena supports the identification of the man and child as Praxiergidai, because there was a close relationship between the priestess and the Praxiergidai,[140] has, I suggest, also no validity; for whoever the man and child may be, it was their manipulation of the *peplos* that determined their proximity to the priestess.

Most importantly, since the man manipulating the *peplos* is wearing a priestly dress,[141] he cannot be simply a representative of the Praxiergidai. In addition, since the image presents this bearded male as a figure almost, but not quite, symbolically equivalent to the priestess behind him, his office was likely to have been almost but not quite symbolically equivalent to that of the priestess at this festival, and this does not fit his identification as a member of the Praxiergidai; for even the office of the *archon* of the *genos* could not have been perceived as almost symbolically equivalent to that of the priestess of Athena Polias.

[139] Steinhart 1997: 476–7.
[140] Ibid.: 477.
[141] See above section 4.

6

City Dionysia, Bakchiadai, Euneidai, and Other *Genē*

1. INTRODUCTION, PROBLEMATIK, METHODOLOGY

In an article published a few years ago Lambert[1] drew attention to the significance of a second-century BC dedicatory inscription, *IG* II[2] 2949, for the understanding of the cult of Dionysos Eleuthereus and the City Dionysia: his argument illustrated the need to consider what, if any, information pertaining to that cult and festival may or may not be reconstructed from this dedication. But I will argue here that his conclusions concerning the cultic realities reflected in the inscription are incorrect.

  IG II[2] 2949 is inscribed on a votive altar in the sanctuary of Dionysos Eleuthereus which is decorated with Dionysiac motifs, satyr masks, and a complex garland that includes vine branches and grapes and ivy leaves.[2] It was discussed by Freeden, who dated it between 123/2 and 121/0,[3] while Lambert places it between 120 and 100.[4] The text, the only trace left in the historical record by the Athenian *genos* of the Bakchiadai,[5] reads as follows:

[1] Lambert 1998: 394–403.
[2] See Parker 1996: 286. For the altar see Travlos 1971: 552 fig. 690. See also Toepffer 1889: 206–7.
[3] Freeden 1985: 215–18 and pl. VIIIc.
[4] Lambert 1998: 403.
[5] On the Bakchiadai, see Toepffer 1889: 206–7; Parker 1996: 286; Humphreys 2004: 264.

Πιστοκράτης καὶ Ἀπολλοδώρος
Σατύρου Αὐρίδαι πομποστολήσαντες
καὶ ἄρχοντες γενόμενοι τοῦ γένους
τοῦ Βακχιαδῶν ννν ἀνέθηκαν.

'Pistokrates and Apollodoros sons of Satyros of the deme Auridai, having organized the procession and having become *archontes* of the *genos* of Bakchiadai, dedicated this.'

Freeden rightly saw that the dedication refers to two separate honours for the brothers, and that the place of dedication and the nature of the object on which it is inscribed indicate that the word πομποστο-λήσαντες, 'having organized the procession', refers to the procession of the City Dionysia; but he wrongly took πομποστολήσαντες to refer to the brothers leading the procession as ephebes[6]—a reading rightly criticized by Lambert.[7] Lambert's own theory is that the dedication suggests that the Bakchiadai played a role in the City Dionysia similar to that played by other *genē* in other festivals, that πομποστο-λήσαντες refers to a gentilicial office; taking the argument further, he also suggested that the Bakchiadai provided the priest of Dionysos Eleuthereus.

I want to present the case against this theory before it becomes established as orthodoxy by default; in the process I shall explore further some aspects of the City Dionysia and the cult of Dionysos Eleuthereus in general. I will not begin with an attempt to criticize Lambert's argument, for such a strategy would inevitably structure my investigation through something which—whether right or wrong—is undeniably a modern construct and therefore an inappropriate 'structuring pattern' because inescapably culturally determined. If an investigation is structured through inappropriate structuring patterns the available data are organized around inappropriate 'organizing centres', and this distorts their meaning (for meaning is created in context) and so corrupts the reconstruction of the ancient realities.[8] To give a crude illustration: someone convinced that a jigsaw puzzle of which most pieces are missing represents a cow may be able to fit a particular piece into that imaginary cow if

---

[6] Freeden 1985: 215–16.
[7] Lambert 1998: 396.
[8] As I hope to have shown elsewhere (see esp. Sourvinou-Inwood 1995: 413–15).

determined to do so, not registering that the puzzle represents a bull whose explicitly gender-specific elements are missing. This is why a priori assumptions corrupt the investigation, whether introduced explicitly, as part of a model, or implicitly, by unconsciously allowing them to structure the scarce data, and why it is therefore necessary to adopt methodologically neutral strategies that block—as much as possible—the intrusion of all such assumptions.

We must, then, begin by asking neutral questions, in this case 'what, if anything, can this inscription tell us about the relationship, if any, between the *genos* of the Bakchiadai and the cult of Dionysos Eleuthereus?' Then, we must adopt methodologically neutral strategies in the attempt to answer them. Since, we saw, strategies based on the deployment of models are not methodologically neutral, reconstruction by analogy is not methodologically neutral; consequently, the strategy that assumes that the association of the *genos* of the Bakchiadai with the cult of Dionysos Eleuthereus—which is what we need to investigate and define—can be made sense of through models based on other associations between *genē* and cults in Athens, is methodologically flawed. For, unless those models are derived from cultic realities identical to those in the cult of Dionysos Eleuthereus, they will structure the data through inappropriate organizing centres and so will inevitably distort the reconstruction of that cult; and since we do not know if the two sets of cultic realities were identical, indeed the model is used precisely for filling in the missing knowledge concerning the cult of Dionysos, this strategy involves an element of hidden circularity.

Two factors make the strategy especially inappropriate in this case: first, the associations between the different *genē* and the cults and festivals with which they were connected varied in intensity; and second, projecting assumptions about running and financing from one Athenian festival to another entails neglecting their individuality and specificities and so is demonstrably corrupting, especially since the City Dionysia was a major arena for elite competition, a shifting arena, reflecting the polis and its ideological preoccupations; this important specificity is of direct relevance to the issue of who participates in its running and the various aspects of its financing. Therefore the notion that, for example, the model of the Oschophoria can be assumed to be relevant to the City Dionysia is flawed.

2. READING THE DEDICATION

The names of the two brothers who made the dedication, with patronymic and demotic, make up the first segment of the inscription. I am not concerned with their prosopography;[9] I will simply say that these names would have been made sense of variously by the different contemporary readers, depending on whether they knew the two brothers personally, or knew of their circumstances and status, on whether, for example, the readers themselves were members of the Bakchiadai *genos* and so on.

The first word following the brothers' names is πομποστολήσαντες. The verb πομποστολέω is first attested in the second half of the second century BC, as is the related word πομπόστολος, which occurs in Delian inscriptions and which, I will argue, does not refer to the same function. πομποστολέω can mean 'conduct a procession',[10] and, with an accusative, 'lead or carry in procession'.[11] πομποστολέω occurs in one other Athenian inscription, in which it is explicitly connected to the Dionysia, on the monument on which is inscribed a decree of 140/39 BC in honour of Telesias of Troezen.[12] The monument was erected by Telesias himself,[13] and the decree is a reaffirmation of the Athenian citizenship that had been granted to one of his ancestors. The inscription lists various functions he had performed for which he was awarded a crown; one of them states that the *boule* and the *demos* awarded him a crown πομποστολήσαντα Διονυσίοις. He was also honoured for having been an epimelete at the Diisoteria,[14] [archi]theoros, and a priest of what is likely to have been a very minor priesthood; for since the monument was erected by Telesias himself, the fact that it was not specified which priesthood he held indicates that it was a very minor one. He had also been a judge at Thespiai.

---

[9] See on this, e.g. Toepffer 1889: 207; Humphreys 2004: 264.

[10] See L-S sv. πομποστολέω.

[11] Strabo 14.2.23 speaks of a road on which πομποστολεῖται τὰ ἱερά, the sacred things are carried in procession, sacred processions are conducted.

[12] *IG* II² 971; Osborne 1981: 213–16 D 102; Lawton 1995: 157 no. 187.

[13] Osborne 1981: 214.

[14] On the festival, see Deubner 1969: 174–5; Parker 1996: 239–40.

The verb πομποστολέω (at the Dionysia) clearly involved a significant—albeit not truly major—office, comparable to the other offices held by Telesias. By contrast, the word πομπόστολος in the Delian inscriptions refers, we shall now see, to a less weighty office. It appears once in connection with Dionysos, in an inscription of the second quarter of the second century,[15] and twice in connection with Zeus Polieus and Soter and of Athena Polias and Soteira.[16] In the last two instances πομπόστολοι are appointed by the priest of Zeus Polieus and Soter and of Athena Polias and Soteira, and those connected with the cult of Dionysos were almost certainly appointed by the priest of Dionysos.[17] There were several πομπόστολοι involved in each instance, and they are thought to have been charged with carrying sacred objects and escorting the victims in the procession.[18] This is consistent with the fact that these πομπόστολοι—whether they were cleruchs or visiting Athenians—were, we know, exclusively Athenian and young.[19] This interpretation also fits the significant numbers of each set of the appointed πομπόστολοι, which Lambert's suggestion ("one suspects" that they had "some sort of organizing/leading role")[20] does not. For about thirty young men leading or organizing a procession is not consistent with what we know about processions, while about thirty young men leading sacrificial animals and carrying sacred objects is a particular crystallization of a common processional modality. Moreover, an office held by dozens of young men in each festival is not prestigious enough to be equivalent to the πομποστολέω performed by Telesias which won him the award of a crown by the *boule* and the *demos* and was correlative with the other offices he commemorates which, we saw, were of some significance. Clearly, then, the function indicated by the verb πομποστολέω as applied to Telesias and the two brothers on the one hand, and the noun πομπόστολος in the Delian inscriptions on the other, were two different crystallizations into technical terms describing different offices.

While, we saw, no occurrence of either πομποστολέω or πομπόστολος earlier than the second half of the second century BC

---

[15] *Inscr. Dél.* 5.2609; see Bruneau 1970: 323.
[16] *Inscr. Dél.* 5.2607-8; see Bruneau 1970: 237–8.
[17] Ibid.: 237–8, 323.
[18] See ibid.: 237–8.
[19] See ibid.: 238.
[20] Lambert 1998: 397 n. 18.

has survived, the two words taken together appear five times in the epigraphical record of this period, and the verb also occurs occasionally in literary sources from Strabo onwards.[21] This pattern of appearance suggests the possibility that πομποστολέω and πομπόστολος may be newly coined terms for new offices. This would be consistent with the notion that they were open—though not limited—to people who were now coming to prominence, such as Telesias. It would not, of course, be legitimate to assume that because Telesias was a 'new man' only 'new men' held that office. But the fact that Telesias did fill this office shows that it was not a gentilicial office since he was a foreigner, and so not a member of a *genos*.[22] The office of πομποστολέω in the Delian inscriptions also occurs in a context consistent with a newly coined term to denote new cultic functions, in that those chosen to be πομπόστολοι were young Athenians who were either cleruchs or visitors, and this would be consistent with the thesis that the name of their office was a newly coined term, for a new office, not exactly a new function, but a function newly formalized into an honorific office.

The view that πομπόστολος was a newly created term for a new office, a newly formalized function, may gain some support from the fact that traditional gentilicial offices involving carrying of various kinds (comparable to that probably performed by the πομπόστολοι) end in *-phoros*.[23] Non-gentilicial offices and ritual duties that were established early also have such endings,[24] not least functions and offices filled by metics in Athens, at the opposite end of the scale from the gentilicial

---

[21] Strabo: n. 11 above.

[22] Though, we shall see, Lambert tries to turn him into one.

[23] For example, the *oschophoroi* and *deipnophoroi*, and the *kalathephoros* from the *genos* of the Salaminioi (*LSS* 19. 46 and 49; see Ferguson 1938: 21, 34, 36–7, 41; Parker 1996: 310–11), the *trapezophoros*, probably from the Eteoboutadai (Istros *FGrH* 334 F9; see Parker 1996: 290); the *spondophoroi* of the Eumolpids and Kerykes (see Parker 1996: 301); the *lithophoros* of the Kerykes (see Clinton 1974: 98; for the text of the honorary decree in which the word occurs ibid. 50–2 and now Clinton 2005: 300); the *pyrphoros* of the Kerykes (see Clinton 1974: 94–5). *Pyrphoros* is also an office in other cults, such as the cult of Apollo Zoster, in which it was said to have been performed by Euripides (*Vita Eur.* I.15–19; see Lefkowitz 1981: 92). The inscribed seat for the '*pyrphoros* from the acropolis' in the theatre of Dionysos calls him 'priest' (*IG* II² 5046; cf. also *IG* II² 3631).

[24] For example *arrhephoros*, *thallophoros* (Ar. *Vesp.* 542–3), and *phallophoros* (Semos of Delos *FGrH* 396 F 24; Sourvinou-Inwood 2003a: 78). The most widespread of these non-gentilicial offices is that of *kanephoros*, to which I will return.

ones.[25] The traditional nature of the -*phoros* offices is echoed in the fact that the -*phoros* ending is also found in deities' epithets, such as Phosphoros and Thesmophoros, and is also reflected in the name of festivals, such as Oschophoria and Thesmophoria.[26] Incidentally, what was probably the closest—albeit not very close—parallel among traditional offices to this reconstructed office of πομπόστολος the (very much more prestigious) office of *kanephoros* was not gentilicial;[27] at public processions it was open to girls of noble families, though their fathers may have had to have been wealthy enough to equip them.[28]

In these circumstances, I submit that the office of πομπόστολος was not early and that both πομπόστολ- offices were newly coined terms for newly created or newly formalized offices that were open (though not limited) to new men. The liturgical component of the more substantial office referred to as πομποστολέω (to which I shall return) would have made it especially appropriate for men like Telesias, the only other person besides our two Bakchiadai brothers known to have performed this function at the Dionysia.

The view that πομποστολέω is a newly coined term for a new office, and one that was open to new men and was not gentilicially apportioned, gains further support from another argument: the history of the office involving πομποστολεῖν, its place in the structure of the City Dionysia, and its relationship to the polis as a whole. Since πομποστολεῖν literally means to conduct a procession, whatever the exact function it corresponded to, it was clearly a function that was either exactly, or roughly, equivalent to, or at the very least overlapped significantly with, that of the *epimeletai* who conducted the procession of the City Dionysia with the eponymous archon. The office, then, either replaced, or, less plausibly, complemented, that of the *epimeletai.*[29] Let us now consider the history of the office that πομποστολεῖν replaced.

[25] For example the *skaphephoroi* at the Dionysia procession (Demetrios of Phaleron FGrH 228 F 5; Suda s.v. *askophorein*).

[26] On the appearance of -*phoros*, -*phoria*, and -*phorein* compounds in cult, see N. Robertson 1983: 245–6.

[27] On the office of *kanephoros*, see most recently Dillon 2002: 37–42.

[28] On the selection and financing of *kanephoroi*, see esp. Wilson 2000: 26, 317 nn. 67–9.

[29] Indeed Lambert himself believes that the office referred to through πομποστολήσαντες replaced the *epimeletai* (Lambert 1998: 402).

According to the Aristotelian *Athenaion Politeia*,[30] the archon ἐπιμελεῖται, has charge, management, of the Dionysia procession together with the *epimeletai*, the ten Superintendents.[31] In earlier times these *epimeletai* had been elected by open vote in the Assembly, and they had themselves paid for the expenses of the procession, while at the time of the composition of the *Athenaion Politeia* they were elected by lot from each tribe, and the state contributed a hundred mnai for the expenses. As Wilson has noted, the relatively small sum given to each epimelete by the city was presumably supplemented by the epimelete's own money, at least sometimes.[32] Subsequently the *epimeletai* appear to have reverted to being elected out of the whole body of citizens, and by 186/5 they were twenty-four, not ten, in number[33]—possibly because it became desirable to share the financial burden between a larger number of people.

This office, then, began with a whole polis reference, which paral-lelled that of the dramatic *choregoi* at the City Dionysia;[34] then the reference shifted to constituent polis subdivisions, the tribes, thus now paralleling the dithyrambic *choregiai*, and in the final phase it reverted to the whole polis reference. This suggests that any office created to replace that of the *epimeletai* would have a whole polis reference (or, at the very least, whole polis articulated through its major subdivisions) and would entail private *euergesia*, benefaction, in combination with some public financing.

Another, earlier change in the financing of the City Dionysia, the replacement of *choregiai* by *agonothesia*, offers quite a close parallel.[35] Demetrios of Phaleron abolished the system of competitive choregiai and instituted one *agonothetes* in charge of the competitions of the City Dionysia and other festivals, a wealthy individual who supple-mented from his own funds those allocated by the polis. It would

---

[30] Arist. *Ath. Pol.* 56.iv.

[31] On the *epimeletai* of the Dionysia, see Wilson 2000: 24–5.

[32] Ibid.: 266, 317 n. 65.

[33] See Rhodes 1981: 627–8 ad 56.iv.

[34] Until the responsibility for the appointment of comic *choregoi* was transferred to the tribes (see Wilson 2000: 24–5, 51).

[35] On *agonothesia* replacing *choregiai*, see esp. ibid.: 270–6. The tribally based competitive *choregiai* were restored in first-century AD Roman Athens (see Wilson 2000: 276–8).

seem that the *agonothetes* also took over some functions previously performed by the archon.[36] It is interesting for our purposes that it is the *demos* that is officially recorded as *choregos* in *agonothesia* inscriptions.[37] This change, then, involved centralization into one man, who symbolically represented the whole polis, a wealthy man offering private *euergesia* combined with some public financing. This is symbolically the opposite modality from that which would have been involved in handing over to a *genos* something that had always been a non-gentilicial polis office—which is what the notion that πομποστολεῖν was a gentilicial office would entail.

In these circumstances, I submit, the facts that the dominant, established, modality of financing at the City Dionysia was *agonothesia*, which was private *euergesia* (with some public funds), and especially that *agonothesia* was referred to as an *epimeleia*,[38] which shows that the two activities were perceived to be closely related, suggest that the presumption should be that any new office that replaced or complemented that of the *epimeletai* was *not* going to be gentilicial, which is symbolically the opposite of this established modality, but something not dissimilar from *agonothesia*. The most likely hypothesis is that only one person filled this office as in the case of the *agonothetes*, one among a restricted number of wealthy individuals. If this is right, we do not know if it was possible for two brothers to combine and count as one, or if our two brothers performed the office on different occasions.[39]

To sum up, a series of separate arguments suggests that πομποστολήσαντες refers to a newly created office that replaced that of the *epimeletai* involving liturgical financing and representing the whole polis. It was not a gentilicial office and it was open to new men. If this is right, it follows that in the eyes of the ancient readers the two brothers' performance of this office would not have been perceived to be connected with the next segment of the inscription 'and having become *archontes* of the *genos* of Bakchiadai'. Indeed, the formulation of the

---

[36] See ibid.: 272.

[37] Ibid.: 273; Parker 1996: 268.

[38] Wilson 2000: 382 n. 50, cf. 317 n. 65.

[39] It may be of some incidental interest to note that two brothers could serve as *epimeletai* together, as Isandros and Mnesitheos, the sons of Echedemos from Kydathenaion, did in *IG* II² 668.23–5.

dedication also indicates[40] that the two brothers are commemorating two separate, distinct honours, the fact that they ἐπομποστόλησαν and the fact that they became *archontes* of the *genos* of the Bakchiadai. In these circumstances, I submit that the inscription's contemporary readers would have made sense of it as follows.

Pistokrates and Apollodoros, sons of Satyros, from the deme Auridai, having filled the office of πομποστολεῖν at the City Dionysia (which involved sending and financing the procession, under the ultimate jurisdiction of the archon, comparably to the way in which the *epimeletai* used to do, but [probably] with a larger element of liturgical financing) and having (also) become *archontes* of the *genos* of the Bakchiadai, dedicated (this altar).

But, it may be objected, is this conclusion, that the office was not gentilicial, not in conflict with the notion that the two brothers who performed it were members of a *genos* whose very name, Bakchiadai, suggests a connection to the cult of Dionysos, and who dedicated an altar in this sanctuary commemorating the fact that they had been archons of that *genos*? Surely, it may be further argued, the fact that the holding of the office 'archon of the *genos* of the Bakchiadai' is commemorated in, and helped motivate, the dedication of an altar in the sanctuary of Dionysos Eleuthereus entails that being archon of the Bakchiadai involved something to do with the cult of Dionysos Eleuthereus.

I will now argue that these objections are mistaken, and that there is no conflict between the conclusion concerning the office of πομποστολεῖν and the rest of the known facts. For the fact that the two brothers played that role does not mean that they did so in their persona as *gennetai*, since it is not the case that *gennetai* only played a role in festivals and cults in their capacity as *gennetai*, in cults connected with their *genos*. For example, in the fourth century, Lykourgos, an Eteoboutad, was appointed a *hieropoios* for the cult, including the procession, of the Semnai Theai,[41] which was a cult connected with the *genos* Hesychidai,[42] and in the fifth and early fourth centuries members of the *genos* Lykomidai were probably

---

[40] As Freeden (1985: 215) rightly remarked.
[41] Dinarchus fr. 4 (*Against Lykourgos*).
[42] On the Hesychidai, see Toepffer 1889: 170–5; Parker 1996: 298–9.

Treasurers of Athena.[43] As for the place of the altar's dedication, the sanctuary of Dionysos Eleuthereus was the most important and prestigious sanctuary of Dionysos in Athens and the fact that the brothers ἐπομποστόλησαν the procession of the City Dionysia gave them grounds for making this dedication at this prestigious sacred space.

I will now consider the *genos's* name. In the second half of the second century BC, when, we saw, new citizens could hold religious offices from which they had previously been excluded, there was a wider change that also affected the *genē*: between the classical period and the 100s BC changes took place in the *genē* and their associations with priesthoods and there was a *genē*-revival in the second and third quarters of the second century BC.[44] It is possible that new *genē* may have been created at that time, and that they may have been given some minor functions that at least partly mimicked the old *genē's* connections with certain cults. A name such as Bakchiadai, probably understood as 'belonging to Bakchos', would have fitted such a context well, but it does not necessarily indicate a connection with a polis cult of Dionysos: a newly created Bakchiadai *genos* may have had no attachment to any polis cult, but may have had a *genos* cult of Dionysos which inspired their name. For a *genos* invented in the second century cannot be assumed to have been focused around a polis priesthood; it cannot be assumed to have been perceived as exactly the same as the old *genē*.

In these circumstances, I suggest that the following alternative explanations would be consistent with all aspects of the reading of the dedication reconstructed here and the realities and assumptions of its cultural context. *One*, the *genos* of the Bakchiadai was a new *genos* which may, but need not, have been given some kind of association with a cult of Dionysos. *Two*, it was an old *genos* connected with another Athenian cult of Dionysos, and when the two brothers became its archons they chose to make this dedication at Dionysos' most prestigious sanctuary because their service at the

---

[43] Davies 1971: 346, 347.

[44] Ferguson 1938: 50–1; Davies 1971: 11; Davies 1973: 229; Humphreys 1983: 43–4; Davies 1996: 630; Parker 1996: 287, 289–90, 291–2; Humphreys 2004: 264–5; [Aleshire and Lambert forthcoming].

Dionysia gave them a connection to that sanctuary. Of course, in theory it could be argued that the total absence of evidence for a gentilicial connection between the Bakchiadai and the cult of Dionysos Eleuthereus does not necessarily entail that there was no such connection. But in reality there is one strong reason for concluding that if the cult of Dionysos Eleuthereus was associated with a *genos* it was not with the Bakchiadai: the fact that, as we shall see in section 3, there is a very strong case for identifying one (fifth-century) priest of Dionysos, and he belonged to the *genos* of the Kerykes, which means that either the priesthood of Dionysos Eleuthereus was non-gentilicial or it belonged to the Kerykes. Finally, it could be argued that if the newly created *genos* of the Bakchiadai had been assigned a connection to a polis cult of Dionysos it could have been that of Dionysos Eleuthereus. I suppose in theory the possibility cannot be excluded, but there is no evidence to suggest that this was the case.

I will now open a parenthesis to consider another, recently proposed, hypothesis concerning the status of the Bakchiadai. In her recent book Humphreys suggested that the Bakchiadai may have been a sub-branch of the *genos* of the Euneidai that had split off from the main *genos* in the second century. She says of the two brothers, "Since they had been involved in organizing a procession, and since Pollux says that a herald for processions was appointed by the Euneidai, it seems possible that the Bakchiadai were a sub-branch of the Euneidai that had split off from the main *genos* in the second century."[45]

She is clearly right to draw attention to the fact that the Euneidai should be taken account of when the relationship between the City Dionysia and gentilicial functions and offices is considered. But her suggestion concerning the two brothers, and the Bakchiadai in general, is, I will now try to show, mistaken. That suggestion is based, first, on the (implicit) acceptance of Lambert's claim that πομποστολεῖν is a gentilicial office, which, I hope to have shown, is wrong, and second, on certain assumptions concerning the role of the Euneidai, which I will now consider—especially since they also

[45] Humphreys 2004: 264.

have implications for the argument that will be set out below concerning the relationship between the *genē* and the City Dionysia.[46] Humphreys believes that the Euneidai "may have been mainly, if not exclusively, associated with the City Dionysia".[47] Elsewhere she notes that the Euneidai appointed the priest of Dionysos Melpomenos, and adds, "who seems to have been associated with the City Dionysia".[48] I will now try to determine what, if any, role the Euneidai played in the City Dionysia. I will begin with a very brief consideration of what is known about this *genos*.

First, they were believed to be descended from Euneos, king of Lemnos, son of Jason and Hypsipyle, and so a descendant of Dionysos, since his maternal grandfather Thoas was Dionysos' son. Second, at least in the Roman period, they appointed, from their members, one of the two priests of Dionysos Melpomenos who had an honorific seat in the theatre—the other, also with an honorific seat in the theatre, was appointed by, and from, the *technitai*, the artists, of Dionysos.[49] Third, the Euneidai were closely involved with music, they were kithara players and, we are told, they provided music during sacrifices and other rituals.[50] Parker asks whether a Euneid was summoned every time music was required at a public festival and suggests that it is more plausible that the lexicographers were overgeneral and that in fact the *genos* only participated at specified rites ("possibly only those of Dionysos Melpomenos").[51] Fourth, according to Pollux,[52] the heralds officiating in processions were provided

[46] On the Euneidai, see Toepffer 1889: 181–206; Burkert 1994: 46 (cf. 44–9); Parker 1996: 297–8.

[47] Humphreys 2004: 229 and 238 n. 41, where she states, "The *genos*' functions seem mainly to have concerned the City Dionysia," a statement for which she refers to Parker 1996: 297–8, who in fact does not say this.

[48] Humphreys 2004: 248–9. She refers to Humphreys 2004: 238 n. 41 for this statement, on which, see the previous note.

[49] *IG* II² 5056 ('from the Euneidai'), 5060 ('from the *technitai*'). On the *technitai* of Dionysos see most recently Lightfoot 2002, with bib. On the inscribed seat of the priest of Dionysos Melpomenos of the *technitai* (*IG* II² 5060) in the front seats of the theatre of Dionysos, see Maass 1972: 128; on that of Dionysos Melpomenos of the Euneidai (*IG* II² 5056) Maass 1972: 125–6.

[50] Harpocr. s.v. Euneidai, attributed to Lysias *Against Telamon*. Cf. Hesych., Phot., *Etym. Magn.* s.v. Euneidai.

[51] Parker 1996: 297.

[52] Poll. *Onom.* 8.103.

by, and from, the Euneidai. Finally, the Euneidai were one of the *genē* that provided Pythaists for the Pythaides of 106/5 and 97/6[53]—to which, incidentally, the artists of Dionysos sent a large number of artists as pilgrims and performers.

There is no evidence connecting the Euneidai directly and specifically with the City Dionysia. However, the nature of this *genos's* cultic functions and their association with Dionysos Melpomenos suggests a possible connection, but one not specific to this particular festival. This *genos* may have been involved in providing music, especially kithara music, in rituals of Dionysos, which may well have included, but would be unlikely to have been limited to, the City Dionysia. This reconstructed connection, then, is not specific to this festival and would involve a role of secondary importance.

Though there is no direct evidence connecting Dionysos Melpomenos with the City Dionysia, two considerations may suggest that in later periods some kind of connection did obtain. First, the fact that the second priesthood of Dionysos Melpomenos belonged to the artists of Dionysos constitutes a connection in itself, since the artists of Dionysos were associated with theatrical performances and so also with the Dionysia. The second consideration is topographical and concerns the area to the north-west of the Agora, which I have discussed elsewhere,[54] and where, at least by Pausanias' time, Dionysos had a space sacred to him. According to Pausanias,[55] what in the fifth century had been the house of Poulytion, in which the profanation of the Mysteries had taken place, was, in his time, a sanctuary of Dionysos Melpomenos, and, in a building described by Pausanias as being situated beyond this shrine, there were clay statues, which, I argued, relate to the persona of the god as Dionysos Eleuthereus, his reception at Athens, and the festival of the City Dionysia. This arrangement of space, then, would connect a sanctuary of Dionysos Melpomenos (where, Humphreys suggests, both the artists of Dionysos and the Euneidai were based),[56] with the nexus of the reception of Dionysos and the City Dionysia. I must stress,

---

[53] See the brief discussions in Burkert 1994: 46; Humphreys 2004: 263 and n. 102.
[54] Sourvinou-Inwood 2003a: 90.
[55] Paus. 1.2.5.
[56] Humphreys 2004: 258, 262 and n. 99. See also Maass 1972: 126.

however, that though the two nexuses are connected, they are also distinct and separate.[57] Also, of course, it cannot be assumed that a second century AD situation also applied in earlier periods, especially in this case, when we know that the sanctuary was post-fifth century. Both connections of Dionysos Melpomenos with the City Dionysia, then, are located in a later period, in a post-fifth-century space and associated with the post-fifth-century artists of Dionysos. Given that there is a semantic correlation between the persona of Dionysos Melpomenos and the artists of Dionysos, and given also that there is no known specific connection between the Euneidai and the City Dionysia, and that the attested links between Dionysos Melpomenos and the City Dionysia are post-fifth century and include his association with the artists of Dionysos, the hypothesis presents itself that the cult of Dionysos Melpomenos became associated with the City Dionysia—where it did—through the *technitai*. That is, that Dionysos Melpomenos, until then in Athens a minor cult associated with the Euneidai, which may or may not have had a minor role in Dionysiac festivals, which may or may not have included the City Dionysia, was adopted by the Athenian guild of the artists of Dionysos as their patron god because he suited their persona, and as a result Dionysos Melpomenos became associated with theatrical performances and so also the City Dionysia. If this is so, then no association may be inferred between the Euneidai and the City Dionysia—other than a possible secondary musical and heraldic function not specific to this festival.

---

[57] On Humphreys's (2004: 258) reading it was the *temenos* of Dionysos Melpomenos that "contained a terracotta relief (?) . . .". But Pausanias' text is clear: the clay representations are not in the sanctuary of Dionysos Melpomenos itself: 'after the sanctuary of Dionysus there is a building . . . in which there are clay statues.' (Incidentally, it seems to me that the formulation ἀγάλματα ἐκ πηλοῦ is less likely to have been chosen to describe a relief; it is a more fitting choice for clay statues.) Humphreys (263 n. 100) also thinks that I am mistaken that Pegasos of Eleutherai was part of the Amphictyon group. Besides the fact that there is no problem about representing Pegasos together with Amphictyon, since Greek representations are mostly not limited to the descriptive narrative mode and the moment-specific scene, Pausanias' formulation indicates that Pegasos, Amphictyon, and Dionysos being offered hospitality are closely connected. They are certainly in the same building and at the very least in close proximity. So, ultimately, whether or not they were in the same group does not matter; this building was associated with Dionysos' reception in Athens and the City Dionysia.

This reconstruction, in which Dionysos Melpomenos is a specialized persona of Dionysos pertaining to kithara music, and not especially close cultically to Dionysos Eleuthereus and the City Dionysia, would be consistent with Burkert's hypothesis which associates the *Euneidai* and Dionysos Melpomenos with a specific kind of cult music, Asiatic kithara music—which he connects with Orpheus and Orphism.[58]

In these circumstances, we may conclude that any association between the *Euneidai* and the City Dionysia was what we may call fully secondary, in that it consisted of a later development involving the artists of Dionysos and perhaps also a secondary role, involving music and perhaps also a herald's role in the procession, at this as at other processions and festivals. If the Euneidai indeed provided music and a herald for the City Dionysia, these functions would have been under the ultimate jurisdiction of the archon and the *epimeletai*, who were then replaced by the men who performed the office referred to through the term πομποστολεῖν. And that is all that the Euneidai had to do with this office.

3. THE BAKCHIADAI AND THE CULT OF DIONYSOS ELEUTHEREUS: A CRITIQUE

Lambert's case deserves further attention, since it is intelligent and, on the surface, persuasive. As we have seen, neither the inscription itself nor the history of the πομποστολ- words supports Lambert's view that it was because they were members of the *genos* Bakchiadai that the two brothers served as πομπόστολοι at the Dionysia. Clearly, then, Lambert's reading of the relationships between the Bakchiadai and the City Dionysia and the cult of Dionysos Eleuthereus is governed by his expectations about *genē* involvement in Athenian festivals—an approach that discounts the specificities of the City Dionysia, above all the fact that it was a major arena for elite competition, which inevitably affected modalities of financing and administering. But this

---

[58] Burkert 1994: 44–9.

argument is further undermined by Lambert's admission that the role performed by the two brothers at the City Dionysia was not an ancestral gentilicial office, but one created in the Hellenistic period to replace the *epimeletai*. For he accepts that the Bakchiadai had not provided "officials known as πομπόστολοι" in the fifth century, and that this office was Hellenistic and that it was an office involving financial obligation. But he constructs a theory according to which "our πομπόστολοι might have replaced the *epimeletai*" known to be involved in the City Dionysia, "the result perhaps of a reassertion of an imagined *patrios politeia* in which responsibility for the procession rested more fully with appointees of the *genos*".[59]

However, once it is accepted that the office of πομπόστολος is a new one, Lambert's argument now inevitably becomes that πομποστολεῖν is a gentilicial office replacing a non-gentilicial office, and so there is no analogy with the gentilicial offices which are based on the *genē*'s traditional roles and cult associations. A further objection is that, as Lambert himself noted, the new office is likely to have carried financial obligation; it is therefore highly implausible that it would have been restricted to members of one *genos*, as opposed to anyone with the ability to pay who was willing to carry the financial burden.

I will now consider what may be described as an implicit argument sketched by Lambert in his discussion of his hypothesis that the *epimeletai* of the Dionysia procession were replaced by a gentilicial office. He mentions the *epimeletai* of the Mysteries in a way that implicitly suggests that the existence of *epimeletai* of the Mysteries restricted to the two *genē* most intimately connected with the cult and festival supports his argument that the *epimeletai* of the Dionysia were replaced by a gentilicial office. However, as we shall now see, the creation and nature of the institution of the *epimeletai* of the Mysteries indicates the opposite of what Lambert wants it to indicate.

The Board of the *Epimeletai* of the Mysteries was established in the mid-fourth century, when it was decreed that the *epimeletai* were to be chosen by the demos, two from all the Athenians, one from the Eumolpids, one from the Kerykes.[60] The formulation both in the inscribed law and in *Ath. Pol.* makes it clear that they share in, and

---

[59] Lambert 1998: 401–2. The quotations from p. 402.
[60] See p. 343 n. 15.

complement the duties of, the *basileus*. Clearly, then, the establishment of this Board involved an expansion of the polis role, a new polis board to work together with the *basileus* (who represented the whole polis) to perform the duties, the *epimeleia* of the Mysteries, for which until then he, the *basileus*, had been solely responsible;[61] and the selection to the Board was in the hands of the demos, with the concession of giving a role to the *genē* connected with the cult. Far from being a parallel to a reversion of an office from the polis to a *genos*, the creation of the Board of the *Epimeletai* of the Mysteries is an example of an expansion of the role of the polis with an accommodation for the *genē* which were very strongly connected with the cult. Moreover, the very fact that the close involvement of the Eumolpids and the Kerykes in the Mysteries was reflected in their accommodation within the framework created and operated by the polis, while in the case of the City Dionysia there was no gentilicial involvement in the institution of the *epimeletai*, also argues against, rather than for, Lambert's case.

Let us return to Telesias, the Troizenian who acquired Athenian citizenship and discharged the function of πομποστολεῖν. Lambert argues that "if 'conducting the procession' at the City Dionysia was indeed a privilege of the Bakchiadai, then Telesias. . . . will have been a member", and the admission of a foreigner to a *genos* and to the other positions that Telesias had held, including a priesthood, is a manifestation of how much has changed.[62] But the notion that a new citizen could hold the offices Telesias held, including what would appear to be a minor priesthood, is an entirely different matter from the idea that a new citizen could become a member of a *genos*, at the core of the self-definition of which is ancestral kinship in the sense of perceived common descent lived out in this land. An even stronger argument is that, in the extremely unlikely case that Telesias had been admitted to membership of a *genos*, it is (given the tenor of the text) impossible to doubt that he would have mentioned this achievement in his monument.

But Lambert took his case further. Having concluded that πομποστολεῖν was a gentilicial office and that therefore the Bakchiadai

---

[61] Clinton 1980: 281 n. 50.
[62] Lambert 1998: 401.

were associated with the City Dionysia, he asked what other officiants at the City Dionysia were supplied by this *genos*. His answer is that the priesthood of Dionysos Eleuthereus was a gentilicial priesthood filled by the Bakchiadai.[63] He argues that the fact that the priest of Dionysos Eleuthereus was never mentioned in polis decrees honouring officiants at the festival "would seem to confirm that the priesthood was probably gentilicial rather than public". He mentions two examples of decrees honouring officiants at the festival of the City Dionysia that do not honour the priest, *IG* II[2] 668 and *IG* II[2] 896, and contrasts them to *IG* II[2] 410. Then he mentions as implicit support for his argument, "the possibility that Hellenistic inscriptions praising *epimeletai* of the Mysteries mentioned only those selected from the people as a whole, ignoring those supplied by the Eleusinian *genē*".

The first objection to this argument is that all priesthoods of polis cults were polis priesthoods, 'public priesthoods'; the two relevant terms of contrast are not 'gentilicial or public' priesthoods, but 'gentilicial or open to all Athenians' (or a non-gentilicially defined segment of them). The fact that they were all polis priesthoods, and that this particular one was an important priesthood for an important whole polis cult, weakens Lambert's argument. Secondly, public honours were in fact awarded to the holders of gentilicial priesthoods through polis decrees, as shown, for example, by the mid-third-century BC decree of the *boule* in honour of the priestess of Athena Polias [Lysistra]te,[64] or the mid-third-century BC decree of the *boule* and the demos for the priestess of Aglauros,[65] or the decree of 20/19 BC and monument for the daduch Themistokles.[66] Finally, the specific decrees and situations he cites cannot support his case, as we shall now see.

Starting with the *epimeletai* of the Mysteries, the notion that the inscriptions Lambert refers to praised only the *epimeletai* selected

---

[63] Ibid.: 398–400.

[64] *IG* II[2] 776.

[65] Dontas 1983 (*SEG* XXXIII 115). I believe her to be the priestess provided by the *genos* of the Salaminioi; see on the problems pertaining to the priesthood of Aglauros Parker 1996: 311; and pp. 152–3 above.

[66] For the decree, see Clinton 1974: 50–2; 56–7 no. 16 (and now Clinton 2005: 300); for the monument, see Clinton 1974: 56–7 nos. 16–17. See e.g. also, for honours for exegetes from the Eumolpids, *IG* II[2] 3490; 3523.

from the people as a whole is not a fact, but one possible (and not the most plausible) interpretation of the fact that Hellenistic inscriptions mention only two *epimeletai*—while, we saw, when the Board was established it was decreed that four were to be chosen by the demos, two from all the Athenians, one from the Eumolpids, one from the Kerykes. The most likely explanation of this state of affairs is that, as has been suggested,[67] the number of the *epimeletai* of the Mysteries was reduced to two in the late fourth or third century. What Lambert is referring to is something that Rhodes[68] mentioned as an alternative possibility, that perhaps the demos had ceased to elect the *epimeletai* of the Mysteries from the Eumolpidai and the Kerykes and that it praised only the two that it did elect. This double hypothesis is less plausible than its alternative, that the number had been reduced. But even if that speculation had been right, it would not have provided a meaningful parallel to the notion that priests of Dionysos Eleuthereus are not mentioned in honorary decrees which honour other officiants because the priest was gentilicially selected. First, because the hypothetical situation postulated for the *epimeletai* of the Mysteries, unlike the hypothetical situation postulated for that priest, would have involved a change that diminished the role of the polis. The *epimeletai* were a polis office which here exceptionally allowed a gentilicial component, which was controlled by the demos who made the appointments; if that control was then surrendered by the polis to the *genē*, which is what the hypothesis Lambert refers to demands, the situation would be entirely different from that of a gentilicial priesthood which, on his hypothesis, was long established. Second, the hypothetical situation postulated for the *epimeletai* of the Mysteries, unlike the hypothetical situation postulated for the priest of Dionysos Eleuthereus, involved a distinction within the same office, a differentiation that marked symbolically a difference which, on Lambert's hypothesis, was ideologically significant, while the distinction postulated for the priest of Dionysos Eleuthereus is a distinction between on the one hand a priesthood and on the other what we may call 'liturgical and/or managerial type' offices.

---

[67] See e.g. Clinton 1980: 282.
[68] Rhodes 1981: 636–7 ad 57.i, see esp. 637.

Let us consider the two decrees mentioned by Lambert as instances in which, in his view, the polis would have been expected to have honoured the priest of Dionysos while honouring officiants at the festival and it does not, because, he believes, the priesthood was gentilicial.[69] The honours in question were awarded in the context of the examination of the conduct of the Dionysia procession and the festival as a whole, and of the officials responsible for it, after a report made by the archon at the assembly after the festival; so, clearly, there is a correlation between making a report, or being 'covered' by a report made by the official under whose jurisdiction one operated, and receiving honours. In *IG* II^2 668 it is decreed to honour the archon and officials for whom he, being in charge of the festival and the procession, had the ultimate responsibility, and so 'covered' in his report, the assessors, the *epimeletai*, and the father of the *kanephoros*.[70] In *IG* II^2 896 the archon's report is only mentioned explicitly in the first of the two decrees it records, with reference to the father of the *kanephoros*; the second decree honours the *epimeletai*, while the archon himself presumably would have been honoured in a separate decree.[71]

Lambert's implicit expectation was that all those who had a significant role in the Dionysia should have been mentioned, unless there was some other reason—which he thinks would be provided by the gentilicial nature of the priesthood. But this expectation takes no account of the correlation between examination of conduct and award of honours and blurs the distinctions between the different relationships of the polis to the various individuals who acted symbolically in its name in various contexts. The priest did not operate under the jurisdiction of the archon, and was not responsible for the conduct of the festival or the procession, his duties and functions belonged to a different semantic sphere and were not 'covered' by the

---

[69] *IG* II^2 668 and 896.

[70] The quasi-liturgical function performed by the father of the *kanephoros* also came under his jurisdiction, for it was part of the procession and we know from *IG* II^2 896 that the archon reported on what the father of the *kanephoros* had done. On the father of the *kanephoros* in the Dionysia procession, see Wilson 2000: 26, 317 n. 69.

[71] For another example of the archon receiving honours at the assembly in the sanctuary of Dionysos after the Dionysia, see ll. 17–19 of the decree published in *Hesperia*, 7 (1938) 100–2.

archon's responsibilities—and report. Therefore, given the observed correlation between report and honouring, we would not expect him to be honoured in these decrees.

This analysis gains support from the decree *IG* II^2 410, to which Lambert contrasts *IG* II^2 668 and *IG* II^2 896. In this inscription the priest of Dionysos and the *hieropoioi* reported to the *boule* on the sacrifices made to Dionysos and to the other gods, and honours were duly awarded to the priest of Dionysos, three further priests, and the *hieropoioi*.[72] Thus, here also there is a correlation between making a report to the appropriate body and being honoured and awarded a crown.

Finally, if it is right that Eupolis in *Aiges* mocked the priest of Dionysos Hipponikos, the son of Kallias, from the deme of Alopeke,[73] the notion that the priesthood of Dionysos Eleuthereus belonged to the *genos* of the Bakchiadai can be conclusively disproved. For this man, Hipponikos II, was a member of the *genos* of the Kerykes, one of the important Eleusinian *genē* who held the *dadouchia*, the office of torch-bearer. Hipponikos II was not himself a *dadouchos*,[74] and so there is no problem about him being the priest of Dionysos. But since he was a member of the Kerykes he cannot also have been a Bacchiad. But is it certain that the priest of Dionysos attacked by Eupolis was Hipponikos? And if he was, was he the priest of Dionysos Eleuthereus or of some other Dionysiac cult?

Eupolis fr. 20 is constructed out of two texts.[75] First, Hesychios ι 292, which reads 'priest of Dionysos. Eupolis in the *Aiges* mocks Hipponikos as having a red face.' Second, Schol. Ar. *Ran.* 308, which speaks of the priest of Dionysos, whom it does not name, as being

---

[72] The priest of Dionysos thus honoured is Meixigenes Cholleides, whom, following Parker's suggestion, Lambert rightly identifies as a priest of Dionysos in the Peiraeus (Lambert 1998: 399 n. 29). See now also Humphreys (2004: 111 and n. 4). Meixigenes was a member of a liturgical family and had also been the recipient of an honorary decree from the Paraloi (Davies 1971: 56–8 no. 1904) and as a priest he had probably contributed from his own funds (see Humphreys 2004: 99).

[73] Eupolis fr. 20 K/A. See on this fragment, Storey (2003: 72–3) together with Nesselrath (2005). On Hipponikos, see esp. Andoc. 1.130-1; Eupolis fr. 156 (from *Kolakes*); Ath. 5.218bc, 12.537ab; Davies 1971: 258–63; Clinton 1974: 47–8; Storey 2003: 180–1, 187, 349.

[74] Davies (1971: 262 s.v. IX) thought that Hipponikos II was a *dadouchos* but Clinton (1974: 47–8) has shown that he was not.

[75] See Storey 2003: 72–3.

pyrrhos, red-haired, and says that Eupolis made a word play between *pyrrhos* and the red flower *aigipyros* in connection with the red-haired priest of Dionysos. Considering that an independent source, Kratinos fr. 492, calls Hipponikos *pyrrhos,* the obvious reading is that Eupolis in the *Aiges* mocked the red-haired priest of Dionysos Hipponikos for having a red face. Storey, however, divided this fragment into two: (a), from Hesychius, which is poking fun at Hipponikos, and (b), which he believes is referring to an unidentified red-haired priest of Dionysos.[76] This reading has been criticized by Nesselrath, who considers it unjustified "as already Hesychius (responsible for 20a) treats Hipponicus and the priest of Dionysus as one and the same person".[77]

As far as I can see, the only concrete argument brought by Storey in support of his view is that Hipponikos' family held the *dadouchia,* "not (as far as we know) a priesthood of Dionysos".[78] But this is not a valid argument against the view that Hipponikos was a priest of Dionysos. First, we cannot be totally certain that the Kerykes may not have been given the priesthood when the cult of Dionysos Eleuthereus was created in the sixth century; then, on the reconstruction which I set out below, by which the priesthood of Dionysos Eleuthereus was non-gentilicial, the problem disappears entirely: a member of the Kerykes could have been unproblematically appointed to this priesthood—especially since this particular member was legendary for his riches.

To turn to the latter question, in what cult of Dionysos did Hipponikos serve, I suggest that in the metatheatrical genre that was Old Comedy the man referred to (in the comedy and so also in the later refractions in our two texts) as 'the priest of Dionysos' was the priest of Dionysos Eleuthereus who was sitting prominently in the theatre, in the middle of the front row, and was certainly brought into the world of the play in other comedies.[79]

In these circumstances, I submit that it is legitimate to conclude that Hipponikos, the son of Kallias, from the deme of Alopeke, a

---

[76] Ibid.: 72–3.
[77] Nesselrath 2005.
[78] Storey 2003: 73.
[79] See e.g. Ar. *Ran.* 297. See for his seat *IG* II² 5022.

Keryx, held the priesthood of Dionysos Eleuthereus. This would entail that the priesthood was not the prerogative of the Bakchiadai. Since it is perhaps less likely that a gentilicial priesthood of Dionysos Eleuthereus would have been given to the Kerykes, I suggest that the probability that this priesthood was held by Hipponikos offers some support for the thesis I set out below, that the priesthood of Dionysos Eleuthereus was not gentilicial, but open to all Athenians.

Eventually Lambert asks if the *genos* of the Bakchiadai could have been a Hellenistic creation, and answers in the negative, because, he says, there is no certain case of such a creation.[80] But this argument is somewhat hollow. For what, given our restricted access and the unreliability of *argumenta ex silentio*, would constitute a certain case of a *genos* being created in the Hellenistic period? What type of evidence would be needed to make such a case? And if no evidence of this kind is available to us, is an argument based on the absence of such a case valid, especially given the changes that had taken place in the *genē* and their associations with priesthoods between the classical period and the 100s BC and the *genē*-revival in the second and third quarters of the second century BC,[81] which would be a context most conducive to the creation of a new *genos*?

4. THE CULT OF DIONYSOS ELEUTHEREUS

I shall now set out a separate argument for the conclusion that it is likely that no *genos* had an ancestral gentilicial connection with the cult of Dionysos Eleuthereus and the City Dionysia. Of course, if members of a specific *genos* always performed certain ritual duties— such as kithara playing or providing a herald for the processions (which is what our sources claim the Euneidai did)—they would also have performed them at the City Dionysia, but this would not constitute a specific gentilicial connection with this particular festival and cult.

---

[80] Lambert 1998: 401.
[81] Davies 1973: 229; Humphreys 1983: 43–4; Davies 1996: 630; Parker 1996: 287, 289–90, 291–2; Humphreys 2004: 264–5.

Gentilicial participation was not the same in all Athenian festivals for which such participation is attested. There is a spectrum of density of *genē* involvement: at one end of this spectrum, represented above all by the Eleusinian Mysteries, are festivals with a very strong gentilicial participation; then, all along the spectrum, are festivals with varying degrees of gentilicial involvement, such as, for example, the Plynteria, Oschophoria, and Skirophoria; at the other end of the spectrum festivals such as the Panathenaia have minimal gentilicial participation. The only *genē* involvement at the Panathenaia[82]—besides minor duties that may conceivably have been performed by members of a particular *genos* in all (or groups of) festivals—consisted in the fact that the priesthoods of its central cult were gentilicial: above all the priestess of Athena Polias, a member of the Eteoboutadai, and her two assistants Kosmo and Trapezo—if it is right that they had a role in the ceremony, and were also Eteoboutadai[83]—and any other gentilicial priestly personnel who had a part in the festival.

Does this differential density represent a random pattern? I suggest that it does not, at least not with regard to the pole of minimum gentilicial involvement which concerns me here. I discussed in Chapter 1 the way in which at the Panathenaia the polis displayed itself as an open system, inclusive of all its own citizens and not exclusive even of non-citizens and foreigners. The *genē* could act for the whole polis, as they did when they held gentilicial priesthoods and other ritual offices, and through other gentilicial involvements in polis cults, and they were subdivisions of the polis; but they were not 'whole polis subdivisions', they did not articulate the whole polis, since only some citizens were *gennetai*; whatever interpretation of their origin and nature we may choose to accept,[84] in the sixth century the *genē* did not include the whole polis, they formed an

---

[82] *Genē* sacrifices at the Panathenaia such as those of the Salaminioi (*LSS* 19. 87) were part of gentilicial cult activity that marked the presence of the *genos* at the festival, partially comparable to the participation of the demes as demes in the Panathenaia (on which see Sourvinou-Inwood 1990a: 315–16 = 2000: 32)—though only partially, for, unlike the *genē*, the demes in their totality did constitute the whole polis.

[83] Istros FGrH 334 F9; see Parker 1996: 290.

[84] On this, see especially ibid.: 56–66.

exclusive segment of the polis. This exclusivity made them less symbolically harmonious with the nature of the festival than the polis subdivisions that articulated the whole polis and, I submit, this absence of symbolic harmony is correlative with the *genē*'s minimal participation in the Panathenaia.

In Chapter 1 I argued that the City Dionysia too was 'Panathenaic' in that it was the other Athenian festival in which the polis articulated itself and, like the Panathenaia, it was a pre-Kleisthenic whole polis festival with a whole polis focus that was reorganized to include articulations through the new polis subdivisions. The Panathenaia had been reorganized, probably in 566/5.[85] The City Dionysia, on my reconstruction, was created around the 530s, under the rule of Peisistratos—with mythicoritual material from other festivals (above all elements from the Rural Dionysia, the Anthesteria, and perhaps also the Delphic Theoxenia) which was redeployed and modified and which also generated new mythicoritual elements, in accord with the religious mentality specific to the cult.[86] The reorganized Panathenaia inevitably included an irreducible minimum of gentilicial involvement, the gentilicial priesthoods involved in the poliadic cult. But the City Dionysia and the cult of Dionysos Eleuthereus were new creations and, since the "panathenaic" nature of the festival was antithetical to gentilicial involvement, we should not necessarily expect to see any such involvement. I suggest that it is unlikely that in the particular circumstances in which the cult was created by Peisistratos the priesthood of Dionysos Eleuthereus would have been given to a *genos*; there is no reason to imagine that Peisistratos, however benign his accommodation with the *genē* may have been, would have had any incentive to hand over to a *genos* the priesthood of a newly founded cult, focused on a new 'panathenaic' festival. I suggest that the circumstances were conducive to the (perhaps first creation of a) priesthood from all the Athenians— with the priest either chosen from all the Athenians or perhaps symbolically from all the Athenians while in reality, at least to begin with, the selection was from a prearranged list of those who

---

[85] See Parker 1996: 89–92.
[86] Sourvinou-Inwood 2003a: 104–6.

could afford any financial burden that may have been incumbent on the priest.[87]

This conclusion, that when the festival of the City Dionysia was created in the 530s no *genos* was attached to it or to its cult, and that the priesthood was not gentilicial, gains some support from the fact that its festival myth does not involve an individual Athenian hero or individual family; on the contrary the reference group, who first rejected the cult of Dionysos, then was punished, and finally, on the advice of the oracle, received the god with honour, was 'the Athenians'. This contrasts to other myths of Dionysos' arrival in Attica which focus on individual Athenian figures, such as the myths involving Ikarios[88] or Semachos and his daughter or daughters.[89] Nor is there any Athenian *genos* claiming descent from Pegasos, as other *genē*,—for example, we saw, the Euneidai—claimed descent from a heroic-age foreigner who settled in Athens.

A contrast between the procession at the Plynteria and the 'bringing in' of Dionysos at the City Dionysia may reinforce the point. As we saw,[90] at the Plynteria the procession to Phaleron was sent out, the statue taken out, and brought back, by the *gennetai* and a unit representing the whole polis, which in the visible evidence was at certain times the ephebes, at others the *nomophylakes*. This is explicitly stated in the ephebic inscription *IG* II² 1011, where in ll. 10–11 the formulation is 'they jointly took out (συνεξήγαγον) Pallas with the *gennetai* and brought her back in again with complete good order, and they brought in (εἰσήγαγον) Dionysos'.[91] The formulation

---

[87] [Lambert forthcoming (a) argues that 'open' priesthoods were not introduced till after the citizenship law of Pericles in 451.]

[88] See Apollod. 3. 14.7. On this myth, cf. also Flückiger-Guggenheim 1984: 108–12; Kearns 1989: 172, 167; Humphreys 2004: 242–3, 259–61, 265–6.

[89] See Steph. Byz. s.v. Semachidai; cf. Philochoros FGrH 328 F 206; and Jacoby commentary ad loc. p. 572. For the late notion that the Dionysos who went to Semachos was not the son of Semele cf. Jacoby commentary ad Philochoros FGrH 328 FF 5-7 p. 269. On the Semachidai as a *genos*, see Parker 1996: 326. See also Humphreys 2004: 229, 257 n. 86, 272.

[90] In Chapter 3, section 3.

[91] This text clarifies the force of συν- in the vaguer formulation of IG II² 1006. 11–12, cf. 1008.9–10. Διόνυσο]ν συνεισήγαγεν in IG II² 1006. 75–6 does not prove gennetic involvement in that procession: the συν- there indicates cooperation between the ephebes and their kosmete, not ephebes and gennetai.

involving the joint sending out and bringing back of the statue of Athena at the Plynteria contrasts with that deployed for the statue of Dionysos, which follows; in the latter the ephebes alone bring in the statue to the theatre, with no co-agent. Though the bringing in to the theatre is a ritual movement of a very different kind[92] from the movements of the procession to and from Phaleron, nevertheless it is significant that no συν- verb is deployed with reference to it.

These formulations and contrasts, I submit, suggest that no *genos* was associated with this movement of the statue, which was effected by a unit representative of the polis. Of course, even if this is right, it does not follow that no *genos* was involved with the cult and festival; but it adds a further little segment of non-gentilicial participation.

5. CONCLUSIONS: A SUMMARY

A series of different, largely independent, arguments converge in their conclusion that there was no traditional gentilicial connection between the *genos* Bakchiadai and the City Dionysia and more generally the cult of Dionysos Eleuthereus. We cannot hope to know, without new evidence, whether the Bakchiadai were an old *genos* or, as I believe is more likely, a new one, created in the context of the *genē* revival in the second century BC. But there is a very strong case against the hypothesis that this *genos* had an ancestral association with the cult of Dionysos Eleuthereus and the City Dionysia comparable to the relationship between other *genē* and other cults. Nor did the *genos* of the Euneidai have a significant association with the City Dionysia; if the Euneidai always performed certain ritual duties such as kithara playing or providing a herald for the processions they would also have performed those at the City Dionysia, but this would not constitute a specific gentilicial connection with this particular festival and cult.

I also argued that there are good reasons for thinking that no *genos* had a special connection with the City Dionysia and that the priesthood of Dionysos Eleuthereus was non-gentilicial and may have been the first major priesthood to have been open to all Athenians.

---

[92] I have tried to reconstruct this ritual and its significance in the context of the City Dionysia in Sourvinou-Inwood 2003a: 67–100.

7

Genē and Athenian Festivals

The reconstructions and investigations set out in this book have, I hope, illustrated, among many other things, the very different ways in which different *genē* were involved in different festivals, more specifically, in the whole polis festivals[1] of the Plynteria, Kallynteria, Panathenaia, and City Dionysia; they also illustrated the varying densities of those involvements. In this final section I will discuss these different ways and densities of *genē* participation and I will also try to determine whether or not it is possible to reconstruct (very tentatively) any parameters that may have been conducive to greater or lesser gentilicial participation in particular cults and festivals. I will first attempt to construct a framework for the assessment of these *genē* involvements in Athenian festivals that does not entirely depend on culturally determined judgements, by setting out a standard of comparison: despite the enormous gaps in our knowledge, we know enough about gentilicial involvements in the cult and festival of the Eleusinian Mysteries to be able to set out some of the main lines of these involvements, to reconstruct a skeleton. Though it is almost certainly the case that members of the Eleusinian *genē* performed ritual roles about which we know nothing, nevertheless, we know enough about their participations in the cult to be certain that the involvements of *genē* in the Eleusinian cult and the festival of the Eleusinian Mysteries belong at the maximum end of the spectrum of such involvements in Athenian cults and festivals.

---

[1] On whole/central polis festivals, see Sourvinou-Inwood (1990a: 310 = 2000: 27). In these places I used the term central, but whole polis carries less baggage and may be less misleading.

The Eleusinian cult, I should make clear, was part of Athenian polis religion from the beginning—of the polis and the cult.[2] The nature of the Eleusinian Mysteries was very complex: it was on the one hand a restricted cult accessible through individual initiation by individual choice and on the other a whole polis festival.[3]

I will now briefly set out the most significant elements concerning the involvement of *genē* in the Eleusinian cult. There were at least four *genē* involved in the Eleusinian cult, the Eumolpids, the Kerykes, the Philleidai, and at least one other *genos*.[4] Of these the two most important were the Eumolpids and the Kerykes.[5] Any adult member of the Eumolpids and the Kerykes could perform the initial instruction of an initiate, for a fee regulated by the polis[6]—correlatively with the fact that the polis had the ultimate jurisdiction in this, as in the other polis cults, and that the *genē* operated on behalf of the polis. The Eumolpids probably recorded the names of the initiates.[7] Also, the Eumolpids expounded on sacred matters concerning the Mysteries. The actual office of Exegetai of the Eumolpids may have come into being at the end of the fifth, or in the fourth, century, but Eumolpid exegesis was older, whenever the office itself was created.[8] In addition, as Parker pointed out, the formulation of the impeachment against Alcibiades for parodying the Mysteries in Plutarch suggests that the Eumolpids and the Kerykes "were seen in a sense as not merely executors but also sources of legitimate religious tradition".[9] On the available evidence concerning the Mysteries it would appear that the Eumolpids and the Kerykes dominated the ritual performances—with some participation of the other *genē*, at least through their priesthoods.

There was a density of gentilicial priesthoods involved in the festival and cult, mostly shared between the Eumolpids and the Kerykes.[10] (Some of these were clearly late, but the development

---

[2] As I have argued in Sourvinou-Inwood 1997a and 2003b.
[3] See previous note.
[4] See n. 10 below.
[5] On the Eumolpids, see Parker 1996: 293–7; on the Kerykes Parker 1996: 300–2.
[6] Law of *c.*460 BC (*IG* I[3] 6; *LSS* 3).
[7] *IG* I[3] 386.161–2; see Parker 1996: 294.
[8] See Clinton 1974: 89–93; Parker 1996: 295–6.
[9] Parker 1996: 294; on Plut. *Alc.* 22.4.
[10] On Eleusinian priesthoods, see esp. Clinton 1974.

illustrates a dynamic of enhancing gentilicial participation.) Of the three major priestly offices, that of the hierophant belonged to the Eumolpids and that of the daduch to the Kerykes, while the priestess of Demeter and Kore was provided by the Philleidai and at least one other *genos*. But there were also several other gentilicial priesthoods. Among the priesthoods of the Kerykes, about which we are better informed,[11] are the sacred herald, the priest at the altar, the *pyrphoros*, the priest *panages*, the *lithophoros*, and three *hymnagogoi*. The Eumolpids provided two or three Exegetai of the Eumolpids, and undoubtedly also some of the priesthoods about which there is no evidence allowing us to identify the *genos* that provided them, such as, for example, the *phaidyntes* and the *hierophantis* of Demeter and the *hierophantis* of Kore.[12] As regards administration, the Eumolpids and the Kerykes, in conjunction with, and in the context of the overall jurisdiction of, the Athenian polis, represented by the *archon basileus*, who was responsible for the Mysteries, controlled the administration of the Eleusinian Mysteries and the cult.[13]

A logical, rationalizing explanation of the dense gentilicial involvement in the Eleusinian Mysteries would see it as the product of particular historical circumstances, the historical moment in which the main features of festival and cult crystallized—on my interpretation in the early sixth century.[14] However, there are two different reasons for thinking that this interpretation would be simplistic and too univocal, so incomplete as to be distorting. First, and most decisively, there is evidence that shows that the dense gentilicial

---

[11] Thanks to a decree in honour of the daduch Themistokles of 20/19 BC (Clinton 1974: 50–2; Clinton 2005: 300), which contains a list of the priesthoods of the Kerykes.

[12] The first attestation of the two *hierophantides* is in the middle of the third century BC (Istros *FGrH* 334 F 29), but their office is unlikely to have been a later addition. For they are almost certainly the priestesses other than the priestess of Demeter and Kore said to be carrying the *hiera* in a decree of 421 BC (*IG* I³ 79).

[13] See e.g. Arist. *Ath. Pol.* 39.ii; see also ibid. 57.i and the law of the mid-fourth century establishing the Board of the *Epimeletai* of the Mysteries which is discussed below (see n. 15). The Eumolpids and the Kerykes with the *archon basileus*, the hierophant, and the daduch supervised the delimitation of the sacred land (*orgas*): *IG* II² 204.12–14 =*LSCG* 32 = RO 58 = Clinton 2005: 144 (mid-fourth century BC). See also e.g. *IG* II² 1230.

[14] See Sourvinou-Inwood 1997a and 2003b.

involvement was not simply the consequence of particular historical circumstances, but was sustained by a mentality conducive to its continuing renewal which was certainly operative, and shaped developments, in the middle of the fourth century BC. For this is clearly demonstrated by the law of the mid-fourth century establishing the Board of the *Epimeletai* of the Mysteries.[15] As we saw in Chapter 6, the creation of the Board involved an expansion of the role of the polis, but also a significant accommodation for the *gene* which were very strongly connected with the cult. This shows that the dense gentilicial involvement in the Eleusinian Mysteries was not simply a consequence of a historical accident; it had not become out of date by the fourth century, a factor that could be neglected when arrangements were adjusted.

The second reason why an explanation limited to the historical circumstances at the time of the cult's crystallization would be partial and insufficient is because there are clear and significant correlations between gentilicial participation and the notion of secret knowledge which is so important in this cult. First, the actual revelations in the course of the ritual of the Mysteries involved, of course, gentilicially appointed priests and priestesses, with the foremost 'revealing' roles played by members of the Eumolpids, above all the hierophant but also the *hierophantis* of Demeter and the *hierophantis* of Kore. Second, as we saw, any adult member of the Eumolpids and the Kerykes could perform the initial instruction of an initiate. Finally, the Eumolpids expounded on sacred matters concerning the Mysteries.

These initiations, revelations, and expoundings involved secret knowledge possessed by the members of the *gene* active in the cult, above all the Eumolpids and the Kerykes, and among these two dominant *gene* much more strongly by far by the Eumolpids. This connects with the cultic belief that Eumolpos, their eponymous ancestor, was one of the princes whom the goddess Demeter instructed in the Mysteries.[16] That is, the (perceived) continuity of the *genos*, of the (perceived) descendants of Eumolpos, guaranteed the uninterrupted continuity of the knowledge passed down the

---

[15] Clinton 1980: 258–88 (Woodhead 1997: 56).

[16] Eumolpos is a complex figure, sometimes divided into two, the Eleusinian and the Thracian. On this figure, see Kearns 1989: 68–9, 114–15, 163.

members of the *genos* from generation to generation, from Eumolpos to the present, and so the integrity of the transmission of the revelation. This belief in ancestral secret knowledge passed down from generation to generation also applied to the other *genē* involved in the Eleusinian cult, though it was the Eumolpids who were clearly perceived to possess by far the greater part of such knowledge. Such a belief is a stronger version of the established Greek religious representation[17] that cults were symbolically anchored and validated through their foundation in the heroic age, when men could have direct contact with, and sometimes were descended from, gods, and when the most prominent and important of them became the heroes of present-day cult, most strongly when the founders of the cult were, as Eumolpos was, the children of gods.

Clearly then, the 'ancestral' aspect of the secret knowledge was very important here; and because in this initiatory, secret cult this secret knowledge and its revelation were of fundamental importance, since in the Eleusinian Mysteries the facet of the festival that may be summarized as 'ancestral secrets transmitted within a restricted group and revealed in initiation' was crucial, there is a clear correlation between the nature of the cult in which secret ancestral knowledge was very important and the very dense gentilicial involvement in the cult and festival. There is also, I suggest, a certain symbolic harmony between the nature of the festival and the density of the gentilicial involvement; the notion of secret knowledge revealed through initiation and the restrictive nature of (a large part of) the festival is in symbolic harmony with the restrictive nature of the groups, the *genē*, whose members officiated in, and administered, it.

There are good reasons then for the strong gentilicial role in the Eleusinian cult. I turn now to the nexus of the Plynteria and Kallynteria. Though members of other *genē*, above all the priestess of Aglauros from the *genos* Salaminioi, had some part,[18] if the main lines of the reconstructions in Chapter 3 are right, it was the

---

[17] I have discussed this set of representations in Sourvinou-Inwood 2003a: 20–2.

[18] The Salaminioi were involved in the nexus of the Plynteria and Kallynteria also in another way: besides providing the priestess of Aglauros, the second honorand, the sanctuary of Athena Skiras at Phaleron, the goal, I suggested, of the procession carrying the statue to the sea, was one of the religious centres of the Salaminioi (see p. 163).

Praxiergidai who played by far the most significant role both in the festival nexus itself and also in the period of abnormality in Thargelion that preceded these festivals, during which this *genos* virtually took over the cult of Athena Polias. They were in control of the temple and the statue during (at least a significant part of) the month of Thargelion; they took over the *peplos* and they dressed the statue in a temporary garment which they provided. Then, on the first day of the Plynteria they (above all the female Praxiergidai) performed secret rites, sacrifices, and other rites, including the removal of the statue's jewellery and of its temporary dress, the covering up of the statue; the Plyntrides, who were undoubtedly members of the Praxiergidai, washed the *peplos*. On the next day the Praxiergidai took the statue to Phaleron in a procession, sharing the ritual responsibility with a unit representing the whole polis, which at some point was represented by the ephebes and at another the *nomophylakes*. At Phaleron the female Praxiergidai who held the office of Loutrides washed the statue and they and/or other female Praxiergidai put the clean *peplos* back on it. As far as it is possible to judge, the priestess of Athena (provided by a different *genos*, the Eteoboutadai) was not a direct actor in the period of abnormality that culminated in, and was 'purged' through, the nexus of the Plynteria and Kallynteria.

The one involvement of the Eteoboutad priestess that we know of does not involve her in the role of ritual actor: in an honorary decree praising a priestess of Athena Polias, *IG* II^2 776, ll. 18–20, there is mention of her allocating to the Praxiergidai for their ancestral sacrifice 100 drachmas from her own resources. This, then, is a voluntary contribution and an involvement of the symbolically distanced and hierarchically superior kind. For her contribution does not entail that she was involved in the performance of that sacrifice, which was ancestral to the Praxiergidai. The role of the priestess here is symbolically closer to that of the polis making financial contributions to a *genos* for the performance of a ritual than of a co-actor in the ritual.

Clearly, on this reconstruction, the density of the participation of the Praxiergidai in the Plynteria and Kallynteria nexus was very high. I will now consider whether this high density corresponds to other aspects of this nexus of festivals. As we saw, the rites performed by the Praxiergidai at the Plynteria included, besides their ancestral sacrifice, also rites referred to as ὄργια ἀπόρρητα, 'secret rituals';[19] therefore there was an 'ancestral secrets' aspect to their participation. This is comparable, but only partially comparable, to the 'ancestral secrets' aspect of the involvement of the genē active in the Eleusinian Mysteries, especially the Eumolpids. Since these rites performed at the Plynteria were secret, they would have been passed on from one generation of Praxiergidai to the next; however, first, the secret rites made up a less significant proportion of the nexus of the Plynteria and Kallynteria than the secret rites did in the Mysteries; second, there is no evidence for the notion, and it is unlikely to have been the case, that they would have been believed to have been based on divine revelation, as was the case with the Eleusinian Mysteries—though it is likely that there was a story that told of the circumstances in which such rites had first been performed in the heroic age; and finally, this secret knowledge was not revealed to outsiders. However, the very fact that secret rites were performed by the members of a *genos* places the 'ancestral secrets' dimension in a central position; this in its turn made the members of that *genos* guarantors of continuity from the heroic age.

This set of perceptions, first, symbolically anchored the rites in the heroic age. Second, the 'ancestral secrets' dimension guaranteed the correct transmission of the knowledge of correct procedures for the conduct of the rites, which ultimately guaranteed the continued existence and prosperity of the polis. To put it differently, the proper conduct of a polis festival depended on the correct preservation within the *genos* of knowledge of the correct practices, as well as, of course, on their proper performance by the relevant *gennetai*.

These two desirable outcomes would have validated gentilicial involvement in the relevant rituals. Therefore, it would appear that in this festival nexus also, as in the Eleusinian one—albeit to a lesser extent—the fact that secret rites were performed was correlative with greater gentilicial involvement. Consequently, it is possible to suggest tentatively that the inclusion in a ritual nexus of secret rites, which inevitably involved the notion of secret ancestral knowledge, was conducive to significant gentilicial participation.

---

[19] Plut. *Alc.* 34. Christopoulos (1992: 27–39) has put forward some suggestions concerning the nature of the secret rites, but their nature does not concern me here.

One fundamental difference between the cases so far considered is clear. In the Eleusinian cult, as far as we can see, the different *genē* played complementary roles at all occasions, including in the Mysteries and the period leading up to the Mysteries, and the *genē* dominant in the cult as well as its administration, the Eumolpids and the Kerykes, played dominant roles throughout. By contrast, in the cult of Athena Polias the Eteoboutadai were the dominant, hierarchically superior, *genos* in all but one cultic context, the exception being the ritual nexus in Thargelion that culminated in the Plynteria and Kallynteria. The actors in that period were the Praxiergidai and the priestess of Aglauros—with the Praxiergidai dominant in the first part.

As far as is possible to judge, the *genos* of the Eteoboutadai, which was hierarchically superior in the cult of Athena Polias, played no role qua *genos* in the nexus of the Plynteria and Kallynteria. Similarly, on the reconstruction offered here, the Eteoboutad priestess of Athena was not a direct actor in this nexus and was only involved in the role of financial donor that was closer to the role of the polis than to that of a ritual actor. I will now argue that, if we reconstruct a map of the interactions of the different visible elements that make up the nexus, and try to reconstruct the fluid contours of the missing elements and their place in that nexus, in a rough approximation of the process of triangulation,[20] we will find that the argument is not merely *ex silentio* and there are good reasons for concluding that the Eteoboutadai did not have a place (certainly not a significant place) in the Plynteria and Kallynteria nexus.

One basic skeleton of that map consists of the relationships between the three *genē* involved in the Plynteria and Kallynteria, placed in the wider context of the cult of Athena Polias as a whole. As we have seen, at the Plynteria and Kallynteria the relationship between the Praxiergidai and the Salaminioi is one of complementarity, expressed in cooperation between the former and the Salaminian priestess of Aglauros. In the wider nexus of the cult the relationship between the Salaminioi and the Eteoboutadai, whenever it becomes visible to us, is also one of complementarity, expressed in the role of

---

[20] As I suggested in the methodological discussion in Chapter 1.

the same Salaminian priestess in relation to the cults of the Acropolis. But insofar as we can judge from the available evidence, especially that provided by *IG* I³ 7, which tells us that the Praxiergidai took over the statue and the temple for a limited period, and thus replaced the Eteoboutad priestess and any role her *genos* may have had in the cult, the relationship between the Praxiergidai and the Eteoboutadai was not one of complementarity, but of substitution.

The other basic skeleton that we need to put in place consists of the structured relationships between particular *genē* and the different ritual contexts and associated symbolic correlations. First, it is clear that the Eteoboutadai, as represented above all by the priestess of Athena Polias, and probably also by the priestesses Kosmo and Trapezo[phoros], belong together with the cult's normality. Second, it is also clear that the Praxiergidai were prominent in, indeed took over during, the cult's period of abnormality, in which pollution and ill-omenedness came into play. Finally, the Salaminioi appear to have had a secondary role, complementary to that of the dominant *genos*, both during cultic normality, in cooperation with the Eteoboutadai, and during the abnormal time of the Plynteria and Kallynteria, in cooperation with the Praxiergidai.

In these circumstances, I suggest that in the reconstructed map of the interactions between the elements of the Plynteria and Kallynteria, the fluid contours shaped by those visible interactions indicate an Eteoboutad absence; they indicate that in the period of abnormality and pollution in Thargelion, the Praxiergidai replaced the Eteoboutadai; during the abnormal and the ill-omened time the Praxiergidai, rather than the priestess of Athena Polias, an Eteoboutad, took control and performed the necessary purifications and other ritual manipulations. The day on which they performed their secret rites was a very *apophras* day, on which no one would engage in serious business.[21]

In the cult of Athena Polias, then, the Praxiergidai performed the symbolically dirty work—though, I must stress, it was no less of a privilege for being 'symbolically dirty'. In this way the priestess of the poliadic cult was kept at a certain distance from the negative segment

---

[21] Xen. *Hell.* 1.4.12; Plut. *Alc.* 34; Poll. *Onom.* 8.141.

of the ritual and was more strongly associated with the positive and the renewal. This is correlative with the fact that the priestess of Athena Polias represented the polis in its relationship with the poliadic deity. Though this priestess was gentilicially appointed, she was nevertheless strongly perceived as representing the whole polis in its relationship with the poliadic deity.

If it is right that the Praxiergidai only acted for the polis in this nexus, and did not have a role in the rest of the cult that symbolically belonged to the time of normality, then the symbolic pollution they incurred would have been kept away from the restored normality and renewal. Such a symbolic insulation would have been facilitated by the fact that, though they acted for the whole polis, this *genos* was nevertheless a restricted group, and so once normality was restored, the Praxiergidai could be conceptually located at some distance from that representative role. Their persona in the Athenian *imaginaire* could move towards its 'restrictive group' facet and away from the 'acting on behalf of the polis' facet that had come to the fore in the nexus of Thargelion.

During the abnormal time of Thargelion, and until normality was fully restored, the Praxiergidai appear to have had, with regard to the cult of Athena Polias, a role, exercised a control, comparable to that which the Eleusinian *gene* had all the time in the Eleusinian cult. So the role of the Praxiergidai is very partially comparable to, but also radically different from, that of the Eleusinian *gene*. The role of the Praxiergidai is limited to abnormal time some of which is ill-omened. In addition, they do not provide the cult's major priesthood—or even any priesthoods of secondary importance such as that of Aglauros.

As far as it is possible to judge, the *genos* who provided the priestess of Athena Polias, the Eteoboutadai, did not play as a *genos* anywhere near as significant a role in the cult of Athena Polias as the Eumolpids and Kerykes did in the Eleusinian cult. They certainly do not appear to have played any role—other than through the gentilicial priesthoods—in the festival of the Panathenaia. I will now set out the argument systematically and try to show that it is not simply a case of an *argumentum ex silentio*.

The one ritual act that we know was performed by 'Eteoboutadai' was that in the procession from the Acropolis to Skiron at the Skira/Skirophoria, the priestess of Athena Polias, the priest of Poseidon

Erechtheus, and the priest of Helios walked out under a canopy called *skiron*, which was carried by Eteoboutadai[22]—obviously a small number of their members. Leaving aside the priest of Helios whose presence is somehow connected with the time of the year and the Sun's functions and operations (note the parasol, which was unlikely to have had a primarily practical function), this act expressed ritually the relationship between the *genos* and the two important priesthoods it provided: the *genos* serves the two important priesthoods, as it were.

They may have played ritual roles that we do not know about, but we have enough evidence to conclude that they were not involved, qua *genos*, in the administration of the cult of Athena Polias and also that at the Panathenaia, other than through the priesthoods, they either did not have any role or a minimal one. In terms of administration, there was no reserved place for the Eteoboutadai on any of the boards involved with the cult, in contrast, for instance, to the role reserved for the Eleusinian *genē* on the Board of the *Epimeletai* of the Mysteries established in the mid-fourth century.[23] As for the Panathenaia, this is a case in which it is not simply a matter of there being no evidence for the involvement of *genē*, but of there being positive evidence for the involvement of what were clearly alternatives to gentilicial administrative participations, units representing the polis. For example, we know enough about the Panathenaia processions, at the Lesser and the Greater Panathenaia, to know that the procession and the festival were the responsibility of polis representatives such as the *hieropoioi* and the *athlothetai*.[24] The Eteoboutadai do not appear among the many attested groups who made up that procession, in contrast to their role at the Skira. This allows us to conclude that there was no role for the Eteoboutadai in the procession of the Panathenaia—or, at the very least, to be excessively cautious, that such participation was almost certainly non-

---

[22] Lysimachides *FGrH* 366 F 3.
[23] See n. 15 above.
[24] See e.g. Arist. *Ath. Pol.* 54.vi–vii, 60 (with Rhodes 1981: 606 ad 54.vii; 669–76 ad 60.i–iii). I am not concerned here with the particulars of these representatives, for example when it was that particular boards of *hieropoioi* were put in charge of the Lesser Panathenaia or the Greater Panathenaia, or when the *athlothetai* took over certain aspects.

existent, conceivably minimal. In contrast, the procession of the Plynteria was sent out, the statue taken out and brought back, by the *gennetai* and a unit representing the whole polis. We also know, from the inscription about the Lesser Panathenaia, that the Eteoboutadai did not play any role in the sacrifices of the Panathenaia and did not receive any portion of the sacrificial meat qua *genos*.[25] They were involved in the festival only through their priesthoods, and, even so, not all priestly personnel involved in the Panathenaia held gentilicial priesthoods. The priestess of Athena Nike who must have been involved in the sacrifice to Athena Nike at the Panathenaia was appointed from all the Athenians.[26]

I have also argued that there was no gentilicial involvement in the City Dionysia—other than any minor duties that may conceivably have been performed by members of a particular *genos* in all (or groups of) festivals—and that the priesthood of Dionysos Eleuthereus was not gentilicial.

Clearly, then, gentilicial participation was not the same in all Athenian festivals for which such participation is attested in the extant sources. There is a spectrum of density of *genē* involvement, at one end of which are festivals with a very strong gentilicial participation, such as the Eleusinian Mysteries, and at the other, the pole of minimal gentilicial participation, are festivals such as the Panathenaia. Between the poles are festivals with varying degrees of gentilicial involvement, such as the Plynteria and Kallynteria, or, for example, the Oschophoria which was administered by the Salaminioi.[27]

In these circumstances, I would suggest that the greater or lesser participation of *genē* in Athenian festivals was, at the very least partly, determined by aspects of the cult. A factor conducive to greater gentilicial participation was an element of exclusivity, which is correlative with the notion of secret ancestral knowledge; a second such factor may have been rites that had significantly ill-omened connotations. The two aspects could be combined, as was the case in the

---

[25] *LSCG* 33 (RO 81).

[26] Sacrifice to Athena Nike: see *LSCG* 33 (RO 81) 20–2 for the Lesser Panathenaia; Parker 2005a: 266–7; her priestess: Meiggs and Lewis 1988: 44; see Parker 1996: 125–7.

[27] See Parker 1996: 310; and more generally on the Salaminioi 308–16; cf. 57–8.

Plynteria, but they did not need not to be, as they were not in the Eleusinian Mysteries.

Because our access to knowledge concerning gentilicial participation in Athenian festivals is very fragmentary and determined by the accident of preservation,[28] this reconstruction cannot be properly tested—and there would be little point in trying to do so with the inadequate evidence that is available. Nevertheless, we are on solid ground in the case of the Panathenaia, which, I submit, is characterized by opposite traits from those that were correlative with greater gentilicial participation in the Eleusinian Mysteries and the Plynteria.

First, there clearly is no element of exclusivity in the Panathenaia; on the contrary, the poliadic festival, the 'panathenaic' festival par excellence, was characterized by the symbolic opposite of exclusivity, a strong whole polis emphasis and the articulation of the polis as an open system. This nature of the festival, I submit, would have helped limit gentilicial participation. The fact that in the Panathenaia the emphasis was on the whole polis would have generated a tendency for selections and developments that privileged structures and institutions with a whole polis reference—whether the polis was one unit or articulated through its constitutive subdivisions. But the *genē* were exclusive groups, not sub-divisions of the polis.

Secondly, we never hear of any secret ancestral knowledge in connection with the Panathenaia, and the time of the Panathenaia was the opposite of *apophras*, a time of joy and celebration, Athenian polis normality celebrated in its most joyful form. This joyful aspect, the opposite of the 'apophrastic' nature connected with greater gentilicial involvement at the Plynteria, may have strengthened the tendency (generated, I argued, by the nature of the festival) for selections and developments that privileged structures and institutions with a whole polis reference.

[The continuous manuscript ends here. A fragment reveals that a discussion of the City Dionysia would have followed. Of a planned

---

[28] For example, our knowledge of that of the Salaminioi in the Oschophoria is due to the fortunate survival of a particular inscription, *LSS* 19. We may get a tantalizing glimpse, as with the very fragmentary inscription *IG* II² 1234, which probably refers to a *genos* and includes a reference to a *telete*.

section of 'conclusions' there survives only a fragment, ending poignantly in mid-sentence with a favourite word:

'The reconstructed picture is not simple and tidy, it is complex and a little messy. This is not surprising since it is the result of many interactions, between parameters in different circumstances and contexts. This does not mean that parameters . . .']

References

Accame, S. 1941. *La Lega Ateniese del secolo IV A.C.* (Rome).

Aleshire, S. B. 1994. 'The Demos and the Priests: The Selection of Sacred Officials at Athens from Cleisthenes to Augustus', in R. Osborne and S. Hornblower (eds.), *Ritual, Finance, Politics: Athenian Democratic Accounts Presented to David Lewis* (Oxford), 325–37.

——and Lambert, S. D. 2003. 'Making the Peplos for Athena: A New Edition of *IG* II² 1060 + *IG* II² 1036', *ZPE* 142: 65–86.

————forthcoming. 'The Attic *Genē* and the Athenian Religious Reform of 21 BC', to appear in J. H. Richardson and F. Santangelo (eds.), *Priests and State in the Roman World* (available online at www.lamp.ac.uk/ric/workin_papers).

Anderson, M. J. 1997. *The Fall of Troy in Early Greek Poetry and Art* (Oxford).

Bammer, A. 1991. 'Les Sanctuaries archaïques de l'Artémision d'Éphèse', in R. Etienne and M. T. le Dinahet (eds.), *L'Espace sacrificiel dans les civilisations méditerranéennes de l'antiquité* (Paris), 127–30.

——1998. 'Sanctuaries in the Artemision of Ephesus', in R. Hägg (ed.), *Ancient Greek Cult Practice from the Archaeological Evidence* (Stockholm), 227–47.

Barber, E. J. W. 1992. 'The Peplos of Athena', in Neils 1992a: 103–17.

Bettinetti, S. 2001. *La statua di culto nella pratica rituale greca* (Bari).

Billot, M.-F. 1997–8. 'Sanctuaires et cultes d'Athena à Argos', *OpAth* 22–3: 7–52.

Blok, J. 2009a. 'Pericles' Citizenship Law: A New Perspective', *Historia* 58: 141–70.

——2009b. 'Gentrifying Genealogy: On the Genesis of the Athenian Autochthony Myth', in U. Dell and C. Walde (eds.), *Antike Mythen. Medien, Transformationen und Konstruktionen* (Berlin), 251–75.

——and Lambert, S. D. 2009. 'The Appointment of Priests in Attic *Genē*', *ZPE* 169: 95–121.

Boegehold, A. L. 1995. *The Lawcourts of Athens* (Princeton).

Bourriot, F. 1976. *Recherches sur la nature du génos: Étude d'histoire sociale athénienne* (Lille).

Bowden, H. 2005. *Classical Athens and the Delphic Oracle* (Cambridge).

Brelich, A. 1969. *Paides e parthenoi* (Rome).

Bremmer, J. (ed.) 1987. *Interpretations of Greek Mythology* (London).

Bremmer, J. 2000. 'Scapegoat Rituals in Ancient Greece', in Buxton 2000: 271–93 (first in *HSCP* 87 (1983), 299–320).

Brulé, P. 1987. *La Fille d'Athènes: La Religion des filles à Athènes à l'époque classique. Mythes, cultes et société* (1987).

Brumfield, A. C. 1981. *The Attic Festivals of Demeter and their Relation to the Agricultural Year* (Salem, NH).

Bruneau, P. 1970. *Recherches sur les cultes de Délos à l'époque hellénistique et à l'époque impériale* (Paris).

Burkert, W. 1966. 'Kekropidensage und Arrhephoria', *Hermes*, 94: 1–25.

——1970a. 'Buzyge und Palladion: Gewalt und Gericht in altgriechischem Ritual', *Zeitschrift für Religions- und Geistesgeschichte*, 22: 356–68.

——1970b. 'Jason, Hypsipyle and New Fire at Lemnos', *CQ* 20: 1–16 (= Burkert 2000).

——1972. *Lore and Science in Ancient Pythagoreanism* (Cambridge, Mass.).

——1979. *Structure and History in Greek Mythology and Ritual* (Berkeley).

——1983. *Homo Necans: The Anthropology of Ancient Greek Sacrificial Ritual and Myth* (Berkeley and Los Angeles).

——1985. *Greek Religion: Archaic and Classical* (Oxford).

——1988. '*Katagogia-Anagogia* and the Goddess of Knossos', in Hägg, Marinatos, and Nordquist 1988: 81–8.

——1990. *Wilder Ursprung: Opferritual und Mythos bei den Griechen* (Berlin).

——1994. 'Orpheus, Dionysos und die Euneiden in Athen: Das Zeugnis von Euripides' *Hypsipyle*', in A. Bierl and P. von Möllendorff (eds.), *Orchestra. Drama, Mythos, Bühne: Festschrift für Hellmut Flashar* (Stuttgart), 44–9.

——1997. 'From Epiphany to Cult Statue: Early Greek *Theos*', in A. B. Lloyd (ed.), *What is a God? Studies in the Nature of Greek Divinity* (London), 15–34.

——2000 = Burkert 1970b, reprinted in Buxton 2000: 227–49.

Buxton, R. 1994. *Imaginary Greece* (Cambridge).

——(ed.) 2000. *Oxford Readings in Greek Religion* (Oxford).

Calame, C. 1977. *Les Chœurs de jeunes filles en Grèce archaïque* (Rome).

——1990. *Thésée et l'imaginaire athénien* (Lausanne).

Castriota, D. 1992. *Myth, Ethos, and Actuality: Official Art in Fifth-Century B.C. Athens* (Madison).

Chaniotis, A. 2002. 'Ritual Dynamics: The Boiotian Festival of the Daidala', in H. F. J. Hortstmanshoff et al. (eds.), *Kykeon: Studies in Honour of H. S. Versnel* (Leiden), 23–48.

Christopoulos, M. 1992. '*Orgia aporreta*: Quelques remarques sur les rites des Plynteries', *Kernos*, 5: 27–39.

——1994. 'Poseidon Erectheus and *ΕΡΕΧΘΗΙΣ ΘΑΛΑΣΣΑ*', in R. Hägg (ed.), *Ancient Greek Cult Practice from the Epigraphical Evidence* (Stockholm), 123–30.

Clinton, K. 1974. *The Sacred Officials of the Eleusinian Mysteries* (Philadelphia).

——1980. 'A Law in the City Eleusinion Concerning the Mysteries', *Hesperia*, 49: 258–88.

——1992. *Myth and Cult: The Iconography of the Eleusinian Mysteries* (Stockholm).

——2005. *Eleusis: The Inscriptions on Stone*, ia: *Text* (Athens) (the reference is to inscriptions by number, not to pages).

Collard, C. (ed.) 1975. *Euripides*, Supplices (Groningen).

——Cropp, M. J. and Lee, K. H. (eds.) 1995. *Euripides: Selected Fragmentary Plays*, vol. i (Warminster).

Connelly, J. B. 1993. 'Narrative and Image in Attic Vase Painting: Ajax and Kassandra at the Trojan Palladion', in P. J. Holliday (ed.), *Narrative and Event in Ancient Art* (Cambridge), 88, 129.

——1996. 'Parthenon and *Parthenoi*: A Mythological Interpretation of the Parthenon Frieze', *AJA* 100: 53–80.

——2007. *Portrait of a Priestess: Women and Ritual in Ancient Greece* (Princeton).

Connor, W. R. 1987. 'Tribes, Festivals and Processions', *JHS* 107: 40–50.

——2000. Connor 1987, reprinted in Buxton 2000: 56–75.

Crowther, N. B. 1991. 'The Apobates Reconsidered (Demosthenes lxi 23–9)', *JHS* 111: 174–6.

Daux, G. 1963. 'La Grande Démarchie: Un nouveau calendrier d'Attique (Erchia)', *BCH* 87: 603–34.

Davies, J. K. 1971. *Athenian Propertied Families 600–300 B.C.* (Oxford).

——1973. Rev. of P. MacKendrick, *The Athenian Aristocracy, 399–31 B.C.* (Cambridge, Mass., 1969), *CR* NS 23: 228–31.

——1996. Art. *Genē*, *OCD³* 630.

Deacy, S. and Villing, A. (eds.) 2001. *Athena in the Classical World* (Leiden).

Detienne, M. and Vernant, J. P. 1974/1991. *Mètis—Les Ruses de l'intelligence: La Mètis des grecs* (Paris, 1974) (Eng. trans. J. Lloyd, *Cunning Intelligence in Greek Culture and Society*, Chicago, 1991).

Deubner, L. 1969. *Attische Feste*, 3rd edn. (Vienna).

Dillon, M. 2002. *Girls and Women in Classical Greek Religion* (London).

Dontas, G. 1983. 'The True Aglaurion', *Hesperia*, 52: 48–63.

Faraone, C. A. 1992. *Talismans and Trojan Horses* (New York).

Faustoferri, A. 1993. 'The Throne of Apollo at Amyklai: Its Significance and Chronology', in O. Palagia and W. Coulson (eds.), *Sculpture from Arcadia and Laconia* (Oxbow Monographs 30, Oxford), 159–66.

——1996. *Il trono di Amyklai a Sparta: Bathykles al servizio del potere* (Aucnus 2, Naples).

Ferguson, W. S. 1938. 'The Salaminioi of Heptaphylai and Sounion', *Hesperia*, 7: 1–74.

Ferrari, G. 1994–5. 'Heracles, Pisistratus and the Panathenaea', *Métis*, 9–10: 219–26.

——2002. 'The Ancient Temple of the Acropolis at Athens', *AJA* 106: 11–35.

Ferrari Pinney, G. 1988. 'Pallas and Panathenaea', in J. Christiansen and T. Melander (eds.), *Ancient Greek and Related Pottery* (Copenhagen), 465–77.

Flückiger-Guggenheim, D. 1984. *Göttliche Gäste: Die Einkehr von Göttern und Heroen in der griechischen Mythologie* (Bern).

Foley, H. P. (ed.) 1994. *The Homeric Hymn to Demeter* (Princeton).

Fowler, R. L. 2000. *Early Greek Mythography*, i: *Text and Introduction* (Oxford).

Frazer, J. G. 1921. Apollodorus, *The Library*, 2 vols. (London).

Freeden, J. v. 1985. '*Pistokrates kai Apollodoros Satyrou Auridai (IG* II² 2949)', *ZPE* 61: 215–18.

Gadbery, L. M. 1992. 'The Sanctuary of the Twelve Gods in the Athenian Agora: A Revised View', *Hesperia*, 61: 447–89.

Gantz, T. 1993. *Early Greek Myth* (Baltimore).

Gourmelen, L. 2005. *Kékrops, le roi-serpent* (Paris).

Graf, F. 1974. *Eleusis und die orphische Dichtung Athens in vorhellenistischer Zeit* (Berlin).

——1985. *Nordionische Kulte* (Rome).

——1996. '*Pompai* in Greece', in R. Hägg (ed.), *The Role of Religion in the Early Greek Polis* (Stockholm), 55–65.

Griffin, J. 1997. 'The Epic Cycle and the Uniqueness of Homer', *JHS* 97: 39–53.

Guarducci, M. 1974. 'L'offerta di Xenokrateia nel sanctuario di Cefiso al Falero', in D. W. Bradeen and M. F. McGregor (eds.), *Phoros: Tribute to B. D. Meritt* (Locust Valley, NY), 57–66.

Hadzisteliou Price, T. 1978. *Kourotrophos: Cults and Representations of the Greek Nursing Deities* (Leiden).

Hägg, R., Marinatos, N., and Nordquist, G. C. (eds.) 1988. *Early Greek Cult Practice* (Stockholm).

Hamilton, R. 1992. *Choes and Anthesteria: Athenian Iconography and Ritual* (Ann Arbor).

Harrison, T. 2000. *Divinity and History: The Religion of Herodotus* (Oxford).

Heberdey, R. 1904. '*Δαιτίς*', *ÖJh* 7: 210–15.

Henrichs, A. 1982. 'Changing Dionysiac Identities', in B. F. Meyer and E. P. Sanders (eds.), *Jewish & Christian Self-Definition*, iii (London), 137–60.

——1991. 'Namenlosigkeit und Euphemismus: Zur Ambivalenz der chthonischen Mächte in attischen Drama', in H. Hoffmann (ed.), *Fragmenta*

Dramatica: Beiträge zur Interpretation der griechischen Tragikerfragmente und ihrer Wirkungsgeschichte (Göttingen), 161–201.

——1994. 'Anonymity and Polarity: Unknown Gods and Nameless Altars at the Areopagos', *Illinois Classical Studies*, 19: 27–58.

Hollis, A. S. (ed.) 1990. *Callimachus, Hecale* (Oxford).

Hornblower, S. 1991. *A Commentary on Thucydides*. Volume I: Books I–III (Oxford).

Horsfall, N. 1979. ' Some Problems in the Aeneas Legend', *CQ* 29: 372–90.

Humphreys, S. C. 1983. 'Fustel de Coulanges and the Greek "genos"', *Sociologia del diritto* 8: 35–44.

——1990. 'Phrateres in Alopeke, and the Salaminioi', *ZPE* 83: 243–8.

——2004. *The Strangeness of Gods: Historical Perspectives on the Interpretation of Athenian Religion* (Oxford).

Hurwit, J. M. 1999. *The Athenian Acropolis: History, Mythology, and Archaeology from the Neolithic Era to the Present* (Cambridge).

——2004. *The Acropolis in the Age of Pericles* (Cambridge).

Jacoby, F. 1954. *Die Fragmente der griechischen Historiker*, iiib, Supplement: *A Commentary on the Ancient Historians of Athens*, vol. i: *Text* (= Jacoby 1954: i), vol. ii: *Notes* (= Jacoby 1954: ii) (Leiden).

Jameson, M. 1965. 'Notes on the Sacrificial Calendar from Erchia', *BCH* 89: 154–72.

——2000. 'An Altar for Herakles', in P. Flensted-Jensen, T. H. Nielsen, and L. Rubinstein (eds.), *Polis and Politics: Studies ... M. H. Hansen* (Copenhagen), 217–27.

——Jordan, D. R., and Kotansky, R. D. 1993. *A Lex Sacra from Selinous* (*GRBM* 11).

Jenkins, I. 1994. *The Parthenon Frieze* (London).

Kearns, E. 1989. *The Heroes of Attica* (London).

——1990. 'Saving the City', in Murray and Price 1990: 323–46.

——1992. 'Between God and Man: Status and Function of Heroes and their Sanctuaries', in *Le Sanctuaire grec* (*Entretiens Hardt* 37, Vandoeuvres), 65–99.

Knibbe, D. 1995. 'Via Sacra Ephesiaca: New Aspects of the Cult of Artemis Ephesia', in H. Koester (ed.), *Ephesos: Metropolis of Asia* (Valley Forge, Pa.), 141–55.

Kokkorou-Alevra, G. 1988. Ἕνα γνωστό-άγνωστο αγγείο του ζωγράφου του Μειδία, in πρακτικά του XII Διεθνούς Συνεδρίου Κλασικής Αρχαιολογίας (Athens), iii. 103–14.

Korres, M. 1994a. 'Der Plan des Parthenon', *AM* 109: 53–120.

——1994b. 'The History of the Acropolis Monuments', in R. Economakis (ed.), *The Acropolis Restoration* (London), 34–51.

Kron, U. 1976. *Die zehn attischen Phylenheroen: Geschichte, Mythos, Kult und Darstellungen* (Berlin).

——1988. 'Kultmahle im Heraion von Samos archaischer Zeit', in Hägg, Marinatos, and Nordquist 1988: 135–48.

——1999. 'Patriotic Heroes', in R. Hägg (ed.), *Ancient Greek Hero Cult* (Stockholm), 61–83.

Kunisch, N. 1997. *Makron* (Mainz).

Kyle, D. G. 1992. 'The Panathenaic Games: Sacred and Civic Athletics', in Neils 1992a: 77–102.

Lambert, S. D. 1997. 'The Attic Genos Salaminioi and the Island of Salamis', *ZPE* 119: 85–106.

——1998. 'The Attic *Genos* Bakchiadai and the City Dionysia', *Historia*, 42: 394–403.

——1999a. 'The Attic *Genos*', *CQ* 49: 484–89.

——1999b. '*IG* II² 2345, Thiasoi of Herakles and the Salaminioi Again', *ZPE* 125: 93–130.

——2002. 'The Sacrificial Calendar of Athens', *BSA* 97: 353–99.

——2008. 'Aglauros, the Euenoridai and the Autochthon of Atlantis', *ZPE* 167: 22–6.

——forthcoming a. 'A Polis and its Priests: The Appointment of Athenian Priests and Priestesses before and after Pericles' Citizenship Law', *Historia* 59 (2010), 143–75.

——forthcoming b. 'The Priesthoods of the Eteoboutadai', to appear in a volume in honour of J. K. Davies.

——forthcoming c. 'Aristocracy and the Attic *Genē*: A Mythological Perspective', to appear in N. Fisher and H. van Wees (eds.), *Aristocracy, Elites and Social Mobility in Ancient Societies* (Classical Press of Wales; working version at http://www.lamp.ac.uk/ric/workin_papers).

Larson, J. 1995. *Greek Heroine Cults* (Madison).

——2001. *Greek Nymphs: Myth, Cult, Lore* (Oxford).

Lawton, C. L. 1995. *Attic Document Reliefs: Art and Politics in Ancient Athens* (Oxford).

Lefkowitz, M. R. 1981. *The Lives of the Greek Poets* (London).

Lewis, D. M. 1954. 'Notes on Attic Inscriptions I: The Praxiergidai', *BSA* 49: 17–21.

——1979/80. 'Athena's Robe', *Scripta Classica Israelica*, 5: 28–9.

Lightfoot, J. 2002. 'Nothing to Do with the *Technitai* of Dionysus?', in P. Easterling and E. Hall (eds.), *Greek and Roman Actors: Aspects of an Ancient Profession* (Cambridge), 209–24.

Llewellyn-Jones, L. 2001. 'Sexy Athena: The Dress and Erotic Representation of a Virgin War-Goddess', in Deacy and Villing 2001: 233–57.

Lloyd Jones, H. 1967. 'Heracles at Eleusis: P. Oxy. 2622 and PSI 3891', *Maia*, NS 19: 206–29 (reprinted in id., *Greek Epic, Lyric and Tragedy*, Oxford, 1990, 167–87).

——(ed. and trans.) 1996. *Sophocles, Fragments* (Cambridge, Mass.).

Loraux, N. 1989. *Les Expériences de Tirésias: Le Féminin et l'homme grec* (Paris).

Lupu, E. 2005. *Greek Sacred Law: A Collection of New Documents* (Leiden).

Maass, M. 1972. *Die Prohedrie des Dionysostheaters in Athen* (Munich).

MacDowell, D. M. 1989. 'Athenian Laws about Choruses', in *Symposion* 1982: 65–77.

Malouchou, G. E. 2008. 'Νέα ἀττικὴ ἐπιγραφή', in A. P. Matthaiou and I. Polinskaya (eds.), Μικρὸς Ἱερομνήμων. Μελέτες εἰς μνήμην Michael H. Jameson (Athens), 103–15.

Mansfield, J. M. 1985. *The Robe of Athena and the Panathenaic "Peplos"*, Diss. Univ. California (Berkeley).

Mantis, A. G. 1990. Προβλήματα της εικονογραφίας των ιερειών και των ιερέων στην αρχαία Ελληνική τέχνη (Athens).

Meiggs, R. and Lewis, D. 1988. *A Selection of Greek Historical Inscriptions*, rev. edn. (Oxford).

Merkelbach, R. 1972. 'Aglauros (Die Religion der Epheben)', *ZPE* 9: 277–83.

Mikalson, J. D. 1975. *The Sacred and Civil Calendar of the Athenian Year* (Princeton).

——1976. 'Erechtheus and the Panathenaia', *AJP* 97: 141–53.

Moret, J. M. 1975. *L'Ilioupersis dans la céramique italiote: Les Mythes et leur expression figurée au IV siècle* (Rome).

Morris, S. P. 2001. 'Potnia Aswiya: Anatolian Contributions to Greek Religion', *Aegaeum*, 22: 423–34.

Murray, O. and Price S. (eds.), 1990. *The Greek City from Homer to Alexander* (Oxford).

Nagy, B. 1978a. 'The Ritual in Slab V-East on the Parthenon Frieze', *CP* 73: 136–41.

——1978b. 'The Athenian Athlothetai', *GRBS* 19: 307–13.

——1991. 'The Procession to Phaleron', *Historia*, 40: 288–306.

Neils, J. (ed.) 1992a. *Goddess and Polis: The Panathenaic Festival in Ancient Athens* (Princeton).

——1992b. 'The Panathenaia: An Introduction', in Neils 1992a: 13–27.

——1992c. 'Panathenaic Amphoras: Their Meanings, Makers and Markets', in Neils 1992a: 29–51.

——1996. 'Pride, Pomp, and Circumstance: The Iconography of Procession', in J. Neils (ed.), *Worshipping Athena: Panathenaia and Parthenon* (Madison), 177–97.

Neils, J. 1999. 'Reconfiguring the Gods on the Parthenon Frieze', *Art Bulletin*, 81/1: 5–20.

——2001a. *The Parthenon Frieze* (Cambridge).

——2001b. 'Athena, Alter Ego of Zeus', in Deacy and Villing 2001: 219–32.

——2003. 'Children and Greek Religion', in J. Neils and J. H. Oakley (eds.), *Coming of Age in Ancient Greece: Images of Childhood from the Classical Past* (New Haven), 139–61.

Nesselrath, H.-G. 2005. Review of Storey 2003, *BMCR* 2: 44.

Nilsson, M. P. 1906. *Griechische Feste von religiöser Bedeutung mit Ausschluss der attischen* (Leipzig).

Oakley, J. H. 1982. 'A Louvre Fragment Reconsidered: Perseus Becomes Erichthonios', *JHS* 102: 220–2.

O'Brien, J. V. 1993. *The Transformation of Hera: A Study of Ritual, Hero and the Goddess in the* Iliad (Lanham, Md.).

Osborne, M. J. 1981. *Naturalization in Athens*, vol. i (Verhandelingen van de Koninklijke Academie voor Wetenschappen, Letteren en Schone Kunsten van België, Klasse der Letteren no. 101) (Brussels).

Osborne, R. 1987. 'The Viewing and Obscuring of the Parthenon Frieze', *JHS* 107: 98–105.

——1994. 'Democracy and Imperialism in the Panathenaic Procession: The Parthenon Frieze in its Context', in W. Coulson, O. Palagia, et al. (eds.), *The Archaeology of Athens and Attica under the Democracy* (Oxford), 143–50.

Palagia, O. 1993. *The Pediments of the Parthenon* (Leiden).

——2005. 'Fire from Heaven: Pediments and Akroteria of the Parthenon', in J. Neils (ed.), *The Parthenon: From Antiquity to the Present* (Cambridge), 225–59.

Parisinou, E. 2000. *The Light of the Gods: The Role of Light in Archaic and Classical Greek Cult* (London).

Parke, H. W. 1977. *Festivals of the Athenians* (London).

Parker, R. 1983. *Miasma: Pollution and Purification in Early Greek Religion* (Oxford).

——1987a. 'Myths of Early Athens', in Bremmer 1987: 187–214.

——1987b. 'Festivals of the Attic Demes', in T. Linders and G. Nordquist (eds.), *Gifts to the Gods* (*Boreas* 15), 137–47.

——1996. *Athenian Religion: A History* (Oxford).

——2003. 'The Problem of the Greek Cult Epithet', in *OpAth* 28: 173–83.

——2005a. *Polytheism and Society at Athens* (Oxford).

——2005b. 'Artémis Ilithye et autres: Le Problème du nom divin utilisé comme épiclèse', in N. Belayche et al. (eds.), *Nommer les dieux* (Rennes), 219–26.

Pelling, C. B. R. 1997. 'Conclusion', to C. B. R. Pelling (ed.), *Greek Tragedy and the Historian* (Oxford), 213–35.

Phillips, C. R. 2002. 'Zwölfgötter', in *Neue Pauly* 12/2: 860–1.

Pickard-Cambridge, A. 1968. *The Dramatic Festivals of Athens*, 2nd edn., rev. J. Gould and D. M. Lewis (Oxford).

Pirenne-Delforge, V. 1994. *L'Aphrodite grecque* (Athens [*Kernos* Supplement 4]).

Pritchett, W. K. 1979. *The Greek State at War*, vol. iii (Berkeley and Los Angeles).

——1982. 'The Calendar of the Gibbous Moon', *ZPE* 49: 243–66.

——1987. 'The παννυχίς', in *ΦΙΛΙΑ ΕΠΗ ΕΙΣ ΓΕΩΡΓΙΟΝ Ε. ΜΥΛΩΝΑΝ* ii (Athens), 179–88.

Redfield, J. M. 2003. *The Locrian Maidens: Love and Death in Greek Italy* (Princeton).

Reeder, E. D. (ed.) 1995. *Pandora: Women in Classical Greece* (Baltimore).

Rhodes, P. J. 1981. *A Commentary on the Aristotelian Athenaion Politeia* (Oxford).

Richardson, N. J. 1974. *The Homeric Hymn to Demeter* (Oxford).

——1981. Review of Pritchett 1979, *JHS* 101: 185–7.

Ridgway, B. S. 1992. 'Images of Athena on the Akropolis', in Neils 1992a: 119–42.

Robertson, M. 1975. *The Parthenon Frieze* (London).

——1984. 'The South Metopes: Theseus and Daidalos', in E. Berger (ed.), *Parthenon-Kongress: Basel, 4.–8. April 1982* (Mainz), 206–8.

Robertson, N. 1983. 'The Riddle of the Arrhephoria at Athens', *HSCP* 87: 241–88.

——1992. *Festivals and Legends: The Formation of Greek Cities in the Light of Public Ritual* (Toronto).

——1996a. 'Athena's Shrines and Festivals', in J. Neils (ed.), *Worshipping Athena: Panathenaia and Parthenon* (Madison), 27–77.

——1996b. 'Athena and Early Greek Society: Palladium Shrines and Promontory Shrines', in M. Dillon (ed.), *Religion in the Ancient World: New Themes and Approaches* (Amsterdam), 383–475.

——2004. 'The Praxiergidae Decree (*IG* I³7) and the Dressing of Athena's Statue with the *Peplos*', *GRBS* 44: 111–61.

Romano, I. B. 1988. 'Early Greek Cult Images and Cult Practices', in Hägg, Marinatos, and Nordquist 1988: 127–33.

Roussel, D. 1976. *Tribu et cité* (Paris).

Rutherford, I. 2001. *Pindar's Paeans* (Oxford).

Schachter, A. 1981. *Cults of Boeotia*, vol. i (*BICS* Supplement 38/1, London).

Scheer, T. S. 2000. *Die Gottheit und ihr Bild* (Munich).

Schmalz, G. C. R. 2006. 'The Athenian Prytaneion Discovered?', *Hesperia*, 75: 33–81.

Sechan, L. 1926. *Études sur la tragédie grecque dans ses rapports avec la céramique* (Paris).

Shapiro, H. A. 1989. *Art and Cult under the Tyrants in Athens* (Mainz).

——1995. 'The Cult of Heroines: Kekrops' Daughters', in Reeder 1995: 39–48.

Siewert, P. 1977. 'The Ephebic Oath in Fifth-Century Athens', *JHS* 97: 102–11.

Simon, E. 1975. 'Versuch einer Deutung der Südmetopen des Parthenon', *JdI* 90: 100–20.

——1983. *Festivals of Attica: An Archaeological Commentary* (Madison).

——1998. *Die Götter der Griechen*, 4th edn. (Munich).

Sourvinou-Inwood, C. 1978. 'Persephone and Aphrodite at Locri: A Model for Personality Definitions in Greek Religion', *JHS* 98: 101–21 (= Sourvinou-Inwood 1991: 147–88).

——1979. *Theseus as Son and Stepson: A Tentative Illustration of the Greek Mythological Mentality* (London).

——1986. 'Crime and Punishment: Tityos, Tantalos and Sisyphos in *Odyssey* 11', in *BICS* 33: 37–58.

——1987a. 'A Series of Erotic Pursuits: Images and Meanings', in *JHS* 107: 31–53 (=Sourvinou-Inwood 1991: 58–98).

——1987b. 'Myth as History: The Previous Owners of the Delphic Oracle', in Bremmer 1987: 215–41 (= Sourvinou-Inwood 1991: 217–43).

——1988. *Studies in Girls' Transitions: Aspects of the Arkteia and Age Representation in Attic Iconography* (Athens).

——1989. 'Assumptions and the Creation of Meaning: Reading Sophocles' *Antigone*', *JHS* 109: 134–48.

——1990a. 'What is Polis Religion?', in Murray and Price 1990: 295–322 (= Sourvinou-Inwood 2000).

——1990b. 'Myths in Images: Theseus and Medea as a Case Study', in L. Edmunds (ed.), *Approaches to Greek Myth* (Baltimore), 395–445.

——1991. *"Reading" Greek Culture: Texts and Images, Rituals and Myths* (Oxford).

——1993. 'Early Sanctuaries, the Eighth Century and Ritual Space: Fragments of a Discourse', in N. Marinatos and R. Hagg (eds.), *Greek Sanctuaries: New Approaches* (London), 1–17.

——1995. *'Reading' Greek Death* (Oxford).

——1997a. 'Reconstructing Change: Ideology and Ritual at Eleusis', in M. Golden and P. Toohey (eds.), *Inventing Ancient Culture? Historicism, Periodization and the Ancient World* (London), 132–64.

Sourvinou-Inwood, C. 1997b. 'Medea at a Shifting Distance: Images and Euripidean Tragedy', in J. J. Clauss and S. I. Johnston (eds.), *Medea: Essays on Medea in Myth, Literature, Philosophy and Art* (Princeton), 253–96.

——1997c. 'The Hesiodic Myth of the Five Races and the Tolerance of Plurality in Greek Mythology', in O. Palagia (ed.), *Greek Offerings: Essays on Greek Art in Honour of John Boardman* (Oxford), 1–21.

——1997d. 'Tragedy and Religion: Constructs and Readings', in C. B. R. Pelling (ed.), *Greek Tragedy and the Historian* (Oxford), 161–86.

——2000. Republication of Sourvinou-Inwood 1990a in Buxton 2000: 13–37.

——2003a. *Tragedy and Athenian Religion* (Lanham, Md.).

——2003b. 'Festival and Mysteries: Aspects of the Eleusinian Cult', in M. B. Cosmopoulos (ed.), *Greek Mysteries: The Archaeology and Ritual of Ancient Greek Secret Cults* (London), 25–49.

——2004. 'Hermaphroditos and Salmakis: The Voice of Halikarnassos', in S. Isager and P. Pedersen (eds.), *The Salmakis Inscription and Hellenistic Halikarnassos* (Odense), 59–84.

——2005. *Hylas, the Nymphs, Dionysos and Others: Myth, Ritual, Ethnicity* (Stockholm).

——2008. 'A Reading of Two Fragments of Sophilos', *JHS* 128: 128–31.

Steiner, D. 2001. *Images in Mind: Statues in Archaic and Classical Literature and Thought* (Princeton).

Steinhart, M. 1997. 'Die Darstellung der Praxiergidai im Ostfries des Parthenon', *AA*: 475–8.

Storey, I. C. 2003. *Eupolis: Poet of Old Comedy* (Oxford).

Tiverios, M. A. 1988. '*ΠΕΡΙ ΠΑΛΛΑΔΙΟΥ ΟΤΙ ΔΥΟ ΚΛΕΨΕΙΑΝ ΔΙΟΜΗΔΗΣ ΚΑΙ ΟΔΥΣΣΕΥΣ*', in *Kanon*, Festschrift E. Berger (Basle), 324–30.

——2004. 'Artemis, Dionysos und eleusinische Gottheiten', *AM* 119: 147–62.

Toepffer, J. 1889. *Attische Genealogie* (Berlin).

Tomberg, K. H. 1968. *Die Καινὴ Ἱστορία des Ptolemaios Chennos* (Bonn).

Travlos, J. 1971. *Pictorial Dictionary of Ancient Athens* (London).

Tümpel, K. 1889. 'Dionysos Halieus', *Philologus*, 48: 681–96.

Verpoorten, J. M. 1945. ' La *Stibas* ou l'image de la brousse', *RHR* 162: 147–60.

Versnel, H. S. 1987. 'Greek Myth and Ritual: The Case of Kronos', in Bremmer 1987: 121–52.

——1993. *Transition and Reversal in Myth and Ritual* (Leiden).

Vian, F. 1952. *La Guerre des Géants: Le Mythe avant l'époque hellénistique* (Paris).

Vidal-Naquet, P. 1981. 'Land and Sacrifice in the *Odyssey*: A Study of Religious and Mythical Meanings', in R. Gordon (ed.), *Myth, Religion and Society* (Cambridge), 180–94.

von Prott, J., and Ziehen, L. 1906. *Leges Graecorum Sacrae e titulis collectae,* ii: *Leges Graeciae et Insularum,* ed. L. Ziehen (Leipzig).

Walter, H. 1976. *Das Heraion von Samos* (Munich).

——1990. *Das griechische Heiligtum dargestellt am Heraion von Samos* (Stuttgart).

Wankel, H., Merkelbach R., et al. 1979–81. *Die Inschriften von Ephesos* (Bonn).

Wesenberg, B. 1995. 'Panathenäische Peplosdedikation and Arrephorie: Zur Thematik des Parthenonfrieses', *JdI* 110: 149–78.

West, M. L. 1983. *The Orphic Poems* (Oxford).

Wilkins, J. (ed.) 1993. Euripides, *Heraclidae* (Oxford).

Wilson, P. 2000. *The Athenian Institution of the* Khoregia (Cambridge).

Woodhead, A. G. 1997. *The Athenian Agora,* xvi: *Inscriptions: The Decrees* (Princeton).

Index